Baba's Kitchen
Ukrainian Soul Food

By

Raisa Stone

Raisa Marika Stohyn

Dear Companion Publishing

www.ukrainiansoulfood.ca

Library and Archives Canada Cataloguing-in-Publication

Stone, Raisa, author
Baba's kitchen : Ukrainian soul food with stories from the village / by Raisa Stone (Raisa Marika Stohyn). -- 2nd edition.

Includes bibliographical references.
Issued in print and electronic formats.
Includes some text in Ukrainian.
ISBN 978-1-4949-1908-5 (pbk.)

1. Cooking, Ukrainian. 2. Food--Religious aspects. 3. Ukraine--Social life and customs. 4. Cookbooks I. Title.

TX723.5.U5S76 2014 641.59477

C2014-900138-X

C2014-900139-8

Dedication

This book is dedicated to my ancestors. You have not been forgotten, and you do not forget me. You exist as far more than shadows. Your hands are upon my head, your songs live in my heart.

Dai Bozha i Slava Ukraina!
Give to God, and Glory to Ukraine!

Table of Contents

Chapter Three

The urgent romantic matter of a full fridge by your bed. Men don't leave at 3 a.m. Because they're scared of commitment. They leave because they're scared of the diet soda and lettuce leaf. Let Baba be your *Mayonnaise Love Expert.*

Chapter Four

Childbirth Rituals: Bum stab a cowardly husband, tame an unruly placenta and introduce a baby to the world of love and mortgages.

Crepe Fillings:

Haul the Butter Goddess around in a sleigh, light fires and throw stale pancakes at politicians.

Chapter Five

Chapter Six

Velyk Den' (Easter) and Spring Equinox traditions: Colored eggs, pussy willow spankings and a monster chained to a rock.

More Easter recipes may be found throughout Baba's Kitchen, for example:

Chapter Seven

Cope with passive-aggression (getting and giving), snake bite, Einstein, Overeaters Anonymous lapses, Presbyterian sex and reluctant bachelors.

Chapter Eight

Avoid bleached blonde poisoning, learn how not to be a lame white person in New Orleans, order a black leather cardigan from the *Black Leather Baba Catalogue.*

Chapter Nine

Make Ukrainian Cocaine, learn a heartwarming Ukrainian folk song: *My Mother Beat Me With a Birch Rod*, tenderize meat under your saddle.

Chapter Ten

Nude encounter groups, cooking with a fly swatter, why your meat balls are too small and JK Rowling is just plain wrong about Dobby.

Chapter Eleven

Sviata Vechera, Koruksun, Rizdvo: Holy Eve, Day of the Dead, and Winter Solstice/Christmas traditions. Talking animals, hungry ancestors, golden sky horses and pudding on the ceiling. Menus for these holidays are referenced to other chapters. Also:

Chapter Twelve

Seduce and poison Nazis, the organic way. Baba is a mushroom picking expert!

Chapter Thirteen

Why the sexy, desperate women on your favorite TV shows are barking up the wrong dog. Lazy varenyky for your lazy self.

Chapter Fourteen

Sabotage hippies and nasty neighbors, be a Cadillac kozak, peel cabbage in a trailer park.

Chapter Fifteen

Baba Riddle: What's the difference between a cheese dumpling submerged in water, and a kid holding its breath?
Answer: Don't wait for the dumpling to turn blue. It won't. Ha!

Chapter Sixteen

Skinny dip with flair, catch trout with your bathing suit, allow men to be men---as long as they keep the massage oil flowing.

Chapter Seventeen

Scurvy Dog Baba gets seduced by a pair of black eyebrows and lives to cook and love again.

Chapter Eighteen

In Ukraina we say, *So long as there is cabbage and potato, house is not empty*. Baba herself never seen house with only these thing. Is usually at least couch and television. But you never know.

Chapter Nineteen

First aid for grated knuckles, permission to eat plenty of fat, what to feed annoying dinner drop ins.

Chapter Twenty

The Ukrainian Banya (Bath House): Spirits and rituals. Why a cold prickly hand on your rump is bad news in more ways than one. Incredible vegetarian dishes for around a dollar.

Chapter Twenty One

Baba tears up a golf course on horse back, the Ukrainian origin of Constitutional freedoms, and the simplest noodle recipes ever.

Chapter Twenty Two

Liven up dry mammoth, whole grains and parties.

Chapter Twenty Three

Part (1) Ivana Kupala: Summer Solstice Erotic Rituals. The village that bathes together, stays together. Sexy Ukrainian songs, talking trees and stalking the elusive fire flower.

Part (2) Non-traditional recipes for pie. Because who would believe a grandma book with no pie? And Baba is so good at making them.

Part (3) Ahhhh. Back to traditional Ukrainian desserts. Drink of the gods, fermented honey cake, wild rose preserves on apple cake. Learn Baba's *First Law of Thermal Underwear*, essential to baking.

Chapter Twenty Four

Baba runs afoul of the Royal Canadian Mounted Police with her opium (or is it?) poppy crop, then gets her man.

Chapter Twenty Five

Deal with yeast infections, baldness, arthritis, colds, bruises, cracked nipples and PMS using common foods and plants.

Get more Baba!
Enjoy extra recipes, and a free newsletter on her website:
www.ukrainiansoulfood.ca

Support Ukrainian authorship:
Review *Baba's Kitchen* on Amazon or Goodreads

Introduction
by
Raisa Stone

Eat well, sleep well, and God must give good health.~Ukrainian proverb

Baba's Kitchen: Ukrainian Soul Food With Stories From the Village is a memoir coupled with traditional recipes I learned from my immigrant family and community. I ate pureed *borshch* as baby food and cut *varenyky* dough (perogies) with a drinking glass as soon as I could reach. My narrator, Baba, is a composite of the personalities who fed me, disciplined me, and told me outrageous, heart wrenching and hilarious stories of the Soviet, Nazi and immigrant experience.

For Ukrainians, a meaningful life is focused on hospitality, the Arts and our relationship with Nature. We express ourselves largely through physical acts of nurturing, pleasure and creativity. Cooking is a significant spiritual ritual which strengthens the bodies and *dushi* (souls) of community, family and of self. It is this spirit I strive to communicate with Baba's Kitchen.

Baba's words, "Ukrainian *yizha dusha*, soul food, is powerful thing. Dusha, soul, is fierce vitality force. It is roaring flame cannot be put out, inside cage of thick flesh and hard bone. Not some kind airing fairy floating around like chiffon scarf. That is Nu Age barfola. Food is to create more life force, make nourishing for your spirit as well as your physical body."

In her inimitable style, Baba describes holidays and folk ways. She presents rituals and recipes for:

-*Maslynitsya* (Mardi Gras). We drive a goddess effigy around town in a sleigh, and throw stale pancakes instead of beads;

-Spring Equinox/*Velyk Den'* (Easter). A monster chained to a rock, a cemetery feast and spankings with pussy willow are all part of our traditions. But no rabbits. Revelations about the sacred symbolism of *pysanky* (colored eggs) include their role in honoring the ancestors, battling evil and protecting the home. Egg recipes incorporate Ukrainian delicacies: horse radish, caviar and pate;

-*Kupala* (Summer Solstice). This is our standing date for the village communal bath, free love, and sexy food like Kozak Honey Mousse;

-*Sviata Vechera/Rizdvo/*Winter Solstice/Christmas. Oy yoi yoi, such a feast you've never seen. Twelve dishes represent the lunar year, while their meatless nature honors our animal friends. We sing carols to Mother Nature, ferment honey cake and bake sacred circle of life bread.

Evocative descriptions of superstitions and rituals abound. From appeasing the mischievous spirits who haunt the village sauna to our annual search for the fire flower, Baba's Kitchen is rife with sensual mysticism.

In a nod to popular culture, Baba takes JK Rowling to task for killing Dobby the house elf. She explains this is a thoroughly neo pagan, appropriated idea; Ukrainians have had house elves for millenia, and they are immortal. An essay on childbirth practices describes the laboring mother sitting on the father's lap, followed by culinary methods for reviving the father. Ukrainian sayings liberally pepper the text. Baba reserves her strongest curse for copyright infringement: "May you be kick by duck!" A person could not sink lower.

Ukrainian culture is essentially one long procession of holidays and rituals. We have a day of Thanksgiving, but discrete celebrations lead up to it. For example: In Ukraine, honey, fruit, wheat and poppy seed each have their own celebratory day. Feasting, singing, dancing and sexual excess is punctuated by *Maalox Day* and *Holiday of Sore Thigh.* Erotic recipes are abundant throughout. Baba teaches the artful use of cheesecake and garlic sausage to entice a lover and keep him in optimum performance condition. Of homesteading background, she is no stranger to animal husbandry practices in mate management. Should one attract a bald sweetheart, her advice is, "Grab his both ear, or you be sorry."

The recipes in Baba's Kitchen have been tested and retested by generations of cooks in Ukraine, my immigrant family/community and myself. You'll find ingredient recommendations that draw from our history as hunter-gatherers, and later, as farmer-herders. Some Ukrainians have never become farmers; Baba emotes romantically about our nomadic *kozak* tradition ("cossack" being the undesirable Russian term).

Though Baba advocates obtaining ingredients in the wild if possible, natural cycles and Ukrainians' evolving relationships with Nature mean I have omitted recipes for horse meat. Ukrainians domesticated horses around 3,000 BC, and treat this amazing partner as sacred. Eating horse meat is a Neanderthal barbarism---unevolved primates with whom we meticulously avoided partnering. Recent DNA studies show that 1-4% of humankind carries Neanderthal genes; they're the ones still eating horse meat today.

As a side note, it is with this passion I pursue the end of horse slaughter. I am the national record holder for signatures to end this brutal practice; my MP read my petition in the House of Commons.

When I was a toddler, I'd no idea the war stories my adopted Baba told me while making me laugh by pushing out her false teeth, would form my view of the world. Who could foretell that her equally strong views on friendly Ukrainian-Jewish relationships would allow me to enjoy a second community? My other Baba's sublime chicken soup would forever leave me dissatisfied with any but made from scratch, preferably using medication-free, organic, happy chickens. I began singing pinfeathers when I was four.

Between these attitudes and the sad fact that my paternal Baba was murdered by the Soviets, I've given the book's narrator a complex and highly opinionated personality. I hope you'll be able to laugh until you cry, and cry until you laugh.

The recipes are homey, nourishing and economical. Ukrainians have, for millennia, prepared an astounding variety of mouth watering foods from basics: potatoes, beets, cabbage, greens, onions, beans, eggs and whole grains. And of course, lots of garlic. As Baba says, “If everyone eating same thing, who care you smell?”

Delicious casseroles are plentiful and largely meatless. Protein and iron-rich white bean pate yields four large large servings for about a dollar (in 2016); I've always been returned an empty serving dish when I bring this addictive recipe to potlucks.

Vegetarians will find much with which to be delighted in Baba's Kitchen. Food shortages caused by war, famine, and natural gathering/hunting/crop cycles have inspired Ukrainian creativity. Because we eat a 100% meatless meal on Winter Solstice/Holy Eve to honor animals, cooks compete to create the most lush buffet with vegetarian recipes.

Unlike some awkward modern recipes that attempt to mimic meat dishes, Ukrainian food is what it is. You'll notice, for example, that *holubtsi* (cabbage rolls) can be made in an almost endless variety, most of them meatless. The addition of meat requires only a small adjustment in ingredient quantities. Since my family experienced life during times of great deprivation, meatless holubtsi are traditional. I didn't even taste them with meat until I was in my 30's!

Many desserts are fruit-based and honey-sweetened. Unexpected recipes such as wild rose petal preserves: Beautiful, simple, and edible upon cooling, delight the senses.

For value and quality, learning to negotiate with butchers, dairy farmers and hippies is essential. Baba is an ace instructor. Shopping takes on a sparkle as she expounds on techniques for turning deli samples into a full lunch (a capacious bra is paramount) and obtaining illicit *smetana* (sour cream).

You will learn intriguing facts about the history of cooking. Inventors of the first clay oven, Ukrainians created the crepe. Baba offers eleven types, with fillings for both main dishes and desserts. Though she cannot offer proof, she insists we invented mayonnaise. It is more accurately mayo-nez, Ukrainian-Frenchish for, "Sauce that go up your nose." As with many recipes, Baba's mayo is made with cold pressed sunflower oil, which gives it the distinctive taste of our national flower.

There are significant health benefits to sunflower oil. A 2005 study at Virginia Polytechnic showed that sunflower has the highest anti-cholesterol properties (phytosterols) of any nut or seed. The *George Mateljan Foundation*, a nonprofit health promotion society, lists sunflower products among the world's healthiest foods.

Baba's Kitchen offers easy alternatives to wildly popular but time-consuming Ukrainian trademark dishes: varenyky (perogies), crepes and cabbage rolls. Baba does teach the traditional way to prepare each dish. Her additional "lazy" recipes and tips shorten preparation and skill requirements by three-quarters, allowing you to cook without frustration. For example, Baba advises throwing a cabbage in the freezer for easy peeling. This eliminates the tedium and overcooking risk of steaming. The cabbage may then be layered with rice and other ingredients for authentic taste without rolling expertise.

Baba is also a recipe creator. Many in this book list simple variations, encouraging you to stretch a bit. When these occasionally veer from the traditional---such as jasmine rice in cabbage rolls or a dollop of curry in lamb stew---Baba insists they are from her school of *Nouveau Ukrainski Fusionski*.

Baba's Kitchen will introduce you to the Ukrainian wheel of the year not only with holidays. As one who grew up with the original Slow Food Movement, Baba encourages a return to natural cycles and use of the home garden. She suggests a variety of fruits and vegetables that are readily available through farmers markets and online catalogues. Even a balcony tomato plant, if of a solid and prolific species, can contribute mightily to kitchen magic. In a nod to economic renewal, Baba's most-touted tomato is the depression-era *Radiator Charlie's Mortgage Lifter.*

Feminist readers will be excited to read of Ukraine's egalitarian roots and their modern expression in our symbols, rituals and attitudes. For example, the Amazon legend is based upon one branch of our female ancestors (the Scythians) who rode side by side into battle with their men. We domesticated horses, were the first women to wear trousers and chose our own husbands once we had killed three enemies. In Baba's mind, this puts a new meaning to the use of extra virgin olive oil. It also speaks of a culture where battered women's shelters were completely unnecessary.

Baba's black Thoroughbred is named Taras Shevchenko, after Ukraine's national hero, “Because all good horse is combination of poet and warrior.” What horse lover can't relate to this?

If you're of academic bent, you'll enjoy meticulously researched historical facts on these and other matters, borne out by the five page bibliography.

The *Ukrainian Medicine Chapter* offers effective home remedies that are enjoyable to use: honey, raspberries, rose hips, oatmeal, plantain and garlic. You will become equipped for any eventuality, from your pet chicken breaking its toe to chafed nipples due to steppe-riding with jacket open.

About how Baba's Kitchen is organized: Chapter and recipe titles are a mix of Ukrainian and English. My object is not to teach you to speak Ukrainian---I'm not fluent myself---but to portray the most common terms for food items. Many of our recipes are so ancient, they do not have a generic recipe category attached. For example, *borshch* is borshch is borshch. A Ukrainian would never call it *buryak zup*, beet soup.

Differing terms for foods or recipes may depend upon the region where they originated. Sometimes even insular family tradition. My people are from the Western province of Haletzia (Galicia), whose capital is Lviv. Ukrainians in Central or Eastern Ukraine may prepare and name recipes differently than in Baba's Kitchen. The Ukrainian language assigns gender to objects, and this creates differences in the names of food items. Many Ukrainians call salad, *salat.* My family feminizes it to *salata.* Salata could also be a throwback to our sad history as Greek slaves. Or a reference to the town of Salata, Poland. Who knows? As Baba says, “Is lost in mist of mysterious history.”

The Ukrainian spiritual world view is reflected in our language: That all things belong to themselves, and are worthy of recognition. Our language reflects this hugely. You may laugh at Baba's lack of articles when she speaks. But “the” does not exist in Ukrainian. We do not say “'the' horse, 'the' cow, etc.” It's simply “horse” or “cow.” A direct relationship with the creature. Saying, “'the' horse,” is as clear a severing of relationship as would be if we said in English, “'the' mother” or “'the' father” when discussing one's own parents! You can imagine how jarring articles are to a Ukrainian. Consciously or not, many do not use articles, even after years speaking English. Though I am first generation (born in Canada), my own relationship with Nature is such that I, too, find articles jarring. Perhaps our treatment of the environment would be different, if every tree was like a beloved friend, just “tree.”

I haven't contrived names for categories that don't exist. In truth, most mixtures have their own name---except for the Ukrainian-Canadian recipes which are Baba's own inventions. Beef is simply *masnyy*, or meat. Some mixed dishes don't have a name at all. To serve meat without supplying vegetables and a starch mixed in or on the side would be considered rude and not too bright.

About meat: We don't eat goat, and mutton is a rarity on Ukrainian tables (excepting the mountain Hutsul people). You'll notice an artificial paucity of pork recipes. I'm not trying to preach. I'm undergoing an internal revolution while trying to preserve my cultural traditions.

While writing this book, I clued into the miserable life led by sows in gestation crates, and the horror of pigs being butchered alive on assembly lines. I have a similar revulsion to chicken factory farming practices, as well as the lives of some beef and dairy cattle. I recently moved back to a farming community, and am shocked to see how many cattle herds are now never allowed outdoors, standing on concrete 24/7. I grew up with poultry that strutted the yard and pastures like small rulers until "the fateful day." The chicken factories don't even have windows! They don't taste very good, either. As I recently rescued a mallard hen with a broken leg, every attempt at recording duck recipes resulted in a vision of her mournful eyes, and a sensory memory of her trustingly snuggling her long neck under my chin. Therefore, no duck recipes.

If you're not vegetarian, Baba urges seeking out that which has been raised and killed humanely.

Some chapters describe Ukrainian holidays and rituals. In this first volume, I have covered childbirth, Mardi Gras, Spring Equinox/Easter, Summer Solstice, Day of the Dead and Christmas. In a future volume, I'll cover Thanksgiving, New Year's Eve and Day, weddings, funerals and birthdays. Oh, and the legend of Baba Yaga, which taught me not to go to scary places by myself---the Ukrainian version of, "Curiosity killed the cat."I have touched upon bread here, and will expand on the plethora of Ukrainian breads in a following book.

Baba's Kitchen: Ukrainian Soul Food went to print as Russia invaded sovereign Ukraine in retaliation for peaceful protests demanding entrance to the European Union. Responses to global condemnation have been nothing short of pathologically narcissistic. Ukraine has been inhabited by civilized people for 44,000 years, and has never willingly ceded to the new state (18th century) of Russia. We are Indigenous people, and endure genocide and oppression, as have Indigenous peoples around the world. To understand the dark humor of my book's narrator, imagine what life is like when Russia is at its worst, with no global media or Internet watchdogs.

Acknowledgements:

God bless every Baba and Didukh, Bubbe and Zayde who contributed a piece of the story or a recipe. Babas Marika and Pawlina, especially. My Mom, Hanya, who let me stain her precious copy of *Traditional Ukrainian Cookery* with beets, butter and honey from the time I could read, and who dances up a *kolamayka* storm. My Dad, Petro, who escaped both a Stalinist prison camp ("collective") and a Nazi labor camp and passed on his gifts with horses and dogs. He insisted I attend Ukrainian language school, listen to and sing our music and read our literature. What irritated me as a child, is a treasure now.

A big hug to my almost-stepdad, Otto Prockert, who patiently endured my teenage mocking of his German background, and who taught me the power of love and redemption. You were the Dad I never had. You'll have to forgive me again, for the *Ukrainian-German Warm Potato Salad.*

A loving nod to those who shall remain nameless because (a) I was too young to remember my family's friends names; or (b) you told me something outrageous at a:

Winnipeg/MontrealToronto/Calgary/Edmonton/Vancouver/Seattle
bus stop/bar/Legion/community center/thrift store/church/shul, then left; or (c) I was sworn to anonymity.

What happens in the Old Country, stays in the Old Country.

Writing is borne afloat by a tribe of other creatives and supporters.

In alphabetical order:

Ann's Perogey Palace, Winnipeg. See Carol Anne and Marylou. The place to visit when even Lazy Perogies are too much work.

Steve and Bill Allen, for encouraging my writing and being all around good guys. Thank you for the comedy and music tapes Steve, and RIP.

Jean Auel, for your "Earth's Children" series, starting with *Clan of the Cave Bear*. It was wonderful to discuss the Ukrainian domestication of horses with you, and be inspired to explore the historical facts upon which your books are based.

Krista Boehnert and other librarians at *Victoria Public Library*,

Downtown branch, who welcomed my storytelling. Also to Esquimalt branch, where the librarians overcame their squeamishness to help me research spiders.

Harvey and Oscar Cantin and families, owners of *Cantin's Drugstore* in Winnipeg. Thank you for your kindness to a senior lady and her granddaughter. The *Chocolate Medivnyk* (Honey Cake) is for you.

Colleen, Chef Extraordinaire and Den Mother to Many, who taught me how to roast peppers perfectly.

CompuserveBooks & Writers Forum. Thank you for critiquing ideas, editing chapters and trying recipes as they emerged, and convincing me of the value of Baba's stories and recipes. In particular, Eve Ackerman, Esme Ann Binoth, Deniz Bevan, Jo Bourne, Marte Brengle, Claire Greer, Diana Gabaldon, Laura Leigh, Barbara Rogan. Kathleen Horrigan for her concept of "mammogrammed" fish balls. A special nod to the *Kid Crit* special interest group, where the character of Baba sprung full blown from my children's story: "Rosie's Rescue."

Twyla Francois and CETFA, Mercy for Animals and *Animals' Angels.* Thank you for educating me on modern factory farming practices.

Victoria Cownden, Gary P. Green, Mary Holland, Jacquie Hunt, Margo McLoughlin, Cat Thom, Tim Tingle. Fine storytellers all. Thank you for your camaraderie and support.

Chris Gardner, whose encouraging words and generosity helped me summon the courage to complete and publish this book. *Start Where You Are*, you said, and I did.

Lina de Guevara and Marianne van der Meij of *Puente Theatre*, who first created the opportunity for me to perform Ukrainian legends and explore Baba's emerging voice.

The staff throughout the *Fraser Valley Regional Library System.*

Morris, Arthur and Bernie Gunn, "The Fabulous Baker Boys" of Winnipeg. *Gunn's Bakery* is where I first tasted the ultimate poppyseed cookie as a tot. My Babas were then nagged to produce this delight on a regular basis. An entire chapter in this book is dedicated to poppyseed, largely due to this sublime experience. When Baba urges use of only genuine rye and pumpernickel bread, it's Gunn's she has in mind. I'm still working on the secrets of your incredible coffee cake and bagels…

Ben and Phyllis Hochman and family, owners of the finest deli in Canada, Winnipeg's *Oasis.* Your early influence on my idea of great food is considerable. I've not been able to find garlic dills, corned beef or pickled herring as good as yours anywhere. I've attempted to duplicate the latter in this book. Also a big warm hug to Sophie, the waitress who served perfect grilled cheese to a happy kid.

Bill Konyk, inventor of the *Perogy Maker*. I looked forward to seeing your smiling face at the Pacific National and Red River Exhibitions.

My soul brothers from the *New Orleans Dirty Dozen Brass Band*: Efrem, Kevin, Roger and the rest of ya big lugs. You blew into town like jazz angels, and convinced me I'm most beautiful when I'm loud and powerful. Wish I was telling Baba stories in the Lower Ninth. Love forever.

Steve Ram's *All India Sweets Restaurant* in Vancouver. Where Baba had the epiphany that Ukrainian food becomes Fusionski when combined with delights such as jasmine rice, coriander and curry. And *Matka Bozha*, traditional cheese patties (*syrnichky/paneer*) with sweet and sour sauce.

Beloved *Santa Barbara Market* on Vancouver's funky Commercial Drive, and the wonderful *Cioffi's Meat Market* on Hastings. Where Baba gets her mixed meat and cheese samples for impromptu lunches. Santa Barbara's immense collection of olive oils gave her the opportunity to experiment beyond the traditional sunflower oil. Who knew Italian goes so well with Ukrainian?

I won't be the judge of who serves the best smoked meat in Montreal, so will thank two regular haunts equally: *Schwartz's* and *Dunn's.*

Maria Alexakis and *The Shadbolt Centre*, for booking me to tell Ukrainian legends and horse stories.

Victoria Kaspryk and the *Ukrainian Cultural Centre of Victoria* for selling my storytelling CD, "Legends of Ukraine and Canada," in which Baba's distinct voice was first recorded.

The librarians at *Vancouver Public Library*, Downtown and Britannia branches, who helped with research and morale boosting. Natalie and Maria, in particular, you are gems. Thanks for the laughter, and for recommending Tony the mechanic to keep my beloved old GM tank alive!

Vancouver Poetry Slam at *Café Deux Soleils* for your "live editing." Most special thanks to Sean McGarragle, Slammaster extraordinaire.

Fernanda Viveiros, who generously gave me her sage advice.

Winnipeg's *White House Restaurant*, for setting the standard in coleslaw.

With *lyubov* (love),
Raisa Stone
Raisa Marika Stohyn

NB: *Baba's Kitchen* is a mix of stories and recipes from Stalinist and Nazi survivors. **Recipe instructions are bolded step by step**, for easy use.

Chapter One

Zup (Soup)

Baba's Ukrainian Borshch

Hello, is your Baba here. I show you how to make special kind borshch, just like in Ukraine. You pay attention and do exactly what I say, or borshch not so good. This is important national food. We say, *If is no borshch, I not even stay at wedding.*

Give self lots of time, because borshch must cook for hours. This not modern original soup from can. Is real thing. Do not use crazy microwave for borshch. This make enough soup for four people for few day. For good party, make two, three time as much.

Borsch and our *Buryak* (beet) *Salata* is one reason Ukrainian so healthy. Buryak is full of iron, phosphorous, Vitamin C, niacin and magnesium. Is also this thing call anti-oxidant.

Now, go get:

Oxtail. Other beef okay if not oxtail, but just okay. Nothing so good like oxtail for rich borshch. If you not have beef cow, you can find in stupormarket or in Chinatown.

***Buryak*, beet**. If you have organic vegetable, so much better for you, the earth and also good tasting. Organic grow in horse manure, and nothing that come from horse can be bad.

***Kapusta*, green cabbage**. No fancy-schmancy red or curly cabbage. Should be size your head. Little bit worm hole on outside leaf okay, let you know not much chemical on plant. Peel away this leaf. Ignore dirty look from store worker. Who making borshch, you or him?

***Morkva*. Some healthy carrot**. If have dirt on them, so much better.

***Tsibulya*. Onion**. Do not use kind already sprouting green at top. She busy having baby, not have time for you.

***Chasnyk*. One head garlic**. Start with usual size, maybe later you like size elephant kind.

***Krop*. Fresh dill weed**. Do not use kind dried up, come in salt shaker. That taste like straw. Pah! I spit on it.

***Fasolia*, little white bean**. These add protein, so borshch can be whole meal. Also turn pink when cooking with beets. Very cute. Later, when you get used to eating borshch, you might add more bean. One cup dry will make double in size, so you know. Do NOT use can bean for borshch. Will turn into ugly mushinski.

Peretz. **Whole black pepper**. Enough so when you cup hand, just fit in your palm.

Little bit cheesecloth, needle and thread to sew whole black pepper in, drop into borshch. You also can use piece thin cotton sock. Make sure is clean, not smell like feet.

Lavrovyi list. **Bay leaf.** Be careful, have sharp edge.

Never mind pronunciation **salt**. Sea salt best. Tiny pinch, like you give friend, then pretend you not know why he mad.

Soniashnyk**, sunflower seed oil**. From soniashnyk, kind we use in Ukraina.

Limon**, Juice from fresh lemon**. Not frozen, not bottled. Fresh.

Xlib. **Two loaf dark rye bread**. The kind so heavy you can use as football. Not modern Canadian white cotton bread.

Maslo**, butter.** If you can get from farm, is better.

Tool: Extra wooden spoon for smack hand of grown up person try to eat borshch before ready. Do not smack little kid, or Baba be mad.

Put on apron, this get messy. **Put water in soup pot about three quarter to top**. Make boil. Make plan stay home that day. You have something to do, I know.

Drop garlic head and oxtail direct in borshch . Do not peel garlic. Let boil for at least four hour, maybe six, until some meat fall off bony part and floating in water. Liquid will make frothing. Keep removing this frothing. When frothing stop, this your second clue meat is cook. **Add boiling water** when necessary, so not run dry. That boiling water, not from tap. Make big difference to flavor. Then **take all bone out of water**. Let bone cool on counter, because meat left make nice snack.

Grate beet, carrot and cabbage into big pile. Make sure wash and peel beet. I don't peel carrot, it kill vitamin. This part I can't tell you, you have to use own brain. Look back and forth from soup stock to vegetable. Liquid should be about three-quarter of pot. You want nice thick borshch, so look if you think vegetable fit in that liquid. Not too much, not too little. Should always be about one inch liquid on top vegetable. If too much liquid, either chop more vegetable or boil liquid more until some evaporate.

Chop fresh dill weed. Give stem to chicken.

Peel and chop onion. Put into frying pan with sunflower seed oil. I not measure oil, nobody so stupid they can't see how much. Fry until onion soft and clear.

Put all vegetable careful in soup pot. Be gentle so they not splash hot water on you.

Drop in little sewn up bag of whole black pepper. Do not be smarty pants, put pepper in without making bag. You be chewing terrible taste later.

Drop in four bay leaf. You can also make little bag for them, or just put in loose.

Pour in dry fasolia, white bean. Can bean will turn to mushinski.

Add salt.

Have cool meat for nice snack while wait for borshch to cook. See instruction below for how to eat with bread.

Make borshch cook two hour. Scoop white bean from bottom of pot, taste if they soft. Blow on them first! They will be pink now. This where you get kid excited about eating bean.

Soup should be thick, almost like vegetable stew. Add more boiling water if too thick. In meantime, **squeeze lemon** and pour into glass jar. **Put butter out** so is soft.

Scoop out black pepper and bay leaf. Throw away. Do not be lazy and leave in or borshch taste funny later. Keep soft garlic to spread on top of buttered bread, if you like.

How to eat borshch:

You think you know how eat soup? Ha! Maybe terrible scary thing from can. Tuck napkin into shirt, because once redness of beet hit it, it not wash out. That why beet make good *pysanka* (Easter egg) dye. Ladle nice thick borshch into bowls. Make sure you get bean from bottom, even you think you not love bean. You will now, Baba telling you this. Take thick slice butter onto dark rye bread. Not this skinny-shminny "spread" butter like is dangerous monster going to bite you. Add one teaspoon to one tablespoon lemon juice to soup. Take spoonful soup, blow on it. Eat soup, take bite bread. Or can dip buttered bread into soup. Try spread little soft garlic on top of butter. Keep eating.

Borshch taste even better, left in fridge overnight. Eat hot or cold.

Ingredient List:

- Oxtail, two pounds. If unavailable, substitute two pounds fatty beef or beef soup bones with plenty of marrow
- Beets, three pounds

- Green cabbage, one medium head
- Carrots, two pounds
- Onion, one large
- Garlic, one head
- Fresh dill weed, one bunch.
- White beans, one cup dry. Do not substitute canned beans.
- Whole black pepper, one quarter cup
- Bay leaves, four
- Salt to taste
- Sunflower seed oil, half cup
- Lemons, three
- Dark rye or pumpernickel bread, two loaves
- Butter for bread
- Square of cheesecloth, needle and thread
- Keep kettle of boiled water handy

Bismasnyy (Meatless) Borshch

Meatless borshch is absolute essential for Sviat Vechir (Holy Eve). Whole meal is *bismasnyy*, meatless.

In next cook book, Baba going to show you two more kind borshch. If she try to cram everything she know in one book, would be like carry two set *Encyclopedia Britannica, Talmud* and *Kama Sutra* around kitchen. Also *Great Ukrainian Songbook and Manual of Expert Sharpshooting Horsemanship*.

Read borshch recipe above. Meatless borshch is require beginner mind, like Ukrainian Zen priestess. If you want to keep life simple and easy, make *Vegetarian Broth*, and just replace oxtail in usual borshch.If you want to learn fancy Ukrainian traditional way, keep on your reading glass. Thing now going out to lunch. Regular borshch take more cooking time, meatless borshch is more detail-orient. If someone say, "Think outside box," Baba going to slap him with wood spoon. She hate these kind expression. THERE IS NO BOX. Never was no box. You, go sit in stupid box by yourself. See how you like.

Start soaking white bean night before. You will need half cup for this soup. You might as well cook all bean at once. In fact, for traditional Sviat Vechir, you better start your cooking maybe two week before. Not counting *Medivnyk* (Honey Cake), which get start even earlier.

Just like with usual borshch, **leave two big lemon on counter** night before.

Next, see chapter on *Mushrooms, Twelve*. **Pour boil water over best dry kind** you can afford. Drain this water to clean mushroom, then soak them in another cup hot water. Should take about half hour till they ready to cook. How you tell? Pinch them. Should feel like your feet when you soak in bath good fifteen minute. If they getting all wrinkle and weird, is too long. **Simmer them** in this same water for about fifteen minute. Put aside and forget about.

Get out your **biggest soup pot**. All cooking will happen inside this magic cauldron, including onion.

Chop up onion and start fry on low heat in *soniashnyk* oil. These day some entrepreneur hippie can even sell you extra virgin soniashnyk. You could pay them what they asking, but usual hippie will barter.

Baba law: is best to barter with your "service" than material good. By time hippie come out of stone trance, he forget you owe him creepy head massage or something.

You got some peeling and chopping to do here. **Peel nice firm beet and cut up in thin strip. Same with parsley root**. Baba beg you, for once don't go digging for this yourself in forest. Parsley root can be easy confuse with poison hemlock, and your borshch will be in village history for wrong reason.

Put vegetable in with onion, along with whole peppercorn in cheese cloth. You can already see taste going to be different from regular borshch. This one taste little more like dirt. You raising eyebrow. Listen, you ever thought maybe your kid is on to something? Ukrainian honor *Syra Mata Zemlya*, Moist Mother Earth, in all kind of way. We don't even put hoe in earth before Spring Equinox, because she pregnant. We kneel and kiss her, but don't dig. And kid is discourage from tapping with stick, like they do. They can eat little bit dirt, though. How you going to stop them?

Cook vegetable for just few minute, until beet is start to soften itself up. **Pour cold water into pot**. Follow Baba instruction from borshch recipe for this. Nothing change about common sense in meantime.

Make thin strip from carrot and dice from potato and small stalking celery. Give leaf from celery to pet duck. They love this. Celery not so much, because silly string get wrap around beak, and duck is not like goose. She not so good at spitting.**Put these intrepid vegetable into soup pot.**

Cook for maybe fifteen minute.

Shred green cabbage and put into soup. She blend taste with these other ingredient like long lost lover. **Cook borshch another fifteen**

minute. Cabbage should still have crispy crunch.

Pour in tomato juice, crush garlic, dill and cook white bean. Add good pinch salt and pepper. If they pinch back, is too much seasoning.

Here is where something get trickier. You going to **squeeze that lemon** and add little splash at time. This borshch is not deep red like other, so bleaching factor is not concern. Ask family in for taste test. Hand stirring spoon over to someone. Stop adding lemon juice when someone make screwy face. It work every time. This way, if someone like more sour, they can add extra to own bowl later.

Baba warning: do not ask dog for taste test. They love borshch, but hate lemon from getting go. You will not find honest opinion here. Good thing is, sometime lemon work better on furniture dog is chewing than hot sauce.

Baba bet you think you done. No way. You forgetting those **Ukrainian mushroom**. They should be cool now, or you did something wrong. Chop them up and add to soup, along with their own personal water.

Make whole soup pot boil, then turn down to lowest heat until time to eat. See regular borshch instruction for how to eat. But most of time, we make this recipe into:

Clear Bismasnyy (Meatless) Borshch

Also is important that if you get help in kitchen for Sviata Vechera, you like who you cooking with. We say about someone we don't like, *I wouldn't make borshch with such a person.*

You can serve meatless borshch clear with *Vushky*. These little dumpling, look like cut off ear and fill with some kind filling: mushroom, *kapusta* (sauerkraut) or fish. Just not meat for meatless. Why I have to tell you? They in same chapter as *Varenyky*. You call "perogy" for some reason. Is probably translation from Polish language.

If you making clear borshch, don't throw in mushroom. Use only they juice and save them for vushka filling. You will feel so clever.

"Clear" mean you going to cook borshch at least half hour longer, then strain out all or most of vegetable. Leave white bean alone. This kind waste make Baba feel bad, even if is only once in year. She add lemon after straining.

She cool these vegetable down with big fan and take as extra offering to her barn animal on Sviata Vechera. Everybody love, but horse make extra gas than usual. You might not want to have romantic ride on Christmas Day.

Ingredient List:

- Dried *boletus* or *porcini* mushrooms, three quarters of a cup. If you can find Ukrainian *bilya hryby*, call Baba
- Cooking onion, one large
- Sunflower oil, three tablespoons. The cold pressed, organic kind will give you the most flavor
- Beets, one pound
- Parsley root, one half of small
- Peppercorns, four
- Keep kettle of boiling water handy
- Celery, one small stalk
- Potato, one medium
- Carrot, one medium
- Dill, one half bunch
- Green cabbage, one medium head
- Tomato juice, three quarters of a cup
- Lemons, two large
- Garlic, one clove
- White beans, one half cup cooked
- Salt and pepper to taste

Smetana (Sour Cream) on Borshch

People, they ask Baba, "What about sour cream on borshch? I go to fancy-schmancy restaurant and skinny borshch come with one beet floating, and big spoonful sour cream."

Baba going to tell you only once: No way, *smetana* on borshch. This Soviet thing. Baba will supply consequence. See *Horseradish Sauce*, under *Dressing, Chapter Three*. Only thing add is lemon juice.

Here is two way to use smetana like independent Ukrainian: go to good family farm that escape stupid government inspection. Must be milk unpasteurized & cow with no antibiotic making terrible taste. Ask for jar smetana. I guarantee they keep in back of cooler, because Canada treat like is some kind drug. If you have to, milk cow yourself. Sing her song what good *korova* she is. If Jersey cow, best kind. Very rich cream.

Cream should be yellow & make sloshing sound in jar, Mason type.

Pay whatever farmer ask, hide in brown paper bag. Better people think you secret drinker, than make betrayal of good farmer.

Bake loaf very dark rye or pumpernickel bread, especially good with caraway seed. Dip bread in sour cream, sprinkle little salt. Eat it. Second thing, put this real smetana on your varenyky, or perohi. Very tasty. Even better, you fry varenyky in butter & onion first. But no sour cream in borshch.

PS What town you living in? Baba need to keep eye on your thing, so you not eating like Soviet.

Kurka (Chicken) Soup

This kind chicken soup so good, make you cry. Also help when you have cold. I thought I know how make best kind, but Jewish neighbor in Ukraina, she stop by and show how to make even better. She say is Jewish penicillin. So this some kind collaboration. Make sure you have all day.

First thing, go to butcher, say you want best chicken. Poke chicken hard with finger, make sure is firm. Also, no purple in skin, this mean chicken bruised from bad treatment before killed. You watch *Criminal Mind*? This terrible thing for chicken. Best kind is organic free range, but very, very expensive. Oy, but taste so good! When Baba live in Ukraina, free range mean, "Run quick to yard and grab chicken before sonumabitch Soviet steal that, too."

If kosher butcher in neighborhood, this very good place to buy. It mean chicken raised and killed with respect, rabbi supervise and say "Thank you" to God for food.

Make sure butcher include chicken heart, liver and *poopitz* (gizzard). This part of flavor. If you so unlucky you have no butcher and buy in stupormarket, also get package chicken livers and so on. Sometime nice guy in back will find all parts for you. I go after I make hair fluffy at salon.

You might need buy new **soup pot. You need so big, barely fit on stove. Fill halfway with cold water and teaspoon salt, start boiling.**

Good news is, never mind waste time chopping chicken in pieces. Only reason to chop is if your pot not big enough. Never mind this diet-schmiet "peel off skin." Is yellow chicken fat that make so much flavor, Jewish friend she call schmaltz.

Take heart, liver and poopitz out of chicken, wash and put in

fridge. You will put in soup later, chopped. In Old Country, we cook these thing with chicken and eat whole, but I go easy on beginner.

Wash chicken. Put whole chicken in boiling water. Adjust to simmering. This mean is bubbling little bit, but not rolling around.

Drop in whole head garlic, do not bother to peel.

Big pinch salt.

Chicken cook all day until meat slide off bones. Every two hour or so, skim broth to take away foam.

Add boiling water when needed. This secret of good soup. Never use hot water from tap.

Chop vegetable:

Large onion, pretty fine. Fry in butter until soft and clear.

Celery. Make very fine piece, or else string get caught in denture.

If you like, **carrot.** Sometime children don't like taste of boiled carrot, so I put one very large carrot (not chopped) into chicken soup for sweet taste. Then I pull out and eat it myself, with butter, salt and pepper. This carrot thing also work with roast chicken.

Parsley. Chop very fine, about half large bunch. Throw out stem.

Turnip or parsnip. Not both, one is bitter enough. See how flavor work? Carrot sweet, turnip bitter, onion and garlic spicy. Yum.

Be very careful, **use ladle to scoop out chicken skeleton**. Some meat will still be on bones, you can scrape off into soup or let cool and have little snack. Scoop out all skin and give to dog or cat when cool. Do not give chicken bone to animal, they choke!

If chicken was very, very chubby and there is three inch fat floating on top, you can scoop out little bit. But make sure leave some, or it taste like terrible diet drink, no point to making soup.

Scoop out garlic head, which now be very soft. **Cut open each clove and drop mushy garlic back into soup**. If you can't stand wait, spread some of garlic on dark rye bread with thick slice butter and sprinkle salt. Call family into kitchen to share garlic and pick at chicken skeleton. Argue who pull wishbone. Argument not over till somebody cry.

Sew or tie whole black pepper and bay leaf in cheesecloth or very clean sock. Sometime I use piece my old bloomer, after good wash. Some Canadian tell me to try modern original pantyhose, but I worry they melt. Drop in chicken broth, along with all vegetable. Do not, under any circumstance, be lazy thing and put spice in soup without wrapping in cloth. You be picking disgusting taste from teeth, whole next week.

Take **heart, liver and poopitz from fridge, chop very fine and drop in soup** for extra flavor.

Cook for one hour.
In meantime, you can cook some kind starchy thing to make soup whole meal:

*Brown rice
*Skinny noodle
*Broad egg noodle, this what my Baba always make herself. See *Lokshyna*, *Chapter Twenty One*. What, you surprise Baba had Baba? You thinking maybe I drop from alien spaceship?
*Steam potato
*Drop noodle

Next day, will be thick layer yellow fat on top soup. You have diet-schmiet mind, you be tempted to skim off whole thing. Do not do this, or soup taste terrible. If you really cannot break yourself of crazy obsession, skim away maybe half fat and thank God you have good food. Baba telling you sure thing, she didn't get really, really fat from eating soup. Neither did you.

Above instruction must be follow for real chicken soup.

Here your option:

*__Peel and chop large potato__, make into small cube, drop in soup one half hour before ready.
*__Chop one head spinach__ into tiny piece. Make sure wash off dirt, first. Or use frozen package, if you so lazy. Use less or no parsley, if you do this.
*__Cut two red, yellow or orange pepper into small piece__ and put in soup. They very sweet, so you maybe can leave out carrot. Do not use green pepper. I hate green pepper!
*__Peel and chop large yam__, put in soup instead of carrot.
*__Add three very small chop yellow zucchini, unpeeled__. Do not use large green ones, they get slimy in soup. If neighbor banging on door trying to give away green zucchini, is good reason. Ask them, "Why you grow this stuff?" If they bring you shopping bag full of zucchini and also "zucchini loaf", you know they both desperate and hate your guts. This thing not real food. When Soviet steal our land, they plant many huge field with zucchini. Then they invent zucchini loaf for Siberian prison camp.
*In bowl soup (not whole pot) try little **cayenne pepper or paprika**, change taste. Hot pepper add to penicillin power if you getting cold

inside your head. It make your blood hot.
***Use white part of leek**, instead of regular onion. I'm not sure make as good penicillin, but sure is tasty if you can afford. Fry in plenty butter.

Ingredient List:

- One whole chicken. Organic, roasting or stewing. Buy according to your budget. Ask butcher to include the heart, liver and gizzard.
- If not included with chicken, buy a package of chicken livers. one half pound
- Garlic, one head
- Salt and cracked black pepper, to taste
- Bay leaves, two or three
- One large onion, chopped fine
- Butter or olive oil, one quarter cup
- Celery, three stalks
- Carrots, three small or two large
- Parsley, one half large bunch
- Turnip, medium or parsnip, large
- Starchy ingredient such as rice, noodles or potatoes

Soup with Vushka

Make *Chicken Soup*, or *Simple Vegetarian Broth*, both under Soup (what you think, under Dessert?) Drop in vushky. Is that simple.

OR

Before you add all vegetable to chicken soup, scoop out just enough broth for you and your friend.

Fry little bit chop onion, white or green, in butter or olive oil. **Add salt and pepper.**

Drop in vushky. Admire how good you are at making little ear. Now **drop vushky and onions into clear broth**. **Eat.** Could not be simpler.

Ingredient List (for two people):

- Soup
- Onion, one half medium chopped OR leek
- Butter, olive or sunflower oil, three tablespoons
- Salt, pinch

- Cracked black pepper, pinch

Beef Stock

Here and there through recipe book, Baba going to tell you to add beef stock. Do she mean brown slopping from tin can? You must be having *zhabahanka*, fantasy. I know you thinking stuff in can is yummy liquid from cook beef. Let Baba read you label: first ingredient is water. Who know from where. Next is salt. Hoo boy, take an awful lot of salt to be list second! Third is hydrolyze plant protein: wheat, corn, soy. This mean floor sweeping at factory. Janitor and his buddy throw into mop bucket with salt. Now we know source of water. And here is some sugar. They steal this from McDonald. Is your stomach making rumble yet?

Finally, we have “beef extract.” This mean cow spit in it. You hope is spit. To enhance this piquant taste is monosodium glutamate, some kind spice---could be anything. No way of knowing. And last, to make cow spit look like something, they use “caramel color.” This is nother way to say sugar syrup that been burn. Probably on janitor truck engine.

Baba going to take you through professional Ukrainian process for beef stock. Like almost anything good, this take all day.

She hope you good friend with your butcher, because you want those meaty bone he giving away to dog. Otherwise, you can start with oxtail, which is richest taste. Second best is beef rib or short rib. Baba hope you not prejudice against short cow. Don't be thinking short rib is inferior. It have lots rich fat for taste. Beef rib is dryer.

Take deep breath and have one more try with butcher. Ask him for “trim.” This is some meat and fat he trim off and maybe will give to you. If you not have this kind nerve, how you going to cook with Baba?

Here come beef stock boot camp:

Put oven rack in middle and make oven 400 degree F. No hotter, or beef bone will have burn spot.

You going to roast beef on **shallow roasting pan. Sprinkle with salt and pepper. Put meat fat side down. Cook one hour**, until they dark as your real hair color. Turn over once.

Baba warning: if you in apartment, have dish towel handy for waving. Smoke alarm will probably come on when you open door. At least it do in my girlfriend old age apartment, where they stacking people like firewood. Day they try to put Baba in one of these, is day she drive her Cadillac off of cliff. And take some horse eater with her.

In meantime, **chop up carrot, onion, celery and garlic**. White part of leek also make your tongue swell in good way. Baba like to add big ripe meaty tomato. If you don't grow your own that make you drool just from smell, don't bother.

Take out your hugest soup pot. If you can borrow cauldron from neopagan friend, all the better. **Heat up soniashnyk oil, and throw in onion and carrot. Stir them around quick** so each piece get its own little oil coat. Now we going to make real caramelization. This mean you keep stirring vegetable around faithful, till they cook in their natural sugar and juice.

Baba know you been to one those all night truck stop. Some them hamburger cook know how to caramelize onion better than any chef she ever seen. Ask for them to grill you cinnamon bun on same place onion been, then slap on butter. After you been out drinking, oy yoi yoi.

Once onion and carrot turning brown, **throw in tomato. Once this turn brownie, toss in celery. Remember, keep stirring**. Because celery have so much water, it won't get as caramelize like rest of vegetable. Not to worry. Be satisfy if it get soft. Be satisfy if you can coordinate all this. Like always with Baba recipe, if something burn, throw it out. If you burn onion, it cost you maybe few cents to replace. Big deal.

If beef is ready, take out and pour fat from pan into heating proof container. See *Roast Beef, Chapter Nine*, for discussion of Ukrainian delicacy, salo, fat. Baba is sure you have reflex to throw out, but we cooking Ukrainian now. You going to save this salo for specialist occasion. Like lunch.

Look your meat over careful like always. If anything is burn, throw away. Do not make false economy. Burn piece of bone or meat will ruin stock and whole day of work. Even Ukrainian dog would not eat this. Especial one been living with Baba and get homemade food. Baba have pet that live twenty-five year and flea is scared of them.

Baba Law: Food is to make body as strong as your *dusha*, soul.

Throw meat into soup pot with vegetable. Cover what you see with cold water, and turn heat up to make boiling. Once it spitting in your eye, turn down to gentle simmering.

Put roasting pan on stove element. Move your *chatchkes* aside first so they don't melt. Oooh, you surprise Baba speaking Yiddish, too? I come from integrate village, *dai Bozha*. Jewish people is real nice to me in Canada, too.

Throw in some water and turn heat to high. Scrape precious leftover brown bit from pan bottom. Again, your crazy reflex going to kick in and you going to want to throw out. Don't you dare. If it make you feel better, this process have fancy name, "deglaze." **Throw these brown scraping into stock pot** with vegetable. Add trim too, if your big eye work on butcher and he give you some.

Add four clove garlic to stock pot. This is what keep flea away.

Sew up peppercorn in cheesecloth like Baba tell you in borshch recipe. You read that first, right? If you like bay leaf, add that. Is matter of taste. Parsley and thyme can be interesting flavor. Is up to you. Peppercorn is non-negotiate.

Beef stock now going to simmer for six to eight hour of your life. This why Baba hope you listen to instruction real careful. You going to be walking back and forth from pool table to skim off crap that float to top of stock. Good thing is, house will smell like Heaven instead of Kraft dinner.

Once stock is done, let it cool. Dump away everything but liquid. Baba mean everything. If there is any flavor left in meat or vegetable, you didn't cook long enough. Is different from borshch, where soup get part of strong lip smack flavor from beet and cabbage.

Strain through sieve. Picky person like yourself might strain through cheesecloth. Pickier person might strain themselves straining.

Is up to you how far you want to boil this down. If you have time, you can keep going another two or four hour to make thick. Then you store in freezer and add water when you need. Super-thick stock can even go in ice cube tray. This is call "demi-glace." Is actual soup syrup you will just grab from freezer to make sauce. If you can find it in there.

Easiest way to skim fat off this stock is to put in fridge.

There. You are not same person as at start of recipe. From tin can alley to real Ukrainian beef stock is super heroine leap. Once you learn to bake bread, chop wood and pickle herring, Baba going to give you some kind certificate. Like those West Coast *therapista*. One weekend in community college and they digging inside your brain and making reiki-schmeiki on your body.

Ingredient List:

- Oxtail, short or beef ribs, four pounds
- Onion, one large
- Carrots, one half pound

- Celery, two medium stalks
- Garlic, four cloves
- Peppercorns, scant hand full
- Salt and pepper to taste
- Water

Hanya's Soup

Baba going to tell you what happen to my friend Hanya one day when she making soup. Hanya live with very difficult husband. Kind one day start beating her. At this time was no such thing "woman transition house." Not that Hanya kind of woman who would leave her home and let crazy man have while she sleep on bunk bed in hen house. No way.

First she try keeping two by four under bed and whack! break his nose while he sleep. But husband not stupid. He catch on after two, three time.

Hanya try everything traditional Ukrainian to make happy home. She tell her *Domovyk*, house spirit, she sorry she ignore him when he pull her hair before wedding. He trying to tell her is going to be abusive husband. Afterward, she wrap bread in white linen and feed Domovyk every day to ask for help. She even hang old shoe from clothing line to make him laugh. But Domovyk say, "Sorry baby, I can only warn. I cannot stop crazy husband."

Hanya pray and pray. Then Hanya husband get sugar diet beet. He very sick, doctor say. Hanya start adding pinch sugar here, then over some month, fist full sugar there. Husband stop beating her. Husband get sicker.

One day Hanya start boil soup on stove. She wonder if her *banyak* going to be home to eat, or if he out at bowling alley with banyak buddy. She need to know how much sugar to add. She go down street. She see her husband shoe outside one door and shade drawn.

Hanya beat on door like storming trooper. "I know you in there drinking vodka with no good goddamn sonumabitch Russian!" she yelling so all neighbor hear. "Your sugar diet beet going to kill you. I so worry!"

Then she smile and go back to stir soup. Little while later, husband come stagger in door and fall down on living room floor. Hanya do nothing. Once soup simmering good, she walk over where husband in diet beet comma. She lean over and yell, "I tell you not to drink with no good goddamn sonumabitch Russian. Now you going to die of sugar diet beet and nobody going to help you."

Husband moan. His finger twitch like he dialing phone. "Oh no," Hanya whisper, "If you think I going to waste good money on ambulance when you drinking with no good goddamn sonumabitch Russian, you got another think in making."

Hanya go back to soup. With home made rye bread, it make very nice meal after funeral.

Hanya's Vegetable Soup

This was kind of soup Hanya made on stove on day of destiny. Is sticking to your rib. Delicious, but sticky rib make it hard to sing.

Invite friend over in case husband not around to enjoy by time you finish.

Fry chop onion, celery, carrot, and chop new or baby potato in enough extra virgin olive or sunflower oil in hugest iron pan to make good sizzle. Vegetable should be soft and firm all one time, just like your heart.

Add *Chicken Soup* broth, exactly as much as fit in 7-11 Big Gulp cup.

Add water, boiled. If straight from tap, make soup taste like from tin can. Why bother?

Add pinch salt and make boil.

Add fine chop parsley.

Bring down to gentle kind simmer. Cook fifteen minute.

While this going on, **chop up big red ripe tomato** from your garden. First, you smell them. This big part of pleasure growing tomato. If some no good goddamn sonumabitch Soviet stole tomato from garden while you sleep, you have my permission to open one pound can style dice tomato. But only if.

Chop up green bean and if you can find, okra. I assuming you people down South reading Baba recipe. In past, we have good recipe and literature exchange program. That Tennessee William, he cook more than cat on hot tin roof. Ha! He Baba's penpal for long time. Fried *Chicken in Cream* is under *Chicken, Chapter Eight*. Boy oh boy, Baba hate redundancy.

If you not have okra, **chop about one cup broccoli very fine**, including stem. Put in soup.

Simmer for another fifteen minute or so.

Baba know you soup beginner. Is temptation to over salt. Here is correction trick: slice up potato and put in soup. It will suck up extra salt.

Fish out potato and throw in compost. Now you ready for any occasion. Good christening, bat mitzvah, engagement party or funeral. Baba always prepared. She teach old Boy Scout leader everything he know.

Serve with nice plate rye or pumpernickel bread, buttered. Large glass horilka for each person at funeral don't hurt, either.

Your option:

***Add fine chop spinach** to other vegetable in oil.
***Add chop red, yellow or orange pepper.**
*Make with *Vegetarian Broth.*
***Add hand full good goat cheese, fresh Asiago or grate Parmesan cheese** to top of soup.
***Try different kind spice**: thyme, oregano or rosemary is good. For rosemary, use only powder so your friend not get little needle stuck in their gum. Why they chewing gum when eating soup? Baba have no idea. They your friend.
***Add bay leaf**.

Ingredient List:

- Onion, one large
- Celery, two stalks
- Carrot, two large
- Baby potatoes, half pound
- Chicken soup broth, four cups OR vegetarian broth, four cups
- Extra virgin olive oil or sunflower oil, half cup
- Boiled water, one cup
- Parsley, pinch
- Salt and cracked black pepper to taste
- Ripe tomatoes, three
- Green beans, half cup OR okra
- Broccoli, one cup
- Pumpernickel or rye bread, buttered loaf

Baba's Ukrainian Minestrone

You going to make vegetable soup like above, only add few thing. This not official Ukrainian recipe. Is *Nouveau Ukrainski Fusionski*, invent by your Baba.

Add bay leaf to chicken broth. Can also cook soup with whole twig of rosemary. Make sure to take out from soup before serving, or someone think they chewing on Christmas tree!

If you have money, **buy leek instead of onion. Chop up white part**. It have creamier taste than onion. If you don't have money, don't whine. Nobody going to lose appetite from, "Oy yoi yoi, I wish I had money for leek instead of plain old onion!" Most people in Canada have taste bud rotten from eating white bread and meat from can. They swallow before even tasting. Remember: they lucky you even feeding them.

Along with dice potato, you can add other root vegetable like turnip.

Cook *fasolia*, white bean. Add same time you put in green bean. Because you don't cook this so long like borshch, you can't add fasolia raw.

Throw in one cup *Lokshyna* (egg noodle), *Chapter Twenty One*. If noodle is fresh, add in last few minute of cooking soup. If you buy this dry stuff in box, is okay because have cute shape you probably can't make at home, like spiral or shell. Whole wheat noodle better for you, if you can find.

Ingredient List:

- Vegetable soup as above.
- Bay leaf, one
- Leeks, two if in your budget. Otherwise, use onion as above
- Turnip, one
- White beans, one cup OR
- Garbanzo beans, one cup
- Noodles, one cup. See Lokshyna
- Good bread, buttered

Horokhivka (Pea Soup)

Green pea is central kind food in Ukraina. We get excite watching pea vine flower, then beautiful green pod growing like little fairy thumb in garden. I like sit on porch with grandchildren and shell pea together.

In fact, I first get idea for this so spiritual cook book when I go to "Free Meditation Session" at New Age church. I am living on West Coast, remember. New Age church tell me they going to show me how to find freedom. They lock all door with us inside. Why this feel familiar? Is because I know about Soviet brainwash tactic. I don't leave yet because I am interest how Canadian do it.

Leader he get up there and he mumbling about this and that. Then he say, "Go to your plaaaaace of peassssss. Go to your plaaaaace of peassssss."

I have fond feeling for pea. I want to do this right away. I run to door and tell security guard to take away chain. He say not until they pass voluntary minimum suggested donation basket.

I tell him I going to pass out in basket, involuntary. This not minimum suggestion, is stone fact. Also I say something about "unlawful confinement" and how this not Siberia. It not even like when Baba do *est.* At least then she know she pay $5000 to be abuse by idiot. And she know where he live. Security guard unlock chain real quick, make big teeth and tell Baba to get some air. Then he lock door even quicker behind.

I go home and start spiritual writing for all your benefit. Be grateful. This not spiritual writing like people who selling this *Law of Attracting.* Baba find what it “attract” is selfish privileged person. You notice they not trying to attract to rebuild Black neighborhood in New Orleans and find home for Ukrainian orphan.

You now in Baba place of peasssssss.

You going to **pick careful through two cup dry split pea**. Take out any rock so they not split your denture. **Wash pea in strainer and soak in water overnight**.

Plan ahead. This excellent recipe to make while you doing laundry.

Next day, **take out big soup pot. Fill with water**. This include water you soak dry pea with. Do not use water you soak bunion in.

Chop onion and fry in butter. Some people add onion to this soup without frying first, but they not real cook like me.

Add split pea, salt pork, onion, dice carrot, chop stalking celery (if you like taste) and salt.

Make boil, then turn heat down so soup is simmer. This mean you can see ingredient tumble around in pot like fruit in slot machine, but not too fast. Or like watching sock in dryer. Why you watching, I don't know. Maybe you can tell rest of us where other sock go. Who else so boring they going to do this?

Cook soup until pea is tender, about same time as it take to do one load laundry, wash and dry.

This assume you wash at home, not on rock in river. About one hour and half.

Peel and crush large clove garlic. Add to soup.

Let ingredient cool for while. Put in blender. If you wait in line at river while some *banyak* untangle his short from tree branch, maybe pea soup is too thick. Add some boil water.

Grate onion. You only going to use tablespoon. While you doing laundry, think hard about what to do with rest of onion. You don't want to throw out and you don't want to smell up fridge for week. This not genius test. I can see your forehead wrinkle. Don't bruise brain.

Brown flour in small amount bacon fat or trimming from salt pork.

Fry grate onion in this.

Pour small amount of soup into fry pan with fat and onion. Mix around till look like green smoothie. I want to make New Age Soviet Meditation Hostage Taker drink this. I going to say to him, "Here your 'plaaaaaace of peasssssss', dum dum."

Anyway, **take green smoothie and pour into soup. Mix around like wild. Make soup boil for very short time. Add salt and crack black pepper**.

Surprise Ukrainian ingredient: **for each person you serve horokhivka, chop half garlic dill pickle in tiny piece. Put in soup**. This special thing, because Ukrainian most gifted pickle maker in world. We win Pickle Olympic every year.

Your option:

*Instead of salt pork, use **nice piece cook ham**. Leave on bone so marrow leak into soup. This give extra flavour.
***Garnish with *Garlic Crouton*,** *Chapter Nine*. I know you going to use crumby sawdust crouton from box. If you do, don't tell people this Baba recipe for horokhivka. I disown you big time. Or use *Fried Lokshyna* (Egg Noodles), *Chapter Twenty One*.
Start with make *Chicken Soup. Use broth as soup base.
Start with *Vegetarian Broth as soup base.

Ingredient List:

- Dry split peas, two cups
- Water, two quarts.
- Keep kettle of boiled water handy
- Onion, one large
- Butter, quarter cup
- Salt pork, half pound
- Carrot, one large
- Celery, one large stalk
- Salt to taste

- Cracked black pepper to taste
- Garlic, one large peeled clove
- Flour or cornstarch, two tablespoons
- Garlic dill pickle, one half for each person's soup

Simple Vegetarian Broth

Baba like to make fun of vegetarian. But really, I try this style of life. One night every year, when Ukrainian prepare meatless dinner. This call Sviata Vechera or Holy Night---Christmas Eve. We not eat meat so Christian can look animal in eye when we thank them for not biting Jesus in stable. Sheep particularly not fond of baby. They just play dumb. I bet you not know this.

One time little girl ask me why wise men not bring Jesus diaper for present. Is very good question. Maybe you can answer for yourself if you Bible scholarship. Let Baba know. Little girl still waiting.

One night in year is not very big "thank you" to animal, I know. Is like when revenue taxation send you Christmas card. Who care? Just make you madder. So Baba want to say, real personal, "Sorry pig. Sorry chicken. Thank you cow."

Now let's eat, fellow hypocrite!

You can make this broth for Borshch, or any kind soup. Except will not work for *Horokhivka* (pea soup), because ham or bacon is part of flavor. What about for chicken soup, you asking Baba. What, you think you going to trick me into answer? No way, hoser.

But I going to make you joke: Why did Baba cross road?
Answer: Because chicken was on other side, trying to run from fate. Hahahahahahahahahaha.

You probably have to be Ukrainian refugee and read Taras Shevchenko* to understand how funny this joke.

Broth:

Boil big pot water.

Drop in head garlic. Not clove. His whole fat head.

Add salt and crack black pepper.

Boil half day. Keep add boil water every time soup reaches half way in pot. If your mother was cook, there will be water line inside.

After four hour or so, **take out head garlic**. Is going to be mushy, but still inside skin. Taste soup. If enough garlicky taste, leave like this. If you love garlic like Baba do, take mush out from head garlic and drop in soup. Or spread on butter rye bread.

***Taras Schevchenko** is Ukraina national hero. We are kind of people who give this honour to poet and artist. Taras go to jail for writing about how is not Ukrainian destiny to be slave. He also write lots beautiful poetry about personal fate. NOT TO BE CONFUSE WITH COMMUNIST. Taras was good guy. In Canada national hero is man who hit puck with stick. This is whole nother story Baba can't be bother with. Even if best hockey player is Ukrainian. Baba have to say, at least Gretzky smart enough to open restaurant after he retire. Even if he have only two his grandmother recipe on menu, and don't write letter back to Baba when she ask for his help with cookbook publication. Pah!

Ingredient List:

- Water, two quarts.
- Keep kettle of boiled water handy
- Garlic, one head
- Salt to taste
- Cracked black pepper to taste
- Good bread, one loaf

Hrybivka (Mushroom Soup)

When Baba come to Canada she concern all her strength going away. Electric stove mean she not chopping wood, chicken in store mean she not swinging ax. And most unfortunate, no *kozaky* mean she not going for run around living room.

She go to gym to do this building body. In Ukraina we do not have people who lift heavy thing and put back down for no reason. In Old Country, is call “work.” We don't look in mirror like while we doing it, neither.

But when in Canada, do as *yolop* Canadian do.

For some reason, Baba attract Black man in gym. They always want to be near her. One day she singing to herself while she working her solenoid. Two them muscle men get into fist fight.

One say, “She sound like Aretha Franklin.”

Other one say, “No man, she just like Mary J. She my girl.”

This kind of thing always happening to Baba. She don't know why.

Both man surround her on bench, throw their arm around her and yell, "Oreo!" This don't bother Baba too much, because these guy drool a little less than other in gym.

Baba decide she going to be their support system at national building body competition. As you know, she is altruism person.

You also know that after man been on stage, he going to be very hungry from strict diet, and very hot from competition. They is pump.

After Baba assist her building body friend getting whole body shave and oil as altruism professional courtesy, she head for hotel kitchen. She borrow ingredient and pot from chef and make excellent hrybivka. This is satisfy recipe that is so easy, too. Perfect for when you want to feed athlete but not weigh him down for action.

Wash fresh, quality mushroom. Slice them up so they attractive and still look like mushroom, not sad little piece of dirt like in can soup. If you using dry, soak for at least two hour before cleaning. Throw out water they soak in. There is funky, which is good for both music and food. Then there is grungy, which is barely good enough for music.

Boil medium pot water and throw in mushroom. Turn to simmer and cook until out jump tasty smell. About fifteen minute.

Let sit on stove until is temperature of hotel room when you just get there. Later, going to be temperature when you leaving. Ha!

Strain out mushroom and keep liquid in pot. Add salt and crack black pepper.

Put kettle on to boiling. Enough for splash into recipe and cup of coffee for you. Baba can tell you is Instant person.

Heat up medium frying pan. Mix around glop of butter or soniashnyk oil with flour until it all turn goldie.

Mix chop onion and crush garlic into butter-flour thing. Trick is to keep scraping around with speculum so nothing stick or burn. **When this mix turn brown, add big splash boiling water**. Stir some more. When everything in pan is smooth like building body man mastoid, **pour into mushroom liquid**. **Also add those mushroom. Make simmering for five minute.**

Baba bring *vushky* in cooler to building body conference. They is little dumpling shape like ear, to drop in soup. Meat filling will give your competitor more energy for after-party.

Your option:

*If you like that Chinese hot sour soup, **add sauerkraut juice** to this soup, last thing. Really, it taste nothing like. Baba just trying to find some cultural common ground. Or put bowl of sauerkraut juice on table so guest can add as they like. Is acquire taste, just like big ripply adenoid on woman.

Ingredient List:

- Fresh mushrooms, one pound OR dried mushrooms, one cup
- Butter, one tablespoon OR cold pressed sunflower oil, one and one half tablespoons
- Flour, one teaspoon
- Salt and cracked black pepper to taste
- Onion, one teaspoon when chopped
- One clove garlic
- Boiling water, one quarter cup
- Sauerkraut juice, one quarter to one half cup. Taste as you add

Soviet Soup

During Holodomor, which is famine Stalin make to murder Ukrainians, we make Soviet soup. We try again during EuroMaidan Revolution.

Ha! Just kidding. They too dry and stringy for good soup. And in 2013, they coated in tear gas we spray on them while making protest. Ha!

See *McCarthy Soup, below.*

McCarthy Soup

Is no such thing. Would be tasteless, anyway.

See *Soviet Soup*, above.

Chapter Two

Salata (Salad)

Baba's Original Garden Salata & Dressing

Hoo boy, we going to have some fun now! This best kind of salata west or east of Carpathian Mountain.

Listen, I know you busy photocopying out of heck from my recipe book. You pathetic orphan. Baba feel sorry.

Not so sorry I not call my RCMP boyfriend deal with you. Is like stealing from your grandmother purse. Baba have something call pull. See *Poppyseed, Chapter Twenty Four.*

This salata recipe so original that no one allow to touch, not even Baba relative. Plug in video and read warning in front of movie. Do this right now. Just like movie-maker, Baba going to send Ukrainian FBI if you copy her recipe. This your final warning before you have to send her quarter million dollar. If you send cash only in small wrinkle bill we keep FBI out of it. Baba letting you off easy this time, poopchik.

Here is how to make best Ukrainian salata in world: **Steam youngest unpeeled baby potato** you can find. **Cut each tiny one only in half** if size of golf ball or smaller. Over time, you learn difference in taste between red, yellow and that kind called "peanut" potato. Order heritage potato from seed catalogue sometime. Russet taste like sand if you use in salad. Is only for bake potato.

Each type give salad little bit different personality. I keep people guessing, "What that Baba going to do now?"

Leave enough time for potato to cool and marinate, at least two hour. Can be in fridge overnight if you like to plan ahead. As if. Put potato in bowl right away when soft. If you leave in metal steamer, potato will start to taste like bad potato-fish. Blech. **Put few spoonful of dressing on potato and toss very gentle**. Now leave them alone to be well adjust.

Go to your garden and pick:

Baby lettuce, arugula, spinach, watercress and any other type green is not poison. Even dandelion green. Fill up your apron. You better not be spraying pestingside anywhere near. Also, do not pick green thing near road. Plant absorb bad chemical from car exhaustion.

Baba warning: If you try make this Ukrainian salata with ugly lettuce from store, kind she have pale green head like insect, whole thing going to be ugly. Don't be credit to your ape ancestor, okay? If you have to buy green thing from store, don't get this kind. At least buy lettuce with personality, like red oak. Mix up different type, as young as possible.

At least two large ripe tomato or whole pile small one.

Big fat juicy cucumber. Size like some man put in vacuum cleaner to try and get. You saying, "Oh, come on Baba. That not true!" You don't think so? My sister work in hospital emergency. She say you would not believe what they mostly fix on weekend. And you wondering why your kid with fever have to wait four hour.

Red, orange or yellow pepper. NOT GREEN. Something is suspicious with taste and texture of green pepper, I don't know what. Only thing I know of that improve by mutation.

One half cauliflower or broccoflower.

Baby yellow zucchini. Under no circumstance green zucchini. For whole political story, see *Chicken Soup, Chapter One*. Baba shouldn't have to tell you this. You reading her life story like bestseller book, right?

Big fat carrot. This you going to grate and sprinkle on salad, not make into piece. Give green part to that rabbit living in your house. Make laughing at how he hop around and wrinkle his nose. If pet rabbit living outside, shame on you. You should go out and live in cold hutch. Then you can die of freezing and depression, too. Rabbit hutch is agriculture industry model for stinking puppy mill. You keep rabbit outside, you no better than puppy abuser. Rabbit is more intelligent than your landlord, Baba promise.

Chive.

Chop up vegetable and tear lettuce. Put in huge bowl with enough room to toss around. Wooden kind best for fresh taste. Just before dinner, **toss in dressing**.

Your option:

*Make this salad with only **fresh spinach leaf**, or mix spinach in with other green for extra iron and more taste.

*Add little bit fresh **Chinese green** from Chinese market.

Baba going to repeat herself now. If I catch you photocopy this recipe or any part this book, you be in big trouble. If I don't catch you personal, then I give you worse Ukrainian curse: *Nai tebe kachka kopne*. May you be kick by duck!

Ingredient list:

- Baby potatoes, one pound. Unpeeled and steamed
- Mixed greens: lettuce, arugula, spinach, watercress, dandelion. If mix is unavailable, lettuce and/or spinach is fine.
- Ripe tomatoes, two large
- Cucumber, large
- Red, yellow or orange pepper, two large
- Cauliflower or broccoflower, one half medium
- Baby yellow zucchini, two small
- Carrot, one large

Baba's Dinner Salata

For complete dinner kind salad, make *Baba's Garden Salata* and add nice slice chicken, ham, roast beef and/or cheese.

Each kind meat and cheese change personality of salad. *Bleu* cheese and roast beef have manly man kind feel to it. Mozzarella and chicken breast very lady lady. Swiss and chicken breast less like lady, little bit more like Baba. Black Forest ham and marble cheddar is like person who have all body part to go. It favorite of my two spirit friend. They say it cover all the base. See *Fried Fish, Chapter Sixteen.*

You can try at deli counter, if you have good one in neighborhood. Ask for "meat end." Sometime you get all kind different type sausage, from kobasa to Italian capicolli, all in one package. Mix and match salad meat.

Baba warning: I know you already. Some day you going to be making good dinner salata. You get all ingredient together, the try to use this whizzing cheese and spamola instead of good stuff. DON'T.

*For another kind dinner salata, **crumble in hard boil egg and try different kind of cheese**. Egg and meat together is overkilled.

Ingredient List:

Same as for *Garden Salata*, above. Add one of the following combinations: roast beef and cheese, mozzarella or Swiss and chicken breast, ham and cheese, hardboiled egg and cheese.

Buryak Salata (Beet Salad)

In Eastern Ukraina, they calling this *Salata Taratuta*. Baba sticking to her Western Ukraina name. Sometime name of recipe is not even official. Is what your family call it. Is good enough for Baba, is more than good enough for you.

Beet salata is popular dish for for *Velyk Den'* (Easter) lunch. Depend how good you make it.

Is almost as many way to make this salata as is region in Ukraina. Baba going to show you more than one. Be satisfy. If you pay attention, she give you more in her next book.

First thing, can beet is out of questioning for any Baba recipe. Can beet is how you learn to hate them. Fresh beet is different from can like reading about sexy romance is different from having one.

Boil two big beet. The more organic the better, so they smell like good earth. See *Beet and Horse Radish Relish (Tsvikli) in Chapter Six* for traditional way to peel.

Grate or slice beet in shape you like. Wait till they cool. Peel them first. Baba hope is not too late for this instruction. Good thing you learn early in recipe book to read everything first.

Grate two big kosher pickle. Jew make best pickle, next to Ukrainian, so this deli is good to visit. If you can dip hand in pickle barrel and feel for firmness, this best kind of deli. If every person doing this, you want to stay away.

Make very fine chopping of two peel garlic clove. Mix with beet and pickle. Add pinch salt.

Stir in big glopping of good home made *Mayonnaise*, in *Salad Dressings, Chapter Three*.

This salad will be pinky when you put in mayonnaise. Is so cute, will make even sulky kid eat beet.

Your option:

*Use ***Horse Radish Sauce***, *Chapter Twenty Two*, instead mayonnaise.
***Mix in small, fine chop, very mild onion or chive**.
*For super spicy like go up your sushi nose, **mix big glump grate horse radish with equal amount sunflower or extra virgin olive oil**. Baba would use almost quarter cup horse radish from her own garden. But you

not Baba. You poor thing.

Ingredient List:

- Beets, one pound
- Dill pickles, two large
- Garlic cloves, two
- Salt
- Mayonnaise, one half cup. Do not substitute salad cream.

Buryak Salata v Krop (Beet Salad with Dill)

Just like with borshch, if you not going to acquire fresh dill, don't start. Go to black market, go to your dealer. Baba don't care what your private life. Just get fresh.

Put several beet in biggish pan with enough water so they not poking out. Put in pinch salt and make boiling. Turn stove down to simmer and cook about forty-five minute, until you can stick fork in easy. Steaming will work too. But not microwave. Ancient root food in microwave is some kind sacrilege. Beet will taste like radio wave.

Drain beet, put in cold water and slip off skin. Make into small cube. If you over-achiever, cut into perfect little cube like you see on beet can label.

Melt butter in big frying pan and stir beet in this. Should only cook two, three minute before you **pour in half cup whipping cream**. Baba know what you going to do with rest of cream. Probably give to food bank. As if. You pouring it in your coffee right now.

Keep stirring beet in cream until it about as thick as half done pudding. Maybe five minute, maybe less.

Add pinch salt and pepper plus squeeze fresh lemon or lime juice. Again, you use frozen or bottle juice, you ruin all your effort.

Take beet mix off from heat. This don't just mean turn off heat. It mean TAKE OFF FROM HEAT. You don't know how many time Baba hear sobbing on her crisis hotline, "But it all crusty on bottom!" Like heat stop as soon you twist dial. This thinking is product of instant-schminstant culture.

Mix in fine chop dill leaf and glopping of *smetana* (sour cream).

Serve salad chill or at room temperature.

Your option:

None. This salata is perfect ecological beet, cream and dill balance. Has not changed since Ukrainian grow beet, milk wild cow and pick dill. And import lemon from south.

Ingredient List:

- Beets, one and one half pounds
- Butter, two tablespoons
- Salt and pepper
- Whipping cream, one half cup
- Fresh lemon or lime juice, one teaspoon
- Fresh dill, small bunch
- Sour cream, two tablespoons

Buryak Salata v Peretz (Peppery Beet Salad)

This salad have little bit more rootsy taste, because you going to bake beet instead of steam or boil. Baking give beet even more extra dimension. Baba making you into cosmic beet astronaut.

Turn oven to 350 degree F and go away till little light go off. Or else your timing going to be off, too.

Bake beet for one hour while you pretending you on aerobicize machine.

After beet is cool, take off peel. Chop into strip or cube. Whatever your artistic soul long for. Don't roll eye at Baba. Cooking is one most ancient art. Baba ancestor run back and forth between pyramid and pottery painting to stove. We build oldest pyramid in world, just outside Kyiv! Didn't use no slaves, neither. Used to be no distinction in importance. Until some *yolop* idiot decide man is better at building/painting pyramid. Just like woman is cleaner, man is "maintenance engineer." What he engineering, Baba want to know. He building Brooklyn Bridge in bathroom? Pah!

Listen careful: **Mix up sunflower oil, apple cider vinegar, and splash fresh lemon or lime juice. Pour on beet**. Do not substitute crap genetic modify oil or blah white vinegar. White vinegar is only so pickle thing don't turn funny color. If you listen to Baba, this will be most killer vinahret you ever taste. You can also use this mix on green salad any time. If you can find extra virgin oil and raw vinegar, people at potluck going to be crying from jealous.

Mix into beet: salt, cayenne pepper, powder clove and powder cinnamon. Can substitute splash Louisiana hottie sauce for cayenne.

Last piece in puzzle is **caraway seed**.

Chill real good. You can serve on bed of lettuce or in nice bowl. Red beet is sexola contrast with green lettuce. Or more show your artsy soul on oak leaf or radicchio. Yellow bowl not only make your eye poke out with happiness, but is beautiful symbol for sun goddess *Kolyada*. If you glance at Sviata Vechera chapter like Baba tell you in beginning, you know what she mean.

Ingredient List:

- Beets, one and one half pounds
- Sunflower oil, one quarter cup
- Apple cider vinegar, two tablespoons
- Fresh lemon or lime juice, one tablespoon
- Salt
- Cayenne pepper OR hot sauce, pinch or splash
- Powdered cloves, pinch
- Cinnamon, pinch
- Caraway seed, one heaping teaspoon

Kartoplya (Potato Salad)

Baba sentimental with Jewish people, and sometime, she attend synagogue. This story that Jew and Ukrainian always fighting is Communist propaganda, made to divide people.

Baba study wonderful Talmud, which is million page of Jewish law. Did you know is illegal for Jew to pee downhill? Should be illegal everywhere, if you asking Baba her life experience.

Anyway, we dance, sing, make lots of party. And always is this woman, she overly nice but have little bit other problem. Only thing she know how to cook is *kartoplya*. She carry potato salad under her arm to every party, picnic, *bat mitzvah* and funeral. Wouldn't be so bad if recipe was different every time. Then wouldn't be rumor was actually same kartoplya she carry over many year. First people stop eating her food, then they avoid her eye.

This not good for her romantic life. All rest of us get lover, and she just sit in corner caressing big bowl potato salad. It get sadder. Soon only lesbian group inviting her, and she is not lesbian. She don't date no one, actual.

Then even they get tired, say they help her if she in abusive relationship or want to spring from closet. But support her right to choose terrible kartoplya is push radical feminism too far.

Baba law. She make up new one every day: don't be that woman. Unless people actual get on knee and beg you with tear in eye for same same, learn different recipe. Keep people guessing. It make them excite to see you.

Baba going to teach you art of both cold and warm kartoplya. Big secret of good taste for cold salad, is make day ahead of time so flavor can blend. *Kartoplyanky*, potato, is pretty bland kind food, so it need time to make love with other ingredient.

Only don't make several month ahead of time, like pathetic woman.

Other big secret is that baby potato or adult potato of red or Yukon gold kind make best kartoplya. This is because they firm. Russet potato have mealy mouth like Canadian government. Canadian motto is, *Peace, Order, and Lie to Ukrainian Immigrant.*

Most Basic Kartoplya (Potato Salad)

Baba going to let you get away with making this bo-ring recipe only one time, for practice. This how Canadian do in 1930, and some never smart enough to stop.

Peel and make in cube six medium potato. Don't matter what color skin. Steam or boil until tender. Oi yoi yoi. Baba already yawning, teaching you what your mama should have show you when you was just little *patichok*, twig.

Let potato cool. If you boiled in water, drain immediate, or potato will soak up water.

Sprinkle with salt, celery seed and vinegar. Baba want to scream: Try crunchy sea salt instead of table salt! Use fancy flavor vinegar, not white!

There. That feel better. **Chop red or white onion into tiny piece and toss in**. **Mix everything with mayonnaise. Garnish with boiled egg half** and Matka Bozha, always that stinking **paprika**. Don't forget **parsley** or you blow whole suburban *hausfrau* thing.

Baba screaming in her head again: make your own *Mayonnaise, Chapter Three* ! Mix mayonnaise half and half with sour cream! If you not make your own, at least pour two tablespoon high quality extra virgin olive in for flavor! Use yummy *Walla Walla* onion! Mix in two teaspoon dry mustard! Throw in teaspoon crack black pepper! Mix in half cup slice olive! Substitute one teaspoon fennel seed for one of celery!

Garnish with caper or *prosciutto* curl or nasturtium petal or olive ring or red pepper curl or small gold statue of boy peeing! Sprinkle with saffron! Anything better than kartoplya Hell Baba feel honorarium bound to describe above.

Put in fridge and make good and cold before guest come. Should be enough for ten people if they like, up to twenty if they don't.

Baba is sweating. Phew. Good thing that is over. Nightmare tonight, for sure thing.

Baba warning: now she teach you be creative, don't be carry away by this one thing. If you think black olive paste will make good mix in potato salad, you so wrong. Whole she-banger will turn gray.

Ingredient List:

- Medium potatoes, six
- Red or white onion
- Salt
- Celery seed, three teaspoons
- Vinegar, two teaspoons

Not really optional: listen well to what Baba is screaming. Add accordingly.

Siberian Kartoplya

Baba calling this *Siberian Potato Salad* because it have frozen pea. Get it? Hahahahahahaha.

This recipe is warm, and little bit different because you going to cook potato with rest of ingredient. Not separate like people in isolate gulag.

Boil water with salt and lump of *salo*, see *Roast Beef, Chapter Nine.*

Make dice from baby potato, skin ON. Baba have issue with skinning baby, even if is only vegetable. She almost puke in First Aid course with rubber baby dummy. But you know this thing about Baba. She have feeling tender like Communist soldier liver, once you marinate and simmer little bit.

Add in clove crush garlic and dice onion.

You going to need patience, because you **keep stirring now and then until potato is cooked**. Do not abandon to go adjust thong. Reach round behind, but stir with other hand. Occasional **add little bit boiling water** so ingredient don't stick together. Ingredient in pan, Baba mean. She find she have to over explain everything to person wearing thong. Sometime is only thing holding brain together.

If what is in thong is all stick together, Baba think you are poor thing. Maybe you should make reconsideration who you socialize with. See *Ukrainski Meditsyna, Babka Plant, Chapter Twenty Five*. If thong is stick to what is stick together, you better have enough medicine to make good soaking solution in bathtub. Don't peel thong out of your *kvitichka* like Bandaid.

When potato is soft, stir in big splash wine or balsamic vinegar. I know thong is still bugging you, so reach round again with ONE HAND.

Stir in pea and crack black pepper. Cook until pea is warm. Yes, pea with no shell, what you thinking? Magic *rusalka* water fairy going to jump from kitchen tap and shell for you? Baba would rather you use fresh pea, but then she cannot make excellent frozen joke from top of recipe. This is problem with being as brilliant joke maker as cook.

Ingredient List:

- Baby potatoes, two pounds
- Boiling water, one cup.
- Pork or beef fat, one tablespoon. As fresh as possible
- Onion, one medium
- Wine or balsamic vinegar, two tablespoons
- Garlic, one clove
- Frozen peas, one cup
- Salt and pepper, to taste

Baba know you is oxygen moron, but **keep Siberian kartoplya warm until serve**. By way, Baba is sick of telling you how to adjust underwear. Go change into decent panty before guest come. In Baba day, only prostitute wear this thing. Is how she signal trick he going to get what he want. All of sudden, excellent feminism get twist into, “Whore for free, right here!” You sending up signal rocket, too maybe?

Why you advertising you going to do what man want, for free? Next thing, you going to be washing his dish. This what thong lead to, Baba telling you. Make man work for what he want, and guess big time if he actual going to get it. This is how you train them, according to their nature. Baba watch both feminist and feminine mystique slide backward till worse than 1950. **She feeling mean, so she going to teach you:**

Ukrainian-German Warm Kartoplya

Baba find this recipe in Nazi pocket after she take him out mushroom picking. He not so good at discriminating what kind not to eat. Ooop. See *Mushrooms, Chapter Twelve*. Baba would claim recipe entirely for Ukrainian victory, but she doubt his mother have same belief system. So she going to give nod to German origin.

Heil potato. Here we go:

Boil or steam six medium potato with jacket on. Cube when cool. Baba relieve you of military peel duty for all potato salad from now on. She know you relieve she relieve. Or can use fifteen to eighteen baby potato. Number is in honor of draft age. **Cut baby only in half**. Such small thing make just tiniest cube root.

Fry bacon to crispness. Drain in sloppy Canadian way so is *salo* left in pan. This fun way to give recipe your middle finger. **Fry onion and flour in this pan**. Now is good time to wipe your mouth from drooling. It make grease splatter.

Mix in balsamic, wine or apple cider vinegar. Soldier mother not write this down, but I bet she approve.

Add beef stock OR mix beef bouillion cube in boil water, not straight from tap. Not even if you have fancy-shmancy water purify machine. Baba say boil, so you boil. Who is leader here? Who teach you to goose step so good? Who your daddy? Ooop again. Wrong audience.

Say to flour lump, "Break it up!" Stir in sugar,crack black pepper, and dry mustard. Simmer only until sauce begin to get thick.

Add kosher salt. Ha! Nazi be turning over in gravy.

Baba would usual add big splash red wine, but she have strong feeling Nazi mother been drinking all through pregnancy. Maybe is not best idea.

Mix all this good thing into potato, which been waiting for it like long lost liberator. **Stir in crumble bacon** real gentle.

Garnish with caper. Why? Because Baba say so. For final Ukrainian victory, **put sprig dill in centre of ring of caper**.

Serve warm only. Otherwise bacon grease will congeal like Reich heart.

Your option:

ABSOLUTELY NONE. Just like Communism, Fascism say everything not compulsory is forbidden.

Ingredient List:

- Potatoes, two pounds
- Bacon, half pound
- Medium onion, one half
- Chives, one tablespoon
- Flour, three tablespoons
- Flavored vinegar, two thirds cup
- Beef stock, two thirds cup OR beef bouillion cube
- Boiled water, two thirds cup (for bouillion cube)
- Sugar, one quarter cup
- Cracked black pepper
- Kosher salt for irony
- Garnish with caper. Caper only. Do you hear Baba?! Only caper. And dill.

Sophisticated Kartoplya

This is potato salad when you feeling adventurous, but not too experimental. You know, like time you buy pantyhose in taupe instead of beige, then call your girlfriend all excite.

If you not Ukrainian or some other good culture, you thinking we wearing loud color babushka and paint each side of house different color because we "primitive." Baba have news for you: until you meet her, you living beige kind of life.

Baba have even more news she know you going to like: Ukrainian invent first house and oven, so we can paint any way we want. We was Neolithic. We live inside super groovy mammoth bone structure, singing and making advance system of politic. Other peoples' baby book only have one page. It say, "Neanderthal child ugly and tough to housebreak." Ha!

This is kind of potato salad you could take to party in Manhattan, if someone ever invite you.

Boil or steam red, Yukon or baby potato. Drain. If big potato, cut into cube. If baby, cut in half.

Pour pickle juice over potato. Chop fine huge pickle. Make sure is garlic dill pickle, and don't let yourself get away with pickle that is soft and limp. This is disgusting. Baba going to send you to buy pickle Viagra.

Mix in chop red or Walla Walla onion. Do NOT use yellow cooking onion unless stink breath is your national custom. Baba don't doubt. **Add large stalking green onion, also fine chop, and fine chop parsley or dill.**

Mix in celery seed. Baba know this is cliché, but it work good for this recipe. Fennel seed can be substitute, but use less.

For dressing, mix up good quality mayonnaise with sour cream. Not this diet-schmiet stuff make you feel depress. Best kind is in *Chapter Three*. **Add glump fancy mustard, sea salt and crack black pepper.**

If you like, mix in two big hard boil egg. OR use them slice for garnish.

Make garnish from something else than parsley. Baba not going to explain whole concept again.

Here is Baba extra touch that make all urban sophisticate people not wearing enough clothes go, "Oooh, aaaah!" P**ut out side dish of chop almond, pecan or sunflower seed**. I say side dish. If you mix in salad, it get soggy like that bad dill pickle Baba warn you about.

Baba warning: take shell from all kind nut first. Fancy party is not place to be making spitting contest like in your workplace. You got in enough trouble for taking bath in sink.

Your option:

*If you so lucky to be stinking rich---or just such people pleaser you don't care if it use whole week grocery budget---**add cup cook crab or shrimp** to salad.
*Same thing for medium jar **artichoke heart**. Pour some oil from jar into dressing, too.
***Pimento** is tasty and have good red color. **Red or orange pepper** also nice accentuate.
Baba Law: DO NOT PUT GREEN PEPPER IN ANY HER RECIPE. DO NOT. DO NOT. DO NOT.
*If you can't afford any of above, **use half cup chop celery.** Not so likely to get you invite back to New York party, so really better to leave out.

Ingredient List:

- Red, Yukon or baby potatoes, two pounds
- Garlic dill pickle, quarter cup
- Garlic dill pickle juice, quarter cup
- Red or Walla Walla onion, one half
- Scallions, large bunch. Use white and green part

- Fresh parsley or dill, small bunch
- Eggs, two large hard boiled
- Celery seed, two teaspoons OR fennel seed, one teaspoon
- Mayonnaise, one quarter cup
- Sour cream, one quarter cup
- Dijon mustard, two tablespoons
- Salt and pepper
- Pecans, almonds or shelled sunflower seeds, one quarter pound

Roasted Vegetable Kartoplya

This is kartoplya Baba feed to creepy hydro meter man so he forget what her Bingo do.

For long time, Baba have dog name Bingo. He is half German Shepherd, half Dachshund. How these two make romance, she have no idea. Probably some *banyak* on YouTube be happy to show you. He provide dating service and chair for them, too. Is ultimate meaning of "backyard breeder," because for sure no one want to see this happen on front lawn.

Bingo is great dog. He have body like Shepherd, but leg like Dachshund. Baba make him harness from upside down horse halter and teach him to pull small red wagon. She always hitch Bingo up when is special on toilet paper and hair color at drugstore. Everyone go away from TV to look at short leg going crazy quick under big body. All neighborhood feed him. Half of time, Baba don't have to buy dog food, just for entertaining value.

One day hydro meter man bang on door so loud, finally Baba answer. What, you telling me you answer door when you not invite nobody? He say this and that in boring snivel servant voice, then he reach for Bingo. Baba say, "Don't touch Bingo, he bite."

Crazy man, he whining, "All dog like me." Then he make some kind snorfle face at dog, would make small baby vomit. Bingo raise German Shepherd lip and show one fang. It sparkle, because Baba brush dog teeth with baking soda.

Baba say, "Bingo don't like you. Don't touch him. He bite."

He reach down and touch Bingo. Bingo bite him real good.

"Ouch!" he scream, "Your dog bite me."

Baba say, "I telling you this. Don't touch Bingo, he bite."

"Ma'am," he say, "You can't have dog who bite. I sue you."

"Sir," Baba say, "Bingo is guarding dog. I teach him to bite on old stuff sock where I paint your face. And Baba warn you: DON'T TOUCH BINGO, HE BITE."

Then she grab hydro meter man by arm and slide chair under him. Out come *Roast Vegetable Potato Salad* along with *Scrambled Eggs with Bacon*, under *Eggs, Chapter Seven.*

Boil baby potato, keep skin on for sentimental reason.

Heat oven to 425 F.

Chop red pepper into strip, red onion into slice, and good kind clean mushroom into mushroom kind of slice. Yellow zucchini is good idea, too. NOT green, even if some dummy try tell you is call fancy courgette. Pah! Propagandist.

Crush two clove peeled garlic. Chop cauliflower or broccoflower into piece as attractive as you know how. Baba not have high hope here, you understand.

Peel beet and make into loaded dice. This type easy to get by casino security, because is lead-free.

Pour extra extra extra virgin olive oil into big mix bowl. How you know if is extra extra extra virgin? When it come out of bottle, it squeak like you did first few time you pretending you virgin. Baba was going to save this for *Ukrainian Meditsyna* section, but she have evidence to believe this information too urgent: Secret is to have bath with some alum salt. Make that floppy *kvitichka* you have, tight like eardrum.

Roll vegetable around in oil. Then roll beet separate with cauliflower, so everything not turn pink. But will be only time your guest see pink cauliflower, and you can be thrill with small distinction in life. If you use broccoflower, will be pinky-green. This perfect for Easter.

Spread vegetable in glass baking pan. Ungreased. Duh. Greasing twice is like that crazy pizza where they say "double cheese." Usually mean they cheap, and was not enough cheese in first place.

Put beet and cauliflower in separate pan, or wrap in foil.

Put in oven forty-five minute, on middle rack.

When potato and all vegetable is cooler than you ever going to be, **flip around with *Plain Vinahret Dressing* or *Lemon Dressing*,** *Chapter Three.*

Add coarse salt and crack black pepper.Serve hot, warm or cold.

Is good ending to this story. Hydro meter man not only drop lawsuit, he roll back number so electric company send Baba check every month. Baba also laughing because is probably only time she not make her bachelor-style scramble egg naked under apron. Naked is for sincerity, not bribery.

Your option:

*If you make plan for once and manage to serve salad warm, **mix in half cup fried, crumble bacon, corn beef or chop *kobasa*** (garlic sausage). No spamming, this just annoy people.
*Warm or cold, **mix in hand full fresh oregano OR dill OR basil**. Not all at once, or taste like big mess.
***Mix in half cup chop black olive** from deli, not from can.
*For last fifteen minute roast vegetable is in oven, put on **shred firm goat cheese**. Not feta, this is not Ukrainian. If you serving salad cold, put on shred firm goat cheese, ***Asiago* or quality *Parmesan*** before serving. Baba find Swiss and *Bleu* a little overwhelming in this salad.

For Bingo Story Part II, see Kurka (Chicken), Chapter Eight.

Ingredient List:

- Baby potatoes, two pounds
- Red peppers, two large. Or one red, one orange.
- Red onion, one medium
- Mushrooms, one brimming cup. Preferably Chanterelle, Oyster, Boletus or Porcini
- Cauliflower or broccoflower, one half medium
- Beet, one medium
- Garlic, two cloves
- Yellow zucchini, one medium or two small
- Extra virgin olive oil, one half cup. Or pomace and olive oil. Cheaper and tasty.
- Salt and cracked black pepper
- Plain Vinahret Dressing or Lemon Dressing, one half to three quarters cup.

Creamed Vegetables

This so easy thing to do to vegetables. It is useful to put inside *Lokshyna Ring* (Egg Noodles), *Chapter Twenty One*, and also to put in blender for baby food. Baba knew someone, she trying to feed baby whole raw food and kid is spitting up more than usual. Baba say, “Duh, really?” then bring over few can jar of cream vegetable. Kid is eating real good now, but will have PTBD, Post-Traumatic Broccoli Disorder, for rest of life.

Melt butter in big pan. Stir in flour real quick with whisk broom. Pour in milk slow, like shoplift costing you something.

Stir in good vegetable, any kind mix: mushroom, red pepper, yellow (ONLY) zucchini, shelled pea, dice carrot, chop broccoli, cauliflower, spinach. Make sure you chop spinach real fine, or will hang from fork like when you go fishing and catch only ugly seaweed.

When Baba first get to West Coast, she figure she going to be real hippie-schmippie. She hanging fresh seaweed on clothesline. It get all tangled with long underwear and make children mad. Especially when neighbor yell, "Ahoy, matey!" every time they out in yard.

Cook until vegetable tender.

Serve with so many thing, Baba not going to list here.

Ingredient List:

- Butter, two tablespoons
- Flour, one tablespoon
- Whole or two percent milk, one cup
- Salt and pepper
- Vegetables, two cups

Ukrainian Kapusta Salata (Coleslaw)

Baba know you thinking, "Nobody have to teach me make coleslaw. I buy bag of shred rusty cabbage in stupormarket and throw around with some mayonnaise from jar."

Baba say to you sincerely, "Blech."

Even though she already disappoint, she going to show you coleslaw with Ukrainian secret ingredient. Also, one thing you leave out so this recipe shine like day sun marry moon.

Shred up green cabbage, size look like it going to fit your big salad bowl. The one you use for company, not the one you putting under dripping trailer roof since 1993.

Shred *morkva,* carrot. The bigger the carrot, the easier is to shred and avoid finger. Finger part in coleslaw can spoil someone dinner.

Chop up mild onion extra fine. Make almost invisible. You going to be tempt to use green onion or chive. Don't.

Baba warning: Green onion go bad faster and will cook with boil dressing. This is beginner mistake. No need for this type mistake with me holding your clammy hand.

You ready for secret Ukrainian ingredient? Okay. First, you going to hold back that celery seed Baba know you dying to add. This create negative space like in good modern painting.

Into that space you going to **throw big hand full poppy seed**. Wow. This not only delicious, but make great visual. Everybody going to be smiling at each other with tiny black poke dot on teeth and lip. Some people going to use as excuse to stick finger in other person mouth. Is Ukrainian ice party breaker.

Toss all ingredient together.

Dressing:

This blow stripe sock off mayonnaise dressing. **You going to boil together vinegar, white sugar, salt, coarse black pepper and oil**. Kind of oil going to determine taste. This mean you can make big variety of coleslaw just by changing oil. Not in car. In recipe. Car going to have to rust on front lawn little while longer.

Extra virgin olive, sunflower or hemp is all Baba recommendation. Hemp is so popular in Ukraine, we say, *Soul can be pull from hell by hanging onto rope from hemp*. We make all kind clothes from it. It not need pesticide, and is extra durable. Baba not like Canadian hippie too much, but she sure grateful they finally bring hemp to this country. They figure it out once they realize is for more than smoking.

Kind of vinegar is next way to determine taste. Apple cider, balsamic or wine vinegar for extra zing zingerama.

Pour hot dressing over salad. DO NOT STIR, JUST POUR. Baba know this difficult when you have technique bless by martini god, but you don't want to encourage any cooking and mushing of ingredient.

Cover up, put in fridge and forget about at least twenty four hour. Yes, Baba know you usually have food sitting longer than that. In this case, is okay. Even you leave three, four day, it just get more transparent and tastier. Stir all ingredient together only when everyone sitting at table drooling like hungry vampire. You the one who raise and invite them.

Your option:

*Dash Louisiana hottie sauce

Ingredient List:

Salad

- Cabbage, one large head
- Mild onion, one very small
- Carrot, one cup grated
- Poppy seed, two teaspoons

Dressing

- Vinegar, one cup
- Sugar, three quarter cup
- Oil, two thirds cup
- Salt, one tablespoon
- Coarse black pepper, one teaspoon

Vegetable Sendvich

We going to make this sendvich like Shevchenko painting on canvas. More likely on prison wall, because that what Soviet do with great artist. Baba not bitter, just not floating round in pink fog with hand over ear like average Canadian.

You going to need:

Big juicy tomato from your garden. Don't be count on store tomato. Better to eat cardboard box they come in. At least have fiber. Use little bit sea salt and you won't tell difference. If you not grow your own tomato, be good neighbor and visit farmer market for vegetable.

Bean sprout. If you not growing your own on kitchen counter, look for kind in package say organic. Bean sprout is especial good at absorbing chemical from earth and air.

Fresh mushroom. Slice thin.

Fat slice aged orange cheddar cheese, for color. I know, I know, is food color. No such thing as orange cow. But you notice Baba stay away from artificial in all other recipe. Give her little artist license here. Recipe is like making painting for her. She is Old Master of Ukrainian kitchen.

Some **very thin slice red, orange or yellow pepper.** Green get slimy and you already have enough orange if you following Baba direction.

Peel and slice tender young cucumber. Here is trick so leftover part not get bitter: chop off end and rub on end until ugly juice squirt out. Wipe off end of cucumber, wrap in plastic and put in fridge when you have taken off as much as you need.

Serve on thick slice black bread. Better if toast. Once you start cooking with Baba, you have to buy wide slice toaster. One time my daughter Odarka come home with this narrow slice Canadian bread and I ask her, "What you want me to do with this thing, play poker?" She always roll her eye and call me "Ukrainian hippie" when I show her eat healthy, but now she middle age and her hair and teeth not falling out like her friend.

This kind bread so healthy, with buckwheat and rye flour. Also blackstrap molasses to build good iron in blood. Best part is fashionable colour. In Ukraina we have saying, *Black is new black*. Also, *Stupid Lenin is new stupid Marx*. But this whole nother story. Make Baba growl like Carpathian wolf.

If you make vegetable sendvich on black bread, everything look more beautiful than usual. Red tomato, green cucumber, orange cheese all stand out nice and sharp like by Ukrainian realist painter Shevchenko.

Spread good heaping size *Ukrainian Mayonnaise*, under *Dressing, Chapter Three*, on both slice bread. Don't be cheap like Anglo Saxophone soup. **Put ingredients on bread. Sprinkle with salt and crack black pepper**.

This sandwich is good when fresh. Get soggy if you leave sitting on counter or in fridge. Sandwich going to be very wide. You have to open mouth to eat, like you singing good song. Not this Canadian "lady lady" little purse lip, she spitting out both side her mouth. Open up and EAT.

Ingredient List:

For two sandwiches

- Tomato, one ripe
- Bean sprouts. One deli package
- White mushrooms, five or six medium
- Aged orange cheddar, four deli slices
- Red or yellow pepper, four medium rings
- Cucumber, half of one small
- Black bread
- Salt and pepper

Chapter Three

Dressing
For
Salads, Vegetables and Meats

Plain Vinahret Dressing

Overnight, put two clove garlic in big jar with balsamic or malt vinegar. You don't have to peel garlic. Just nick clove with knife. You can even have big permanent jar going with garlic vinegar. Pour what you need in with jar of oil when you making salad.

Be careful, because if you not see garlic floating in bottom, this vinegar look like good strong beer. On other hand, this not bad thing if you tell children this is beer and give them each glass. Is easier than trying to rescue alcoholic once he get going. Baba is anarchist social worker. Ha!

Before putting on salata, mix with extra virgin olive oil or sunflower oil. I like very strong, so make about half and half. Some people have weaker personality, so they use more oil than vinegar. Some people so gutless, they eat with no dressing and have Communist and Nazi for friend. Baba not invite them back to her table.

Throw in sea salt and crack black pepper.

Add hot pepper sauce or cayenne pepper for zing zing taste.

Shake jar real good.

Your option:

*White vinegar is not option. Tasteless. Insulting to Baba salata. Is only for some kind woman name Muffy.

*If you really, really need to eat salad but really, really cannot have so much garlic on breath in middle of work week, you have Baba secret permission to **use garlic salt instead**. But also make sometime with real garlic. Make big difference both to taste and to your good health.

***Check out vinahret mix in *Spicy Beet Salata recipe*,** *Chapter Two*. Baba mia!

Ingredient List:

- Garlic, two cloves
- Balsamic, wine or malt vinegar. Proportional
- Extra virgin olive oil or sunflower oil. Proportional
- Salt to taste
- Cracked black pepper to taste
- Hot sauce, two dashes OR cayenne pepper, half teaspoon

Lemon Dressing

Oy, this dressing going to taste like Heaven!

Leave four lemon on counter overnight to get warm. This free up juice inside. No one want to give you what they got when they shivering with cold. In first place, you have to buy lemon with thinnest skin. This kind have most juice.

You going to do opposite of *Plain Vinahret*, above. **Pour extra virgin olive oil or sunflower oil into big jar**. Do not use canola crapola. **Throw in two clove peeled, nicked garlic**. Or more, if you going to stay in all weekend with man who also eat this.

Squeeze four lemon to make one cup juice. Under no circumstance use lemon juice from jar or frozen kind. May as well eat brake fluid from old Datsun.

Add two dash hot pepper sauce or half teaspoon cayenne pepper. Then sea salt and crack black pepper.

Add brown sugar or melt honey.

Shake everything together real good and toss into salad.

Ingredient List:

- Lemons, four with thinnest skin available
- Extra virgin olive or sunflower oil, one half to one cup
- Dash hot sauce OR cayenne pepper, half teaspoon
- Salt, one teaspoon
- Cracked black pepper, one teaspoon
- Brown sugar OR honey, one teaspoon

Smetana (Sour Cream) Dressing

Ukrainian love this recipe because is so naked taste. It give us chance to show off two of our treasure: how good is cream from our cow, and egg from our hen. Canadian in city don't understand this is big deal. Think of it this way, sweetheart. When you wearing some funny hat from store, have swishola feather and maybe flippy-floppy pansy, you want whole world to notice. When we steal egg and milk, we want whole world to notice, too. Baba almost say cow and hen want you to notice, but really, they would rather keep these thing to themselves. This is not some kind veganzola spiel, just uncommon sense. We have ceremony to say thank you to animal on *Sviata Vechera* (Christmas Eve).

Mix up flour with salt and dry mustard. If you like sweetie sweetie, **mix in big glop sugar.** If not, make it small glop.

Here is Baba trick: icing kind sugar make easier mix.

Beat two big egg yolk into dry stuff. The more fertilize and free range and organic egg is, the better. In Ukraina, we just call this "normal."

Splash in vinegar. White is okay for now. One you get to be smetana expert, fruity or wine flavor can be part of your repertoire.

For piecing together resistance, **add smetana**. Since Baba tell you this is naked recipe, is worth your while to drive out to farm for real stuff. Everyone going to judge you on this quality. This is reality therapy with your Baba.

Pour dressing into double boiler. This is conniption where water boil underneath pot on top, so cream don't get burn taste. Baba hear this call ruling of thumb. Just don't stick thumb in, or it will be sore. **Keep stirring dressing until it get partway thick**. About like when your instant pudding is three quarter set. If you wait that long before drinking.

Put smetana dressing in fridge overnight. Next day, it will be tangy for: steam vegetable, cold meat, baby potato, toss salad or salad not toss so good.

Ingredient List:

- Flour, one tablespoon
- Salt, pinch
- Dry mustard, one teaspoon
- Sugar, one to two teaspoons
- Egg yolks, two
- Vinegar, three tablespoons
- Sour cream, one cup

Smetana Horse Radish Dressing

If you think *Smetana Dressing* is over moon, you will cry when you taste this.

After dressing is chill, **mix in big glop fresh grate horse radish**. If you like cute pink color, also add small spoonful fine grate beet.

Ukrainian Mayonnaise

Baba laugh at big debate about origin of mayonnaise. Some French king suppose to make for his chicken last minute before riding into battle. Or Roman thug have brainwave, how he going to hide taste of spoil meat.

Pah! Is just another example of man trying to take credit for great invention. Truth is obvious. Some Ukrainian baba was taking jar of *soniashnyk*, sunflower, oil to her son home. Also a few her most excellent egg from good laying hen. Horse get spanky-spunky, jar and egg break in saddlebag. It take her few minute to calm spirit horse down. Of course this baba stick her hand in bag to make damage assessment for insurance company. Then she lick her finger. Mayonnaise is born.

Even snobbola modern French chef admit soniashnyk, our national flower, is best oil for this sauce. Ukrainian so generous, we let them have little bit credit. "Mayo-nez" is Ukrainian-Frenchish for "sauce go up your nose."

You ready to get blow dried away? Here is Ukrainian favorite dressing:

Mix together salt with dry mustard and sugar.

Remember Baba trick: icing sugar blend better in no-cook recipe.

Next trick: Sprinkle in just several grain **cayenne pepper**.

Take two yolk from your prize hen egg. If you don't have such valuable possession, this is one those time is worth taking drive to farm and beg for some.

Beat these room temperature egg yolk with no mercy. Add splash fresh lemon juice.

Take half cup cold press soniashnyk oil and add just one dropping at time. This is non-negotiable. **Keep up beating with whisk** whole time. Oil and egg will start to get thick like thief.

Trick number three: Add another half cup oil, little bigger dropping at time. **Make alteration with vinegar.** Pattern is oil, vinegar, oil, vinegar, until is all used up. Keep beating. Mayonnaise will now be nice and thick, official Ukrainian-style.

Store in middle of fridge, not coldest part. Or mayonnaise will have separation problem, then divorce. If this happen, you can try emergency repair. Beat up one more egg yolk, then beat into mayonnaise. Success will depend on how far gone is marriage.

Eat mayonnaise on green salad, fried potato and cold vegetable. Is traditional Ukrainian thing to put out big tray cold meat and vegetable at party, with mayonnaise in side dish. Cold chicken is in particular desirable. Because egg is raw, pack dish in ice or fresh snow. Ice chipping from inside freezer will do trick, but won't win you raving for attractive display.

Baba also use to make her hair sparkly. Put good glop in hair first thing, then hang around house for hour. Shampoo, condition, and hair will have life on its own.

Ingredient List:

- Salt, large pinch
- Dry mustard, one half teaspoon
- White sugar, one half teaspoon
- Cayenne pepper, less than a pinch
- Egg yolks, two large
- Fresh lemon juice, one tablespoon
- Sunflower oil, one cup. Organic and cold pressed, if available
- White vinegar, two tablespoons

Baba's Favorite Mayonnaise

I call this Baba Favorite because it is. Why? It have hefty feel like udder on young milking goat;

Since it have cook egg instead of raw, you can leave out on table longer;

It have tangy smooth taste like Ukrainian mayonnaise, but stick to meat better. This mean it won't run out end of your grill kobasa sandwich.

Baba hear you now. “Oh! Oh! Where is recipe for kobasa sandwich? Is not in stinking index!”

Poopchik, “grill kobasa sandwich” *is* recipe.

This mayonnaise not so great for hair conditioner. Will not rinse out.

There is two way to prepare egg. First is for expert, second is for you.

Expert is going to separate six egg in perfect way, then poach egg yolk till they hard. Baba asking you not to pretend, for your own good. If you never poach egg in your life, you going to use up at least dozen and half before you get it right. You will end up crying in bathroom. And what you going to do with all them white part? Make mayonnaise, shynka and gallon of meringue all in one day? Sure.

Baba law: If you have that kind cookbook always asking you to do impossible thing without explanation and practice, throw out. This kind of book is big bully. If you having boss who do same thing, get nother job. He one sick joker.

Just **boil six egg and dig out yolk with spoon**, okay?

Once yolk is cool, press this part through sieve. Do not use hand drill. This seem quick and easy, but will cause regret.

Mash yolk with dry mustard, salt, pepper and glop white sugar. Like usual, icing sugar melt easier.

You now going to **beat in soniashnyk oil, few dropping at time**. Baba going to give you unintelligible freedom of choice: **use fresh lemon juice OR white vinegar**.

Make altercation with oil and lemon, just like in Ukrainian mayonnaise. Keep beating like you caught Stalin lurking in your outhouse.

And when Baba say you can leave this dressing on table longer than regular mayonnaise, she don't mean all night. Is still better to put on ice. Be *bon vivant*, not bon slob.

Ingredient List:

- Egg yolks, six medium
- Dry mustard, one tablespoon or more to taste
- Salt, one half teaspoon
- Pepper, pinch
- Icing sugar, one half teaspoon
- Sunflower oil, slightly more than one third cup
- Fresh lemon juice or white vinegar, two tablespoons

Baba's High Octane Mayonnaise

Sometime you making romance with hot man, and you thinking, “Matka Bozha, can't get any better.” Then he do something make you swallow your teeth and fall halfway out from bed.

This describe taste of *Baba Favorite Mayonnaise* when it go High Octane.

Make recipe like above, but also cook two of the egg white. Chop this in tiny piece. When you mashing yolk, mash in these white.

Now zoom all the way to part where **oil is completely mix with lemon juice. Then boom! Mix in big splash sour cream and fresh grate horse radish**.

You did not expect that, did you?

Keep some this special mayonnaise in little fridge by bed along with kobasa sandwich on rye bread. And grape. Cheesecake, too. With no fork, because you going to feed lover with hand. And vodka. Nice cold vodka. Your boyfriend going to stay for breakfast, for sure.

This is one place woman make mistake. Man leaving at four in morning is not always running from "intimate." You kidding me? They crazy about morning romance. That is when lighting is good. No, *dorahenka.* Sometime man leaving early because he know woman only have some kind low calorie soda and lettuce in fridge. Of course you familiar with that part where he say, "Got any beer?" and open fridge door. He is not always looking for beer. He is checking out entire content.

If was nothing there, he remember. He jump from your bed and go straight to *Denny*, meet his night shift pal and eat two plate "Cave Man Special." He brag about how he make you squeal. His friend make girlie imitation and slap his back. Guy in next booth laugh. You see how this lack of preparation snowball. Your new boyfriend start to think of whole experience as more like sport game than romance.

Keep him in your bed! Right food is ultra important. If man don't poke around before *lyubov*, make little suggestive opening of fridge door, just like you did with trashy blouse in bar. Then he will stay and make you squeal again. If you anything like Baba, you will have trouble getting man to leave so you can have life.

Improve your odd. Listen to your *Mayonnaise Love Expert* Baba.

Ingredient List:

- Baba's Favorite Mayonnaise, above
- Egg whites, two
- Sour cream, three quarter cup
- Fresh, finely grated horse radish, one quarter cup

Med v Mak (Honey Poppyseed) Dressing

In Ukraina we have saying, *Don't hang diaper on line after dark.* This can have meaning whatever you like.

Baba decide it mean you should be inside house, safe from predator, making *Honey Poppyseed Dressing.* This is versatile thing you can put on green salad, cold meat or potato.

Other day Baba in stupormarket, looking at salad dressing ingredient. She especially interest in these natural-shmatural kind with label look like it drawn by five year old. This supposed to make you trust manufacturer. Label screaming, "Fat free! Very tasty anyway!"

Of course it don't need no fat to taste good. First ingredient is "high fructose corn syrup." Here is where your mind bend some more. Is organic high fructose corn syrup . Please notice is not whole ear of corn or piece of fruit. Is just crap.

Here, Baba show you how to make something tasty and healthy.

Mix together liquid honey, Ukrainian mayonnaise, Dijon mustard, poppy seed, salt and pepper.

Just when you think you can't stand no more deliciousness, Baba crank up volume. **Add splash good quality dry red wine or balsamic vinegar**. This work because Dijon mustard have wine taste. Is like boosting bass on your amplifier for *zhabava*, real party extravaganza.

And by way, Ukrainian word *zhabava* for party literal mean, "Forget about it!" Make this dressing, and soon you will see world through pair of rose color bloomer.

Ingredients:

- Liquid honey, one third cup
- Ukrainian mayonnaise, one cup
- Dijon mustard, one tablespoon
- Dry red wine OR balsamic vinegar, one tablespoon
- Poppy seed, two tablespoons
- Salt and cracked black pepper, one quarter teaspoon each

Chapter Four

Nalysnyky I Mlyntsi (Crepes and Pancakes)

Childbirth

When Baba job in village was wise woman, she help make birth for baby.

Baba like to show up at door with not only knife and herb, but good food. Woman in labor can't cook, and husband almost forget to eat. Beside, he play super important role. In Ukraina, is no pasty-face man running around in waiting room with cigar or using video camera so whole neighborhood can get gross out later. You know Baba going to make him work lots harder to get baby out than he did getting it in.

First thing she do is send him out to pick female hemp plant.

Sometime before she even get there, Baba can see baby future. After he born, she know much more by shape of face, mole and eye color. If both parent eye is blue and baby is brown, for sure is going to be big explaining in family later. Baba is pretty good geneticist.

So baby will not get stuck, Baba walk around house and untie all knot. In curtain, in string, in that mop you call "family pet." She yell out window at priest to open partition door inside church. For big finale, she blow air up chimney in case *Did Moroz* (Old Frosty) is stuck from last year. You should do this for your Santa Claus, too. Then Baba throw thick rope over roof beam so woman can hold on. She going to be standing up and sitting down. Is kind of obstetric pull up.

If she having extra hard time, or just if she want to, woman sit naked on husband lap. She facing away while he groan with her and rub her belly. How he inspire to do this?

Some Ukrainian woman not only have bow and arrow in bedroom, just like you. She carry short, sharp dagger, which she got during Turk invasion. This come in several feminine color and is for bum stab. If husband not doing his job, she do little reach-around. Soon, he become voluntary helper. He even give her little shake now and then, so baby will fall like slimy apple from tree. Very cute;

He know is his job when Baba walk through door and give him eagle eye.

Believe Baba, when some schmuck visit Ukraina and try to get investment for nightclub have this thing call "lap dance," everybody just stare until he want to die.

Baba is gentle midwife. When baby come sliding out like big red jellybean, she don't give spanking. This is insult to baby spirit, and can break delicate spine bone. She get on chair and tap its feet on roof beam. Then it know it live in house with everybody else and one day will have mortgage. It start to cry very hard. Baba reward it. She tie up umbilical cord with female hemp plant, so baby will know life have all sort potential. Then she wipe him off with piece of her quality home made bread. Hold butter.

If baby look weak, Baba blow breath of divine life into its mouth. She make sure she eat garlic first, so baby will have will to live as good Ukrainian. Sometime this work, and sometime fate take over. This is life. Ukraina not like Canada, where every story supposed to turn out perfect. Sometime baby is only meant to be on earth for few minute or day, to make some sort transformation in family. This is spiritual life with real faith, not one where doctor is God.

After she give baby to mother and make sure it have good suction, Baba go bury placenta out in yard. She add money, bread and salt for welcome and luck. She do this fast so nobody get no New Age hippie idea and start mailing piece of placenta to friend. One most shocking thing Baba ever hear is when she just get to West Coast and hippie invite her to placenta-eat party. Baba she say no, she don't have good recipe. She want to puke. "But it going to be fry with ketchup," they tell her. I tell them we is not living in Holodomor, terrible Stalinist famine. This is take munchie way too far.

If is one thing Baba learn as midwife, when you play fast and loose with placenta, no one win.

Baba go back in house and start molding baby into human being. This is first time he get full body massage so all connecting tissue is healthy. She rub his hand and feet, press chin, pull nose and pass her hand over baby two eye. This call "peeling open eye" so baby can start to see world like is. At this point, he cry even harder. Baba wrap him up in linen for comfort and to start him get good taste in clothes. It take more than birth to make human being.

Mother is lying there while milk is draining out. She get little bit tired of "ooh" and "ah" over baby. Her stomach start growl and she want attention for herself. Father is still curl up in corner, cover in goo and sucking thumb. Ukrainian man is tough, but is still man.

By way, female hemp plant go in midwife coffin when she die. She is bury with great honor, and with piece of thing that help her get life in first place. Strength of hemp also help her be good dead ancestor for next generation. Baba going to be bury with big bunch hemp and haunt you forever.

If house is very cold, Ukrainian woman also like to give birth on top of *pich*, or stove. This not so weird like you thinking, Canadian-brain. Ukrainian pich have long ceramic counter beside cooking surface. Pipe go underneath and warm this. Is where sick and old people sleep. Is best seat in house. Also great place is in *banya*, or bath house. This is sacred steam room where we forget our problem. This also allow midwife to put her feet up after long labor. See *Kasha, Chapter Twenty.*

Is time for Baba to make one her favorite thing for occasion. Nalysnyky, or crepe, perfect combination of elegant and nutrition. Is also one very first thing ancient Ukrainian people ever bake when we invent oven many century ago.

Nalysnyky i Mlyntsi (Crepes and Pancakes)

Basic Nalysnyky Recipe

Nalysnyky is what French call "crepe" so they can pretend is theirs after they steal from Ukrainian. Since we invent oven, is no way.

Use energy you would use to spank new baby into **beating up four egg. Make them foamy. Mix with milk and boil water, cooled**. Don't get lazy and use all milk. Then your crepe will be tough and you will have to give to dog. Mind you, is not bad distraction to stop him from digging up placenta. This was big embarrassment at Baba first birth. Is even worse for single mother trying to snag husband. Okay, you should actual save some nalysnyky for dog.

Add sift flour and pinch salt. Mix up till is smooth sailing.

Put dab butter in small pan, about six inch. Make hot, but not so butter burn. You going to have to practice before baby is born, okay?

Pour in juuuuust enough batter to cover bottom of pan. You want very thin cake. Wave pan around so batter move, and you don't have to flip over the cake. Then they will be like melting in mouth. Take cake from pan as soon as edge turn brown and top part is bake.

Butter pan again for each cake. Don't be cheap thing.

Next you going to put some kind tasty filling inside nalysnyky. Is protein kind, vegetable kind and dessert kind. Once you decide which food group you represent in life, **roll up each cake with brown part on outside**. Because otherwise is no point making brown. If you not experience at such thing as rolling tight cigar, Baba let you tuck in end before rolling up.

Put roll in butter baking dish, and sprinkle butter bread crumb between layer. If you like, use plain butter instead.

Cover and heat in 325 degree oven for half hour. Take off top for last five minute for final suntan.

How many this serve? It depend on how good they are and what kind filling you use. It make about twenty cake. Something tell Baba fewer Canadian going to eat kind with pig brain than with mushroom or fruit. But she going to be nice and tell you how to make both.

Buttermilk Nalysnyky

For *I don't know what it is but I would kill you to find out taste*, leave out usual milk. Instead, use **buttermilk. Add teaspoon each baking powder and baking soda to dry thing.**

Lazy Nalysnyky

Your Baba so sweet to you. She always showing lazy way out. If you have new mother in bed and new father in coma, here is what you can do.

Whip up usual nalysnyky recipe. Spread filling on each one, then make stack. Bake with glump of butter on top.

Or, **Baba give you permission to not even bake**. **Spread crush fruit between layer**. Some good one is blueberry, raspberry or strawberry. Or fresh peach. Pitted cherry is excellent and Ukrainian favorite. Baba going to go all out and give permission to use frozen fruit, thaw. Can fruit is gross. Don't even think about can pie filling, or Baba reach out from page and slap your soft spot.

Put butter or buttered bread crumb on top. Maple syrup is not Ukrainian thing, but it really work. Cut nalysnyky stack in wedge.

How to make buttered bread crumb: Slide bread crumb around in melt butter. Big deal.

Get lazy nalysnyky to people as fast as possible.

Baba warning: Do not feed to baby. It will make him all sticky. Kid is sticky enough, believe me.

Baba find out interesting thing in Canada. In Ukraina, she use rye or pumpernickel bread to wipe new baby. This clean him up not too bad and give him blessing. But Wonderbra bread actual make better sponge. Baba recommend real bread for ritual, and surreal kind for absorbent. She even keep sponge bread beside change table, along with wrench (*see Baby Food, Chapter Five*). You knew it was good for something.

Ingredient List:

- Eggs, four large
- Two percent milk, one cup
- Water, one quarter cup boiled and cooled
- Sifted flour, one cup
- Salt, half teaspoon
- Buttered bread crumbs

Hryb (Mushroom) Filling

Chop up apron full delicious Ukrainian mushroom. See *Mushrooms, Chapter Twelve*.

Cook them real good in butter. Add tablespoon very fine chop onion and cook too. Onion should be mushy for delicacy. You can put onion in heavy kind freezer bag and use rolling pin. Or put on floor and roll over with office chair. Baba is here to make your deepest dream come true.

Pour in real sour cream and mix around with mushroom and onion. By now, neighbor will knock on door to return hemp he borrow. His nostril will be two time normal size and making twitch. He will pretend he don't know is dinner time. Tell him to send his wife to baby welcome party and bring good gift.

Let mix cook little bit so flavor fall in love. **Sprinkle with little bit salt and coarse pepper. Add fine chop fresh dill**. If not fresh, forget it. May as well use green sawing dust.

Spread filling on nalysnyky, roll and bake like Baba tell you in first recipe.

Serve with *smetana*.

Ingredient List:

- Mushrooms, two cups chopped fine
- Onion, one tablespoon
- Butter, two or three tablespoons
- Smetana, three tablespoons
- Fresh dill, one teaspoon
- Salt and pepper
- Sour cream for topping

Savory Syr (Cottage Cheese) Filling

You ready? We go all in big rush.

Make mashing with: dry cottage cheese or farmer cheese, egg yolk, whip kind cream, big pinch dill and small pinch salt.

Make groaning like woman in labor so everyone think you working so hard at this easy thing.

Spread on nalysnyky and bake like Baba already tell you several time.

Your option:

See *Syr* Dip under *Syr* *(Cottage Cheese), Chapter Fifteen*, for all sorts idea of thing to add to cottage cheese filling. Really, you could make a different kind of cheese filling every day for month or two. Until family get thing call “nalysnyky fever” and try to chop each other up with ax.

Ingredients:

- Dry cottage cheese, two cups
- Egg yolks, two
- Whipping cream, two tablespoons
- Dill, one teaspoon,
- Salt

Sweet Syr Filling

This is good substitution when you feeling like *syrnyk* (cheesecake) in big hurry. This could possible also revive new father. You may have to sit on floor and feed by hand.

Mash up dry syr. Do not use cream cheese, or baking will turn into white puddle.

Mix in two large egg yolk. This help hold thing together, which you needing right bow. Is so many dangerous way this recipe could fulfill proverb, *Opustyv svit I portky*, he drop the world and his pant. English literal would be, Let all hang out. You be sorry if you let any recipe do this.

Splash in vanilla or good rum. Aftershave is terrible idea.

Mix in icing sugar and give taste. If is not sweet enough, add little bit more. **Put in pinch cinnamon and salt in so small pinch** like you would use to pick up misbehaving ant. Apparently is evidence that cinnamon lower blood sugar. You should be okay to eat half this recipe yourself now, Baba think.

Spread on nalysnyky. Roll up, dot with butter and bake.

If you figure heading off sugar diet beet is lost cause, top baked nalysnyky with more ice sugar and even whipping cream. And berry. Or chocolate sauce.

Your option:

***Add hand full raisin** to filling.
***Add half cup pitted cherry to filling**. If you use sour cherry from jar, add extra ice sugar. Save some cherry for topping.

Ingredient list:

- Dry cottage cheese, two cups
- Eggs yolks, two large
- Vanilla, one half teaspoon
- Icing sugar, one quarter cup
- Cinnamon, one quarter teaspoon
- Salt

Kapusta (Cabbage) Filling

Oy, this filling tasty and can have many variety with different meat.

Fry grate onion in butter until it go all softie.

Shred large size green *kapusta*. Baba try this in paper shredder. It work first time. Very nice, even piece come out. But people start complaint about funny smell and rust on shredder teeth.

Baba law: If you going to make innovation, clean up good afterward.

Fry cabbage with onion, salt and pepper until it feel tender but not mushy. Like good dog who lean against your leg, but don't have nauseate runny eye.

Toss in pinch caraway seed. Caraway is tasty and also good defense against making gas.

Baba warning: Don't get smartypants idea and think cabbage recipe mean you can use tomato juice for sauce like with *holubtsi* (cabbage rolls). Ukrainian cooking is magic. Is lots like African music. It seem simple because over many thousand of year, it get baked down to essential note. But when you not African and try to improvise on this singing, you fall flat. Baba know this is terrible pun. So don't write letter to her about this. She put letter in shredder with cabbage.

Your option:

Now she give you warning about making improvisation, Baba going to make leeway. Is okay to improvise within Ukrainian bound and little bit more. To cabbage filling, you can **add fine chop *kobasa* (garlic sausage), summer sausage, crisp bacon, ham, mushroom, corn beef or hard boil egg.** Not all at once, or going to taste the way WASP free jazz sound. If you making for new mother, she just going to burst out crying.

Ingredient list:

- Onion, one tablespoon
- Green cabbage, three cups
- Butter, one quarter cup
- Salt and pepper
- Caraway seed, quarter teaspoon
- Sour cream for topping

Meat (or Vegetarian Substitute) Filling

Baba bet her sweet patootskie you never hear of crepe with meat filling. You can use any kind ground or fine chop meat: turkey, chicken, beef, pork, bison. Sky is limit. Maybe you even shoot fresh goose from sky. Ha! Like you have any good aim. Baba know you have trouble just spitting tobacco in can. You always blame on wind rocking trailer.

Fry ground meat with extra virgin or soniashnyk oil and small onion.

This seem like lots meat. But is because you going to fry meat until dry like you make boss martini when you kissing his *sraka*. Meat will shrink. **Drain fat from pan, and stir in big splash home made broth. Cook till meat is again dry**. Is these little touch that make recipe Baba teach you superior to neighbor.

Stir in good slop! smetana. Add salt and crack black pepper.

Bake and serve with more smetana. *Duzhe smashno.* Very tasty.

Your option:

*If you use your fever imagination, you can make endless filling from meat, fish and poultry with different kind broth, gravy or sauce.
*Try with *Dill, Smetana and Green Onion*, *Mushroom* or *Horse Radish Sauce*, under *Pidlyvi* (Sauces), *Chapter Twenty Two.*

Ingredient List:

- Extra virgin olive or sunflower oil, two tablespoons
- Onion, one small
- Cooked meat or substitute, one and one half pounds
- Broth, one quarter cup
- Sour cream, two tablespoons
- Salt and pepper
- Sour cream for topping

Pig Brain Filling

This filling have some kind of vitamin haven't been discovered yet.

Press one set raw pig brain through sieve. If you can't imagine self doing this, don't start recipe. Nobody going to bum stab you.

You still with Baba? **Mix in mushy onion, salt and pepper**. I was going to say "to taste," but she is proud you come this far in becoming Ukrainian. She not going to push it.

Spread on nalysnyky and bake for forty minute instead of thirty. Half-bake brain is unbeautiful thing.

Top with smetana or any sauce like for meat filling, above.

Ingredient List:

- Pig brains, one set
- Onion, one teaspoon
- Salt and pepper
- Sour cream for topping

Orange Sauce Filling

This one fancy-pantsy filling you can make for *rodyny*, which is all-woman party after baby is born. This is where Ukrainian have big wisdom. Is personal Revolution.

Canadian make stupid party where everybody frustrate because they don't know if to buy blue or pink. So they buy ugly Walmart thing in crazy yellow, which make all baby look like it have bad complexion. Even worse, they buy bad shoe. Baby don't have to cry near as much as you think it do. Is fashion issue.

At least if you have party after, you not only know baby sex, but shoe size.

Melt butter and let cool little bit. Don't stick your tongue to check. Use finger.

Mix butter with: icing sugar, fresh lemon juice, fresh orange juice and big pinchola orange zest. If you can pry away from new father mouth, **add sherry.**

Use wooden spoon to make orange filling so creamy delicious, you lucky if it get to party.

Spread on nalysnyky. Use plain butter instead of bread crumb. Bake.

Top with smetana.

Ingredient List:

- Butter, three tablespoons
- Confectioner's sugar, one half cup
- Lemon juice, one tablespoon
- Orange juice, one third cup
- Orange zest, half teaspoon
- Sour cream for topping
- Optional: one teaspoon sherry

Med (Honey) Filling

Med is sacred Ukrainian ingredient, because bee is 007 spy for God. Bee travel many thousand mile and bring back blessing in its sweet poop.

There is spiritual lesson in this. Whenever you thinking about someone, "Eat poop!" you imagine them eating honey. This is better for your soul. Is one of Baba serenity prayer. Next one is, *Don't think about yesterday, don't worry about tomorrow, and don't be big jerk today.*

Baba number three serenity prayer is, *Oy Syra Mata Zemlya, oh Moist Mother Earth, please help me shut up.*

If you can find unpasteurize honey, so much better. Don't rat on beekeeper who give to you, or Baba and God be mad.

Melt butter and mix with liquid honey. If you beginner, use light taste honey. If you going to real Ukrainian party, use buckwheat.

If you think this alone is enough to make heaven, surprise. **Mix honey butter with big pinch lemon or orange zest, juice from half fresh lemon, juice from half small orange, and half cup crushed pecan or walnut**.

If you recognize this as kind of baklava, you almost right. When Greek and Turk took Ukrainian as slave for many century (9th to 17th) they learn this recipe from us. But of course, ours is better, because Ukrainian is world master beekeeper. And slave always know more about master than master know about slave.

Top with smetana.

Ingredient List:

- Butter, one quarter cup
- Honey, one half cup
- Orange or lemon zest, one half teaspoon
- Fresh lemon juice, one teaspoon
- Fresh orange juice, one teaspoon
- Crushed walnuts or pecans, one half cup
- Sour cream for topping

Apple Filling

Serving apple recipe to man in Ukraina is one way to tell him you love him. You could say is opposite of throwing pumpkin at reject suitor.

Take out core and peel tart apple. Slice up. If you using crab, don't peel. You can also use Baba "apple *horilka* soak method" like in apple pie recipe instead of adding liquor later. Your choice, poopchik. See *Desserts, Chapter Twenty Three*.

Melt butter in largest pan. Because Baba have flexible mind, she going to suggest you even use Chinese wok. You need to **fit whole grocery bag full of apple in pan and stir around**. You will be happier camper if they not continual falling on floor and you not dusting off cat hair before throwing back in pan. **Keep adding butter until all apple is soft**.

Stir in brown sugar or splash liquid honey. Before you do face plant in pan, **add big splash good brandy or dark rum. Stir apple around another five minute**.

Horilka is going to reduce, but not enough to serve to alcoholic. This is one recipe Baba recommend you don't put in blender for baby.

But would still be good without horilka, Baba is going to take educate guess. Again, use flavor syrup idea from pie recipe.

Put apple filling in big bowl and mix in pinch each cinnamon, nutmeg and clove. Here you need some patience. Let filling cool to bathwater temperature before spreading on nalysnyky. Is good time to go put few more stitch in those rainbow baby bootie.

Top with good farm smetana.

Your option:

*After apple filling nalysnyky bake, you can **top with ice sugar, crème fraiche or whip cream**.
*Go to pie recipe for **fruit filling** idea. Is unlimited to your imagining.

Ingredient List:

- Tart apples, ten large or twenty to thirty crab
- Butter, three quarters cup
- Brown sugar, one third cup packed OR liquid honey, one quarter cup
- Brandy or dark rum, one quarter cup
- Cinnamon, nutmeg and ground cloves, one quarter teaspoon each
- Sour cream for topping
- Optional: icing sugar or whipped cream for topping

Maslyanitsya

Maslyanitsya is Ukrainian *Mardi Gras*. We have big party with butter goddess. Butter is maslo. We make ton of delicious round pancake to symbolize sun coming back after winter. We do not eat ground hog like Canadian.

Ukrainian always been really big on sleigh ride. We put straw figure of goddess Maslayanitsya in sleigh and even take her on sliding toboggan. At this festival, we steer sleigh horse in semi-circle path like sun across sky. Rider on horse go around village with torch to symbolize same thing. In meantime, masquerade bystander throw snowball at sleigh rider. Rider throw stale pancake back. Is too cold to show tit like in New Orleans. We have to find different kind of amusement. Mind you, Baba was brave girl and she have strange kind frost bite to prove this.

At midnight, we strip clothes off straw figure and burn her to say, "Bye bye, winter, we not miss you." Long time ago, this was not exactly butter goddess. She is compromise Ukrainian feel we have to make with Christianity. Real goddess is *Kostroma*, whose name mean "bony." We get tired of bony old winter and burn it up. Word "bonfire" in English mean "bone fire." Is way to chase away evil spirit and invite good one. Ashes get cover in snow for first fertilization of field. We also burn leftover pancake. Which is best thing for it.

Mlyntsi (Pancakes)

Baba know you think pancake come from stupormarket package. Sure, just like best kind soup. Blech. Why you not just eat chalk dust and smack lip?

Sifting is very important. It make right blend of ingredient. **Sift with baking powder, salt and sugar**.

Here come liquid. Pour in melt butter, two egg and milk. Do not sift. You would be cleaning sieve forever. One time my daughter Stefania call me. She whining because she sift liquid thing. By time she call, it make hard crust. She been sitting and trying to poke out from hole with toothpick for three hour. Baba didn't say her children was genius. Successful, but not genius. Don't get these two thing mixed up. Is like assume university degree make you smart.

Heat casting iron pan and melt butter just so is sheen like sweat on your forehead. Let few drop of sweat fall into pan. If drop dry up immediate, pan is too hot. If drop go flat, is too cold. When drop is round shape, is time to pour batter in. Be grateful to Baba for teaching you perfection. **How much batter? To make thin cake three, four inch across.**

Top of cake will make bubble. Do not panic. This suppose to happen. **Just flip over once and finish cooking**. This is only time you look at stupormarket package. It show you what color brown shade *mlyntsi* should be.

Serve mlyntsi with smetana, maple syrup, fruit syrup, preserve or honey. Yes, honey is liquid. You ever seen honey come out from hive in solid chunk? Maybe near Chornobyl.

Your option:

***Add one cup blueberry or saskatoon to batter**. This is good kind self-contain berry. Other berry will spread out and stain entire cake red. For even more interesting taste, **add one teaspoon grate lemon peel**. This call zest, because is zesty.

***Add one cup fine chop apple to batter**. If your family don't like crunchy thing, fry apple in butter little bit first. Baba don't peel apple if she don't have to. Rosy apple look cute, green apple is good if you have little boy who like to pretend is bug in food. Baba is last thing from sexist; she just never met little girl who pretend same thing, okay?

*Try with any **fruit based *Sauce* or *Dessert*.**

Make extra recipe so you have enough pancake to throw at maslyanitsya holiday. Baba do this one week ahead so they good and stale. Then they make decent flight trajectory from Mardi Gras sleigh. Baba even have flight simulator in her basement. She practice all year. If you don't mind to waste good sauce, this make nice mess in bystander hair. If you send media release ahead of parade, your politician will probably be in front row. Some politician always in front row, especial if they have to shove person on crutch to be there. You get Baba picture?

Ingredient list:

- Flour, two cups
- Salt, one teaspoon
- Sugar, one teaspoon
- Baking powder, four teaspoons
- Butter, two tablespoons
- Large eggs, two

- Milk, one and one half cups
- Butter for frying
- Topping of choice

Hrechanyky (Buckwheat Pancakes)

Sometime Baba think buckwheat is love of Ukrainian life. Is extremely nutritious food, actual not related to wheat. Is more of a nut, just like you. Can have much more protein as wheat, which make it superfood. Is pretty easy to find in grocery store, these day.

Hrechanyky is name for buckwheat pancake we usual only make for Maslyanitsya. Is kind of tricky to make. You have to whisper sweet something to these cake so they rise. Baba want to make sure you is up to big challenge.

This is yeast raise kind of recipe. Oooh is scary. Don't be worry, even Ukrainian sometime fail at this. We write song about it, where pancake just sit there like when your husband *Ebay* Viagra shipment is delay.

Scald milk and let cool. How to do this? Make milk boil, but stop it before it do. This get rid of protein that keep pancake from rising. Stir milk entire time. Watch milk never boil.

Dissolve white sugar in warm water. Sprinkle on one tablespoon yeast. For your information, this is how much in one those little package. Let this stuff hang round for ten minute.

Then all of sudden, you going to **mix yeasty mix with these next ingredient: Sift together white or wholewheat flour with buckwheat flour. Add salt and sugar**. If you not living in country, hippie store can get for you. They also going to try and sell you spelt, quinoa, and seaweed pre-chew by Tibetan yak herder. But one thing at time.

Baba law: New Age hippie is awful good at retail. They make big eye while they take all your money. Don't be fool by dilate pupil. Is not cause by honesty, believe me.

Beat up three good egg. Take off shell first. Mix with melt butter, NOT stinking margarine. This is butter goddess festival, remember? Margarine is almost like bringing ham to Hanukkah party. Baba know you. You say, "But was on sale!" Pah! Cheapsnake.

Mix egg and butter with scald milk.

Now beat up everything together. Baba mean everything, but not kitchen sink. Batter will be creamy so you will want to lick. Don't. This is precision recipe.

Cover up batter with clean dish towel and go do something useful for almost two hour. Oil change is about right. Is important you leave batter in warm but not hot place. Sunny kitchen counter is good. So is inside cool stove. Use fat felt pen to make note with many exclamation mark so no one turn on stove.

When you come back fifteen minute before two hour, degrease your hand. **Boil milk, stirring whole time**. If it burn, throw out or you will ruin recipe. I know this bother your cheapness gene, but grit teeth.

Stir up batter real good along with boil milk, then let sit for ten minute more. Baba hear you groaning and sighing. Look, this is ritual recipe with ancient meaning. If you looking for instant-schminstant, why you even start?

Batter will be thin. You cook just like mlyntsi, above.

Is traditional to **serve with butter and smetana**. Or can use other topping like Baba suggest before. Between you and me, Baba don't throw hrechanyky at nobody. They too much trouble to make. Stick with plain mlyntsi for throwing, hrechanyky for impressing guest.

Before Baba forget, this is super nutritious food to give new mother. Will help her make super rich milk.

Ingredient list:

- Basic yeast mix
- Granular yeast, one tablespoon (one package)
- Warm water, three quarter cup
- White sugar, one teaspoon
- Batter mix
- Milk, one cup scalded and cooled
- White sugar, two teaspoons
- White or whole wheat flour, three quarter cup
- Buckwheat flour, two cups
- Eggs, three large
- Butter, two tablespoons
- Milk, one cup boiling hot

Chapter Five

Baby Food

Now you know all about good food for nursing mother. One day, that baby will chew nipple little too hard. Mother will scream and start stuffing its face with other food. What kind food will work? Here is story:

One time I work for rich woman who refuse to change her own baby diaper. This because she have mental illness call "weirdo." Baba cure her. I tell you how.

I always keep wrench by baby changing table, just in case. One day baby make spectacle of poop. I yell to his mother, "Quick! Is emergence!"

She come running. I grab her by wrist and stick hand in warm baby shit. Then I pick up wrench and smash down on rich woman hand. She dance around screaming like her stock option go down, then put all finger in mouth. After that she okay, never cover nose and complain again. Baba cure her of hating innocent little baby shit. Crazy woman.

What is point of this story? Is this. When you have baby, is your full time job. Baba not trust baby food in can, so she tell you this: BUY GOOD BLENDER. Put little bit boil water in with food, and you going to make happy, healthy baby.

Almost any recipe Baba show you can be baby food, as long as not spicy.

Here is Baba favorite recommendation, in order of book chapter:

-*Borshch*. This is staple baby food. Just don't staple baby.

-*Vegetable, Minestrone, Pea* and *Mushroom Soup*

-Skip *Salata*, except those with *Kartoplya* (Potato). Is superkabalisticexpialidocious nutritious, but lettuce get watery in blender and baby just not going to eat! For complete veggie nutrition, feed borshch.

-*Nalysnyky* (Crepes) with filling.

-*Yitysy* (Egg) recipe, except *Pickled*. You don't want pickled baby hanging out at bar.

-Any *Kurka* (Chicken) or *Masnyy* (Beef) recipe, except leave out one with lemon. Baby will make old man face and spit at you.

-*Hryby* (Mushrooms) recipe

-*Varenyky* (Perogy) of course! Baby must learn taste for this Ukrainian staple early. They will probably not like sour kind, like plum or *kapusta* (sauerkraut). You don't want these ingredient in diaper, believe Baba.

-*Holubtsi* (Cabbage Rolls). Not going to get more nutritious than this, especial with meat or big protein kasha (buckwheat).

-*Riba* (Fish) can be acquire taste, so go easy on baby. Again, pickled fish is not to mess with till kid is older.

-*Pechenya* (stew). Duh.

-Potatoes, Grains and Beans. Lots ideas here.

-*Lokshyna* (Noodles) not only great baby food in blender, but is favorite food for teaching baby to eat on their own. Will end up in hair, wall and in your face, so make kind you like best to eat.

-Forget *Pidlyvi* (Sauce). Longer you can keep baby knowing about this extra thing and McDonald's, happier your house will be.

-Next in book come whole ton dessert. Of course you can feed to baby any kind but alcoholic, but is no reason to make sweet tooth before kid even have tooth. Longer you can hold out on feeding dessert, is better.

Baba advice: teach kid about dessert with good fruit. Fresh is best kind, or make low sugar dessert like *Sugarless Pie*, *Uzvar* (Compote) or *Yabluchnyk* (Apple Cake). Always use honey for sweetener before sugar or some terrible phony sweetener, make hand grow out from forehead.

Also, since you at least smart enough to ask Baba advice: don't let your baby grow up to be cowboy.

If you buying all baby food at store, may as well save money, you lazy bone. Go to pet food aisle and get big bag Baby Chow. Ha!

Chapter Six

Ukrainian Spring Traditions

Velyk Den' (Great Day)
Ukrainian Spring Equinox and Easter

Pysanky is Ukrainian tradition many thousand year old. Is woman sacred obligation to write blessing on egg every year. She then give away as many as possible.

This not ritual like some kind weirdo modern thing these people make up who dancing with crystal on head and moaning in park. One day they Greek god, next day they some kind rootsy-tootsy Gypsy. Only can't sing.

They should try keep up dancing, singing with me and other women at Ukrainian festival. They think they New Age. Ha! I show them Old Age.

Listen and I tell you pysanka story. You have my permission read this to children. Is good for them understand how to fight evil.

Is terrible monster live deep in cave. Probably more ice cold bunker like Hitler have, only near Kremlin. He chain to rock since beginning of time. This monster look like cross between that Bugs Bunny Tasmanian Devil and politician who have fierce orange eye so close together, look like only one in middle forehead. You know who I mean. Eye is narrow like mind, so you can always tell. If you follow this voting advice, you never wrong. No, eye can't be orange. This is color of Ukrainian liberation. Correction. Eye is Soviet red. Also, monster is little bit too hairy to be normal. This not always true for politician, good or bad. Use your discrimination.

Monster have ear that hang low, pimple on thigh and bad breath. He film himself for *YouTube*.

He is guard by three goddess call *Zorya*, or stars. They is goddess of dawn, goddess of dusk and goddess of midnight. They also decide people fate.

Every spring, ugly monster send out demon into four corner of earth. They scout to see if people still loving each other, still writing blessing on egg and giving them away. If so, monster sad. He stay chain to rock another year.

If we stop writing blessing on egg, happy monster break chain and pow! He fly loose with demon and destroy whole world.

This why egg written with symbol for all sort of good life thing: sun, animal, plant, cross of four direction, vine and Baba Spider, she who weave Universe.

Why egg? Is eternal shape of cosmos and sun. Tell us life continue always and that monster never going to win. But we have to fulfill sacred obligation to planet and our Creator.

When you making pysanky, you blow out inside for amulet against evil. If someone wishing for baby, you leave yolk inside. Never boil egg. Inside must stay alive. You don't want to eat what come out when you blow. Will have dye in white and yolk, so can be toxic. If you draw ancient spiral shape on egg, spiral will trap evil and not allow to escape.

I know you going to run to Internet to find out how to make these beautiful egg. Is better if you find Ukrainian baba at cultural centre or church who show you how to make. Is also meditation that go with this. You supposed to meditate for whole day on blessing before starting to write on egg. Also not fight with no one for this time. Baba have to admit, sometime she fail this spiritual test.

These women who make so beautiful pysanky not allow to do this any other time of year except for one month before Easter. This add to spiritual power of egg. Over lifetime, a woman pysanky get a little better each year. Is good reminder that her ovary and uterus important, too. Is not just thing for childbearing, then throw away. Egg shape is eternal also inside woman. Baba is supporter of *HERS Foundation For Women.*

Many uses for pysanky: Girl give one to boy she like. We put in furrow and under beehive for fertile crop. We keep in house to turn away lightning and fire. Only thing you not do is eat. Is really, really bad luck to intentional break shell sacred amulet.

Other good Ukrainian springtime ritual is you and friend cut pussy willow branch and spank each other. This to let pussy willow know you notice it getting fuzzy and blooming to celebrate spring. You say blessing, *May you be tall like willow, healthy like water, and rich like earth.* Baba take exception to “tall” part. But at least we never crazy enough to say “thin.”

Then you make tea from pussy willow to stop stinging sensation. This how Ukrainian invent aspirin. Special trick to this: if you get priest to bless pussy willow first, you can even do spanking inside church. Maybe you like to do this, maybe not. I don't know everything, it just seem that way.

Why we do this? Very long time ago, cruel farmer put several kitten in sack and try to drown in river. Mama *kitsya,* she sitting on riverbank and making such crying! Willow tree take big pity. It reach branch into water and rescue as many as not drown. It tell mama to chew on its branch to ease her pain. Next spring, regular willow burst into fuzzy bud to remember kitten who drown. When you spank, you transfer heart compassion, fertile egg and healing of aspirin to friend. If you want more than this, eat a pussy willow bud, call *kotyk*, or kitten.

At same time you spanking each other, some men make big bonfire at edge of village to warn demon they not going to find people neglecting tradition here. These fire also light way for ancestor spirit to come home for Easter dinner. Ukrainian have so many ancestor, we never have leftover.

Ukrainian *Velyk Den'* basket get bless in church. In old day, is roast suckling pig and sacred bread so big, we have to take wagon. It require whole lots *hrin*, or horse radish, to make cleansing of body and spirit. We don't bother with Guinness World Record for bread, even though we know we would win.

After church, family gather around family grave and eat lunch. We leave all leftover for ancestor, along with pysanky for blessing. We eat colored egg at lunch too, call *krashanky.* They one solid color. Very beautiful if color made from beet juice or tea. Instruction here: **www.ukrainiansoulfood.ca**

We throw shell into river, to let Nature know we not forget her on Great Day. Shell travel down to ocean, where all soul live. This how we bless ancestor collective conscious. That Jung guy, he taking credit. Pah!

We mostly call this holiday Velyk Den'.

This is traditional menu for Velyk Den':

- Always boiled *yiytsy* (Eggs), but you can improvise with one of Baba many creative recipe in *Eggs, Chapter Seven*
- *Shynka* (Ham), recipe below
- *Kobasa* or other tasty sausage
- *Syr* (Cottage Cheese). Plain or another one of Baba smooth recipe, *Chapter Fifteen*
- *Khrin*, horse radish
- *Buryak i Khrin (Tsvikli)* beet and horse radish relish, recipe below
- *Syrnyk* (Cheesecake), under *Desserts, Chapter Twenty Three*
- *Paska and Babka* bread

In Volume II cookbook, I going to show you how to make Paska and Babka, Ukrainian spring bread. You so lucky to learn this from real Babka. In fact, in next book Baba going to show you several kind bread. Right now publisher is waving her arm, yelling, "Stop already! You have so much wisdom we is run out of paper!"

In this book, you going to learn how to make *Shynka* and *Buriak Relish/Tsvikli* for Velyk Den' dinner.

Shynka v Med (Honey Baked Ham)

Shynka is indisposable dish for Velyk Den'. Because this fact, Ukrainian try to not get too friendly with pig. Baba have strategy. She only raise her own for pet. Little baby pig is too cute. She give them each name and cannot make into ham later. She end up with whole herd of huge pig, eating her out from house and home.

So she buy eating pig every year from farmer friend. Is cheating, she know, but you feel same way after you see movie Babe. At least Baba not demanding you make whole roast pig, like in old day. Oy. For same reason, duck is even out from questioning. Baba have so many good friend from duck, especially after she make brave rescue of mallard hen with broken leg. Hen family teach her wise quack. Ha!

This going to be work of art. **Get yourself about ten pound ham by whatever mean is necessary. Take off the top skin, but leave the fat underneath**. Fat is supposed to drip into meat while cooking.

Here where your artistic talent come into question. Look this way and that, then **cut diamond pattern into top surfacing of meat**. Don't cut deep! Only like when you bluffing in sword fight.

Don't draw individual diamond. Baba know someone who try. She come back several day later, and this person is collapse on top of ham, moaning. Make all diagonal line one way, then other.

Put oven rack on bottom rung. Heat oven to 325 degree F.

Put ham in big roaster pan. Use pastry brush or that new paint brush been sitting there three year, and put coat of Dijon mustard on ham. Keep coat light and even, like you painting huge toenail some sexoid color.

Baba secret: if you put aluminum foil in roaster first, you won't have to yell at no one to scrub it later. This recipe get damn gloopy, and if honey burn at all, oy yoi YOI.

Dump brown sugar and big glop liquid honey in pan. Cook on

low heat just till sugar melt. Use brush to give ham good glazing.

Baba know she going to have to send you to read *Artist Way*, but try to focus. **Stick whole clove only in every second diamond**. Part of being artist is not overdo.

Pour unsweeten apple, orange or pineapple juice in bottom of roaster. DO NOT POUR ON HAM OR HAM WILL EXPLODE.

Baba making *zhart*, joke. You don't want to wash off your three layer installation art: clove, mustard and honey/sugar glaze.

Baste ham every half hour or so.

When you take out of oven, let hang out on top of stove for fifteen minute or so. Ham will exhale and not fight so hard when you try to carve.

How you know is ready? Baba, of course, know by instinct. She give you dispensation to buy meat thermometer. Pork is tricky thing, dead or alive. **Inside of baked raw ham should read 160 degree F. If precook, should be 140 degree F**. If ham have bone, be careful thermometer not resting on this. Then you only get ham bone temperature, not meat.

Make sure oven is heated up whole way so ham will get crispy. **Cook about twenty minute to half hour for each pound raw ham**.

If you buy precook kind, there will be direction on package. Some only precook, some also been smoke.

Oh. You throw out package. Have fun in dumpster dive.

Serve with any kind sauce have horse radish in it. Especial traditional is *Beet and Horse* Radish *Relish*, below. Excellent with *Baba's Favorite Mayonnaise, Chapter Three*. Plain or horse radish variety.

Your option:

*Put **large pinch cinnamon** in pan when cooking honey and fruit juice.
*Add o**ne half cup red wine or dry cider** to juice.
Use juice from *Uzvar, under *Desserts*, *Chapter Twenty Three*, instead of other fruit juice.
***Use juice from your pickle fruit** instead of other fruit juice: raspberry, peach and so on.
***Use buckwheat honey** for strong Ukrainian taste.

Ingredient List:

- Ham, raw or precooked, ten to twelve pounds
- Cloves
- Brown sugar, one cup

- Liquid honey, one half cup
- Dijon mustard, one quarter cup. Some may be left over
- Apple, orange or pineapple juice, one cup
- Meat thermometer

Buryak i Khrin or Tsvikli (Beet and Horse Radish Relish)

Beside pizazz taste, this relish have advantage of being pickle in only twenty-four hour. Again, is Ukrainian kitchen magic. When false story making woman who stir cauldron into evil witch, is way to degrade woman power. Especially of older woman. Baba going to tell you all about true Ukrainian origin of *Baba Yaga* in next book. Just you wait.

Right now we getting on with this recipe. Is uber-traditional for Velyk Den'. We eat along with shynka that been glazed within inch of life, above.

Some Ukrainian also call this dish *tsvikli.* Different region than Baba.

There is easy way to prepare these beet, too. Cut stem off beet, leaving one inch for handle. Leave root alone. Scrub. **Boil or steam until you can easy poke fork i**n.

Put beet in cold water and use stem handle to help slide off skin. **Chop off root**.

Make beet coarse grate. Good thing about this vegetable is it hide blood, so you don't have to be too careful like with potato.

Grate fresh horse radish. Don't rub eye while doing this.

Mix together beet and horse radish. You will laugh at beautiful color, like you can only make yourself. Next thing, you will be dyeing your own clothes. Sure, when your checking account is in overdrive.

In medium size pan, mix together pickling spice with vinegar, salt and white sugar. Make boiling, then take off from heat. Once you is past being amateur Ukrainian, try wine or apple cider vinegar. But not today. Wait till next year, when you not so worry about exploding jar or how to grate beet.

Make straining of this pickle soup over beet and horse radish. This is where you can justify self for those screen window still leaning against porch six month later. Use for strainer you don't have. **Mix whole thing together** best way you know how.

See *Oseledets (Pickled Herring)* under *Ocean Fish, Chapter Seventeen*, for **how to sterilize jar.**

You will need about five cup size jar. Always prepare couple more, in case is relish left over. What, you going to shovel raw mix into mouth if you make miscalculation?

Put relish into jar and seal. Okay, here is truth. Speedy Gonzalinsky pickling mean this relish don't keep so long. Will last about one week in fridge. Baba hear your disappointment. You was hoping would be fine addition to your pickle cellar you spend all year building. Sorry, no luck. But perfect for huge dinner party, or you can give away to someone you trying to bribe.

Ingredient List:

- Beets, two pounds
- Fresh horse radish, one quarter cup grated
- Salt, one teaspoon
- Vinegar, one cup
- White sugar, one quarter cup
- Pickling spice, one teaspoon
- Eight ounce sterilized jars, five

Chapter Seven

Yiytsy (Eggs)

Baba going to show you many thing to do with egg.

First I tell you story about thing that happen to my friend Serge in outhouse. Later your mind will catch up and you will see how these thing intimate relate.

Serge go to Africa like he always want. Everything fine. He dance, he sing, he make photo of hippopotamus. But Serge terrify of snake. Everywhere he go, he ask, "Is snake here? Is snake there?"

Serge not see no snake for month; he start to relax. One night he go to outhouse. Just when he settling in for good time, he feel sharp bite on his *dupa*. Serge have social work degree so he know this not positive thing. He go running screaming through yard, "Snake bite me! Snake bite me!"

His African friend make him lie on table, face down. He let them make criss cross on sraka with sharp knife while he biting on wood stick. Some very, very good friend draw straw, then loser suck poison out.

Then men go out with stick and net to outhouse. One of them look very careful down hole with flashlight. They hear, "PWAAaaaaak, PWAAAaaak, pwaaaKAAAAAK!"

Next thing, big white chicken jump up from hole.

They take chicken from outhouse and next day have egg for breakfast. Serge never hear end of it. He have to leave not just country, but all of Africa because in village, they not so stupid from TV like here. They know when thing is genuine funny, and soon everyone know.

Here is simple egg recipe, you could make even if you spend night so terrible as Serge and his friend.

But first, **Baba tell you egg secret:** To make nice sunshine yolk balance right in centre of egg, take all egg out of carton and put in bowl overnight. Because they happy resting sideway instead of standing on head, next day all yolk will be obedient. Your neighbor be making crooked egg, and your egg be perfect. You laughing, they crying. That is life. *Dai Bozha*! Give to God! God Give to You!

By way, this good time to make toast with horilka. God like that, Baba find. Why you think they always guzzling wine in church?

Baba learn this law of egg physic from Mrs. Einstein. We correspond for many year while she inventing *Theory of Relative Dropping In For*

Dinner, and universal law of Husband Take Credit for My Science, too.

Dilled Eggs

Heat extra virgin olive oil or butter in iron fry pan that have lid that fit. I know you probably have to go to store for even this simple thing. I say "have to." This not option.

Ask everybody, "How many egg you want?" Don't listen to all different order: over easy, sunny side, and so on. You have enough to do. You not truck stopping waitress.

Crack egg into pan. Be very gentle. Do not crack yolk. Put lid on pan and steam egg for while. Probably three minute. Is okay to peek, especially when you is beginner.

If you this kind of person like to be environmental, put egg peel in blender with little bit water, then put mix on house plant.

In meantime, **chop fresh dill.** How much how much you always asking. Depend how many egg, like I tell you. This nothing like making plastic surgery on your friend.

Okay, plan to put large pinch fresh dill on each egg.

Put lid back and allow dill to steam on top of egg for minute or so.

Serve like usual, with good toast.

Very good with **spoonful fresh farm smetana** (sour cream) on top. If you have this thing, **tasty with caviar or herring roe**. In Canada, Baba find wonderful Greek thing called *taramasalata*, taste something like herring roe. Is fish egg. I call "poor woman caviar."

Ingredient List:

- Two or three eggs for each person
- Butter or oil to fry eggs
- Fresh dill, one bunch
- Sour cream, one tablespoon for each egg
- Toast

Deviled Eggs I

This great recipe for party. Or if friend ever suck poison from your *sraka*, you should take over this thing to her. And much, much more. Probably you should also make roaster *holubtsi* and big bowl *varenyky*.

I promise you is not yawn type thing like these Canadian devil egg. They little bit paprika and big deal. I supposed to throw up hand and ooh and aaah like I am pretending to love everything at wedding shower. Next I put paper plate with ribbon on my head and get piercing in belly button. Sure. Same day I put rose on Stalin grave.

Have platter and big bowl ready.

Here is next Baba egg secret: take egg you going to boil out of fridge at least half hour before using. Then hot water hitting cold shell will not make crack. Also is better if you not take egg directly from under chicken sraka. Egg that is little bit older will peel easier. And you not make chicken mad so she peck your dupa like my friend Serge. Ha!

Boil one dozen egg till hard, five minute. Recipe will be disgusting if yolk is running.

If you have patience to be super cook like Baba, you should **boil water furious, then turn off immediately. Let egg all sit in hot water with lid for half hour** while you read book. This make white part more tender than when you keep boiling.

Have bowl of water fill with ice cube waiting and put egg in there. Let sit while you engineer rest of ingredient.

Heat butter in iron fry pan. Cook two chicken liver and two chicken gizzard. Gizzard is chicken belly button, *poopitz*, only chicken not really have belly or button. We make up all sort of thing in Ukraina. We are amusing people. Baba call someone she like *poopchik*, which mean "dear little belly button."

If you poor thing who not have own chicken or stupormarket that carry gizzard, use four chicken liver instead. If you not have this either, is time to think serious about move to another town.

Cook real well, but not till dry. Liver should have narrow pink stripe inside and be juicy.

Fry white or red onion in butter left in liver pan. Add more butter if you have to. Fry till onion has transparency, but not burning. Did you chop onion? Good! You learning something from Baba. Why I so sarcastic, you want to know. I was not sarcastic before I move to Canada and try to explain how real thing work, okay? Is like some kind bad karma debt.

When liver is cool, put in blender with extra virgin olive oil. Run till pasty and smooth. Be careful you turn off blender before using spoon to push down liver inside glass. Even better, unplug completely and make sure use wooden spoon. I know you, smarty pants girl. You going to use first thing handy---big metal spoon with blender running.

You crack off blender blade and ruin chicken liver, too. *Chy ty z byka vpav*? Have you fallen off an ox?

Egg will now be cool and ready to peel. Here is one your favorite thing about Baba. Just when you think she told you everything she know, she teach you another trick.

Baba secret for peeling egg: Take egg out of ice water bowl. Tap tap tap gentle on counter so egg is crackly all over. Put back in water. Water will go underneath shell and help slide it off. Do with each egg, why I have to tell you?

If you ruin any egg, save it to make crumble on top salad. Or eat for snack.

Slice each egg in half long way and put on platter.

Using spoon, take yolk out each egg and put in big bowl. Easier if you use soup spoon with round edge. **Mash yolk with onion and liver paste. Add dash good vinegar, like balsamic, wine or apple cider**.

Throw in three good pinch each salt and crack black pepper.

Push filling into each half egg. Do not over fill, or guest going to get stain on nice suit. Probably you not going to have enough to over fill, anyway. I know you eating spoonful filling for each one you put in recipe. Sometime I eat so much of recipe is nothing left for guest. Is call, "Bane of top flight cook and lapse member *Overeater Anonymous*."

Keep in fridge until you ready to serve.

Ingredient List:

- Large eggs, one dozen closer to expiry date than not
- Bowl of ice water, large enough for one dozen eggs
- Two chicken livers and two gizzards OR four chicken livers
- Butter, one quarter pound
- White or red onion, one half chopped
- Extra virgin olive oil, one quarter cup
- Balsamic, wine or apple cider vinegar, dash
- Salt and cracked black pepper

Deviled Eggs II to Infinity

This time you going to boil, **cool and peel dozen egg** just like above. This where you dying to put yolk with mayonnaise. You can, if you like, and will taste okay. If you make own mayonnaise, will taste like real food. See *Ukrainian Mayonnaise* under *Dressings, Chapter Three.*

Hellman not too bad, either. Especially new kind made with olive oil.

Baba beg you, please not crappy salad dressing or you be Canadian cliche. Worst thing is tofunaise you bought from old hippie at farmer market because you feeling guilty for something. Who know what? Don't write to Baba about your "feeling" and don't even bother open that jar. Blech.

But---Baba telling you to get farmyard smetana, the yellower the better. **Use big fork to mash yolk with cream** for genuine Ukrainian taste. Mash until smooth and creamy, mash until you never want to see egg or cream again. Discipline yourself. Keep mind on how impress your guest going to be. Use the good side of your brain. This mean add cream a little at time and make sure filling not turn into soup. Cooking is science AND art, okay?

Add salt and course black pepper.

Here is different thing you can put in egg mix. Just no boring paprika!:

***Two to four teaspoon grate horse radish with two teaspoon Dijon mustard** will blow off top your head. Use red color kind horse radish so will be beautiful like pysanka (Easter egg). Or **add few drop beet juice**. Not food coloring, then egg just look strange. I call this *Ukrainian Sushi Egg*.

You can play game with this kind egg at party. Put out big dish horseradish or tube *wasabi* paste and dare guest to put biggest lump on top. This good game for people who say they quit drinking. They still like to walk on edge and play drinking game without drinking. People who prefer to stay alcoholic can follow each sushi egg with vodka shot.

Remember Ukrainian proverb, *Pyaniy svichku ne zasvitym*! A drunk can't light a candle! So be careful who you make assignment to in your house.

***Half cup crisp bacon, fried, fine chop kobasa (garlic sausage) or summer sausage**. If you not trying to stay faithful Ukrainian, try thin slice prosciutto, capicolli, or dry salami from Italian store.

***Hand full fresh dill chop very fine**. For sure you can't use dry dill from jar. Your guest will be spitting green flake all night and talk about you later. Not in nice way.

***Hand full fresh basil chop very fine**. You should be growing on windowsill, anyway. If purple basil, will make devil egg even cuter.

***Hand full fresh chive chop very fine**. Do not use purple flower at top.

*Piquant taste: **Two tablespoon fine chop sweet pickle, olive, OR pickle pimento**. Not all at same time, what you thinking?! If you using olive, firm kind from deli is better. But green from jar taste okay. If you like black olive, do not use one from can. This have terrible taste. Use only fresh.

*For short time every spring in west coast of North America, there is magic thing call **Walla Walla onion™**. Mild like apple. If you can find, chop two raw tablespoon fine. Do NOT confuse with any other kind onion, or will be kind of party where nobody kissing. Nobody want that!

***Three tablespoon tiny sliver red or orange pepper**. Not green. Green is icky. Can combine pepper with basil leaf, chive or Walla Walla onion.

*For fish taste, **mix in half cup crab flake**. If you not have much money, use mash sardine or that pollock color pink to look like crab. But warn guest in case they allergic. If you like, mix in two teaspoon horseradish or one tablespoon raw Walla Walla onion for zing zing.

DO NOT mix in tomato, grape jelly or blowfish. DO NOT get fancy and make devil egg suspend in jelly salad. That just disgusting. Jelly salad disgusting. If you make for party, everyone eat little bit for polite sake and hate your gut. Don't be this kind of hostess, dorahenka.

Baba law: is okay to make half one kind and half another kind with almost any recipe. Especially if you make something guest might be allergic to. So you could make half fish kind devil egg, half dill only. Or half chicken liver, half basil only. This also make people pretending to be happy vegetarian, actual happy. They can eat meat kind egg and pretend they thought it was all vegetable. What you care? Everyone have little lie in life. Better they cheat little bit with your loving kind cooking, then sneak to McDonald after party and drop dead from explode artery.

Garnish any kind devil egg with parsley or fine chop chive. Once Baba get too creative and garnish with pine branch. People laugh. Everything get worse when tree ornament start falling on top, too. Look like we have to stay boring with garnish till Baba think of breaking news update.

Wait. Baba brain is waving. It tell her you can garnish with purple flower from chive, so this thing already moving. Wait again. Instead of stupid paprika, try orange nasturtium flower. Also herring roe or caviar. Caper, too. Or little swirl black olive paste. Baba brain go rest now.

Ingredient List:

- Eggs, one dozen closer to expiry date than not

- Bowl of ice water
- Sour cream or quality mayonnaise, one half cup
- Salt and course black pepper
- Any of the fillings and garnishes described above
- NO paprika, you cliche hound

Just when you think Baba reach end of egg rope, **here is Ukrainian *Egg Magnus Opium*:**

Deviled Eggs With Mushroom Caps

This recipe so exciting, Baba drooling in cleavage. She going to tell you very fast.

While you making stuffed egg, also **fry at same time one dozen very big mushroom cap in butter**. NOT margarine. **Brown one cup rye or pumpernickel bread crumb in butter**. NOT margarine. Scrub good your best glass baking dish so it sparkle, because you going to serve from it.

Make oven 350 degree F.

How you going to do all this at same time is your business, poopchik. Baba tired from trying to teach you physic.

Baba warning: Mushroom cap not so good with horseradish or piquant style devil egg. Excellent with all other kind, so why you crying?

This combination going to make guest moan.

Baba warning: Always there will be one passing-aggressive woman patting ten inch waist and whining you making her fat. No matter how much you keep this kind of person off guest list, someone always bring her along. They probably scared of her. Put on big fat lying smile and tell her everything you cook is "negative calorie." Idiot love that kind of speech. If she look skeptic, tell her how to burn calorie scrubbing party dish.

Pour mushroom sauce into baking dish. Sauce must cover bottom, but not drown egg. See *Mushroom Sauce* under *Hryb, Chapter Twelve*. Is very first mushroom recipe. Please tell Baba you not thinking you going to use can mushroom soup. Baba not that kind of girl, and this not that kind of recipe book.

Put all devil egg in baking dish. One mushroom cap go on top

each egg. Two will look like you trying too hard.

Sprinkle top of egg with buttered bread crumb.

Put baking dish in oven for ten minute. Baba warning: do not try to serve on separate plate, or whole jigging will be up. This recipe too delicate to move. If you cleaned baking dish like normal person, will be no shame putting out on table.

Ingredient List:

- One dozen deviled eggs. Plain or with various fillings described in *Deviled Eggs I and II to Infinity*. Except horseradish and piquant.
- Attractive baking dish to fit twenty-four egg halves.
- Large mushrooms, preferably oyster, chanterelle or other tasty, fancy type. One dozen. Cap should be large enough to cover one half egg, or nearly so.
- Butter, one half cup
- *Mushroom Sauce*, one and one half cups
- Rye or pumpernickel bread crumbs, one cup

I know you thinking, "That Baba going to run out of egg idea now, she so smarty pant." Not even close. She going to teach you to make

Ukrainian Eggs in Cream

This beautiful dish for any time. Is good substitute for that Egg Benedict Arnold fancy neighbor always cooking. And less complicate to make, as long as you have delicate touch.

For two people after big night:

Have **four large egg sitting ready beside stove. Also empty saucer**.

Take out **medium size pan** that actually have matching lid. If glass lid, even better.

Baba surprise: Don't use butter!

In heating pan, blend flour with half and half cream. Make look like that paste your kid always eating.

Pour in more cream. Mix in good with paste.

Add salt and vinegar. Can be white, if you even keep such thing in home. White vinegar is only for setting dye in pysanky (Easter eggs) and making *Pickle Egg*. Baba prefer wine or balsamic. She down to earth person who is vinegar snob. Small thing like good vinegar, oil and crack pepper make whole difference to recipe taste.

Now PAY ATTENTION. You going to make cream boil. Have to watch careful.

As soon as cream boil, turn heat down to simmer. This mean three or most four on stove dial, not, "If I turn to nine, whole thing be ready faster." This how you make disaster before, remember?

Break each egg ONE AT TIME into saucer. Launch egg sideway ONE AT TIME into hot cream. Be gentle like you rocking new baby pig by wood stove, not throwing boyfriend stuff out from window.

Cover partway with solid lid, or completely with glass lid. Keep watch on egg until white is nice and firm. Next there should be kind of film over yolk.

Keeping gentle, gentle hand, **use spatula to put egg on two plate. Pour cream from pan over top**. Baba know this sound bland, like some kind scary Presbyterian sex. Here is how to spice up:

Sprinkle top of egg with pinch salt and crack black pepper. Baba now going to break her "no paprika" rule from devil egg recipe.

Sprinkle one of these topping on top. I like saying that. Be very spare; meaning don't pile on so much topping you break yolk:

*Paprika**
***Fresh basil**
***Fresh dill**
***Fresh oregano**
***Sun dry tomato**
****Fresh only* Asiago, Swiss, firm goat or good Parmesan cheese**. Not cheap powder kind crap from bulk aisle. What kind cheese is taste good sitting in open air, Baba ask you?
***Fresh chive, fine chop**
Thin slice *lox from Jewish deli. Baba know you dying to use herring or chunk cheap salmon, but don't. Is too heavy for egg yolk to support. Is like what happen when you put waterbed in lousy apartment. Uh oh. Midnight moving again.
***Prosciutto**
***Saffron**
***Caraway seed**
***Cilantro**

No law (yet) against putting out several kind these topping on table, so guest can pick and choose. Sometime is good to feel like rich person, even if for only several minute.

Baba special sub option: You understand Baba invent most of these topping and mixing, is not from Old Country. She very proud. After you take egg out from pan and cream is still sitting there, mix into cream one these thing:

Two tablespoon fresh Asiago, firm goat, Swiss, Parmesan or Bleu cheese**. ***Paneer from India Town also good. Cottage cheese will not work. Is too runny.
***Hand full fine chop fresh dill**
***Half cup dry crumble bacon, fine chop kobasa or summer sausage**
***Half cup very, very thin slice good quality mushroom** you already fry in butter.
***Half cup fresh or can, sweet precook shrimp**. If frozen, thaw before putting in recipe. Here is shopping hint. Frozen shrimp is cheap like Soviet borshch at China Town.

Baba warning: don't get carry away with cute dry shrimp you see in basket out front. They extreme salty. You need Chinese cook to show you how to prepare. I know this shock you, but Baba not educate in this particular area.

Chinese shred pork is different story. Is so good right out of box, Baba take to movie and give to grandchildren instead of popcorn. Sometime with popcorn. To each her own thing, okay?

Back to recipe. After you mix in your choice of flavor, **pour cream over egg on plate**.

Sorry, vegetarian poopchik, tofu not going to work. Will just make uber-bland.

Baba can tell you want to get fancier and fancier. If you going to use whole hog, you can combine one these cream mix filling thing with one kind topping. But not lox and sausage. That kind of marriage lead to quick divorcing.

Ingredient List:

- Four eggs for two people
- Flour, two teaspoons
- Heavy cream, two cups
- Balsamic or wine vinegar, one teaspoon
- Salt and cracked black pepper
- Any of the toppings mentioned in the recipe
- Toast or toasted whole wheat bagel. NOT English muffin.

Scrambled Eggs

Baba know you already know how to make plain scramble egg. Break egg, mix in little bit heavy cream, throw in hot butter pan, scramble with fork, eat with toast from good dark bread. Delicious.

What you not already know is you can mix in any kind ingredient from *Devil Egg* or *Ukrainian Egg in Cream*, above. Any time, you can substitute *salo* (quality beef or pork fat) for butter in pan and on toast. This is traditional Ukrainian taste. See *Roast Beef, Chapter Nine.*

Salo is especial good if you trying to put weight on for hard winter, or trying to get sick dog/man to eat again. Like brave new world, is not?

Here is two more scrambled recipe that make you like super-Uke:

Scrambled Eggs with Tomato and Onion

Before you throw egg in pan in your usual carefree way, fry one tablespoon fine chop onion in butter for every two egg. Add in sun dry tomato and fry till soft. Ukrainian usually use nice, fresh, very firm tomato from garden. But if you not growing your own special kind, tomato usually too watery for recipe. Sometime stupormarket Roma tomato is firm enough.

If you looking for good kind seed, Baba fall in love with American heritage tomato call *Radiator Charlie Mortgage Lifter*. You will find in Burpee seed catalogue, only they take away romantic name of "Radiator Charlie," and is call only "Mortgage Lifter." Maybe Charlie unhappy in catalogue. Baba not sure. She is going to petition President to make this official *Economic Stimulus Tomato.*

Burpee also have extra-sexy Ukrainian tomato, call *Black Krim (Crimean).* You eat one these, you know so much more about Ukrainian *dusha*, soul.

Make sure you using extra butter for both extra ingredient and egg. Like I say in *Scrambled Egg*, can substitute salo for butter. But not for cream in egg mix. Duh again. Baba have to be constant explicit. You would not believe what kind dummy is out there. They should make book, "Dummy for Dummy". Then all dummy can meet and have their own country by themself, leave rest of us alone.

Make egg/cream mix, add salt and crack black pepper. Pour

on top of onion and tomato. Cook very gentle. Use only fork to mix ingredient, not barbeque spatula. This way egg stay tender and creamy.

Top with caper. Serve with toast.

Ingredient List:

- Two eggs for each person
- Heavy cream, two tablespoons
- Sundried tomato, one large tablespoon or one half very firm fresh tomato
- Chopped onion, one tablespoon
- Butter or salo, two tablespoons
- Salt and cracked black pepper
- Optional garnish: capers

Scrambled Eggs with Bacon
(or, How to Bring a Bachelor Down)

Hoo boychik. Now we really getting down to primal Ukrainian-style.

For every two egg, chop up four slice bacon or salt pork. Don't be shy. This simple kind trick is especial impressive to hungry man who wonder if he should marry you. Listen to Baba. When man not thinking about hot sex, he thinking about next best thing. And you going to give to him like L'il Kim. You know thing is getting hot when I start rap. Baba in da *house.*

I seen crusty PhD professor down on knee after I cook him this simple thing.

Prepare egg mix only after bacon is cook.

Fry bacon/pork until crisp. Add fine chop onion, fry little bit. Pour off most of fat, except for about tablespoon. You going to cook egg in this salo. When man smelling this, he be drool down his polyester shirt. Ignore drool. DO NOT give bib. You want man who looking for wife, not for second mother. Ick.

Mix up egg with cream. If you do too early, mix will separate. This bad omen for marriage.

Pour over bacon and mix gentle with fork only. Egg should still be creamy, not like you buy at Canadian tire.

Never mind fancy-shmancy garnish. Serve with smile. Baba find over and over again, proposal come more quick if you naked under apron.

Also, just because you serve him this food, don't mean you have to accept proposal. Is okay to use just to make man hot.

If you not so sure you want this bachelor after watching way he swill his horilka, can also **add half cup good firm cheese for every two egg**. See egg recipe above for suggested kind.

Baba warning: Cheese make pan harder to clean. If you going to be boinking bachelor over long weekend, you don't have time for this. Unless you make him wear apron while you sit and watch.

Ingredient List:

- Four eggs (you're going to eat too!)
- Heavy cream, one quarter cup
- Bacon or salt pork, eight slices
- Onion, two tablespoons finely chopped
- Toast

Optional: cheese, one cup

We going to take little break from kind of egg recipe you expecting. **Baba show you**

Pickled Eggs

Baba know you sitting home like good Canadian woman and not going to bar. Unfortunate, you missing out not only on dancing, but on pickle egg. Men eat these like row of pig at trough while they shooting whiskey and acting like big shot. Is pathetic. Now I let you in on woman secret.

First, moan and groan to everyone how you making big special effort for this recipe. Really, it save you time over long run making snack. Is kind of thing when husband or kid come in door and whining, "What is there to eat, Mama?" you can throw at them and it not leave mark.

Here is how:

You going to need **two big pot and one medium size**.

Boil six egg. How you do this special? Put in pot and cover good with cold water. Make furious boil. Shut off heat and let stand thirty minute. Put in bowl ice water, wait ten minute and peel off shell. See best instruction under *Deviled Eggs*.

Now Baba going to ask you to be coordinate. I know is genius level exercise for you, but try. While egg boil, take out another pot. **Boil together for three minute: vinegar, water, colorful kind pickle spice, salt, garlic and brown sugar**.

Baba relax her standard here. You can use white vinegar, because you not going to directly drink. You not suppose to, anyway.

Slice up small onion. For once, Baba telling you do not cook this. You should be surprise.

You going to boil third thing in huge pot: big glass jar with tight lid. Submerge in hot water and boil ten minute. Use tong to take out from hot water.

Put egg and raw onion in glass jar.

Pour other ingredient over top.

Let sit in fridge at least twenty four hour before you dip hand inside. Otherwise will not bounce when you throw at family. Then you can not make, "Heh heh, only joking," face while you being passing-aggressive. Actually, nothing passing about this.

GARLIC ALERT: Sometime garlic will turn funny blue or green colour when pickle. This okay. Is just holding breath inside liquid.

EGG ALERT: Sometime egg will turn brownie colour when pickle. Like lousy family counselor say, "And that is O-kay."

If you like pink egg, replace water with beet juice. Boil beet, use juice. Not *KoolAid.*

Ingredient List:

- Six eggs
- White vinegar, one cup
- Water, one quarter cup
- Pickling spice, one tablespoon
- Salt, one half teaspoon
- Garlic, one large clove
- Brown sugar, one teaspoon
- White onion, small

Perfect Plain Omelet

One time my twelve year old granddaughter come home from school very sad. “Why you making such crying?” Baba ask.

"Because," little Rosie say, "They think I so stupid, they teach me to make tea and cinnamon toast in Home Ick class."

Of course Ukrainian child insulted! By time Rosie six years old, she can not only ride horse bareback, she already help make varenyky (perogies), cookie, borshch and pie. "Rosie, any boy in this class?" Baba ask

"No," she say. "They all in Shop and Graphic Art."

Baba's head feel like it going to split up and fall right off shoulder. Baba sit Rosie down and remind her Ukrainian is matriarch society. We have several thousand year history of woman training horse and riding into battle with our men. None of this, "You stay home while I ride, sweetheart." Our Scythian ancestor used to say, *Woman is not woman until she kill three man in battle*. She could then choose her husband. This where legend of Amazon woman come from. Also why Ukrainian women win gold fencing medal in Olympic and World Woman Chess Championship. Weak female was old meaning of "virgin."

Then crazy Western society twist this so Amazon woman is some kind man-hate weirdo. Do Baba seem like man-hate weirdo to you? You better answer correct, or she take out her bow and arrow. She love men and enjoy almost every minute.

More on this subject later. Rosie can not only show any boy what to do, she also toss damn fine omelet. Because Baba show her how:

First secret of good omelet is to make each one separate, only two egg at time. Otherwise it get too heavy. For large family, sometime Baba get four fry pan going at same time. She not expect Canadian to be this coordinate. Start with two.

This little bit different than making scramble egg. Omelet is not creamy, omelet is light like feather bed. How you do this? **Use milk or water to mix two egg instead of heavy cream.**

Add salt and crack black pepper.

Put dab of butter in medium fry pan, swirl round. Keep heat low down. Whole bottom of pan should be nice and coat, like when someone rub massage oil on you. Baba prefer pirate. She tell you that story in *Ocean Fish, Chapter Seventeen.*

Pour egg into pan. Use speculum to lift omelet around edge and let liquidy part flow underneath. Just like when you putting on makeup foundation. Baba have news for you. At certain age, you not need *Elizabeth Ardent.* You need good sandblasting. This not contrary to feminism. You should be able to do job yourself.

When omelet is firm but not too brown, make fold neat like plastic surgeon after makeup trick stop working.

Serve super hot. Can garnish with crispy bacon or *kobasa* (garlic

sausage) and orange slice.

What we do about little Rosie, you want to know? Baba go march down to school and enroll her in Shop and Graphic Art, that what. Then Rosie and Baba give demonstration in Phys Ed. While lame kind gym teacher showing some crazy thing like dance with hoop, Rosie and Baba shoot with bow and arrow from horseback. Performance end with Baba on horse, upside down picking handkerchief off ground with denture. Rosie make super finale standing on horseback, waving sword. She shouting, "Next year, I am Olympic girl, only never in Russia!"

She never have to do Home Ick again.

Real feminist is something you make happen, not say you "believe" in.

Ingredient List:

- Large eggs, two for each person
- Milk or water, two tablespoons
- Salt and pepper
- Butter, two tablespoons

Mushroom and Cheese Omelet

See Baba lecture note on *Hryb (Mushrooms), Chapter Twelve.*

Now we have that understanding, you can make decent mushroom and cheese omelet:

Fry slice mushroom in butter, big hand full for each person. **Turn off burner and leave sitting there**. Unless you getting good at making many omelet at once, and need all burner. Go to street perfomer and learn this juggling. Ha!

No, really, is okay to take mushroom off stove and put in bowl. Baba let you off of hooking this time.

Make *Plain Omelet* recipe like above. After you tip pan and egg flow under egg to cook---you sure you get this?----put mushroom and your favorite cheese on ONE HALF of omelet. Baba see you tugging on ear and have puzzle frown. This is so you can fold omelet with filling inside. This is why you having big problem closing your sock drawer whole life.

Baba law: When you fill thing to top, is no room for more. Except your brain.

Your option is to make filling from:

***Kobasa and hard cheese**. Unbelievable with firm goat.
***Chop red or yellow pepper and cheese**. Can also add mushroom. Can add mushroom to anything.
*You can pour over with delicious ***pidlyva*** **(sauce)**, like *Sour Cream & Horse Radish, Chapter Three,* or *Honey Onion, Chapter Twelve.*

Baba warning: If you go over the border with too many filling, you need more egg. Two kind ingredient work with two egg. If you use three or four ingredient, cut back on each filling portion OR throw in one more egg. No more than three egg in one omelet, or omelet will become unmanageable in pan. Baba have faith you get this. Once you stay up all night with calculator.

Ingredient List:

For every two people

- Plain omelet recipe, with two eggs
- Mushrooms, half cup sliced
- Hard cheese, quarter cup
- Chives, quarter cup

Chapter Eight

Kurka (Chicken)

Roast Kurka

First, see *Chicken Soup, Chapter One*, for how to shop for kurka.This same thing, only you need buy larger chicken. Read whole recipe first.

Take out little package with heart, liver and poopitz. Wash and put back inside chicken.

Wash chicken, put in fridge until you finish chopping vegetable.

Take out biggest roasting pan. You need room for lots vegetable plus chicken. Maybe get huge one from dollar store. **Preheat oven to 350 degree F**.

When you finish chop one kind vegetable, first pile in huge bowl, not in roasting pan.

Cut up bunch spinach after make sure dirt washed off. Or, be lazy and use frozen spinach. This one time, I let you use crazy microwave. Put frozen in for about 5 minutes, then drain water before put in roaster.

OR

Cut up broccoli in small piece. You can use stem part, chop very small. Don't waste good food!

Chop onion in tiny piece. Regular onion or Spanish kind or big red one.

Chop red pepper, make ring, then chop ring in half.

Peel and cut up turnip, size like baseball. Make sure you cut off little hair, like coming from old man ear. Make turn your stomach.

Wash carrot, cut off green end but leave whole. Carrot make chicken taste sweet. So good.

Put kettle water on to boil.

Wash and slice *pidpanky*, is tasty kind Ukrainian mushroom. Or try what call *oyster, boletus, porcini or chanterelle*. Last resort, use brown or white kind, regular from stupormarket.

Baba warning: Some kind mushroom is poisonous. Do not go pick with someone who don't like you.

Fry mushroom in butter and little bit crush garlic.

Poke knife hole into two big clove garlic, do not bother peel.

Two, three large, clean potato can go into roaster whole, cut in half, or any way cut up you like. Do not remove skin, this where vitamin are. If you can afford little new baby potato, so much tastier. Especially organic. And if you find potato somewhere called *peanut*, write me letter. I been looking for long time. One time weird bachelor feed me, but I don't want to call him. Another time, one Baba fan promise special UPS to Canada from US. Baba wait and wait. She notice she get some kind letter at post office, but she figure is always best to ignore summons. Finally, two week later, fan ask, "You get my peanut potato, Baba?" It turn out that despite Baba teaching her how to get life, she get cheap at last minute and send regular mail. These peanut potato more like dry pea. Is sacrilege, I am telling you. Don't be this kind fan. Send Baba gift FedEx special delivery ONLY.

Or, poke knife whole into potato skin, and put on rack below chicken. One for each person, why I have to tell you?

Now you have not only chicken, but red thing, green thing, pink thing, white thing, brown thing and orange thing. That how to make good nutrition.

Take chicken from fridge, put breast up in roasting pan.

Pour in boiled water, room temperature. Not from tap. This make delicious chicken juice.

Arrange vegetable around chicken, as much you can. Broccoli always go on bottom, or else little flower will burn. **Shake on little salt, lots crack black pepper**.

Put two thick slice butter on vegetables. Not this sickening spray diet fake thing. Blech.

Once oven light go off, slide chicken in. Don't forget put in potato to bake.

Large chicken cook about two hour. How you tell: take chicken out, wiggle leg. It should be very loose. Cut knife into breast, down to bone. Should be no pink juice, or you make self sick. Is no such thing as "chicken medium rare."

To make brown skin, take lid off roasting pan half hour before chicken finish cooking.

How to eat roast kurka:

Take piece you like. You might like use bowl instead of plate, because this get juicy-loosey. Get good chunks potato from roaster or rack. Put butter on. Use large spoon, take all kind vegetable. Use ladle to take chicken juice and pour over everything. Taste and shake on more salt and crack black pepper, if you like.

Take out whole carrot and give to yourself for reward. You did all work, right? Put on butter, salt and crack black pepper. If others want, make them wash dish.

Make sure you eat rubbery end chicken bone. This build your bone, instead you buying all kind expensive calcium.

If you find road kill eagle or vulture, remember to stew just little longer to make tender. This extra work will make up for itself, because you can make good flute from their bone. Ukrainian been doing this twenty-five hundred year. See *Road Kill Stew, Chapter Eighteen.*

Next day, hopeful chicken will be cold. Instead of reheat, is traditional to make attractive slice and serve with *Ukrainian Mayonnaise*, under *Dressing, Chapter Three*. And please, Baba begging you, do not serve with that white salad dressing from jar. She don't want no one to think she tell you to ruin lively chicken recipe with Presbyterian blandorama.

Ingredient List:

- Roasting chicken, one whole
- Spinach, one bunch OR one package frozen
- Broccoli, half pound
- Onion, one large
- Red, yellow or orange pepper, one large
- Turnip, one medium
- Carrots, three large
- Water, three cups boiled
- Chanterelle, oyster or the best you can afford, half pound. Can substitute dried mushrooms. Follow instructions on package
- Butter, half cup
- Crushed garlic, one clove or more to taste
- Potatoes, three large OR baby potatoes, two pounds
- Salt to taste
- Coarse black pepper to taste

Honey Lemon Garlic Roast Kurka

Shop and make chicken and vegetables like above, except this time, put whole head garlic inside chicken. Wait. Read again. I didn't say, put your own head inside chicken. That is just silly. You do not have to peel garlic.

Leave big lemon on counter. Warm lemon make more juice. Thin skin best kind.

When chicken halfway cooked, take out of oven and squeeze lemon juice onto chicken.

Pour one cup honey on chicken and vegetable. Try different kind honey. Buckwheat very strong and good, this another Ukrainian secret. Make bee drunk, like little stripe *kozak*. Fireweed have beautiful taste. Clover is mildest kind. Sprinkle chicken with black crack pepper.

Put back in oven for one hour.

Ingredient List:

- Roast Chicken, as above
- Garlic, one head
- Lemon, one large
- Honey, one cup
- Cracked black pepper, two teaspoons

Kurka in Cream with Dill

See *Chicken Soup, Chapter One*, for how to shop for chicken. This time you have to be double smart, because you going to make two chicken instead of one. If you chopping something into many piece, I say keep going. May as well have firewood for winter instead of just one hot weekend. If you short of money, get five pound package chicken leg or thigh.

Baba make it easy on you this time. This one those rare kind recipe look and taste very elegant when really Baba hardly make you work at all. Excellent to impress boss or to stall Bolshevik police.

Heat oven to 350 degree F.

Chop up chicken into logical piece: leg, breast, thigh, back. Easier if you get knife or cleaver sharpen just before start this project. Put into big roaster or glass pan.

Chop up onion and fresh dill weed. Put around chicken piece. Does not have to be beautiful arrangement.

Mix good thick cream 50/50 with boil water. Pour over chicken. Farm cream best, but I know you not going to walk to barn and milk cow or goat. Probably you going to drive one block to 7-11 in your bathrobe and curler. Everybody talk about it and you don't even know. If this your intrepid strategy, might as well get kind of cream you whip. If you not have raw cookie dough to tide over, buy little extra whip cream and some sugar. You going to comfort yourself while you hopping from foot to foot waiting for good dill chicken.

Add salt.

Cook for one to one and half hour. You know is ready when no pink juice run from part of chicken you poking. Try breast and leg both. Sometime one ready before other. One time I dating plasterer, and he show me how his technique for stroking woman body same as for his work. You stroke even all over, and go back and forth to make sure she done in every place. He even give blue collar seminar in this technique, Baba not joking. She know some interesting men. Is same strategy for cooking. Go back and forth, leg to breast, breast to leg, and make sure is done.

In meantime, steam potato, cook rice or boil *Lokshyna* *(Egg Noodle), Chapter Twenty One*. If you not too busy eating bowl whip cream.

This recipe make enough for your guest or to feed small country. Depend on size of chicken, what you think?

By now you thinking, "I get it. To make recipe Ukrainian, all I have to do is add dill. Dill ice cream, dill pizza, dill spaghetti."

Wrong. Baba tell you this, you so wrong. If this what you thinking, we going to have to start over and explain Ukrainian *gestalt*, poopchik.

Ingredient List:

- Chicken, two whole or five pound package of thighs and/or drumsticks, according to budget
- Onion, one large
- Fresh dill weed, one bunch
- Thick cream, two cups. Half and half or whipping cream
- Water, two cups boiled
- Salt to taste
- Starchy ingredient to pour chicken pieces over. Rice, noodles, potatoes, your choice

Kotleta Po Kyivsky (Chicken Kyiv)

Before she teach you this famous Ukrainian recipe, Baba going to first ask you to read *Roasted Vegetable Kartoplya (Potato Salad), Chapter Two.*

That where you meet Baba German Shepherd Dachshund cross dog

Bingo. Actually was two dog, exactly like twin. Baba get Bingo first, then rescue his brother from crazy people who keep him on short chain and starve him.

Because Baba so famous wherever she go, stupid dog hater people find her and call RCMP. You understand that just because police always visiting Baba, don't make her bad person.

Anyway, this time is not Baba RCMP boyfriend who show up to make investigation. Is two other police officer, not so handsome. They say, "We going to have to take dog you stealed, Baba."

Baba have two twin dog sit beside her. They both stare real good at police officer. Baba open chain link fence gate very little bit, just so *Guard Baba on Duty* sign rattle. She say in voice sweet like sucklehoney, "Go ahead, make Baba day. Take which one dog you think is stealed."

Bingo raise his German Shepherd lip.

Police officer talk with head together ten second, then come back and tell Baba, "Ma'am, we think is more civil than criminal case. Have nice day."

Bingo stop growling, and Baba go inside to make *Kotleta Po Kyivsky*. She invite police officer to eat, but for some reason they not interest.

How to make for two people and two big dog. Two small dog can share one piece:

Leave butter out overnight. If you have dog taller than Bingo, put butter up on fridge. **Next day, mix butter with two clove crush garlic, fresh chop dill, chop fresh chive, and good pinch salt and pepper. Add lemon juice**. Real stuff, not bottle kind that taste like peroxide.

How Baba know peroxide taste? She once have to suck this thing from head of friend who get bleach blonde poisoning. Is not something Baba do every day.

Baba warning: Neither should you.

Count butter mix into four piece, wrap and put into freezer. You want butter to get firm like your boobala was before you get mix up with crazy aerobic. Might take two hour for butter. We both know your boobala hopeless. Who care?

This next part messy. Maybe you should put on leather cardigan like Baba have. It stretch real good across chest and do up on one pearl button. My children make special order from this *Black Leather Baba* catalog. Cardigan come with lambskin bloomer and support hose, almost two for one price. Was even better deal than they think. They not know catalog belong to their Baba.

If you wearing something underneath cardigan, Baba don't know why. What, now you going to pretend you not desperate housewife? Roll up sleeve before starting on chicken.

Take two big boneless chicken breast and cut each one in half. Put between two piece wax paper and give good pounding like with tenderizing *Bytky* beef in *Chapter Nine*. You have to be little more gentle with *kurka* (chicken) so it don't break, but it should get thin like ugly celebrity. If you decide you going to go route of just putting out on highway, make sure you wrap in very heavy plastic, kind mattress come in. This special useful information if you going to make lots of this dish for party.

Baba warning: When you letting traffic do work for you, you still can't read magazine and drink horilka. You have to watch so no one jump out of car and steal. Is all kind chicken thief these day, Communist or not. All TV station pretend democratic event not happening. You think someone going to watch your *kurka*? Ha!

Heat oven to 350F.

Take firm butter mix from freezer. Put one piece in centre each skinny chicken breast. Roll up butter inside chicken real good with same technique you using to stay inside leather vest. **Make tight with wood skewer**.

Beat up egg with water. Dip each chicken roll in this and make dusting with flour like you powdering baby bum. **Roll in stale bread crumb**. Baba mean, roll chicken in bread crumb. You want to roll in it, this your thing. Don't be making lie that Baba advising such foolishness. But if you going to go for it, throw whole bucket bread crumb on floor. No use doing thing half way. Enjoy your crunching.

Grease up baking dish and put chicken in oven for 45 minute. Leave cover on. **Bake 15 more minute so chicken crust get nice and brownie-gold**. Is good idea to take chicken from oven to remove cover. Baba know you already have several oven mitt with burn mark. Stop it, she telling you.

Cut into one piece chicken, make sure is no icky pink juice.

Serve with *Mushroom Sauce*, under *Hryby, Chapter Twelve*,or *Dill Sauce*, under *Pidlyvi (Sauce), Chapter Twenty Two* and *Lokshyna (egg noodles), Chapter Twenty One*.

Oh please, Baba beg you, don't be thinking can mushroom soup is substitute for real mushroom sauce!

Garnish with lemon slice and parsley or caper.

Your option:

*Put half teaspoon cayenne pepper in with butter mix.
*Use hand full fresh chop parsley instead of dill. Will not taste so

Ukrainian, but maybe we ease you into ecstasy.
*Put hand full fresh shred Asiago, Parmesan or firm goat cheese in with butter mix.

Ingredient List:

- Boneless chicken breast halves, four. Pound to one quarter inch thickness.
- Butter, four tablespoons
- Fresh chives, one tablespoon
- Salt and pepper
- Lemon, one half
- Garlic, two cloves
- Dill, small bunch
- Flour, one quarter cup
- Egg, one large
- Fine dry bread crumbs, one half cup
- Wooden skewers, four
- Mushroom or Dill Sauce
- Lokshyna
- One lemon, four sprigs parsley or half jar capers for garnish

Kotleta Po Kyivsky New Orleans

Make like Ukrainian recipe, but use parsley instead of dill.

After you roll up chicken, put in fridge for half hour so inside is stuck together.

Instead of baking, **put one half cup sunflower or olive oil in big frying pan**. Heat up for minute on medium before you slide in chicken.

Fry chicken five minute on each side. Cut partway into chicken meat and make sure is done. You don't want guest to barf.

Serve with Louisiana hottie sauce.

Garnish with Mardi Gras bead. No, not really. Why you always want to look like you trying too hard? This call being lame white person. If you want be hip like Baba, garnish with piece of levee and make donation to rebuild New Orleans.

Venison (Olenyicha) Winnipeg-Kyiv

Use fresh deer meat instead of chicken. Baba invent delicious thing first time her Ojibwe boyfriend drag home deer. Substitute **big pinch fresh sage** for dill to get real wild Prairie feeling. About quarter pound meat for each person. If you going to use caribou or moose, make sure to soak in lemon overnight to make tender. Pluck out guard hair with your good tweezer or electrolysis unit.

Beef Donbas

Beef Donbas is name for region in Ukraina. **Prepare just like *Kotleta Po Kyivsky*, but use quarter pound boneless steak for each person**. Use whatever cut you can afford, because you going to pound life out of it.

When your best friend idiot husband who never been past his drainage ditch make sound like sick machine gun and ask, "Is this 'Beef Dumbass'?" you make big phony smile and say, "Yes sweetheart. I cook special for you."

Kotleta Po Kyivsky with Bacon and Asparagus

You going to add two thing to make this good thing little bit different.

Baba warning: Be prepare for pee to smell strange from asparagus. Is no polite way to say this, and Baba not going to try her usual diplomatic. But oh, so delicious!

Make butter mix like above. For four chicken piece, fry eight slice bacon. Drain *salo* (fat) and let cool.

Steam twelve asparagus, tip only. Taste more tender if you use little baby asparagus. If you thinking about "vegetable rights" at this point, you been reading too many hippie magazine. Chill your head. You have to eat something sometime.

When you roll butter inside chicken, **also careful roll two bacon strip and three asparagus tip into each chicken breast half**. Why two bacon and three asparagus? Baba tell you to start with eight and twelve, and now you throwing up hands. Oy yoi yoi. Can you do math on Crackberry? Good! Please note Baba subtle sarcasm.

Cook like in first recipe.

Now, be little bit tasteful. Do not garnish chicken with more asparagus or anything else green. Matchie matchie is for Nazi Nazi. Ha!

Use lemon slice, orange nasturtium petal or purple chive flower.

Ingredient List:

- Asparagus tips, twelve
- Bacon, eight strips
- Garnish as in recipe

Fried Kurka in Cream

This recipe for all you US Southern bella bellas who think you know about fry chicken. Baba show you something so delicious that Tennessee William write about it. He was Baba pen pal, because she have so much to teach him about woman and food. One day he make play about bad time in Baba marriage. He call it "Chicken on Hot Tin Roof." Baba say she very flatter, but this title not too sexy.

Take frying kind chicken and cut up into piece. Or, if butcher good looking, make him do it while you read to him from other Tennessee William play, *Streetcar Name Odesa*. Baba make all butcher she know yell, "Stella!" several time. What you think, she going to give them her real name?

Mix flour with salt and pepper. Roll chicken piece in this. Make sure is good and coat on all side. Nothing sadder than naked fry chicken.

Turn oven to 300 F. What this have to do with fry chicken, you want to know. See, Baba told you she going to show you something different. Hold on your horse.

Fry chicken in big casting iron fry pan in plenty butter. Make sure it get good and brown all over. Here is where some you Canadian reading this start twitch and reach for spray can of diet fat. Slap yourself. All you will have is sticky mess and terrible taste.

Put fry chicken in casserole dish. Baba now give you freedom of religion. You choose if you pour **smetana**, OR one cup sweet cream. See? Is like two for one sale around here.

Sprinkle with salt and pepper.

Bake in oven about half hour. Obvious thing, cooking time depend on how good you fry, and how big is chicken piece. Stick knife in each piece and make sure no pink juice running out. One time Tennessee

William cute boyfriend not do this test before serve chicken. Uh oh. Lots screaming in house. Oh well, at least it become inspiration for *Suddenly, Last Summer*.

Serve chicken on rice or *Lokshyna* *(Egg Noodles), Chapter Twenty One*.

Your option:

***Chop up some good vegetable** very fine and add to cream sauce. Mushroom, red or orange pepper, chive all tasty.
***Add hand full fresh dill** to cream sauce.

Ingredient list:

- Frying chicken, three or four pounds
- Flour, one cup
- Salt and pepper
- Butter, one half cup
- Cream, sweet or sour, one cup

Chapter Nine

Masnyy (Beef)

Huliash (Goulash)

Huliash is real old time thing, very simple to make. Is what strong horseman *kozak* eat. I have for lunch on day I ride horse hanging upside down from saddle, kozak-style. I also pick up handkerchief with teeth. Make sure leave couple hour between eating and riding. Also I wear damn good restraining bra, design by university engineering department. I am sportwoman, not idiot asking for black eye. Putting duct tape on flap flap armpit skin not bad idea either.

Here we go:

Chop good beef into good size chunk for chewing. Can use any cut, from chuck to quality sirloin. Depend on your budget. I show you how to make tender and taste very good no matter, so don't be worry.This first kind basic. In *Son of Huliash* (below), I take you fancier.

Take out cooking pot. Best kind have steel bottom. Aluminum not good.

Fry chop onion in big lump *salo* or butter, then put in dish.

Brown meat chunk in same butter as onion. Keep stirring. Put onion in meat and add: paprika for nice orange color, salt, crack black pepper, caraway seed, hot water----make sure has boiled. Hot water from tap ruin taste.

Make these ingredient boil. Stand over stove while it happen. "Watch pot never boil" is for Canadian cook. Is excuse to walk away and let everything boil four hour while they playing cricket or some crazy thing. All this food taste like glue. Gray meat, gray pea, gray carrot. Blech. So I'm saying, watch pot already and have faith.

As soon as this boil, turn down to slow simmer. This mean low heat and you only see one thick bubble once in while, like I see when children take me to tar pit. One of them husband he mumble something about, "Maybe she stay with dinosaur and not come back." Is okay. I make him very special recipe, only enough for one serving. He not ask for second. Now my daughter happy married to next husband.

Cover pot. Simmering should take about one and half hour. You will know is ready when meat tender and only tiny bit liquid left in pot. But do not let burn. **You must lift lid every twenty minute** or so, look and stir. Use oven mitt, poopchik. If you have boobala like mine, also use restraining bra like I mention.

Serve huliash over *Lokshyna*, *(Noodles), Lokshyna Chapter Twenty One*. Why they say home made? Someone making them in garage?

Also put bowl of hot sauerkraut on table.

Your option:

*If you not have time to make noodle---mean you spending too much time at bingo hall. Ha! Baba know you busy doing important thing. You can **steam baby potato for ten minute** or so instead. Do not boil, they too delicate. Leave peel on for taste and vitamin. Cut potato in half and pour huliash over top.

***Pour huliash over brown rice, millet or *Kasha*,** *under Grains, Chapter Twenty.*

***Serve with *Ukrainian Garlic Bread*,** *this Chapter.*

Ingredient List:

- Beef, two pounds. Whatever cut you can best afford.
- Onion, one large
- Butter or bacon/salt pork fat, one quarter cup
- Paprika, one half teaspoon
- Salt and cracked black pepper
- Caraway seed, one teaspoon
- Hot water, one half cup, and keep kettle boiling
- Lokshyna
- Sauerkraut as side dish

Son of Huliash

Do everything I tell you like in recipe before. Only this time you going to make more fancier. You taste this, your eye going to pop out from head.

Add to simmering ingredient:

As many fresh, clean mushroom as you can fit in hollow of apron.

If tiny button kind, leave whole. If large, slice. Try different fancy kind. **Fry in lots butter first**, till mushroom looking little bit transparent at edge.

Man size fist full clean, chop fresh dill. Leave out stem. If you not lying you really can't find fresh, add dry dill. Don't tell no one.

When *Son of Huliash* ten minute away from cooked, stir in room temperature real *smetana*---sour cream from farm. If you can't get real thing, plain yogurt can be just as good.

Never mind store kind smetana. Is all white jello. Better if thick organic or home made kind. Whatever you do, do not use fruit flavor.

Serve like above.

Your option:

*Can add either **chop fresh spinach, baby green pea, red or orange pepper**. Broccoli and carrot will come to your mind for sure, but this make huliash weird texture. Don't even start with green zucchini. Blech. Baby yellow zucchini may be okay.
***Chop onion so long slices** like in Chinese stir fry.

Baba warning: don't add all these thing. Secret of great huliash is keep flavour simple. Just add mushroom and one extra kind vegetable. If you add all, this first of all put too much liquid into huliash, and it is really become *Beef Stew*.

See? **Big difference between huliash and stew** is that (a) huliash very simple in flavour and (b) it thicken itself without flour or corn starch.

Ingredient List:

- Same as for Huliash, above
  plus
- Mushrooms, one cup sliced
- Fresh dill, one small bunch
- Sour cream, one cup

Zayitz (Meat Loaf)

Ukrainian name for meat loaf mean "mock rabbit." Why we make fun of poor rabbit I don't know. Is lost in mist of mysterious history.

Meat loaf is versatile thing. Can eat hot or cold, in sandwich or in bare hand if you like standing in cold light of fridge at night. Don't lie, we all done it. I have special tearing cloth house coat for doing it. Maybe some day you join me and world can be as one.

I show you how to make plain and how to make stuffed kind.

Plain Zayitz

Tell butcher to grind round steak and lean pork. Be watching with your eagle eye whole time, he not mixing in pig hoof or cow tail to add weight. Anytime you buy meat already ground in package, you have no idea what is inside.

One time I find three yellow chicken beak in "ground chicken." I take back to store, manager look at me real cold. He say, "What you trying get away with, Baba? You pay for only one ground chicken, here is proof you get three." I spit in his eye.

Soak dry bread crumb in milk. Use good rye, whole wheat or pumpernickel bread and at least two percent milk, not this skim stuff looking like someone drool in water glass. Pah!

Chop and fry small onion in butter until looking cooked but not burn.

Beat up one egg with fork. Wash fork right away or be sticky job later. Unless you have dog or cat with small tongue that like to lick between fork tine.

Turn oven to 350 degree F.

Put on your rubber glove and grease loaf pan. What other kind pan you think you use, bundt cake? Sheesh.

Melt butter or *salo* (beef or pork fat).

Keep rubber glove on and mix:

Bread crumb, onion, egg, lemon juice, salt and pepper with ground round steak and ground lean pork.

Make nice loaf shape inside pan. Pat pat pat to make all smooth and pretty. Do not try to make look like rabbit. This not sculpture class at local community centre, poopchik. Like time Baba take Fine Art class and crazy instructor turn out to paint only house. Baba give him piece in her mind, and he have nerve to tell her she have no perspective.

Use pastry brush to put melt butter or salo all over top of loaf. This going to make tasty crust.

Cover loaf with aluminum foil and put in oven one hour.

Go check your stock option.

When twenty minute up, take meat loaf from oven and pour hot

soup stock over it. Cover up and put back in oven. Do this again twice more in next twenty minute. Then leave aluminum off for last fifteen minute of baking.

When you think should be done, big surprise. Is not done! This why you love cooking with Baba instead of boring business person who give you all the fact. **Now you mix flour real good with sour cream and pour over meat loaf**.

Put back in oven one more time. **Let cook maybe ten, fifteen more minute so cream have time to soak in**. Don't tell me I am indefinite. I am artist.

Take loaf out of pan real careful. Use two tools to remove so not fall apart in middle.

Put salt and pepper in sauce at bottom of pan and mix real good. If some piece of meat fall in sauce and make ugly lumpy, use strainer. Don't strain yourself. Ha!

Cut meat loaf into thick slice and pour sauce over top.

Your option:

*Instead of sour cream, pour half cup **good thick tomato juice** over loaf.
***Use ground chicken instead of ground pork**. If you like spicy spicy, use quarter pound mild meat and quarter pound kobasa (garlic sausage), summer sausage or Italian sausage.

Ingredient List:

- Ground round steak, one pound
- Ground lean pork, one half pound
- Stale bread crumbs, three quarter cup
- Whole or two percent milk, one cup
- Onion, one small
- Butter, three tablespoons
- Egg, one large
- Lemon juice, one tablespoon
- Salt and pepper
- Butter or meat fat, one tablespoon to brush onto meat loaf
- Pastry or large paint brush
- Hot beef or chicken soup stock, one half cup
- Flour, one tablespoon
- Sour cream, one half cup

Stuffed Zayitz

Baba going to teach you stuff yourself with stuff meat loaf. Make recipe like I show you above. I am going to be up in front with you. Is two way to make stuff meat loaf. You can:

1) Pound down whole meat mixture on wax paper so very wide. **Spread stuffing on meat, then roll up** like when you hide dead body in carpet. **Seal edges and put into grease loaf pan**.

This technique require nerve and skill. Do if you can handle it. Or;

2) *Linyvi* (lazy) kind. Press half meat mixture into grease loaf pan. Spread stuffing on top, then press other half meat mixture on top. Not so fancy, but taste good too.

Different kind of stuffing:

*Bread and cheese. **Mix one cup grate sharp cheddar with one cup bread crumb, two tablespoon butter and beaten up egg**. If you in big hurry, can even just cut cheese into long slice and use stuff technique #2. Better with tomato sauce than sour cream.

***One cup *kasha* (buckwheat) with fried mushroom**, under *Grains, Chapter Twenty*. Mix one beaten egg in with kasha to hold together.

***One cup kasha with one cup sharp cheese**. Also use egg for binding.

***One cup green olive with pimento or good black olive**. Do not use black olive from can. Go to Greek deli and get real thing. While you there, pick up big bar olive oil soap to make hair and skin shiny. This one my secret why twenty year old men still chasing Baba. Also, soak your denture *every* night.

***Fry one cup mushroom in butter**.

*If you commit to being like Ukrainian, use **one cup sauerkraut**.

***Peel and slice hard boil egg, about six**.

So every time you make meat loaf, family not groaning they eating same thing. Is always different.

Ingredient List:

- Meat loaf recipe
- Waxed paper

Stuff with any of the ingredients in recipe

Bytky (Pounded Steak)

Bytky is Ukrainian noun for "beaten up thing." One day when I meet you, we sing together folk song, *Byla Mene Mati, Berezovim Prutym.* It mean: "Mother beat me with birch rod/ because I hang out with soldier all night."

This great mother/daughter bonding tune, like you can't find on radio in Canada.

If you squeamish kind person, put on rubber or latex glove, clean.

Trim fat off edge round or chuck steak. Sprinkle large heavy cutting board with season flour. If you beginner, season flour mean you put in salt and crack black pepper in bowl of flour, mix real good. Later when you experience like me, you can add all sorts thing like garlic salt, thyme, paprika, saffron and so on. You could even get fancy like my East Indian friend and make masala. But not right now. We is on Ukrainian Central Time. Today just use salt and pepper.

Wipe steak with damp cloth so flour going to stick. Put steak on cutting board and cover with heavy dusting season flour.

Pound steak with meat mallet as hard you can. Pretend is politician who cut down your pension plan. **Turn steak over and pound some more. Keep turning and pounding until all flour is absorb into meat** and you know you not going to need anger management course. If you actually see face of politician in meat, call newspaper to take picture. If turn into face of *Matka Bozha*, Mother of God, go on TV and tell people send you money.

Other option is trick I learn from kozaky: **put tough steak under saddle and ride on all day**. Guarantee it be very tender. If you don't like flavor of sweaty horse and leather, put in plastic bag first. Baba like this flavor. It remind her of younger day and younger kozak.

Baba see you curling your lip. Learn to take advice from woman whose people are first to train horse in history, okay? We also invent cheese by galloping round with horse milk in saddlebag. AND clay oven, so we not always have to be squat around outside in rain and snow.

If you think Ukrainian is primitive, listen to Baba: my ancestor inventing all these thing PLUS complex system politic and architecture while some people we don't talk about (Viking criminal forefather of Russian) was hairy hunchback in cold cave, chewing on raw sheep gut. Want to argue with Baba about this? Meet me at oldest archaeological site in world, near Kyiv. We also invent writing, 22,000 year ago.

Heat oven to 350 degree F.

Cut steak in strip.

Take off rubber glove now, or heat going to make melt on your hand. One day I going to make huge profit telling people so obvious thing.

Fry chop onion in quarter pound butter. Why so much? Because once you take out of pan, you going to brown meat in this butter.

Take out onion from pan. Fry meat for about five minute.

Add back onion. Put in clove crush garlic and cup boiling water (not hot from tap).

Bring to boil, then turn off heat. Pour in casserole dish. Cover and put in oven for one half hour.

Be careful when doing this: if you confident, just pull casserole partway toward you and add half cup smetana. If you little bit clumsy, take casserole from oven to top of stove and add there. **Stir into meat and cook maybe fifteen minute more**. If sauce look scary thick, add spoonful boiled water at one time to make thinner. Sorry, you going to have to play this with your ear.

Serve with steam or bake potato and nice salad. Ukrainian garlic bread also good.

Your option:

***Make with humanely raise pork cutlet instead of beef. Do not use veal** where they are mean to baby calf. Baba also wondering about how men grow up in Canada. Obvious, she is not vegeaquarium. But in Ukrainia, we believe is sad thing to kill baby calf to eat. We cry. Is hard work, and we rather forget about when finish. Why is your men chasing baby calf around in thing call rodeo---on day off? Don't he have nothing better to do, like make love or dance? Sheesh. Big sissy.

Ingredient List:

- Round or chuck steak, one pound per person if big eater, one pound per two people if small eater.
- Onion, small
- Flour, one half cup
- Salt and pepper, one half teaspoon each
- Butter, one quarter cup
- Garlic, one clove crushed
- Keep kettle boiling
- Sour cream, one half cup

Ukrainian Pepper Steak

I eat something like this one time at big hotel. I never eat exactly this in Haletzia (my province), but I think they steal it in spirit, because it sure taste Ukrainian. You see recipe call French this and Italian that, but when they steal from Ukraina, they just don't put any country origin on menu. Is one good way to obliterate people. Did you know Ukrainian invent crepe? We talk about that in *Nalysnyky, Chapter Four*.

Make *Bytky* steak like above, slice in strip. Put meat aside. Is still raw at this point.

Chop up bell pepper, different color for fun. **Slice onion thin. Put on rubber glove and chop up hot pepper**. You know I stickler on everything fresh, but this time I let you get away with using dry hot pepper or cayenne instead. I hate this burning feeling. Especially I hate cleaning glove, which nearly impossible after hot pepper. Guess I never going to publish "Baba Cook in Mexico Cookbook." This make me feel wistful.

Peel garlic and chop off bristle end.**Clean up mushroom and slice thin** like your last date wallet.

In iron skillet, melt butter and extra virgin olive oil together. If you think one these thing good tasting, you going to be over moon with this brother-sister act. Think of it as *Osmond sauce*. Frying these two thing together allow you to use higher heat while still keeping butter taste. Oil have higher burn point than butter.

Add onion to butter-oil and fry till nearly clear.

Add garlic clove and chop pepper. Watch careful so garlic don't burn. If it do, start over. Good cook always be willing to lose cheap kind ingredient to save more expensive. Don't throw out goat with bathwater.

When garlic looking mushy, grind into butter-oil with fork. Do good job, be proud yourself.

Take all vegetable from pan with kind spoon have hole, and put in bowl. Say to vegetable, "You wait here. I be back."

Put steak in pan and turn heat to high. Brown very quick, turning piece with long fork.

When meat look half done, add mushroom real quick. Toss these ingredient around together. Throw meat and mushroom into bowl with lonely vegetable but leave liquid behind.

Turn heat to low. Swallow some red wine from bottle, make sure is fresh. **Pour wine into pan**. Take another swallow wine to be sure. Add beef bouillion cube. Did Baba just say this? No way. **You should add one cup your real *Beef Stock*** like I show you. See *Soup, Chapter One*.

Mix in flour.

Keep mixing and scraping pan to make gravy. Should take about ten minute. Do not leave for bathroom. Do not answer phone, especially if cell phone. Is call that because is frying your brain cell worse than hot pan. People soon be walking round with big smoking hole in head, paying big buck to use someone else brain. You have this kind of money? Then smarten hell up.

If you watching careful like human being, you going to see if gravy too thin or thick. Add boiling water or little bit flour, depending. If you using cell phone, you won't be able to figure out. Dial 1-900-ASK-BABA. Only $4.99 a minute.

Put vegetable and steak into pan and mix around a minute. Taste and add salt and crack black pepper if it need.

Serve with rice, steam potato or *Kasha*, under *Grains, Chapter Twenty*.

Ingredient List:

- Make Bytky
- Red, orange and or yellow bell peppers, three large
- Onions, two large
- Hot pepper, one half OR tablespoon cayenne or dried hot pepper
- Garlic, four cloves
- Mushrooms, one brimming cup
- Butter, one tablespoon
- Extra virgin olive oil, three tablespoons
- Red wine or sherry, three tablespoons
- Beef stock, one cup or beef bouillion cube, one. Or teaspoon *Bovril*
- Flour, one tablespoon
- Keep kettle boiling
- Salt and pepper

Ukrainian Garlic Bread

This bread made on theory no such thing too much garlic.

Put butter on counter to get soft.

Take loaf fresh Ukrainian or Jewish rye, pumpernickel or black bread. Use serrate bread knife and slice loaf lengthwise. I put between knee, but this work good for me from many year riding horse and telling man what to do. You might be safer asking family member to hold down end of loaf while you slice. Is your call, poopchik.

Peel several clove garlic. How many, you want to know? Experience Ukrainian use maybe six or eight for loaf of bread. You just apprentice, so start with five.

Use garlic crusher or chop in tiny piece and crush with fork. **Put garlic in soft butter and mix real good. Add pinch salt**. Better if you do this several hour before you spread on bread, for flavor. Do not use garlic salt on top of this. Yes, I know you think this is state obvious. You would not believe what Baba have to endure from beginner.

Spread garlic on both side of bread loaf. Fifteen minute before you taking Bytky or other main meat dish from oven, put garlic bread on broiler pan and put in oven. Some people put in aluminum. I think this wasteful. Just make sure pan is larger than bread. Duh.

Do not do not DO NOT use white bread for this. Ukrainian steak going to be insulted. Whole flavor match will be water down.

Ingredient List:

- Butter, one quarter pound
- Decent bread, one loaf
- Garlic cloves, five
- Salt

Garlic Croutons

These cretin excellent for add to salad. There is two way you can make.

1. If garlic bread is left over, which Baba doubt, chop up next day and put in salad.

2. Follow close what Baba say next:

Read my instruction for buying good bread.

Leave bread out on counter for couple day to get stale. Put mouse trap beside so nobody touch. If they don't see mouse trap, at least you find out who is big thief in house.

Cut up stale bread in cube.

Melt big lump butter in fry pan. Add two clove crushed, peeled garlic. Mix around bread cube in butter until they looking yellow. Like your eye when your drinking catch up to you. **Add salt**.

Add dill, basil or parsley. Make sure to chop so fine you can barely see. When Baba son Boryslav was little boychik, he like to take my fine chop green thing onto plate. He would sit at table and pretend he is Great Blue Whale eating krill by sucking green thing through teeth. My family always been very science-oriented.

Mix around some more. Now you have decent homemade cretin.

Ingredient List:

- Butter, one quarter pound
- Decent bread, one loaf
- Garlic cloves, two
- Dill, basil or parsley, one tablespoon
- Salt

Roast Beef

Baba going to teach you to make roast beef like out from this world. If you can buy beef label free range, is better. This kind cow chase each other around all over countryside. Have lots fun, maybe even fall in love, have marriage, before butcher, well, you know. Also, they eat healthy grain and not shredded newspaper. Then you not in danger from "mad cow." You eat crap, you be mad too.

Whatever kind of roast you afford, you can make so tender by:

Day or two before cooking, put in glass or ceramic pan. Not use metal until roasting. Any kind metal or plastic give meat strange taste.

Mix together enough tasty kind vinegar and virgin olive or soniashnyk oil to cover roast halfway.

Try apple cider vinegar. This very strong, and also good for make shiny hair and make my arthritis feel better. Also some neighbor come over with fancy-shmancy kind, called balsamic. Fruit flavor vinegar good, too.

Every few hour, turn roast over in this sauce, called *vinahret*. They use this word in Paris, but we sophisticate people talking here. We let French have some our words from Ukraina.

When you feel like cooking, **peel as many garlic cloves** as strong you like. Nick each clove with knife.

Turn oven to 350 degree.

Fry chop onion in butter, put in roasting pan.

Wash baby potato, put in roasting pan. Do not peel.

Wash and chop red pepper in ring, put in roasting pan. Get rid that little label tell you where pepper born. Usually California, so who care?

Wash and slice fresh mushroom and put aside.

If you like **bake potato,** you can put beside roast, on rack. Don't have to bother wrap in tinfoil, this wasting American thing. Just poke hole with knife and put on rack. Potato turn out just as well cook, with crispy jacket.

Take roast from fridge, pour away vinahret. Do not drink, or you be sorry. Baba know you not do this, but there all kind of *banyak* in world. Mean "head empty like pot," would drink anything.

If roast don't already have nice coat of fat, you going to have to lard it. Push salo deep in cracks in meat. Deeper. Don't be baby, go, "Oooh oooh oooh, icky raw meat." Just do it. Chopstick is easiest way to push lard in. Decent butcher will give you salo. Indecent butcher will make you beg.

Do same thing with peel garlic clove.

If you like strong taste, **rub whole roast with dry mustard**. Little milder, rub with kind mustard you put on hot dog. You shouldn't eat hot dog, not so good like garlic kobasa. But I know you do. Don't lie to Baba.

Put in oven. Take cook as long as takes for how big it is. There strange little rule here: if you like roast pinky-red, cook 15 minutes per pound, plus another 15 minutes on top that. If you like more browner, cook 20 minutes per pound, plus another 20 minutes.

When you take roast from oven, let sit on top stove fifteen minute, kind of settle and get itself ready to be eaten.

In meantime, **fry mushroom in plenty butter**. Serve beside.

Take all vegetable from roaster while hot, and serve with roast. What left, put in fridge container. Glass best.

Next day, there will be layer of beef fat on bottom of roaster. We call this *salo.* We like this so much, another name is "Ukrainian cocaine." These day in Ukraina they eating salo with chocolate. Wait till no Canadians with diet-shmiet looking. Rub piece of garlic on dark, and I mean dark, rye bread. Then scoop beef fat onto bread. Use little bit salt. I would only eat this if meat come from organic free range cow.

You can also save salo to fry or scramble egg in next day.

Salo make hair shiny and keep your hip flexible. By all mean possible, do not let hip dry out. How you going to dance and make love with rusty hip?

Ingredient List:

- Roast beef

For every five pounds of roast:

- Extra virgin olive oil or sunflower oil, one cup. Cold pressed organic is best
- Apple cider or balsamic vinegar, one cup
- Beef suet for larding, one quarter pound
- Garlic cloves, five to eight
- Onion, one medium
- Baby or mature potatoes, one pound unpeeled
- Red bell peppers, two medium
- Dry mustard, one tablespoon
- Mushrooms, two cups
- Butter, one half cup

Shashlyk (Shishkebob)

You like werewolf? At the same time is proto-Slav Scythian people riding horses and inventing bow and arrow (and pants) to become real Ukrainian, is neighbour tribe call Neuri. Like all Nature people, they make ceremony where they go inside animal mind to become One. They wear cloak and mask to understand fierce wolf. This is part of ancient way to communicate with animal. Ukrainian people would not be able to hunt successful or domesticate horse and wolf without speaking with animal. Baba co-author Raisa do this every day. Some people, like your rotten neighbor, have to make story from beautiful thing. So they make lie about these people becoming wolf, and then start blame for them causing animal killing all over countryside. This is how story of "werewolf" start.

Greek historian Herodotus who make document during his weird life from 484 to 425 BC, not only start werewolf rumor, he claim Neuri tribe was driven out from land by giant serpent invasion. Ukrainian people know that (1). Don't trust history by same people who make you slave and steal your recipe; and (2). sound like old Herodotus maybe sitting around in crusty robe too long and smoking some that hashish kozaky throw on steam bath fire.

Don't forget, he is part of culture that say king of Arcadia Lycaon slaughter his son and give to Zeus as gift. Merry Christmas! Zeus make him big present too. He turn him into werewolf. Happy New Year! Is where word "lycanthrope"come from. These people need to get life, Baba serious about this.

Werewolf story is also make excuse right till today, for vicious person to organize massive wolf kill. They make wolf evil, which is big fat lie. Wolf is beautiful wild soul. Corporation and ugly man hate wild soul.

Baba once have neighbor in Canada with Arctic wolf. Wolf love Baba so much, she learn to unlock door, sneak out and walk with Baba at night. Then story about werewolf start in neighbourhood, so Baba and beautiful wolf have to cool relationship.

This recipe is in honour of all wolf and maybe one, two werewolf (not really exist). They love to share shashlyk with us, only they eat raw. Shashlyk is old school meat recipe. Original, chunk of meat was cook on kozak sword. You don't have sword? Use stupid wienie stick, see if Baba care. When you feed to wolf, don't use no stick at all.

Most traditional is leg of lamb, but you can use any kind of meat and even mix up different kind. Must be fresh. Frozen meat you chip from freezer will fall apart on sword.

Buy freshest meat. Save some for dog and cat. You one those people feeding vegetarian to cat or dog? Something deep wrong with you. Shameful business. Go get homeless hamster, rabbit or horse. She be glad to eat your vegetarian, instead of poor innocent carnivore.

Hardest part is **cutting meat into cube** measure about two inch on side.

Make marinade from: soniashnyk (sunflower) or olive oil, dry red or white wine or vodka, vinegar, boiled and cooled water, crushed garlic, whole peppercorns.

Baba Secret: Most recipe counsel putting salt in this marinade. Shashlyk cube is so small, salt will suck life from meat. You get kind of shrinkage like when boyfriend take cold shower. Put salt and pepper on table, and let your guest add to nice juicy finish product.

Marinate the meat cubes for at least two hours. In meantime, cut some vegetable you like into about four inch piece. Red or Walla Walla mildest onion, hot house pepper and fresh mushroom work best.

Drain marinade and turn meat this way and that on mechanic paper towel to make dry. Water on surface going to make spitting on grill.

Run sword or skewer through all meat cubes. Make altercation with vegetable piece.

Take good clean stiff small paint brush and **put oil all over meat and vegetable.**

Arrange shashlyk real nice on broil pan, and put under broiler or on grill.

On grill, use hardwood for most authentic Ukrainian flavor. Keep flame very low so you not char veggie. In Ukraina, people who can afford meat, grill real shashlyk all over place same way North American make disgusting hot dog from floor sweeping and pig lip.

Will take about **15 minute** to cook. Every 3-5 minute, **baste shashlyk** with juice that run off in pan, or with more oil.

Try to arrange little bit attractive on nice plate, with **lemon and tomato slice**. Better to make lemon wedgie, because some experience eater like to squeeze this onto shashlyk.

How to eat shashlyk:

If you is person who stuck tongue to metal pole in schoolyard, stick sword in mouth and eat that way. Will be just as good result for your health. Baba shaking her head when she watch Canadian trying to eat shashlyk from skewer, then grabbing mouth. Even nomad kozaky have some kind plate or piece bread, and wolf is more graceful.

How to eat like civilized person: brush meat and vegetable onto bed of rice. **Nice side dish** is smetana (sour cream) and chopped green onion for dip. Have salt and crack black pepper on table. Baba grandchildren once make disaster with onion dip from store, but is at least they stop texting while reaching for shelf.

Ingredient List:

- Two to three pounds of your preferred meat(s), plus enough to feed the wolves.

Marinade:

- Sunflower or olive oil, one half cup
- Dry wine or vodka, one half cup
- Boiled and cooled water, one half cup
- Wine or balsamic vinegar, one half cup
- Crushed garlic, One or two cloves
- Whole peppercorns, five

  Optional: bay leaf

Shashlyk Vegetables:

- Fresh mushrooms, hot house peppers, onion
- Lemon and tomato for garnish

Make donation to wolf conservation.

Chapter Ten

Sichenyky i Zrazy (Meat Patties and Meatballs)

When Baba get to BC, her children decide they going to get rid of her Stalin and Hitler trauma. They get brilliant idea to send her to this thing call "nude encounter group."

At that time Baba English was not perfect like now. She think they say, "Nude counting group." Baba never have no problem with counting naked people. Is her hobby on Ukraina beach. She have no idea how this help with nightmare, but she think, "Maybe same as counting sheep, only better because so much more expensive."

Baba get there on camp bus. She is lull into false sense of security because everyone like to sing *99 Bottle of Vodka on Wall* with her. Then she find out she supposed to be naked in pine needle forest. Right away she thinking these people not so smart. Naked is for home, beach and work.

We make lots good screaming. Most people is rolling round in pine needle like idiot, yelling, "I hate you mother! I hate you father!"

Baba make better use of time. She build two big ugly dummy of Stalin and Hitler. Body is sandbag and head is cabbage. Therapista nod their head and say, "Very constructive," in tight little simper voice. Then Baba escape to town and bring back rifle. It take some time to get in good position. Lucky for her, right breast tuck under armpit just fine. Baba blow these dummy to bit. She credit lesson by Ludmilla Pavlichenko*. She think her therapy is big success because she feel so much better.

Therapista get alarm face and make football huddle. Baba get sent home by herself on camp bus. She sing *99 Bottle of Vodka* with bus driver.

When she get home, she find pine needle is even crazier idea than before. She have to pay professional to remove. So she send bill to nude encounter people and ask for $5000 refund.

They ask, "How you feeeeeeeeel about that, Baba?"

Baba send them picture of needle removing operation and write, "Feel this!"

They write back, say, "We already do. That is what $5000 is for."

Baba rolling around on ground, yelling, "I hate you, therapista! This feel almost as good as shooting fascista.

Lucky for her, this nude encounter group remind her of all good meat patty and meatball recipe she know. And this is good for you.

**Ludmilla Pavlichenko is Ukrainian sharpshooter who kill 309 Nazi by herself. Baba decide to ignore she is part of Red Army. Life in Ukraina is complicate. During Soviet and Nazi time, nobody sure who is enemy. Also, Ukrainian Army liberate Auschwitz-Birkenau..*

Sichenyky (Meat Patties)

Sichenyky is common in Ukrainian home like hockey puck and McDonald is in Canadian. Use of good milk in recipe make patty moist without needing lots of *Salo*, under *Beef, Chapter Nine.*

I know you getting alarm over how much beef and pork fat Baba use, so she going to ease your healthy conscience here. No salo. Only beef, pork and butter. *Nazdarovya*! To your health!

Throw bread crumb in big bowl and mix with best milk you can stand. Ideal would be whole Jersey milk. Everything downhill from there. Allow to soak few minute while you file nail. This one those recipe you going to need rubber glove if you squeamish.

Good fashionista news: black rubber glove is now in *Black Leather Baba* catalogue.

Traditional, when Ukrainian raise own meat we mix in ground beef, pork and veal. Baba have tiny bit big problem with veal that raise in crate. So cruel to little baby calf, make her sick. She would rather march in animal right parade then teach you this recipe. Which is what she gonna do. In fact, she going to drop down in helicopter right outside your house if you buy veal. She going to wear her fighting bloomer, also from Black Leather Baba catalogue. Those *Raging Granny* always try to get Baba to join. She think they have great political idea, but their costume is booo-ring.

If you can't get humane kind veal, substitute more beef or pork. In fact, Baba not sure is such thing as "humane" veal. Even better, farm raise buffalo or wild game. Very yummy.

Mix in grate onion, beaten up egg, salt and pepper.

Make sichenyky into flat patty shape. Sometime my kid and grandkid make starfish. They even take out cookie cutter, then cry when meat make weird expansion in frying pan. Better to avoid this.

Dip each patty into fine bread crumb. Make crissy crossy shape

on each with butter knife. This not only fancy, it help them cook faster. One day McDonald going to beg Baba for patent, and she going to laugh in their face. After she pocket several million dollar.

Turn oven to 350 F.

Cook patty in hot butter. I know you jonesing to use salo, but butter is best thing. If you really desperate, Baba meet you on corner and sell you black market salo from under her polyvinyl trench coat. You getting idea here that maybe Baba own part interest in catalogue? Call **1-900-BlackLeatherBaba**. I know is too many number. So what. It sound like you surprise Baba have her own phone exchange, poopchik.

Ne takiy ya durna yak ty mudra! Baba not so stupid as you are smart!

I know you going to have to reread this several time to get it. Take your sweet time.

When patty is cook, put in baking dish. This is one of those Baba recipe that go extra mile for extra delicious taste idea.

When all patty is cook, cover them in baking dish with lid. Which you probably don't have. Okay. This one pathetic time, use aluminum foil. **Bake in oven twenty minute.**

How many sichenyky this make? Depend on how big you make. Some people always running around with measure tape. Not Baba.

Baba already covering her ear from your whining. "Why I have to bake when I already fry, Baba? Why can't I use orange margarine, Baba? Why is sky full of paratrooper, Baba?"

Because baking make extra delicious flavor blend of all kind meat. It also balance moist centre of meat mix with dry outside. Really, you have to go to trouble of making before you become believer. Ukrainian invent oven several thousand year ago. We know many thing about chemistry you don't, so don't question Baba.

Serve patty with:

****Mushroom Sauce***, under *Hryb (Mushrooms), Chapter Twelve* or
****Cream, Dill, Horse Radish & Sour Cream*** **or** ***Honey Onion Pidlyvi*** *(Sauce), Chapter Twenty Two*

Baba don't know why she bother with these primo instruction. You just going to slap on two piece Wonderbra bread with stinking ketchup.

Ingredient List:

- Ground beef, pork and veal substitute, one third pound each
- Bread crumbs, one cup

- Whole or two percent milk, one cup
- Onion, one small
- Egg, one large
- Salt and pepper
- Butter, one quarter pound
- Sauce of your choice
- NO KETCHUP

Zrazy (Ukrainian Meatballs)

This not particular pleasant thing to cook as soon as you get home from nude encounter group. For two or three week you might feel like you seen enough burned meatball for lifetime. Get over it. If you not eat every time something was disgusting in world, you be dead anorexic in no time.

Baba confession: She lose some appetite herself after ugly naked lawyer talk to her. She have no idea can be freckle in some kind place like he show her.

Okay. Is time to thank God for repress memory and think about feeding yourself.

Make meat sichenyky recipe like above. Meat taste better if you buy in chunk, then ask butcher to grind. Don't be fool and buy package ground meat, unless you can't afford to do this. Baba have her own meat grinder ever since she convince her *Domovyk* house elf to clean this thing for her. You probably don't have so strong spiritual power.

Baba get tear in eye just like you when that JK Rowling kill her Dobby. But not for long. House spirit getting kill is thing call “pathetic fallacy.” Also really bad research of neo-pagan. Now she busy appropriating Native American spirituality. Stop crying, because spirit is immortal. Baba guarantee you this. We have same same house elf in my family since we first build house from mammoth bone twelve thousand year ago. They get marry, have baby and move in with each our new family. So cute when Domovyk hang out wash, too. Only thing is, they like mini Sasquatch. Hairy all over except for face. So you sometime have to pick long hair from clean sheet.

How you get Domovyk to move? When you ready, put out empty suitcase. They crawl in. At new home, lure Domovyk out with Ukrainian dinner.

Baba hear on BBC News that Russian accuse Rowling of model

Dobby after Prime Minister Putin. She wonder why they make laughing stock by point this out. In contrast, Ukrainian elf is quite handsome. As is all our political leader. You seen Yushenko and Tymoshenko? Woooo-eeeee. That what Baba talking about. Poroshenko also have sex appeal. Russian KGB so jealous, they try to ruin Yushenko face with digoxin.

Back to recipe. Instead of patty, make meat into many ball. Roll them round in hot butter pan until they even brown all over. Is like when you put down plastic sheet on beach and roll in suntan oil. That way you know everything get bake. Only don't get sand in your meatball. Ha!

Turn oven to 350 F.

Put meatball in baking dish. Pour home made hot beef or chicken soup broth on top. Use only enough so meat ball is cover half way. Is really no point using vegetarian soup. Might as well have diet drink with your banana split. Baba hate hypocrite.

Bake in oven half hour.

Serve with good Ukrainian sauce like above. Why Baba bothering to write this, she don't know. You probably going to eat right out of baking dish so you have good sad story for your Overeater Anonymous meeting. Is not quite so sad as that woman who eat meatball straight from garbage, but she not so lucky to have Baba teach her how to binge with class.

Ingredient List:

- Sichenyky recipe
- Boiling hot soup broth, one half cup
- Sauce of your choice

Zrazy v Khrin
(Ukrainian Meatballs with Horse Radish Stuffing)

Now this is advance Ukrainian cooking. My god, it have it all. Meat, horse radish, butter, sour cream, and even Baba permission to add *salo* and dill if you like.

You going to be envy of whole party. These lame Canadian show up with blah same old meat ball floating round in same old sauce. In fact, is sometime literal same old sauce. Some them take home leftover to freeze. Then they throw old stuff in blender to start next recipe. No wonder everybody going to fight with fist over your zrazy.

You so lucky, because this kind meatball have its own built in dramatic saucearama.

Make meat sichenyky recipe one more time. You know you loving it.

Making stuffing is harder part: you going to have to **press two hard boil egg yolk through sieve**. If you going to cheat and use fly swatter, make sure is clean.

Mix egg with big helping horse radish, as fresh as you can find. If none in your garden, jar kind mix with beet juice make very nice color stuffing. Cover yourself in polyvinyl apron so as not to make red stain on blouse. Do Baba have to tell you one more time where you can buy this thing? No? Good. You learning.

Make soft butter or salo and mix with soft bread crumb. Salt. Mix this into egg and horse radish. Have kleenex ready. By now is possible you sneezing from snorting horse radish and just general excitement.

Here is where your brain have to become flexible like Ukrainian one. Listen careful. **Put on your black rubber glove and shape meat into many small ball.** About size of pony testicle. Now with one big smack of that flyswatter, make into patty. If it take two smack, no harm intend.

Put spoon full of stuffing in middle each patty. Plop! Fold edge of patty over stuffing. Make into nice tight envelope.

Turn oven to 350 F.

Baba warning: If you find you not have enough meat to fold over, is because you shape them size of your ex-husband who make false claim. Don't be afraid to start over with patty or relationship. Sometime this is only way to get life.

Now make ball or egg shape with meat, stuffing already inside. **Fry them to good brown color in hot butter**. You going to want to drink this butter, it smell so good. If any left over, pour on your popcorn. Like my friend Katya say about people who worry on calorie, "Damn the tuxedo!"

Line up these meatball in baking dish.

You not finish yet. And there is subtle difference from regular *zrazy*. Baba see you faltering in endurance. How you think you would have survive in ancient Ukraina, you can't get through this recipe? Pah! You are recipe tourist.

Boil half cup home made soup stock in same pan with one tablespoon flour. If you did use fat for popcorn, you going to need to melt more. Serve you right for not reading my recipe whole way through before starting procedure. **Keep stirring to make thick. Sprinkle with**

salt and pepper.

Add best kind smetana. Mix till sauce is like brownie velvet and you drooling to drink straight from pan.

You forget all about lonely meatball sitting there waiting, Baba know. By now you probably sucking up sauce with one those spoon straw from Slurpee.

Pour sauce over meatball. Cover baking dish and cook half hour.

Your option:

***Add fresh fine chop dill** to sauce.
***Chop fancy mushroom**, fry in butter or salo and put in sauce.

Baba law: Don't all of sudden get clever and make *Horse Radish and Sour Cream Sauce*. In cooking, always blend mild with hot, and smooth with crunchy.

You should be grateful Baba teaching you all this. Sometime she just shake her head and remember word of great Lviv writer Stanislaw Lec, "Dealing with undersized individual deforms the spine."

Ingredient List:

- Sichenyky recipe
- Egg yolks, two hardboiled
- Butter or salo, one quarter pound
- Fresh horse radish, one third cup grated fine
- Soft bread crumbs, two tablespoons
- Salt and pepper
- Flour, one tablespoon
- Soup stock, one half cup
- Sour cream, one half cup

Spinach (Vegetarian) Sichenyky

This is excellent vegetarian recipe. Baba know some of you love her story and only read meat recipe for this reason. Is just like training dog. Here is your next big food reward, so SIT:

Wash, steam and drain two big bunch spinach. See *Lokshyna & Spinach Casserole, Chapter Twenty One* for what to do with stem.

If you want best drain kind spinach, squeeze in between clean towel.

If you already use up all towel in house making your hair that color don't fool nobody, Baba have brilliant suggestion. Go to hardware store and buy mechanic hand towel on roll. Super absorbent, because is made to soak up grease from car. I guarantee will work for your cooking, wiping up dog mess and popping ugly pimple. If you have good timing, can finish all this before guest come.

Chop spinach into tiny bit.

Fry chop onion in butter, and mix with spinach. If you can afford, make substitute from leek. When Baba first move to Canada, man always saying, "I am taking leek." I think he is going out to garden. Then he come back with nothing, and she mad at him. Next time she follow him, and hoo boychik, is she sorry her English was not so good then.

Have medium size bowl with crush bread crumb waiting. Waiting for what? **For medium size bowl with egg. This egg should be mix up with fork and have splash water add**. Tell these two bowl to sit patient and wait for their turn.

Mix onion and spinach with big fat bread crumb, splash thick cream, beaten up egg, salt and pepper. Let this sit around for ten, fifteen minute while you go wipe off face from mess you make mixing. Mechanic towel is also good for this.

Time to put on your fancy rubber glove again. Unless you really like feel of slimy vegetable in hand. Baba didn't think so. **Make many small patty shape** with your mixture.

This is why two bowl of stuff been waiting! **Dip each patty in crumb, then egg**. Here is superkabbalisticexpialadocious trick. **Listen again to Baba: First dip in crumb, then egg, then bread crumb AGAIN.** Do not skip step, or patty will not taste Ukrainian. Never forget you learning from person whose ancestor invent first oven.

Fry in butter until beautiful brownie-gold. It make Baba cringe, but she have duty to publisher to tell you: Fry on both side.

Serve with some kind good sauce not out of stupid jar:

**Mushroom Sauce*, see *Hryb (Mushrooms), Chapter Twelve* or
**Cream, Dill, Horse Radish & Sour Cream* or *Honey Onion Sauce,* under *Pidlyvi (Sauce), Chapter Twenty Two*
Or, Matka Bozha, *Sour Cream & Green Onion Sauce.*

Ingredient List:

- Spinach, two cups cooked
- Butter, three tablespoons

- Small onion, one half
- Large eggs, two slightly beaten. Dilute one with two tablespoons of water
- Cereal or whipping cream, one tablespoon
- Salt and pepper
- Bread crumbs, one heaping cup
- Crushed bread crumbs, one half cup
- Butter, one quarter cup

See also *Mushroom Sichenyky* in Mushrooms, Chapter Twelve

Chapter Eleven

Winter Solstice

Koruksun, Sviat Vechir I Rizdvo (Day of the Dead, Holy Eve & Christmas)

Day of dead for Ukrainian is *Koruksun* or Winter Solstice, when sun is in sky shortest time, December 21st.

Baba love this holiday for three reason: is one more time for ancestor worship, it have lots good dancing and everyone appreciate her cooking even more than usual.

Hors is name of old sun god who is dying. He turn into brand new sun goddess, name Kolyada. She get dress to nine and hitch up her several golden horse to gallop across sky. This is positive gender role model for children, too. Unfortunate, someone turn powerful, generous golden goddess into Santa Claus with sleigh. Man in drag taking powerful woman place. What else new? Last time Baba went to her church, she wondering if priest have Ferragamos under that robe.

In meantime, Ukrainian spend ten whole day making good party. This last until New Year Eve, when it become some other kind party. We deal with that later. Baba know Canadian have short attention span from short holiday.

We like to go to graveyard and light big fire to keep ancestor warm. Also at crossroad to invite wandering ancestor and repel crazy demon. At Maslyanitsya (Fat Tuesday) we make "bonefire" to burn bone. At Koruksun we make bonefire to warm bone. Is subtle but big difference. You going to have to build bridge between right and left brain, poopchik.

When we not lighting fire or stuffing face, we make ritual circle dance holding hand. Is too cold for village to bathe together in river like at holiday of *Ivana Kupala* (Summer Solstice). You got to make do.

Children dress up in costume and go to people house to sing song about season. These beautiful song all about how Baba Spider weave universe and how special is earth, moon, sun and star. Our kid don't yell, "Trick me or treat!" Ukrainian not too tacky people. Everyone have little gift of candy and sometime money for them.

At same time, some people believe Saint Nicholas wandering around making miracle, especially helping animal. Ukrainian not too big on almost-stranger giving present to our kid. You could say this is under emphasize. We give gift to our own and neighbor kid. Beside, we don't have stinking Walmart. How you going to hide from kid that you been carving him wood horse for six month?

Next come hugest feast time, call *Sviata Vechera*, or Holy Eve.

I know what you thinking if you not Ukrainian. "Baba, you have Hollow Weenie and Christmas all mix up!" No way. Baba is one who get it straight. I tell you how was original way. When Christianity come, they install rabbi Jesus, make holiday shorter and kick sun god Hors and Kolyada into cheap seat. Baba teach you how to have complete experience of Slavic culture.

At end October, we is still lying around groaning from extending of Harvest Festival. We have short break call *Maalox Day*, then go straight into *Koruksun*, which is Day of Dead. Day after Sviat Vechir would be call Christmas morning in Canada. Mostly we just nursing food hangover and talking about New Year party. Baba love Jesus, he is cool cat. She sometime have big little problem with people who say they follow.

All these thing mix together make one boomerang bonanza of holiday. Ukrainian party all year long, when not putting in overtime at work.

How much you like holiday start date of December 21st depend on what you prefer, make love in day or night. Baba only care she have great lover and warm place to lie down.

Baba warning: Cold lover and cold bed is bad like sitting on cold concrete. Will give you *vovk na sraka*, wolf in bum.

Food on Holy Eve is unbefunkinglievable. Even though type of recipe and ritual vary from region to region, one thing stay always same: you have to use ingenuity to make twelve meatless dish. These food stand for twelve month, zodiac and twelve apostle. Is also for size twelve shoe *kozaky* use to kick Nazi *sraka*. Don't get Baba start on that.

Okay, she start herself. Was one battle in western Ukraina where kozaky defeat Nazi tank on horseback. Baba was one them, dress in man drag. Modern times is not like Scythian, when women have equality.

Before Sviata Vechera feast, woman spread hay all over floor and on table while everyone make animal sound. Moo, cluck, bleat. Baba has special talent for horse neigh. For some reason, this make Canadian man hot. She don't know why.

And by way, tablecloth go on top of hay, not under. Unless you some kind slob. Don't forget to put clove garlic on each corner of table. Also under cloth. Add second tablecloth for ancestor.

Seating arrangement by marry woman is to put single woman in middle of table, to help her find husband. If don't like this woman, she seat her at table corner. If she suspect this woman making floppy eye at her own husband, she seat her out in snow.

Twelve meatless dish is spread out on table. But before anybody eat, they all go out to stable to thank animal for providing everything for family rest of year: loyalty, labor, entertainment, egg, milk, meat, wool, hair and manure for crop. If guest from city, some them still try make animal noise. This don't go over so big when some guy in suit say, "Oink oink," at pig. Pig think he is stupid, because pig know fluent Ukrainian. Some is even English bilingual. We make sure of this, because English is international language of pig business.

We feed animal *kutya* (grain and honey pudding), plus mix part of our meal into their feed. They talk to us. Because Baba never eat horse, duck or goat, they talk to her every day anyway. What they say, you want to know. First, "Thank you for not eat me." Then they give forecast of political election and beauty tip. If you not have animal to honor, make big donation to animal rescue shelter. But first check their book, make sure some Communist bureaucrat not stealing money and killing nice dog. Is special place in gulag for these people.

Then man of house spread his arm to sky and call Perun, who is thunder god. He say, "Bad thunderstorm, evil spirit, if you want my home, come get it right now." Then he wait and say, "Put up your duke right now! No? You not coming cuz you scared cat, huh? Fine. Then don't bother come round any other time of year. You not come when I invite as guest, you not welcome anytime. You are rude."

Wife, she cross her arm and say, "And that go for me, too."

Children make chorus. They say, "Yeah."

Back at table, is one place sitting empty for ancestor. Also, *didukh* (grandfather) from harvest is in room corner. This sheaf of wheat where ancestor live. If you have fireplace, ancestor is in fire, too. In fact, is no place you can get away. They in your house, your garden, your office, your car. Don't be worry. They close their eye when you making rude kind scratching. Unless your ancestor is maybe some kind weirdo.

We make sure to blow on and brush seat of chair so we don't sit on ancestor. This can make awkward occasion.

Because Winter Solstice is continuation of Ukrainian agricultural wheel of year. You give biggest blessing when you wish for someone large crop. In some family, father stand behind stack of wheat at dinner table and play peeking boo. He say in big thunder voice like Perun, "Can you seeeee me?"

Family say, "Yes *tato*, we can see top your bald head."

Father reply, "Next year, wheat crop will be so huge, you will not see me. Also, I pay for good toupee."

Child in house watch out window for first star to appear. No one can touch food till this star twinkle down. Is sign from God, mean, "Let's eat!" Star are pathway to other world. If at any time Ukrainian lucky to see falling star, it mean angel is coming to retrieve soul from earth. Wishing on this is nother way to respect ancestor. Your wish go right up to heaven and come true.

Man throw spoonful of kutya up to ceiling. The bigger the piece that stick, the more luck family will have. If you sitting under where it fall down, you have worse luck. That stuff make hair like cement. Is kind of fashion call "kutya punk." You don't want this.

Why is Ukrainian hospitality so centre on food? For one thing, only *nychysta syla*, evil spirit, don't eat. Skinny-shminny, "None for me, thanks," kind of person scare heckola out of healthy Ukrainian. We make sign of four direction cross behind your size two skirt and skeleton arm. Meatless dish is not only to honor animal. Is only way Ukrainian can fast and eat at same time. You not going to find any those hollow eye saint around here. Our saint come in form of nice fat Baba and Didukh. Baba going to be canonize any day. She should be, all this patience she showing for you.

What kind food we can make if everything meatless? Hoo boy, table is groaning like when you making third try getting up from couch. We have saying, *A table bends from a meal.*

Just remember, you can't have no *salo* or other kind animal fat. Vegetable oil is okay. Ukrainian not some vegan-schmegan, but Baba show you alternate meatless version of each these Sviat Vechir recipe. You going to pick twelve of these to make. Twelve dish is to honor twelve lunar moon. Christian also honor twelve apostle. We have:

Non-negotiable dish. Sometime is because is part of sacred ritual, sometime because you would just look stupid if you didn't serve:

- *Kutya, Chapter Twenty*, is part of ritual.
- *Meatless Borshch,* under *Soup, Chapter One*. with meatless *Vushka, Chapter Thirteen*
- *Varenyky* (Perogies)---savory kind, but without dairy or meat.
- *Meatless Holubtsi (Cabbage Rolls), Chapter Fourteen*. Baba prefer *Kasha* (Buckwheat) filling for Sviat Vechir. Rice is good too.
- *Fasolia: White Bean with Garlic*, hot or cold dip, *Chapter*

Twenty

- *Mushroom dish, Chapter Twelve*
- *Kolach* (braided sacred bread), below. Part of sacred ritual.
- *Uzvar,* which is stew fruit, *Chapter Twenty Three*. You also drink juice and call it *Pyva Bozha*, Drink of God. This recipe usually mark end of main meal, because someone always spill serving dish all over himself.

At least one kind fish. Baba suggest:

- *Baked Stuffed Fish* (with no butter) *Chapter Sixteen*, or
- *Pickle Herring, Chapter Seventeen*

Not mandatory, but tasty:

- *Kapusta i Horokh* (Sauerkraut and Pea Casserole), *Chapter Eighteen*. This dish is delicious to have, but you won't look stupid if you leave out. If you craving *kapusta*, sauerkraut, but already have too many dish, make kapusta vareneky!
- *Salata* is optional, but would count as one dish. Baba know table look strange to non-Ukrainian without salad, but remember borshch is vegetable stew, anyway.

Pick some dessert to round out twelve dish:

- *Medivnyk (Honey Cake), Chapter Twenty Three*. You have to start this early in season! Is non-negotiable
- *Pampushky (Filled Doughnuts), Chapter Twenty Three*. Is almost non-negotiable. Look, if you amateur, you might not want to attempt, even if is very traditional. Is no Ukrainian Krispy Creme outlet, so you can't just pick up bag of doughnut quick before dinner. **You have other option like:**
- *Nalysnyky* (Crepes) with sweet filling, *Chapter Four*
- *Perakladanets (Coffee Cake), Chapter Twenty Three*
- *Makivnyk (Poppy Seed Roll), Chapter Twenty Four*
- *Varenyky* with dessert filling, like plum or cherry, *Chapter Thirteen*

Here is your dispensation for animal fat. Baba know you was worried: once main dish dinner is over, is officially next day, or Christmas! Just like how Jewish people divide day by sundown. This mean you can eat dessert with butter, and put cream in coffee. Ukrainian purist jury is still out on if you can reserve savory verenyky for dessert, so you can eat with smetana. Baba make judicial decision. She would say this is cheating on faithfulness to animal. Save for breakfast.

Horilka don't hurt, and this is time to bring out your fanciest. Like lip smack liqueur and favorite flavor vodka. Bread and horilka recipe going to be in Baba next cookbook. With exception: In centre of table is gorgeous braid bread, call kolach. Baba going to teach you this.

She like to give caroler *hrustychky,* which is type of crunchy doughnut with icing sugar. All them end up with white frost on face, so cute.

Another great thing about this meal is, never no leftover. By end of meal, Baba still slapping people hand so everyone get enough varenyky. When she see Canadian eat turkey sandwich for six month after Christmas, she laugh like Solstice banshee. Is sad, really. She don't understand why you making such nauseate surplus. Can't be that hard to breed small turkey. You just put together short lady turkey and short man turkey. Baba don't mind most short man, why should lady turkey be fussy?

After dinner come caroler. We sing, both with and without them. We sing so strong, would make your good eye water. Most part this *kolyadka* is several hundred year old, but Baba write chorus about weaving star together. Ukrainian should feel free to pass around rest of song. Is serious copyright issue in chorus. Is going to be on television, you will see. One day we all going to honor golden goddess Kolyada again:

Before there was a world,
There was Baba Spider
Weaving the stars together
She made a web where people could live
She fed everyone
She brings all good things

There are three friends
Caught in her web
The shining sun
The bright moon
And the light rain
To make things grow

Weaving the stars together
She brings all good things

Weaving the stars together
She brings all good things

© BABA. Don't you forget!

Baba Spider weaves the web of life
She gives us the beauty of her designs
So all people can be together
Be kind to spider
And she will bring you good luck

Weaving the stars together
She brings all good things
Weaving the stars together
She brings all good things

© BABA. Don't you forget, too!
© 2011 Raisa Marika Stohyn/Raisa Stone

Baba co-author Raisa write entire book call "Rosie's Rescue", all about this legend. Is very good bedtime kind of reading. You buy some book, okay? **Keep up to date with Baba and Raisichka at www.ukrainiansoulfood.ca and www.reisastone.com.**

You didn't sing loud enough, you. Baba once read, "Sing like no one listening, dance like no one watching." Why is this, you have rotten teeth and no fancy pair red boot? You sound like poor thing. Here is Winter Solstice/Koruksun recipe to cheer you up. We give these out to caroler, too:

Hrustychky (Icicles) or Verhuny (Sweet Nothings)

Again, this two different name for same thing, from different region in Ukraina. We going to make about fifty of these thing. When people say "melt in mouth", this what they mean. Is pretty easy recipe, but is little trick at end. If you kind of girl can tie knot in cherry stem with tongue, you be done in no time. If not, going to be extra ten minute.

Take out big bowl. Baba making it easy. This recipe all happen in one place. **Beat up egg yolk and gradual pour in white sugar. Mix in *smetana*, white flour and salt**. Your eye is getting all big. Baba said recipe was cheery, cute, tasty and easy. Not healthy.

Mix in brandy or rum. This keep dessert from absorbing as much oil in deep fryer. Rum extract not going to work, and no, is no avoiding deep fryer. Get over yourself.

Put lots flour on counter or pastry board. Knead like when kitten making big mess on your sweater. **When dough get smoothie, put cloth on top and go have tea. It only need ten minute rest**, so don't get too comfortable.

Roll out this dough very thin, because it going to hold its breath and puff little bit in hot fat. You would too. **About one eighth inch thick. With very sharp knife, cut dough into long strip one inch wide**. Yes, Baba know. You going to have to cover dough and run next door for sharp knife.

You back yet? **Cut dough on diagonal about three inch. You going to have all these piece in front of you look like diamond**. Is not diamond. Don't be fool.

Make slit in each piece, pick up each end and pull through like bowing tie. If you scratching head, stop. You have flour all over head. We just got kutya out from there. If you was using sharp knife to scratch, you maybe already notice.

If pulling through both end of dough is too much, only pull one end, then fold it back. This way you will not break so many. Remember what Baba say about skill with cherry stem. Is just to make interesting shape. Relax already.

Heat fat in deep fryer to 375 degree F. Sunflower oil is real good. This is Ukraina national flower.

Drop in few hrustychky at time, then use slot spoon to scoop when they goldie brown color. No, brandy or rum did not repel ALL oil, Miss Diet Head. **Put out paper towel** just like for bacon.

Baba law: Is better nutrition to make crazy indulgence only on holiday, than to stop at fast food place all time. Avoid these place, then don't feel guilty when you eat sugar and fat now and then.

Baba law also: Fat repel alcohol little bit, alcohol repel fat little bit.

Sprinkle hrustychky with icing sugar. Pretend is snow. They look little bit like tasty icicle. One time Baba daughter Odarka use that spray can snow, because this is way Odarka do everything since birth. Baba love her, but is sometime dismay. Anyway, that work out so good, Baba make her and other kid punch hole in each one and hang on tree.

Hrustychky is excellent hot, but is just fine cool. You can make ahead of time for guest or caroler. If you taking to friend house, put in paper bag. Will make your heart thump how grease make stain on brown paper. Baba know you know exactly what she mean.

Baba warning: Maybe you better double recipe so some is left for guest.

Ingredients:

- Egg yolks, four
- White sugar, two tablespoon
- Sour cream, two tablespoons
- White flour, one and one half cups plus extra for rolling
- Salt
- Brandy or rum, one tablespoon
- Icing sugar, one half cup

Kolach

Kolach mean "circle of life bread." Yes, Baba know you think that *Lion King* invent. Please. What else is on? Be serious person for once. Kolach is from word *kolo*, or circle. It also symbolize life-giving sun---which is what Solstice is honor. You can see relation to name of sun goddess, Kolyada. Life giver is round. Family circle is important, too.

This bread is center piece of table at Sviata Vechera and at dead person memorial. Parent present this to bride and groom at wedding. About only place this circle bread don't show up under Ukrainian arm is at childbirth and Mardi Gras. This is because we replace it with round golden pancake, *Nalysnyky, Chapter Four*. Ha! You thought you had Baba by her shortest hair. No, poopchik. Ukrainian is in constant circle of life. Even our flag is about this. Blue sky over gold wheat.

At Sviata Vechera, we have special challenge. We actual bake three level loaf stack one on top of other. This give you three time prosperity, health and happiness. Sprig of evergreen tree go on bottom one for even more eternity. Is against law of physic, but Baba don't care.

We then stick fat white candle in centre and light.

Baba riddle: Why we light this candle?
Answer: To call ancestor!

Baba know you getting tired of all this work to call your ancestor. She thinking of marketing high pitch whistle for lazy person. One blast, and ancestor come running and panting. Is easy, like some kind Twelve Step program. Make confession, beat chest and say prayer. Boom! By grace of God listen to only you, all your problem is gone. While rest of world is struggle with war, disease and famine. Must be because your skin is like lily, attract such good luck.

Baba have little big issue with 12 Step concept of "old timer," too. This is person who keep hand off bottle for twenty, thirty, forty year. They boil whole year of ritual and festival down to boring Step, then make these old timer into ancestor. Ha! No, dorahenka, they not necessarily ancestor. They just old people who not drinking. Get realistic.

Here come our kolach:

This take most of day. All good ritual procedure do.

Before you get all work up, TEST YOUR YEAST. Do not go into denial if it is stale. For your good information, one package yeast= one cake yeast = two tablespoon yeast. Baba give you permission to use candy thermometer. Most time she don't believe in measure this, measure that. But this recipe is like sending you up baking Olympic creek without paddle.

Boil kettle and let water cool. Stir one teaspoon white sugar into one cup warm water, about one hundred degree. Sprinkle two package yeast over water, then shove over to side of counter for ten minute. It should get all bubble like good champagne. If champagne is flat, send someone to store for fresh. Is absolute no magic wand you can wave to revive sick yeast. Is like giving Jaw of Life to dead goldfish.

If yeast is good, you off to racing. **Take out hugest mixing bowl. Pour three tablespoon white sugar in two cup warm whole milk and stir**. Milk should be about one hundred, maximum one hundred ten degree. One day you be able to tell with elbow. Not today.

Add yeast mix to milk and stir.

Beat up egg, the more organic and rich the better. Best if fertilize. Remember this is circle of life bread. Is magic spell.

Baba law: More trouble you take to make ritual food, the better blessing you and family will have.

Sift three cup flour. Sifting is yet nother way you show respect to grain that give life.

Put egg, salt, soniashnyk oil, and flour with milk. Stir in that bubbly yeast. Beat whole thing until is no bubble left. Got it? Lots of bubble in yeast, no bubble when mixing is done.

Here is trick: dough will mix better if you keep stirring in same

direction. You can also say blessing over this. Or maybe Baba is asking too much.

Cover with clean towel. Okay, we take break here while you find such thing.

Leave dough in warm place for rising, one hour. Inside of oven is good for draft proof. If you leaving on counter, put pet bird in cage. Is old saying, *Bird in bread is terrible bad luck.*

Is actual no such old saying. Baba make it up. Is true, though.

Dough should be double size. If not, go away for another hour.

Here come your big surprise: **mix in six more cup sifted flour**. Yes, six cup. This not some amateur cake-in-a-box we making here. But do it one cup at time!

Knead dough. This is real good exercise for bicep, tricep, deltoid and abdominal. You knead bread for ten minute, it replace your ironing pump. Every spring, Ukrainian women parade around village in off-shoulder blouse with lots red bead to show off upper body. Whooo-eee. Is lip magnet. Baba buy those dingle dangle earring from Gypsy, too.

You know you are done kneading when dough is like rubber ball and not sticking to bowl. **Now lift it up into larger bowl you coat with oil. Roll it round** so whole thing is nice and oily.

Cover bowl with clean towel. Go away for about one hour.

When you come back, **dough should be double in size**, look like big fat stomach. **Punch dough in stomach and walk away**. If it try to follow you, walk faster. **Let it rise again little bit, maybe to one third again bigger**.

You got that? Dough have three rising before baking: one with little bit flour, one to double with lots flour, and then one minimalist rising.

Braiding and baking kolach:

There are several way to bake kolach.

Neatest method need **springform pan**. This kind have buckle on side. If you have three such pan, even better, because we making three loaf. **Line pan real good with parchment paper that you put butter and flour on**. Then kolach pop out easy-peasy. This not Ukrainian expression, by way.

Divide rest of dough up into three part. **Take one part, and divide that into three**. If your kid is home from school, maybe they can figure it out.

You going to roll out each these last part into rope, about long as your arm. Do not get dough stuck in armpit. This call "job hazard."

Probably better if you shave real good and don't use chemical deodorant, just in case.

Braid these piece together. Divide next third of dough into three and braid that together. Same thing with last piece dough. Got it? You have three piece braided bread altogether.

Once you get skill like Baba, you can roll out rope so is thicker in middle part. This look really cool once kolach is bake.

Put one these braided piece in pan. Make sure you turn end of braid under so it not go blooey in pan. If you putting more than one loaf in oven at once, make sure is room between. Kolach going to rise to double size. "Rise" mean it spread sideway, too. You hope.

Cover dough again and leave until it double in size, about one hour. No cheating. How you know is risen enough? Make your finger wet. Not from spit, from tap. Sheesh.

Give dough poke in its fat stomach. If this make permanent belly button, dough is risen.

At this time, you will freak out because is gap in centre of braided loaf. IT GOING TO DOUBLE AGAIN IN OVEN, OKAY? Gap will disappear.

When dough is almost double, heat oven to 375 degree F.

In meantime, **beat up egg with little bit warm water. When dough is ready, paint this glaze on top each loaf with pastry brush**. If you using paint brush, do not use kind soak in turpentine.

Sprinkle poppy seed on top each loaf for even more life and fertility symbol.

Bake about one hour.

Other method of baking:

Roll out and braid dough like Baba say.

Put two loaf on butter baking sheet. Baking stone is nice, too. Leave lots room, just like when planting hemp. Is more chance with this method that kolach going to overlap and make Siamese twin. Your choice, your party, poopchik. **Cover and let dough double in size. Use belly button test like before.**

Make glaze and bake like above.

And for Kolyada sake, put rack in lower third of oven. Do not try to save time by making duplex. You going to have to do two session of baking to make third loaf, and that is that.

Put third unbake loaf in no-draft place and cover until its time. Or borrow neighbor oven.

How you know when bread is bake?

Baba know you going to be fool. Bread will start to look goldie-brown pretty early because of egg glaze.

No. **Bake one hour**. If you absolute sure is done, turn loaf over and make tap tap tap with clean knuckle on bottom. No one should answer. If they do, hang up. Ha!

Then **make pinching test on bottom of bread**. If it feel firm, it is done. If not, put back in for ten minute and watch closely. This mean replace burn out bulb in oven for once.

Make cool on wire rack for at least one hour before stacking and any kind slicing. Don't forget small evergreen branch on bottom layer, or you cheat yourself of luck.

There your Sviata Vechera kolach. Break bread and eat when official meatless dinner is over, because it have butter and milk. Make sure you leave at least one layer overnight for ancestor to eat themselves.

Baba going to go lie in hammock now. Oi yoi yoi, is harder teaching you, than making twelve kolach.

Ingredient List:

- Candy thermometer
- Parchment paper
- Springform pan
- Sugar, one teaspoon for yeast
- Sugar, three tablespoon for milk
- Dry yeast, two envelopes
- Boiled water, cooled to 100 degrees, one cup
- Warm milk, two cups
- Eggs, two large
- Salt, one tablespoon
- Vegetable oil or melted butter, three tablespoons for bread
- Butter to grease pan
- Cake flour, nine cups

Glaze

- Egg, one large
- Warm water, one tablespoon
- Dry poppy seeds, two tablespoons
- Clean, dry pastry or paint brush

Clean up after Sviata Vechera

Should be hardly any leftover. After all, you put out heaping plate for ancestor, too. Leftover bread have special ritual to show respect: kiss the slice and throw outside for wild bird to eat. You will wait till next day to do this with leftover kolach, so ancestor have time to digest first. If you eat on Sviata Vechera like most Ukrainian do, is not going to be Tum left over for them.

Get children to sweep up all hay from table and floor. Carry this outside with *didukh* wheat sheaf. You going to light another fire, and whole family going to jump over and make New Year wish.

Baba law: make fire low and jump high.

Joyful Solstice everybody! And yes, Baba know she make up that greeting. So if you Ukrainian and grumpy, don't write her about this. Her publisher only pass on letter where people telling her how wonderful she is, anyway. He is fast learner.

For people who is in general disgruntle state, Baba say, "Go get gruntle."

Chapter Twelve

Hryby
(Mushrooms)

Baba going to teach you all about cooking *hryby*, mushroom. This very Ukrainian thing.

Most important, ask someone who know about mushroom to go to woods with you. Must be expert and someone who like you. Otherwise, you can be poisoned. Back in Ukraina, Baba like to wear berry stain on lip, wink at Soviet or Nazi soldier and take into woods as far as possible. Then I feed him mushroom. Oop, is wrong mushroom. Oop, is dead Nazi. You think you and your girlfriend know how to laugh? You not been nowhere, sweetheart.

Or else you not so brave, go to stupormarket and buy good kind mushroom. Worst kind is white ordinary. Best variety is call *bilyi hryb*. In stupid Canada, everything is so mix up. You can usually only buy kind of mushroom close to Ukrainian in Italian store. Is call *porcini* or *boletus*. If you can't find, try instead kind called *chanterelle* or *oyster,* much more flavour. Dry *shitake* is tasty, but maybe have too strong flavor. Is your good guess. If you find Ukrainian mushroom call *pidpenky*, you double lucky. Go buy lottery ticket, too. Pidpenky is call honey mushroom.

If you get dry *porcini/boletus*, you going to have to soak in hot water hour or two to make soft. They usually have some dirt, so you going to pour away water you soak in. Or can use to soak bunion. Baba don't know if mushroom water have medicinal property, but it make your feet smell tasty.

Hrybova Pidlyva (Mushroom Sauce)

Start making this sauce very soon before dinner. Wash those mushroom with kind little brush you use on nail after gardening. If you not know what the hell I'm talking about, use soft toothbrush. Some mushroom they grow in manure. Which is nothing wrong, animal manure is friendly thing. Just not good to eat. Do not use this toothbrush on your teeth later.

Do not put in dishwasher or you be blowing bubble out your nose.

Slice up two apron full mushroom.

Start boil kettle water. Let cool little bit. Just like with make soup, secret good sauce is never use water straight from tap. If you can find water from well, even tastier.

Chop onion. Put mushroom and onion in big fry pan, medium heat, with butter. When onion almost clear color, add one clove crush garlic. Stir for one minute, then take out from pan with big spoon that have holes. Take out mushroom, too. Put in bowl.

Turn down heat little bit. Stir into this "all purpose" flour with fork, very fast, until it all turn beautiful brown color like romantic cow eye. Very slowly **pour in boil water**, keep stirring. This time, **use whisk**. If sauce too thick, pour in more water.

Put onion and mushroom back into frypan with sauce. S**prinkle salt and coarse ground black pepper**. Keep sauce on very low heat. If get too thick, add more water.

If you like, can add splash cooking sherry, especial if you going to pour sauce on good steak.

How to eat mushroom sauce:

On top *Kasha *(buckwheat), Chapter Twenty*
***With *Deviled Eggs with Mushroom Caps*,** *Chapter Seven*
***On top boil, steam or fry potatoes**. Especially good with tiny baby kind.
On top *Varenyky (Perogies) instead of butter. Especially good with potato kind. Can try sour cream with this, too. For Sviata Vechera, meatless Holy Eve, use soniashnyk or hemp oil instead of butter.
*Make what in Canada call **"stir fried."** Chop red and orange pepper, snow pea, broccoli, all kind vegetable you like, and fry quick in oil until soft. In meantime, steam nice potato with thin skin. Leave jacket on. Cut up and put in vegetables. Pour mushroom sauce in and mix together.
***On top rice**.
***On top steak**.

Big secret to make best tasting: Let mushroom sauce sit on rice, slice potato or whatever else you eat long enough to soak in. None this last minute ladle-schmadle. This sauce freeze pretty good for three, four month.

Ingredient List:

- Mushrooms, four pounds

- Cooking onions, two medium
- Butter, one quarter pound
- Garlic, one clove
- Flour, three tablespoons
- Salt and coarse black pepper
- Boiling water, one half cup. Keep kettle boiling
- Optional: splash of sherry

Easy Pickled Hryby

Make sure mushroom you choose not been near nuclear radiation like is happen in Ukraina and Japan.

Use one pound small button kind mushroom, fresh. Do not let me catch you trying mushy kind from can, taste like tin. Clean real careful so cap not come off stem.

Boil big kettle water. Put mushroom in big pot, and pour water so they are cover. Add two pinch salt and cook so simmering for fifteen minute. This mean not quite boiling, but looking like it spitting at you little bit. Pop pop pop!

Drain water from mushrooms into heat proof jar so you not waste. Can use later for delicious soup. **Leave mushroom on counter or fridge to cool while you boil big sealer jar ten minute**. Make sure jar is completely under water and both inside and outside get boil. And use tong, not bare hand.

Slice up small white onion. If your eye water, use google like I tell you in recipe for *Chicken Soup, Chapter One.*

Put layer onion in sealer jar, then layer mushroom. Layer, layer, like you building brick wall or saving whole month laundry for later. Leave little room at top for liquid. You not filling gas tank on boyfriend credit card, poopchik. This classy recipe.

In pot, mix two third cup vinegar with one half cup water, six whole black pepper, bay leaf, big pinch salt and big pinch sugar. Make boil, then quick! turn down so it just simmer ten minute.

Put this mix through strainer and make cool.

After mix cool, **pour on top mushroom in jar**. Add enough extra virgin olive or soniashnyk oil to fill almost to top. Put on cap.

Leave mushroom to pickle for twenty four hour before eating.

Get to work on your good soup with leftover liquid!

Your option:

***Try different kind vinegar**. Balsamic, wine, apple cider. If you use balsamic, no need to add sugar to liquid. Balsamic sweet.

Ingredient List:

- Small mushrooms, one pound
- Keep kettle of water boiling
- Salt, two teaspoons
- White onion, one small
- Vinegar, two thirds cup
- Whole black peppers, six
- Bay leaf, one
- White sugar, one teaspoon
- Extra virgin olive oil, one quarter cup (approximately)

Hryby i Smetana (Mushrooms with Sour Cream)

This one most popular traditional recipe, because it combine some our favorite food: mushroom, dill and good smetana. This recipe could have own TV show, "Forest Meet Barnyard with Baba."

Baba going to produce this show right after cookbook get publish. You friends with any TV people she can call? She know they love to hear from her.

One time Baba was on series TV show as Ukrainian dancer. But other girl, they dump tar on her costume because she is so star quality, camera always on her. At that time, Baba was stupid enough to think, "Go along to get along." She figure in old age, she deserve her own show.

Wash and slice mushroom. Cook onion in butter, but not till it get brown. Just soft and receptive to mushroom. **Pour in mushroom and cook till it look cook**. Baba not being smartypant. Cooking time depend on type of mushroom. Some is skinny, some is fleshy like your thigh. If mushroom burn, you know you was wrong.

Take out big bowl. Mix flour with smetana until is smooth like cellulite cream. Yes, Baba know she making fun. Only is backward what you think. In Ukraina, we is sane people. We think voluptuous thigh is beautiful. Cellulite cream is big rip off and you hate yourself. When Baba was fourteen, handsome boy tell her he fall in love with way her strong thigh flex on horseback. You listening? This is sanity.

Now stir in rest of smetana. Pour in mushroom and onion. Cook and stir until this mix juuuuust start to boil, then turn down to simmer. About "three" on dial. Baba refuse to give you microwave instruction because is just not appropriate. Microwave is where you should cook your cellulite cream.

Crush one half clove garlic. Here is how also to make seduction into marriage proposal:

One way to crush garlic is to put under board between mattress and box spring. Invite boyfriend and do some bouncing. While you making romance, smell of garlic will creep out. Boyfriend will associate your talent on mattress direct with excellent cooking. Is no better formula to get engage. After, lead him straight to kitchen and feed him this recipe. Then use your hand to feed dessert.

Add crush garlic, salt and pepper to mushroom and cream. Let simmer five minute, then add fresh mince dill.

Pour this recipe over *Lokshyna (Egg Noodles), Chapter Twenty One, Kasha, Chapter Twenty,* rice or potatoes. Can be one your meatless dish for Sviat Vechir.

Is also excellent side dish for so many other recipe, from chicken to beef to *Holubtsi, Chapter Fourteen.*

If all this fail to impress your guest or boyfriend, Baba give you bonus prize. When she sign your book, she put your real name and your friend will think you actual talk to her.

Ingredient List:

- Mushrooms, one pound
- Sour cream, one cup
- Small onion, one
- Butter, one quarter cup
- Flour, two tablespoons
- Garlic, one half clove
- Salt and pepper
- Fresh dill, one teaspoon

Fried Hryby

This is very simple mind recipe. Even Baba daughter with Master degree can make.

Wash and slice mushroom into thin piece. Put aside. Fry dice

onion in sunflower oil, extra virgin olive oil or butter until onion is goldie color. Man you love will already be standing behind, saying, "When is going to be ready?"

Don't lift apron at this point, or you burn recipe. **Shove onion aside in pan and throw in mushroom. Then put onion on TOP of mushroom**. This way, onion be done just right, because it in control of the cooking. Tell boyfriend this is natural order of thing, you show him later.

Sprinkle recipe with coarse black pepper, then put on lid. Let cook on low heat for ten minute. Mushroom juice will flow out and mix with oil or butter. They will cook themself real good. This is also natural order.

Mix up mushroom real gentle until they reabsorb some their own liquid and are delicious brown color. **Sprinkle with little bit salt**.

If you and man are not already on kitchen floor, immediate use mushroom same way as in recipe above. Baba thinking reheat may be necessary.

Ingredient List:

- Mushrooms, one pound
- Onion, one small
- Oil or butter, one quarter cup
- Salt and pepper

Battered Hryby

For this one you going to use very cute small mushroom. Wash mushroom, but for first time in your long non-lustrous career, **DO NOT SLICE**. If they wet, put on mechanic towel for super-absorbency. You don't want piece flimsy paper towel to cling to mushroom.

This is recipe with several step, so listen close to Baba:

Dip each one mushroom into flour mix with salt and pepper.
Dip each one mushroom into beat up egg dilute with splash water.
Dip each one mushroom in fine bread crumb.

You see? Genius of Ukrainian recipe is this double dip. Is like when expert makeup artist put on both good cream and powder blush, so it last eighteen hour. Not using that cheap crap from dollar store, either. Beauty is no place to make economy. We say, *Miser pay twice.*

Kiss your boyfriend, because for sure he still going to be hanging round after last mushroom recipe.

Turn oven to 350 degree F.

Fry all these dip mushroom in plenty butter. They going to turn goldie like sun.

Next step going to surprise you. We not done with these mushroom yet.

Arrange them in baking dish like they delicate flower. Put pinch each salt and pepper, and bake without cover for about five minute.

Serve as party favor or along meat dish.

Baba bet you think some Canadian pub invent fry vegetable. Ha! As if they think of this. They steal recipe from Ukrainian, but make such beautiful thing ugly. They not do the double dip and fry in good butter. They use same week old fat as for stinking french fry. Worst of all they fry cheap slimy zucchini. Lousy oil and zucchini is both Baba kryptonite. Just remember that.

Ingredient List:

- Small mushrooms, one pound
- Egg, one large
- Warm water, two tablespoons
- Flour, one cup
- Fine bread crumbs, one cup
- Butter, one quarter cup
- Salt and pepper

Baked Hryby

This recipe even simpler than fry mushroom and so elegant. Even Baba daughter who get PhD can make! Is so quick, you going to **preheat oven to 350 degree F** right now.

Wash large mushroom and cut each only in half.

Arrange overlap mushroom piece in long, presentable baking dish. Uh oh, Baba should have warn you about "presentable" part.

Take little bit care and time with this arrangement. Should be graceful like when blackjack dealer fan out card. Don't be making innocent eye here. You know exactly what Baba talking about.

Boil heavy cream. Watch careful and keep stirring whole time.

Sprinkle salt and pepper. Put small piece butter here and there on mushroom. Pour cream over top.

Bake in oven for half hour.

Take out with your best oven mitt, not one have ratso stuffing leaking from end. Yell, "Hot stuff coming through!" Someone should have put big coaster on dining room table. Someone else should make good joke about how mushroom is not the hot stuff. If not, then you hostessing wrong crowd, dorahenka.

Put out serving spoon. Guest can eat naked like it is, or ladle over starchy thing.

Your option:

***Add crumble bacon**, deli corn beef, kobasa (garlic sausage) or dice ham to baking dish.

Ingredient List:

- Mushrooms, one pound
- Salt and pepper
- Butter, one quarter pound
- Heavy cream, one half cup

Baked Hryby with Goat Cheese

Every Ukrainian have goat, even if only for decoration. Why you laughing? Some Canadian *banyak* have pink flamingo or rusty car. At least goat will lick your face. Sometime you get lucky and she make milk. Then what cheese you can have for cooking! Oi yoi yoi, it make Baba taste bud do small ecstasy dance. But we don't eat goat. They is person.

This is one more recipe need presentable pan and good mitt.

Butter small square baking pan.

Turn oven to 400 degree F.

Slice tomato from your own patch very thin. If you not have tomato patch, is time to change where you live. Oh well. Best kind tomato at stupormarket is "organic on vine." Cover bottom of baking pan with these slice.

Wash and slice mushroom very thin. Make card sharp layer on top of tomato. Sprinkle salt and pepper.

Brown bread crumb in butter. Remember how much taste is add by good deli or home bake rye, pumpernickel or black bread. Do not use Canadian cotton or chain store bread. **Brown crumb slowly so they not**

burn.

Sprinkle these crumb on top of mushroom. Smack your lip, but we not done yet.

Baba hope you already had presence of mind to make goat cheese. Don't tell her you didn't read recipe through before starting. She don't want to hear about these kind problem. Baba don't want to hear about any kind problem. Her day of being warm nurturer is over, maybe you can tell. You take her order or go marching somewhere.

Make crumble of firm goat cheese on top. Bake without covering for twenty minute.

Pull same routine out to table as in *Bake Mushroom*, above.

Ingredient List:

- Mushrooms, one pound
- Firm medium ripe tomatoes, two medium
- Salt and pepper
- Coarse rye bread crumbs, one half cup
- Butter, two tablespoons
- Butter for baking dish
- Firm goat cheese, two ounces

Hryb Sichenyky (Patties)

Mushroom sichenyky is for when you been eating too much meat lately and need tasty substitute. Baba try vegetarian Canadian patty from Vancouver hippie restaurant. Hoo boychik, they complicate. You have to cook this kind bean, that kind lagoon. Then you put some kind grain you can't pronounce in special order grinder until you going to pull hair out, you so hungry. No wonder restaurant charge about million dollar. They also try to make you think you being ecological hero, to spend so much money.

Here is pretty simple patty, by Baba standard. If you use gourmet mushroom, is going to be little bit more expensive. But at least won't take time you could use to ride horse or cook holubtsi.

Clean up mushroom. Baba discover oyster mushroom in Canada. She have to say is exceptional for sichenyky. Drain water real good and give them pat on head so they pretty dry.

Chop mushroom very fine and put in big mixing bowl. This is good time to take down food processing you have hiding in closet since three year ago. Forgive husband for buying this on your birthday and get to work. How you think he feel when you buy him book call "Cure for Male Rug Pattern Baldness"?

Throw hunk butter in big frying pan on medium. This is four or five on radio dial. Speak of devil, turn on polka music. Don't be so serious.

Chop up onion so piece is almost invisible. Fry for couple of minute until they yellow. If they get brown, throw out and start over.

Baba law: Always better to sacrifice cheaper ingredient for more expensive one. Or one easier to make than thing that is complicate. This is why politician should go to front line of war instead of our kid. But that is controversy for different book.

Pour onion butter into mushroom. Don't throw pan into sink just yet, even if you obsession-compulsive.

Throw in soft bread crumb. Is better if they rye, pumpernickel or black bread. Then you have something!

Add fine chop parsley or dill. Fresh, like always.

Beat up two medium egg. Add to mushroom mix. Egg is plaster going to hold these sichenyky together. Recipe is like building house, only different. You can't eat two by four.

Sprinkle in salt and pepper.

Mix up all ingredient, then take out your opera glove to make small patty. Enjoy squishing between finger. Not really. Rubber or latex work better.

Here come more that double dipping like in *Battered Mushroom* (above) that make Ukrainian food outrun all other. No one will ever guess why your recipe seem so easy, but have extra layer of flavor. Is like our personality: seem simple and friendly on top, but have subtle archeological layer you never dig through in whole lifetime.

Beat up nother egg with splash cold water.

Have medium bowl ready with dry, fine bread crumb. Don't be fool by this kind bread in stupormarket say thing like Winnipeg Rye, but weigh about as much as duck eyelash. Take yourself to real deli. Get bread with substantial income and hopeful future. If deli not have crumb, dry bread yourself. Baba can see you flapping eyelid like you never have stale bread in house before. This time, you have permission to do it on purpose.

Throw more butter into frying pan you left on stove. Put on low heat.

Dip patty into bread crumb.

Dip patty into egg.

Dip patty into bread crumb.

This is not misprint.

Fry patty in butter until they look done. They will get golden tan and tiny bit crunchy.

Sichenyky can be serve by themself, with green salad, vegetable plate or good soup. They have that kind personality like woman who don't always give good grammar, but she able to get marry five, six time. Get along with everybody. Maybe too much.

Your option:

***Try with any kind sauce in Baba *Sauce* chapter**. Mushroom sauce is too matchy-matchy.

Ingredient List:

- Mushrooms, one pound or equivalent dry
- Onion, one tablespoon
- Butter, one quarter cup
- Eggs, three medium
- Cold water, two tablespoons
- Soft bread crumbs, one cup
- Salt and cracked black pepper
- Fresh dill or parsley, large pinch
- Stale bread crumbs, one half cup

For more Sichenyky recipes, see Chapter Ten
For Hrybivka(Mushroom Soup), see Chapter One

Chapter Thirteen

Varenyky i Vushki (Perogies and Ear Dumplings)

Varenyky In North America, call Perohi (Perogies)

Call up all female friend and family to make varenyky. Is good time to gossip with girlfriend. I watch this sexy TV show, and all the time those women drinking drinking drinking, but not make varenyky. They need more thing to keep hand busy, you want my opinion. Also more delicious thing to eat, they so scary skinny. Man in Ukraina would scream and run away, you show him one these women. He think, "She not have appetite for life!" No wonder they have so much trouble find husband. That red hair one, I think she Ukrainian. Once she have baby, she start to look beautiful, have some round part on woman body.

They so selfish. Why they not making big bowl varenyky and pot of borshch, take to eat for poor people? You never see these woman doing good thing. All the time they starving, sitting in bar looking for investment banker, like fox trying to steal chicken. Men with no soul. These dry guy. They not dance *hopak* for these women, how she know he have energy in bedroom? Why she fall in love with bureaucrat, no creative talent? Why they not find good farmer? Even is gardener in Central Park, man in touch with life. These skinny-schminny, they barking up wrong alley.

Between you and me, you can also drink horilka while making varenyky, but then they turn out funny lopside. Better to wait until dinnertime. Okay, I get off my box of soap now and we make good food.

Varenyky with Cottage Cheese Filling

You going to need whole top of table, old clean bedsheet, good wooden spoon and lots of time to make. Just like anything good, you have to practice to make perfect ones. This recipe make about thirty varenyky.

First kind varenyky dough. This is traditional:

Sift white flour into big bowl to make fine. Make hollow well in bottom of flour. Warm milk, just so warm as you would make for baby bottle. Use wooden spoon, **Mix milk in this well with salt and one egg, beat up**.

Second kind varenyky dough:

This kind is stickier, so maybe you need more experience to do, after you get good with first kind. **To ingredient in flour well, add mash potato and soniashnyk, sunflower oil**. This dough will stay soft, but harder to roll out. Make more tender varenyky, once cooked.

Put hands into this and squeeze, just like milking cow. This called kneading dough. Mix with hands as quick as possible, or dough get tough. Dough is ready when feel smooth and not sticking to side of bowl.

Put dough aside for one hour, so it have time to think about becoming varenyky. This called *Varenyk Meditation*. Those New Age people not know what they missing. They eat my varenyky, they think they already having past life. You have cup tea now. Remember what I tell you about what drinking horilka do to your cooking.

Filling:

Chop onion very, very small and fry in good butter. Don't be cheat and use margarine, or not taste like real thing. Is traditional to cook in *konopli*, hempseed oil for Sviata Vechera instead of butter. Soniashnyk is other kind you can use.

Rub dry cottage cheese on sieve to make very fine. In some place you can buy this cheese called *Farmer Style*. If not, get kind from stupormarket. **Mix with onion and butter.**

Don't do this to all varenyky, because some people don't like. **Put to side maybe one quarter of cheese filling, and chop little bit very fine krop, dill weed, into this**. I call this *Extreme Varenyky*. Next time you can also try add clove crushed garlic. I call this, *Taste So Good, Who Care You Smell?*

Remember I tell you to have **whole top of table? That because you going to spread flour on at least half**, so dough not stick. **Spread bed sheet on table**. Better if clean and no flower type pattern to confuse you, "Where my varenyky?"

Sprinkle flour on sheet. Take dough from fridge, and tell friend to get rolling pin, do hard work. You supervise, they divide into four pieces. Roll each piece so dough about one-quarter inch thick. Your job to make friend laugh, so they not mind.

This most fun part: you and other friends **cut dough into nice circle with upside down water glass.** Not shot glass. Children like this very much. **While other piece dough wait their turn, cover with damp cloth, so not dry out**.

Put about tablespoonful of cottage cheese filling inside centre each circle. Make sure not spread filling to edge, or dough will not seal. You will know if you use right size spoon once you pinch sides together. Pinch, pinch, pinch, pinch. Make very firm seal, or they explode in boiling water and your whole day ruin.

Baba now going to teach you two varenyky pinching trick no one else will:

Smear little bit warm water on dough circle at edge so will stick better.

Start pinching varenyky at horn of crescent moon toward middle, not from middle outward. If you start in middle of moon, by time you get to horn, varenyk is going to look like Longhorn cow.

Once you almost finish pinching into little half moon type shape, **boil water in biggest pot you got. Put in pinch salt**. Boil enough varenyky at time so just same size as rim of pot. About twelve. When they getting ready to eat, they float to top of pot. This take maybe six minutes. When they floating, boil five more minute. **They done when all puffy from holding breath in water**. Be patient with varenyky. They little crescent moon shape to symbolize Ukrainian respect for lunar calendar.

In meantime, varenyky waiting their turn should be cover with clean cloth that have flour on it so they don't make sticking. Then they won't be dry thing. This is great idea any time you working with large quantity of dough waiting to be cook.

Take from pot with spoon have hole in it, so water drain from varenyky. **Put in colander. Toss very gentle with little oil, so they not stick together. Put them in large roasting pan with lid. Put in warm oven until all varenyky cook.**

How to eat:

You going to eat some right away, won't be able to help yourself. Will be like inhaling. Like President Obama say, "That is whole point." Baba not sure he talking about varenyky.

Have some butter sitting outside fridge, so nice and soft. Put little butter on varenyky, then good *smetana* from farm.

When you calm down little bit and able to chew food, you can do this: **fry lots butter in big pan. Chop onion into it. Fry varenyky until they have brown crispy outside.**

Can also add ring or small cube kobasa to frying pan. Baba guarantee people line up outside house when they smell all this cooking. Send your children out to sell things you can't dump on eBay.

To freeze varenyky: Clean out big flat space in freezer. Put verenyky, not touching, on oiled cookie sheet. Put in freezer. Write note on your hand, "Varenyky in freezer, don't forget!" When they freeze good, take from cookie sheet and put in plastic freezer bag or Tupperware. To save room, put out in snow bank.

Ingredient List:

- Regular dough
- Clean bedsheet
- Wooden spoon
- White flour, two cups
- Milk, one half cup
- Egg, one
- Salt
- Extra flour for sprinkling on table
- Sunflower seed oil for tossing varenyky

Potato dough. To above, add

- Mashed potatoes, one half cup
- Sunflower seed oil, three tablespoons

Cottage Cheese Filling

- One medium onion, chopped fine
- Butter, two tablespoons
- Dry cottage cheese or Farmer cheese, two cups
- Dill weed, two tablespoons

For each type of dinner varenyky, you'll need kobasa , fried onions and smetana. In whatever quantities seem reasonable. Also a huge pot of salted boiling water to cook them.

Non-Dairy Dough

Varenyky so tasty when you add different kind fat and Ukrainian kobasa. But if you cooking this dish for Sviata Vechera, everything have to be meatless. You can use oil. But no smetana, butter, kobasa, bacon or chicken fat. Serving animal fat for this holiday is like you offer Orthodox Jewish friend cheeseburger. Uh oh. Not kosher.

Mix up in huge bowl with salt.

Mix soniashnyk or konopli oil with warm water. Where I going to get hempseed oil Baba, you want to know. Is available in healthy food store. Is also big export business in Manitoba of hemp product. West Coast think it so advance, but while they getting all stone, Prairie person is making good legal business. Ha!

This warm water should be boil water you let cool. Not from tap where is strange fish making romance in tank.

Pour oil and water over flour. Make kneading motion. If dough way too sticky, add little bit flour. But don't go overboard, because too much flour make dough tough. Really, you should phone 1-900-ASKBABA for personal life coach.

Ingredient List:

- All purpose flour, six cups
- Salt, two teaspoons
- Hemp or sunflower oil, one quarter cup
- Boiled water cooled to lukewarm, three cups

Potato Filling

Make dough just like I tell you.

For potato filling, I tell you little secret: boil four huge or six medium huge potato inside skin, peel when they cool. This make peeling easier.

Fry onion in oil or chicken fat until they crispy brown. Add chopped chives, white and green parts. Leek good, too.

Shred cheddar cheese. Some people like mild, I think everything get better with old age. Or can use dry cottage cheese.

Mash potato very well. Mix with onion and fat from pan. Add one or two clove crushed garlic.

Mix cheese into onion, add salt and pepper.

Put tablespoon filling in dough. Remember: do not spread to edge, or verenyky will not seal.

Cook like cheese varenyky, above.

For Sviata Vechera, leave out cheese and use only oil for frying. Substitute extra cup potato and flavor with small bunch fine chop dill. Or you can go overboard on onion, leek or chive. Is still going to taste *duzhe smashnyy*, very delicious!

This potato filling, with or without cheese, is recipe you can serve on day you not feeling well and don't want to bother making pincharoni varenyky. Just smush everything in bowl and throw in front of family.

Garnish with cell phone so they notice something is happening.

Ingredient List:

- Potatoes, four huge or six medium, peeled
- Large onions, three chopped fine
- Sunflower oil or chicken fat, one quarter cup
- Chives or leeks, one bunch chopped fine
- Cheddar cheese, one cup OR
- Dry cottage cheese, one cup
- Crushed garlic, one or two cloves
- Salt and pepper

Kapusta (Sauerkraut) Filling

Make dough like I tell you. Better if you make *kapusta* at home. If you have to, buy kind in glass jar, never never kind from can. Blech. Acid thing in metal taste like garbage. Remember kapusta is pickle, but still raw. Taste much better if you cook a little before put inside dough. Then it get tender and mild.

Fry bacon. Save fat. When bacon cool, chop in little pieces.

Drain kapusta very well. Chop in little pieces. Sprinkle little pepper. No salt. Kapusta salty already.

Chop onion very fine, fry in bacon fat or butter. Add kapusta and fry few minutes. Add teaspoon caraway seed. This the spice make rye bread taste extra special.

Put kapusta, bacon and onion inside dough and pinch. Cook like cheese kind.

You can also fry kobasa, Ukrainian garlic sausage, in salo or oil. Put that inside varenyky with kapusta, instead of bacon. Veggie substitute sausage is fine thing.

For Sviata Vechera, use extra cup kapusta instead of meat. Fry in soniashnyk or hemp oil instead of with butter.

Ingredient List:

- Sauerkraut, two cups drained
- Bacon, one half pound fried. Reserve the fat OR

- Half cup butter
- Pepper
- Onion, one medium chopped fine
- Caraway seed, one quarter teaspoon
- Kobasa fried in butter, lard or oil can be substituted for bacon. Or use veggie substitute

Hryb (Mushroom) Filling

See *Vushky* (miniature dumplings), below *Fish or Meat Filling*

Linyvi (Lazy) Varenyky, Cheese Kind

This kind lazy thing you see only in Canada. If you ask me, is like eating soup from can, but all grandchildren say, "I have no time, Baba. I need do fancy hair, Baba. I too busy taking over corporation, Baba." Pah! *Kasha nasha, tativ borshch*, Baba say. *The kasha may be mine but the father made the borshch.*

In case you not guess, this mean some them my children and grandchildren more like male side of family. Which male, you want to know. Mind own beeswax and get into good fertility ritual, you.

But you know, I try *linyvi varenyky* once or twice. Like some thing in life, it taste pretty good if you close eye tight.

Here we go. **Rub dry or Farmer Style cottage cheese through sieve. Beat up egg and put together with cheese and melt butter and salt. Mix up** together until it all look like one yellow thing.

Add flour, mix it up until feel like soft dough. Make sure you feel with hands. If too squishy, add another half fist flour.

Sprinkle flour on kitchen table. Make dough into long shape like sausage. Only skinny sausage, like from cheap pig. Is best you deserve, making this thing. Press roll with hands to make kind of flat. **Make crissy-crossy kind design on top dough with knife. Turn over, and make crissy-crossy on bottom. Cut into triangles by make slanting. Put on oiled plate or cookie sheet, so not stick.**

Boil very big pot water with one teaspoon salt. Drop a few lazy varenyky in boiling water at time. They cook about four minutes. When they ready, they tell you by holding breath to be fat puffy. Take from water with holey spoon, put in colander to drain.

Melt butter, about two third size your fist.

Put varenyky in big bowl with melted butter. Keep them warm until all cooked.

Can fry in onion and butter, just like varenyky made by normal people, not like you and my grandchildren. Use smetana too.

Can also put buttered bread crumb on top: fry stale bread crumb with butter. Can add chop dill to this.

Ingredient List:

- Dry cottage or Farmer cheese, two cups
- Eggs, three
- Butter, one half pound
- White flour, one and one half cups
- Buttered or oiled pan to keep pieces from sticking together

Linyvi (Lazy)Varenyky, Potato Dough

Hoo boychik, Baba can't believe she is showing you second kind of lazy type varenyky. This kind not only easy, but very cheap to make. Don't even tell anyone I told you how to do this. Make my neighbor laugh. This something like Canadian hash brownie, only better.

Boil four large potato. When they cool, peel off skin and make into dice.

Start boil water in very huge pot. Mix together egg, milk, flour and salt. This make kind of dough.

Drop dough in water by teaspoonful. Boil for five minute. They make little dumpling.

Put half pound butter in pan. Yes, Baba say half pound. Potato drink butter like crazy. **Chop onion fine and fry in butter. Put potato dice in butter with dumpling. Fry until potato brown and soft. Put smetana,** maybe will taste like food.

Ingredient List:

- Large potatoes, four boiled, cooled, peeled and diced
- Egg, one
- Milk, half cup
- Flour, one cup
- Onion, one medium chopped fine
- Butter, one half pound

Dessert Varenyky

Varenyky with fruit is good dessert. While your relatives have ladder out picking crab apple for pie, make sure they also pick you tasty sweet plum and cherry.

You can also shake tree, make some fall down. Watch you head. **You need about eight to fifteen fat plum for this recipe.** If you more ambitious than average Canadian, pick six more plum for to make sauce. Read whole thing to find out why. You have to taste them before start to cook. If they sweet, you won't need sugar. If they not sweet, each one need one teaspoon sugar.

Make half as much dough as for dinner varenyky. This make about fifteen.

Roll out dough like I tell you. **Cut fifteen circles.**

If plum is small, cut into side and take out stone. **Put one teaspoon brown sugar or honey inside plum, close up.** Remember what I tell you: if plum already sweet, don't put sugar. **Put plum in dough circle and pinch pinch pinch.** If plum come burst through dough, you know is too big, okay? Not to be worry. We fix up next one.

With big plum, cut in half. Put one teaspoon brown sugar or honey in middle. Put half plum on dough circle. Pinch pinch pinch edge.

Cook just like cheese varenyky. I warning you, don't try eat with onion, garlic or kobasa. That just crazy. Some people like little bit butter. I like make *Plum Sauce, Chapter Twenty Two.*

Ingredient List:

- Make one half the varenyky dough recipe
- Plums, eight large or fifteen small
- Sugar or honey, one half cup

Berry Varenyky

You can make dessert varenyky with many kind berry: try blueberry, saskatoon, raspberry, strawberry. If you West Coast hippie-shmippie, try blackberry. Just don't put those funny kind weed inside. We grow that stuff in Ukraine, called hemp. But we use only for making rope and clothes, not for making stupid.

Make dough. Use two cup fat berry, put big tablespoon full inside

circle. Sprinkle little sugar and little flour or cornstarch on berry. Cook.

Ingredient List:

- Make one half the varenyky dough recipe
- Clean, hulled and pitted berries, two cups
- Honey or sugar, one half cup
- Cornstarch or flour, one quarter cup

Other Fruit

Make dough.

Use two cup peel, slice apple or cherry. Try sour cherry, if you can find. Usually in big jar at stupormarket. Use sugar that make sense with how sour is fruit, okay?

If you thinking about trying pear, grape or orange in varenyky, stop yourself.

Ingredient list:

- Make one half the varenyky dough recipe
- Clean, hulled and pitted apples, cherries or sour cherries, two cups
- Honey or sugar, one half cup
- Cornstarch or flour, one quarter cup

Vushky

Vushka mean "little ear." Is because you make these thing something like varenyky. Difference is they very tiny and you pinch pinch pinch edge so they look like ear from dwarf. *Vushky* is plural ear.

Then you plop! into soup like fancy dumpling. Into clear borshch and mushroom soup is traditional. But is so delicious, soon you will put little ear in all different kind soup. You can trade filling around between varenyky and vushky, too. Is like Ukrainian Rubik cube.

Here is what happen last time I make vushka:

One day Baba get tired of watching people turn cap backward and wear baggy pant all by themself. I go into hippity hop store and ask,

"How Baba become gangstah?"

They sell me Tupac shirt, hang down to my lambskin support hose. Then they tell me I have to bring back body part before I official become gangtsah.

This not part of Baba life plan. I thought gangstah mean I get to dance like breaking. I know how to throw babushka on ground and spin on head. It help if you have hair in bun. This act like kind of cushion. Mall store gangstah say this not possible at Baba level of initiation. What they could be thinking? I spend whole life dancing *hopak* and *kolomayka* like maniac. In high heel red boot with wild kozaky kicking all around me, yet. And these guy think I can't dance like breaking.

I go home and make pot of vushky. I take pot of ear back to hippity hop people and say, "There your body part. Now I am Shark gangstah." They laugh and say, "Baba, get hip. *Westside Story* is old school."

I say, "No, is old age. I make vushky and be in Shark gang, just like in movie. Anyone who can be gangstah, dance and sing at same time is Ukrainian in heart. Now eat good cooking and be chill."

They taste my vushky and tell me I am official gangstah Baba. I smile like I am thrill. Between you, me and fence post, dorahenka, these people in store never seen body part in their life. I am refugee from Stalin, and I know innocent when I see. Turn out I also know what is real gangstah.

Yo. What is up, poopchik? Pass *out*.

How to make vushky:

Make dough like Baba show you for varenyky, first recipe in this chapter. But this time, roll out dough very, very thin and cut them into square about dimension of your pointing finger on both side. How thin to roll? You will be able to see filling through the dough once cooked. If vushka was real ear, you would see wax. Don't take this literal.

Put spoonful of filling in middle and pinch. Dough will wrinkle when you boil. Is so simple you going to screw up if I don't tell you again: cook just like varenyky. Will make two, maybe three time as many vushky as varenyky with same recipe. Duh.

Drop vushky in soup. Is usual to do this with *Meatless Borshch,* under *Soup, Chapter One.*

These next two filling is traditional, but you can also use any filling I show you for varenyky, including dessert. Reverse visa, too.

If you hosting party for rootsy tootsy intelligentsia at art gallery opening, tell them is *Van Gogh Soup.*

Ingredient List:

Make dough just like for varenyky. Vushky use same filling, proportionately. And vice versa. So if you half the dough recipe, half the filling recipe. **One varenyky dough recipe will make sixty to one hundred vushky.**

Vushky i Varenyky Fillings

Hryby (Mushroom)

This extremely simple filling to make. Is fine for meatless Sviata Vechera meal. Just substitute hemp or soniashnyk oil for butter.

Chop onion real fine and fry in butter.

Clean and chop mushroom. Add few extra so you can do as many taste test as you need. **Add to pan and fry until look done.**

Season with salt and crack black pepper.

Take pan off heat and beat in raw egg yolk. Throw white on floor for dog to eat. It make lousy omelet without yolk.

You can put this filling in half of vushka and add chop fresh dill to other half of filling. Not everyone lucky enough to have "dill gene" that can handle great food. Poor slob.

Ingredient List:

- Make varenyky dough
- Onion, one medium chopped fine
- Butter, three tablespoons
- Mushrooms, two pounds make four cups when cleaned and sliced. Buy the fanciest quality you can afford. Do NOT use canned.
- Salt, one teaspoon
- Cracked black pepper, one half teaspoon
- Egg yolks, two raw
- Fresh dill, one small bunch chopped fine

Fish or Meat Filling

Again, so easy to make. And for one time I let you even use leftover. You going to need your energy make all those tiny ear.

Fish kind is another tasty and surprise filling for Sviata Vechera. Use oil, not butter. Grind up fish or meat, any kind you like.

Baba warning: do not combine fish and meat. Is no such thing as surf and turf vushky. Blech. See *Holubtsi (Cabbage Rolls), Chapter Fourteen* for recipe you give to your enemy.

Try: Ground beef, ground chicken, regular chicken. Baba see your hopeful dopey face, but hot dog and *Spam* not going to work. Kobasa taste great when you mix with other meat. If you too broke for kobasa, you can buy meat end at deli. Chop up good and mix in with cheaper meat. Veggie type sausage also going to work.

Almost any lake or ocean kind fish work, except kind from can. Don't make people sick.

Juries is out on Fukushima, but Baba want you to be careful. Only use kind of fish have his own two eye. Not three. And especial don't eat fish look like Sochi bear, model after Putin. Creepy eye in middle of his forehead. Give Baba nightmare.

Cook onion in butter, then mix with meat or fish.

Make little bit moist with two egg yolk, good thick gravy or Cream Sauce, under *Pidlyvi (Sauces), Chapter Twenty Two.*

Add salt and pepper. Like with mushroom filling, can add fresh dill.

Your option:

*For gangstah initiation and Hallowe'en, **add red food coloring** to vushka dough. Or black---say is petrified ear.

Ingredient List:

- Make varenyky dough
- Fish OR meat, two cups ground and cooked. Your choice: perch, sole, red snapper, halibut, catfish, cod, bluefish, trout, flounder. Canned fish and meat are out of the question.
- Onion, one half chopped fine
- Butter, two tablespoons
- Salt, one teaspoon if not using a salty meat like kobasa

- Pepper, one half teaspoon cracked
- Egg yolks, two OR gravy, one half cup
- Fresh dill, two tablespoons chopped leaves

Your option with all type varenyky and vushki: mix sour cream gentle with caper. This is more Baba Ukrainsky Fusionski. She doing lots fusing lately.

Chapter Fourteen

Holubtsi
(Cabbage Rolls)

Meatless

Holubtsi mean dear little pigeon. You probably call cabbage roll. This sound not too romantic. When I make holubtsi, men line up on village street. They say, “Oh Baba, can I be little pigeon in your hand, too?”

I send them chop wood. They come back and give me foot massage with big rough hand. Then I make sound like pigeon. *Croo, croo, croo.* Maybe then I feed them. Ha!

I show you how to make holubtsi like real Ukrainian. First, get neighbor to come over and help. This long job. Also, taking core from cabbage is boring. This first kind have no meat. Stalin steal our cow and pig, and for long time I only make without.

This not make me vegetarian. So don't be telling all your hippie-shmippie friend, “Go see Baba.” I live in BC with grandchildren. I drink horilka and stick nail in tire of Volkswagen van for big kick. Then I put pedal to metal in my Rocket 88. I help my grandson take engine from boring Oldsmobile and fit in my red '68 Caddy for real ride. They call me *Cadillac Kozachka.*

This recipe make twenty or thirty pigeon.

Baba going to show you two method for peeling cabbage:

1. Take core from big head cabbage. Use very sharp knife. Make small “v” beside core on two side, then cut down and make wiggle wiggle wiggle until core come out. Also is patent tool for doing this, if you can find. Not sure if invented by Ukrainian. Probably. We invent helicopter, xray, immunology, pants and horse tack. So why not paring tool?

Put head cabbage in biggest pot and steam or boil on low until outside leaf look soft. Watch careful. If cabbage get mushy, you have to go back to store. No exception. If you really smart, you buy two head cabbage in first place.

2. Clean out your freezer so have room for head cabbage. This way might look easier, but Baba not so sure. Look inside freezer first. Put whole head cabbage in plastic bag. Stick inside freezer and leave alone for at least forty eight hour. OR, if is middle of winter, lock it in trunk of that junky car in front your trailer. Don't forget where you leave it, or in spring your relative will have to move out of car because of smell.

This mean you have to plan ahead. So again, not easy.

Take cabbage out from freezer and bag night before. Put in colander thing and let thaw without disturbing. If you make disturbance, cabbage might believe it better off without you.

Next day, take out core like Baba tell you. Cabbage leaf will almost fall off by themself. Have clean towel waiting, because leaf will be wet.

Peel and chop three medium or two large onion. Here is trick so you not cry: when daughter not home, go steal swimming google. Kind make her look like bug eye insect. Only not tell her she look like this. Wear before starting to peel onion. Also, can peel onion under cold running tap water. Then wash hand with soap, rinse, and rub hand along metal tap until smell all gone. This trick on tap also work for garlic smell.

Fry onion in butter until they looking clear and whole kitchen smelling.

Wash google and put back. I warn you: when daughter find out, she scream and cry. What you care? Is in interest of science.

Cook long grain white rice or brown rice with just enough water to cover. If you usually use four cup water, use just two. Watch rice. You want to be only cook enough to soak up water, but still a little hard. Brown rice have more B vitamin and very good for woman hormone.

Mix rice with onion. Put salt and crack black pepper. Do not use crazy ground pepper from dollar store. This tasteless. Holubtsi very cheap to make. Spend little bit money on good pepper. Even better, you buy whole pepper and make good looking man grind for you.

Baba law for compromise: Put half of rice and onion mix in another bowl. Mix in chop fresh dill for real Ukrainian taste. Some people have twisty kind taste bud, not like dill so much. Tell them, “Eat other kind,” then don't invite over again.

Grease large roasting pan (size like you roast chicken) with *soniashnyk,* sunflower oil. We call flower this because she follow sun around all day with her face, so beautiful. Line roaster with largest cabbage leaf, make nest for little pigeon. So cute.

Big surprise this recipe: NO GARLIC.

Spread big clean sheet on kitchen table. Not same one you use for varenyky (perohi), or they be jealous each other. Beside, if you clumsy and splash tomato juice on sheet, then where your varenyky be? Put big greased roasting pan close by. Not on chair, or some stupid neighbor sit in it. People always screaming, "Lawsuit!" so be careful with this thing.

But maybe your dupa get stuck in pan, you be mad, too. I think they make too big deal, anyway. Last time this happen, I try explain grease make it easy to slide out. But she not listen. Next thing I know, shyster at door with some kind paper, saying, "People Court." And they say this some kind democracy. Worse thing, I have to start over greasing roaster for holubtsi.

Baba can't believe she saying this, but is better than yet nother stupid lawsuit: **Let rice, kasha and any other filling get Joe Cool before you put into cabbage leaf.** Hot filling is hot. You can burn yourself. Also, water is wet. Wet water will make you wet. Knife is sharp, butter is greasy and how high is moon.

And you can be sure, you ever sue Baba, she going to write about and talk about on national TV and in magazine. You like one these story be about you, *diurna* loser, go ahead.

You and neighbor take cool cabbage leaf, spread on sheet. With big spoon, put filling inside. Tuck end inside leaf and roll, roll, roll. If you already know how to make own cigar, you be finest kind holubtsi cook. I like small dessert cigar, soak in plum horilka call *slivovitz.*

Use eye like eagle, look this way and that to judge how much rice to put. I know you get upset, say, "Baba, I need measurement!" Look, poopchik, no such thing as government regulation cabbage leaf size. Use brain to measure, okay? If you put too much rice, it spill from end and baby pigeon be ugly thing. If you put too little, you have anorexic pigeon. There your measurement. Pah!

Make neighbor help you put holubtsi in bottom roaster, tight against each other. Put seam on bottom, so they not unroll. Pigeon cuddle lots in nest. Make layer.

Heat oven to 400 F. Put aluminum tray on rack, bigger than roaster to catch juice overflow. Kind you use when baking large turkey. Later, you thank me for this. Later, you thank me for everything.

When roaster two-third full, pour big can of tomato juice on holubtsi. Same size can as when dog get spray by skunk, not size you always pouring in Bloody Mary. You can also try some this V-8 juice mix half-half with tomato. Just don't pour any in V-8 Cadillac, or you be sorry.

Baba warning: if holubtsi are all the way to top, you need bigger roaster! This time I let you transfer some to another roaster. Go buy real roaster for next time.

Make sure is room for juice to bubble, or you have mess in oven. Pigeon not duck. Can't swim! So use enough juice to cover about two-third of holubtsi. Cover with left over cabbage leaf. Snug like in bed.

Put lid on roaster. Cook for half-hour at 400 F, then turn down to 350 F for one and one half hour.

How many holubtsi will you make, you asking. If you was more intimate with cabbage, you would know it have about twenty leaf.

Your option:

*For extra tongue tingle, **use boiling soup or mushroom stock instead of water to cook rice.** This is Baba tip you can use almost anytime, except in coffee. Gross.

***Use scalded milk instead of water, and add quarter cup butter to rice.**

***Substitute jasmine** rice for sweeter taste. This is part of Baba *Nouveau Ukrainski Fusionski* menu.

Ingredient List:

- Clean bed sheet
- Huge greased roasting pan
- Two large cabbages. One is a spare
- Onions, two large or three medium
- Butter, three tablespoons
- Long grain brown or white rice, three cups dry
- Fresh dill, one bunch chopped fine
- Salt, half teaspoon
- Cracked black pepper, half teaspoon
- Tomato juice, 32 oz. can. Can mix with V-8 for variation in taste

Hryby (Mushroom) Holubtsi

See *Mushrooms, Chapter Twelve*, for how to pick mushroom. If you have to buy at stupormarket, get best quality you can afford: Ukrainian *bilyi hryb* or *pidpenky*. If no such thing as usual, buy: *oyster, chanterelle* and so on. Desperate last resort is scary white kind, no taste. You have to fry in lots butter and some garlic to make taste like food. Sorry, but those Chinese dry mushroom have wrong taste mix for holubtsi too, so don't get wild idea and ruin recipe.

If you broke but really drooling for mushroom holubtsi, mix gourmet mushroom with white kind, half to half.

Make just like Baba show you in recipe above. But this time **cook only two and half cup rice, not three.** This leave room for mushroom, got it? You going to chop apron full of nice clean mushroom and fry real good in butter and onion.

Baba going to let you substitute extra virgin olive oil for other kind holubtsi if you want, but not this kind. Mushroom have to make partnership with butter to bring out best taste.

Mix onion and mushroom in with rice. Divide mix in half and stir hand full chop dill into one half.

If you didn't listen to Baba and used 100% cheap mushroom, this is point where you feel sorry. Recipe just not smelling like you want to eat with bare hand. Baba say, make sign of cross and continue. Go in bathroom, look in mirror and make phony smile like when police come. You going to need this smile when you serve cheap mushroom holubtsi. Also when you have nerve to ask Baba to sign this book. If you tell her you use can mushroom, she going to let pen explode on front page and your too-tight blouse, poopchik.

Baba law: is always better to serve plain thing than bad fancy substitute.

Ingredient List:

- Clean bed sheet
- Huge greased roasting pan
- Two large cabbages. One is a spare
- Onions, two large or three medium
- Butter, one half cup
- Long grain brown or white rice, two and one half cups dry
- Mushrooms, gourmet. One to one and one half pounds chopped
- Fresh dill, one bunch chopped fine
- Salt, half teaspoon
- Cracked black pepper, half teaspoon
- Tomato juice, 32 oz. can. Can mix with V-8 for variation in taste

Kasha (Buckwheat) Holubtsi

For surprise taste with high protein, use *Baked Kasha recipe, Chapter Twenty*.

Exception: bake for only thirty minute before putting kasha in holubtsi, or will be too dry at end of recipe.

Two cup dry kasha will make six cup cook. This is equal to using three cup dry rice.

Can use tomato juice like above, or pour two cup smetana over holubtsi. **Fill roaster one third full** with some kind broth. About two cup. Can be vegetable, chicken or beef.

If some neighbor at Ukrainian hall always making people "Ooh" and "Aaah" over her usual holubtsi, buckwheat kind with sour cream will steal her thunder thigh. Don't try to tell Baba you not enjoy when you find her crying in washroom. Bonus point if you pretend to comfort.

Also try *Smetana Sauce with Green Onion* in *Pidlyva* *(Sauces), Chapter Twenty Two.* In this case, you not going to have to simmer sauce. Pour smetana sauce on top of holubtsi before cooking. Oy Bozha.

Ingredient List:

- Baked Kasha Recipe, Chapter Twenty
- Broth, two cups
- Smetana or Smetana Sauce with Green Onion, UNCOOKED

Kasha i Syr (Cheese) Holubtsi

Here is Baba intrepid invention:

Mix four cup cook kasha with two cup dry cottage or Farmer cheese OR five cup cook kasha with one cup old age cheddar or firm goat cheese.

Is tasty with tomato juice or sour cream sauce.

Kasha i Hryb (Mushroom) Holubtsi

Make substitute of five cup cooked kasha for rice in *Mushroom Holubtsi* recipe, above. Leave out dill. This is not soulmate with kasha.

Either tomato juice or smetana sauce is lip smack territory with these holubtsi.

If you want absolute outrageous holubtsi that going to be blue ribbon prize win in any kind fair, **mix in half cup shred old age cheddar or firm goat cheese with kasha and mushroom**. No reason you can't do this if you using rice, too.

Holubtsi with Meat (or Vegetarian Ground Beef)

Make mostly like I tell you before. But this time you going to **make only two cup rice or other grain, not three. Then mix in with hand one pound raw ground meat. Add salt and pepper.** If you squeamish kind person, put on rubber glove before mixing. Probably better to wash glove before using again for wash dish. My granddaughter go to this Food Safe. Next thing I know, never mind wash glove, she even spraying bleach on dog. Use your reasonable mind.

Any kind meat okay: beef, pork, lamb. Lean is better. In Canada, I like very much ground bison or venison. Moose and caribou not so good for holubtsi. Ground sausage very good too, mix with half mild kind meat. If you use kobasa (garlic sausage), have strong taste.

If you is broke, get package of meat end from deli. Sometime you find real expensive thing in there: proscuitto, corn beef, etc. Baba is regular hand slapper at deli on weekend, when other people reaching in there like cow fighting over lost cud. Do not use kind that have any kind "loaf" like chicken or turkey. If it look like *Spam*, it is. Blech.

Mix one-quarter pound sausage chopped fine with three-quarter pound other kind meat. You can mix any kind: lamb with beef, beef with pork and so on. Lamb have no cholesterol, too.

Once you make perfect holubtsi, some neighbor will be jealous. Usually kind of neighbor, she flipping hair around and act like her grandchildren better than yours. She call police when you hang bloomer on line, then smile in your face. She make sweety-sweety in neighbourhood and make bomb in her kitchen. She is Soviet in heart.

What Baba hate most is this kind person force me to be sneaky to survive.

Here how: do not tell neighbor what kind meat is perfect combination. Tell her secret is to send husband to lake, catch some kind fish. Then grind fish into holubtsi. Even better, if you live on West Coast, tell stupid neighbor, "Best kind holubtsi filling made from salmon and lamb. I telling only you this secret. Shhhhhhh." She will learn lesson, big time I am telling you.

Rest of recipe and cooking is same like meatless holubtsi, above.

Your option:

*You feel fancy? Instead just one kind rice, mix with this Middle Eastern **cous-cous, or crack wheat** (bulgur). These kind have to be soak in hot water, first, to make soft before add to rice. **Canadian wild rice** great and not have to be soak. But expensive.

***Add sprinkle chop fresh dill to all holubtsi, or just few.** Put ones with dill on one side roasting pan, so you know which kind.

***Add sprinkle caraway seed** on top.

***Chop *pidpanky*, nice Ukrainian mushroom, fry in butter and add to rice.** Or try *chanterelle, oyster* or some other fancy kind at stupormarket.

***Use this V-8 juice instead plain tomato.** I don't know what juice have to do with my Rocket 88 engine, but I find many strange thing in this country.

****Yves* company make real good veggie ground hamburger and sausage.** Baba used to buy *President Choice* and other Loblaw brand until she find out they sell horse meat, and also promote *Top Chef Show*, make horse meat. Baba organize BIG boycott. Horse is her heart. Soviet steal and slaughter three million horse. Watch out PC, you make big sacrilege. Horse god not going to forget you.

*Warning of big mistake: my sister get clever and use this clam and tomato juice. Don't bother. You have Baba permission tell jealous neighbor do this.

*Next big mistake: don't use tomato soup or ketchup instead tomato juice.

Ingredient List:

- Two large cabbages. One is a spare in case you rip the leaves
- Onions, two large or three medium
- Butter, three tablespoons
- Long grain brown or white rice, two cups dry
- One pound lean chopped meat: beef, pork, lamb, venison, bison. OR three quarters of a pound ground beef and one

quarter pound kobasa or other strong sausage.

- Fresh dill, one bunch chopped fine
- Salt, half teaspoon
- Cracked black pepper, half teaspoon
- Tomato juice, large can. Can mix with V-8 for variation in taste
- Clean bed sheet
- Huge roaster with lid

Linyvi Holubtsi (Lazy Cabbage Rolls)

These good kind holubtsi for when you tired rolling, and everyone tired of you bossing them to roll. Make for yourself, and tell everyone, "You not help, you not eat."

Use same ingredients like above. Only this time, don't bother core cabbage, thank God. Just make shred. If you even lazier, buy shredded package from store.

Cook onion in hugest fry pan, with butter. When almost done, add shred cabbage. Stir until it wilt little bit.

Put in salt and crack black pepper.

Pour in tomato juice and stir.

Don't need sheet on kitchen table this time.

Heat oven to 350 F.

With big spoon, put layer of cabbage and onion on bottom of biggest roasting pan.

Put layer of rice, or rice mix with other kind grain.

Another layer cabbage, another layer rice.

Pour more tomato or V-8 juice until two-thirds covered. See above for bubbling instruction.

Make topping from butter bread crumb: take cube stale bread and toss in fry pan with melted butter. Can also toss with chop dill.**Cook one hour.**

Your option:

***Add chopped kobasa** or good ham. Canadian bacon tasty, too.
***Add chop fresh dill** or sprinkle caraway seed.

Ingredient List:

- Skip the bed sheet
- Huge greased roasting pan
- Two large cabbages. One is a spare
- Onions, two large or three medium
- Butter, three tablespoons
- Long grain brown or white rice, three cups dry
- Fresh dill, one bunch chopped fine
- Salt, half teaspoon
- Cracked black pepper, half teaspoon
- Tomato juice, large can. Can mix with V-8 for variation in taste
- Buttered stale bread crumbs

Chapter Fifteen

Syr (Cottage Cheese)

Because Ukrainian have such close relationship to cow and goat, we always thinking, "What exciting thing can I make from same old stuff? Always this cheese cheese cheese coming out from cow and goat, and I eat. Day after day. Enough to drive you out from mind."

Baba joking. We so spiritual people, we never tired of what we have. Except for: hair, shoe, dress, car, house, furniture, job and some time, husband. Also poverty, flooding, Chornobyl radiation and our Evil Neighbor, Russia.

You going to laugh when Baba tell you how simple is this recipe. If you running your behind for lunch or friend drop over with gossip and you not have time to cook, make

Syr Dip

Mix one cup dry cottage cheese or farmer cheese with half cup good smetana. Or, one cup two percent OR whole cottage cheese with quarter cup smetana. Think for minute. I know you catching on. By way, farmer cheese is not cheese made from farmer. If you try this crazy thing, he going to run too fast for you to catch.

Add salt or garlic salt. Add real garlic if friend who drop by is business rival, and she have to go back to work after lunch. If she ask, "Is this garlic?" say, "No, is negative calorie soy granule. New overprice product from *Lululemon*, you yuppie-hippie yoga face."

Serve with good rye or pumpernickel bread, toasted. Tasty to dip bagel and those artisan crisp, too. Not so bad with corn chip. Or Cheezie. Even ketchup flavor potato chip. Wait, Baba getting carry away from being your Good Nutrition Hostess.

Put cheese dip on:

*__Steam baby potato__
*__Brown rice__
Lokshyna *(Egg Noodles), Chapter Twenty One*
*__Rice stick__ from China Town

**Kasha* *(Buckwheat Porridge) Chapter Twenty*

Baba know you not exactly dipping when you put dip on top of something, but don't let stupid semantic get in way of good food. What she suppose to do, print same cheesy recipe twice and give two different title?! Might as well become cheesy romance writer. Blechorama.

You can also mix into cheese dip:

***Fine chop chive**
***Fine chop fresh dill**
***Crumble bacon**
***Soy bacon bit**
***Fresh Asiago or Parmesan cheese.**
***Pinch caraway seed.** This match caraway seed on pumpernickel bread. Very fashionable. Match better than your purse and shoe, Baba betting.
***Fine chop black or green olive.** Fresh only for black olive. Kind in can not worth giving to food bank, even if you mean spirit kind of person who donate worst food there. Don't be liar. Baba been to food bank once or twice. Also to thrift store where you giving shirt with armpit stain. Just remember: Goddess Berhenya watching, poopchik.
***Mix in teaspoon coriander or curry powder.** This not particular Ukrainian, but Baba have mind open like your thigh in college.

Ingredient list:

- Dry cottage cheese, one cup OR
- Creamed cottage cheese, one cup
- Sour cream, one quarter to one half cup. See recipe for explanation of varying amounts.
- Pinch salt or garlic salt
- Rye or pumpernickel bread

Syr Spread

You going to have to listen close to catch subtle difference here from *Cheese Dip.*

Take dry cottage cheese and add just enough smetana to make moist and you not choke.

Mix in any of option in *Cheese Dip*, above your head. Spread on bread.

This is spread, like Baba say. Too stiff to put on rice or noodle. If you dip potato chip while you watching TV, chip will shatter and make itch in cleavage. Sure, like you watch TV full dressed. This why they call "boob tube." Ha!

Syr Halushky (Dumplings)

If you thought Baba was generous teaching you *Lazy Varenyky* (perohi), you not know extent of her hospitality. Baba is sure you scratching scab on head and saying, "These dumpling no different from lazy varenyky!"

Try to practice subtle positive discrimination once in your life, okay?

You be thrill to hear you don't have to make soup to drop these dumpling. They stand out on their own.

Halushky is Ukrainian kindergarten but so delicious, you be Top 40 smash hit at next party. Everybody going to talk about you like they do when my friend Halyna take one piece silk cloth, wrap around her figure with no panty or bra and have best sexy dress at party. When she wave hand and say, "Oh, no no, was simple really," no one believe her.

Because she don't want no one to believe her, get it?

Going to be same reaction with these halushky:

Leave chunk butter out overnight so is soft.

First make butter bread crumb. Toss crumb in butter in hot pan. Brown under broiler.

Press cottage cheese or farmer cheese through sieve so cheese is fine fine.

Mix with soft butter and two egg yolk. Don't get insane diet mind on Baba here. Egg white dumpling is not going to get you admire at party, poopchik.

Start huge pot of water boiling furious. Add pinch salt.

Mix cheese with cream of wheat. Of course dry. We not all of sudden going to put down cheesy buttery yolky thing and eat creepy bland cereal. Cream of wheat is only binder. **Put in just enough so is easy to shape cheese mix into many small ball. Do this on board with flour.** It make about two dozen. Depend on how you handle ball.

Drop halushky gentle into boiling water, only few at time. They going sink to bottom. Don't be worry. They only stay down there so long as they can hold breath. Just like when mad kid hold breath and say they going to die. Pretty soon they coming up for air. All you have to do is stand there with arm crossed and foot tap tap tap. **Every once in while give little stir,** just like I know you can't help giving kid little poke.

Baba joke: What is difference between mad kid and halushky?,
Answer: Don't wait for halushky to turn blue. It won't.
Hahahahahahahahaha.

Put cooked halushky in colander to drain. Use big spoon with hole.

Melt butter. Put drained halushky in nice serving dish, pour butter on top. Toss very soft so all covered in butter.

Sprinkle with butter bread crumb. Put dish of smetana on side so guest can help themselves. This is place where you bend little bit to stupid Canadian diet mind. Put out one dish real sour cream, another you tell people is low fat sour cream. Does Baba really go out and buy two kind? Is Pope waterproof? Entertainment is all smoking in mirror.

Your option:

*__Fry clove crush garlic__ in pan with bread crumb
*__Add garlic__ when you melting butter
*__Add fine chop fresh dill__ to melting butter
*__Fry white or red onion,__ toss with cooked halushky
*__Add fine chop fried kobasa__, summer sausage, corn beef or crumble bacon to final product. Yves company make very good veggie kind.

Ingredient list:

- Dry cottage cheese, two cups
- Egg yolks, two
- Softened butter, two tablespoons (for cheese mix)
- Uncooked cream of wheat, one third to one half cup
- Salt
- Melted butter, half cup (to pour over halushky)
- Butter, two tablespoons (to make buttered bread crumbs)
- Pumpernickel or rye bread crumbs, one cup
- Sour cream, one cup. Full or low fat according to your conscience

Crazy Gourmet Syr Halushky

Use same ingredient as above. Hold on your horse, we about to go overboard. This not traditional Ukrainian, but Baba is addict for all different kind of cheese. She is great inventor, which you already know.

To cottage cheese mix, add: fresh Asiago, shred Parmesan, firm goat, Swiss or cheddar. Cheddar can be mild, medium or sharp. Why they call sharp when is impossible to cut with, Baba don't know. Is another mystery of stupid English language. Nothing is call what is. Whoever invent this language have sideway mind instead of good straight one, like Ukrainian. We say ax is sharp, cheese is strong or mild.

Cream cheese is silly idea. Cream cheese halushky going to make explosion in pot. If you free spirit experimental kind person, bleu cheese can work if very firm. Baba would try only few of these, see if you like taste. Softer kind bleu cheese also will explode. Blue spore on kitchen wall not too appetizing.

You going to have to adjust amount for cream of wheat, depend on how dry or sticky is extra cheese. **Mush halushky good with hand**; ball should feel like young sheep testicle. Will make two dozen ball, more or less.

Cook just like ordinary halushky. Can always make half and half kind, like in Baba law under *Deviled Eggs II to Infinity, Chapter Seven.*

Ingredient list:

- Make *Cottage Cheese Halushky*
- Preferred hard cheese, one half cup
- Sour cream, one cup. To use on side.
- Buttered bread crumbs, one cup

Syrnychky (Cheese Patties)

If you looking for light alternative to hamburger patty or veggie burger, here is. And this blow slice sandwich tofu out of bathwater.

Press cottage cheese or farmer cheese through sieve. If you too lazy bone to press cheese through sieve, go to India Town and buy *paneer*. Ask nice person at front desk which one in fridge is patty, instead of solid block. Otherwise you back at squared one and have to press it yourself. Like you suppose to.

Dip paneer patty in flour, then fry.

Mix sieved cheese real good with two egg yolk and whip cream. You can't buy only one tablespoon cream; Baba hope you invite her over for whatever plan you make for rest of carton.

Add salt.

Have cup flour ready. Add only little bit at time to make syrnychky stick together. No, we not using cream of wheat like in halushky (cottage cheese dumplings, above). Flour make nice brown crust on patty. Cream of wheat just lay there like Presbyterian on honeymoon.

Here is where your big "freedom of choice" come in. Uh oh. Baba know you like TV to tell you what to do, but Ukrainian cooking demand you use brain cell. Ready? You can make few patty big enough to put between bread slice, OR can make small, cute patty people will just eat in hand. This recipe make up to two dozen small one, or eight to twelve large. This is estimate. You think Baba have time to stand over you and make sure how many?

Fry patty in butter pan until goldie-brown. Flip over, even though you yakking on cell phone and bored already with frying just one side.

Put in attractive serving dish. Smetana is in side dish.

Your option:

Dip small syrnychky into *Plum, Tartar* or *Honey Onion Sauce, *Chapter Twenty Two*. If you like more zing zing taste, mix **teaspoon balsamic vinegar** into plum sauce.

*Even though basic ingredient is cheese, you can still be holy hog and top burger-style patty with **strong taste kind cheese:** Bleu, sharp cheddar, Swiss, firm goat and so on. And of course any kind good topping you usually put on burger: **tomato, lettuce pickle, bacon.**

Syrnychky not marry well with relish, ketchup or mustard. Is too sophisticate for this kind plebian nonsense. Is good *Hryb (mushroom) Sichenyky* in *Chapter Twelve.*

Ingredient list:

- Dry cottage cheese, two cups OR paneer patties
- Egg yolks, two
- White flour, one half cup
- Butter, one quarter cup
- Sour cream, one cup

Chapter Sixteen

Riba (Lake Fish)

Baked Stuffed Riba

Baba going to teach you how to catch, stuff and bake fish. It always taste better if you catch yourself, not buy from row of staring eye in stupormarket. If you like to swim in lake like Baba, all the better.

One day I make mistake and not catch any fish. This because I like swim naked and not too careful. I swim swim swim about one hundred feet from beach, then take off bathing suit and tie around my leg. Where you think I put, on my head? Oh. I forget. We in North America.

Last summer I leave grandchildren with babysitter so I can have solo swimming adventure. I see this kind cooler like made from styrofoam float on middle of nice warm lake. I want to focus on goal to swim to. And maybe catch fish with my teeth, like in Ukraina. Or maybe have to use hand, now I have stupid denture.

I stand up in water to do this fancy-shmancy running like racehorse in swimming pool. I am bucking naked and my belly and boobala holding me up real good. If you got those things, you not need stupid floating belt like anorexia women at intelligentsia swimming pool.

I am running real good, and every once in while, dip eye under water to see if trout underneath. No luck. But I thinking run-swim to cooler is real good workout, and maybe inside is sandwich and beer. Sun feel very nice on naked back, and lake water churn on my legs.

I get real close and reach out hand to open white box. My mouth watering, tasting what is inside. My hand getting closer closer till almost touching, then pop! up come head from water. Is big-eye man in glass window mask. I squint my good eye and see cooler is really oxygen air tank, and this man is attached. He look real surprise, like why big naked Baba is going to turn off my oxygen air?

I flip round in water like crazy woman and run real fast back to shore. Good thing man he too surprise to follow me, because he not so good looking in mask.

I not catch one single stupid trout that day. I too upset from run-swim all that way and not get no beer or ham sandwich. Too bad, today you not get lesson in how to catch fish with teeth. Buy from store already. I going home to shake sand from bathing suit. I so wild on way back to beach I forget to untie from leg and it drag on bottom. I put on fast and get crazy rash on *kvitichka*. See *Yeast Infection* under *Ukrainian Medicine, last Chapter*. Never mind my trouble. **We going to cook:**

Take large fish, maybe three pound for four people. Take away gut and scale or get someone do for you, you big baby. Leave head on fish. Throw gut to chicken in yard. They will go like nutcase, squawk and peck. Dog will get in there too. I warning you, don't let him lick your face later. Just like you not let him after he polish his silverware.

Rub coarse salt all over fish, inside and out. Sea salt best, as fish will feel friendly.

You going to make stuffing and bake fish. This why recipe called *Baked Stuffed*, okay? Big surprise.

First make dice from celery, only don't paint on small dot. Ha! You think Baba shoot Vegas crap without taking home good joke?

Chop onion size of league hardball.

Wash good mushroom and slice. Better to pay little more and get tasty kind like chanterelle or oyster.

Turn on oven to 400 degree F.

Fry these vegetable in lots butter, about size very big cow eyeball. I should not have to tell you this, but make sure enough butter left in pan to make bread crumb soak.

Mix these thing with bread crumb. Only don't use this white cotton call Wonderbra bread. This only for stuffing if you not gifted like Baba on top. Use good rye or pumpernickel, not stale. You want it soft. And listen, don't believe these big store bakery who say they make "Winnipeg Rye" or real Ukrainian bread. If you want good kind bread, line up and fight with fist like real person at neighborhood store: Ukrainian, Polish, Jewish, Italian.

Use your hand to mix, don't be squeamish thing. Put in pinch salt and pepper.

Shove whole dressing thing inside fish. I know, I know, his eye staring at you. Ignore, is good for your character.

Take big needle and fat thread and sew up dressing inside fish if you know how. If not, call neighbor for smelly job. Promise you feed her. Next time.

Melt butter in pan and brush all over fish. Keep ignoring his staring eye. **Sprinkle fish all over with flour.** Can use white, whole wheat or rye. Make dusting with **paprika** for pretty red color. If you caught rainbow trout, this even more beautiful.

Lift fish real careful and slice three gash on each side. Three is for Father, Son and Holy Ghost, ancient secret Ukrainian blessing. Close your eye and hum until you dizzy. Make prayer for thanking fish and also so you go to Heaven when you die like fish. Not really. This so fish not explode in oven. You so gullible New Age person, I can see you nodding like this all meaningful information. This why teaching you to cook so much fun.

Put on greased pan and bake about 45 minute. Poke fish at 30 minute to make sure. If juice still running out at 45, bake 10 minute more. I charge big money to hold your hand, so try to think. Call 1-900-ASKBABA if you need help with calculation.

In meantime, you going to **baste fish few time with fifty-fifty mix melt butter and water.**

Before serve to guest, take away thread or some slob going to use for dental floss, I guarantee. He marry to your best friend, so just don't think about them making romance.

Slice lemon for guest to squeeze on fish. Put out bowl of good fish sauce you make yourself. See *Tartar* or *Dill Sauce,* *Chapter Twenty Two.*

Your option:

*Throw in **tablespoon chop dill leaf** to dressing. Not stem. Use fresh! Don't combine with any other kind spice.
OR
***Two tablespoon chop fresh parsley.** This good for your sex organ. It give you energy to run in water.
AND
*Tiny pinch **savory seasoning, powder rosemary or powder sage.**
*For stuffing, use **heaviest kind of rye or pumpernickel bread.** Never, ever white bread. Ick.
*Try different kind onion: **chop fine green scallion or red Spanish.** Also amazing thing Baba find on West Coast is **Walla Walla Washington onion.** Can also eat on sandwich with just mayonnaise and cheese, so mild. Not to confuse with "onion from Walla Walla River." This is marketing baloney. Must be genuine.
*Mix in **one small chop red, orange or yellow pepper** with vegetable.
*Mix in **small bunch chopped spinach.** Try different combination of veggie, just like you do with many boyfriend.

Ingredient List:

- One lake trout, three pounds
- Celery, one half cup
- Onion, one medium
- Butter, one half pound
- Mushrooms, one half pound
- Bread crumbs, two cups dark
- Paprika, salt and cracked pepper
- Lemon wedges
- Salt pork or bacon, eight slices
- Large needle and coarse thread
- *Tartar* or *Dill Pidlyva (Sauce)*

Alternate Stuffing for Riba

Make rice. Brown is better for your nutrition. Jasmine is sweet, and out from this world.

Chop onion and fry in butter until is clear like Baba instruction.

Beat egg. Not too much, just like one-time light spanking.

Mix egg into rice and onion. Add salt and pepper.

Add rye, pumpernickel or whole wheat bread crumb. Mix in shot glass size melted butter.

If you creative person, **can also add different type chop vegetable** like I tell you above: pepper, spinach, mushroom. Only stay away from green zucchini. I tell you all about this Soviet plot in *Chicken Soup, Chapter One.*

Shove stuffing inside fish and sew up. Big deal. Bake.

Ingredient List:

- Brown rice, two cups cooked
- Onion, one small
- Egg, one large
- Salt and pepper
- Bread crumbs, one heaping cup
- Butter, one quarter cup

Optional: chopped vegetables as in recipe

Fried Riba

Okay, so next time Baba go to lake she not get into stupid involvement with no scuba men and oxygen air tank. I hear how he telling lie at party, about big naked Baba and how he she almost kill him. Good for you, Baba think. You be so lucky she interested enough to kill you, boychik. Get life.

This time I park around other side lake and take bathing suit in hand to use for fish net. This work best if part of suit made of black mesh. With red rose down side so fish think is some kind fancy bait. Bikini not work unless you at least have boobala size like mine. So use your best one-piece and eat heart out jealous when you see Baba in person. She have to be careful leaning over soup, or this be double-dipping. Ha!

Baba paddle paddle paddle out to middle lake, so nice and warm, and soon fat rainbow trout see red rose and bite bathing suit. I scoop him real quick. He fighting inside suit like he going to tear my mesh. This look like what is in Tom Jones pant when he dance.

Baba yell, "Don't you try nothing, crazy fish!" and drag him back under water real quick to part of beach there is no people and hit him on head with rock. Don't worry, fish head empty anyway. I not be surprise one day catfish is big time politician. Most them look that way already. Some of them, I'm not saying who, also have eye so close together they looking even more like some kind ugly fish.

Now we cooking! Clean and scrape scale like I tell you above. Cut into fillet, which mean pull small bone away from meat. Use your long nail or if you don't have, try good pair tweezer. You can borrow from girlfriend, don't tell why. Just wash with lemon juice after to take away stink.

Cut up fillet, sprinkle with sea salt and let sit half hour while you polish nail some good color.

Baba warning: don't use kind with glitter, it flake off in fish and everybody mad at you for leaving fish scale in recipe. Use three coat of polish and give lots time to dry.

Put beaten up egg with a little bit water in bowl.

Pour white or whole wheat flour in another bowl. **Cut up fillet into small piece and dip in flour so coated good. Then dip fish piece in egg.** Keep firm hold. Maybe you even use tong, if you know such thing.

Last, make very fine bread crumb. Can be whole wheat or rye. Or you can use corn flake. Put hard stale bread or corn flake in heavy duty plastic bag, kind you use to bury small animal in garden. You know what I'm talking about. Is terrible thing when dead hamster fall out from bag in front of grandchildren. They making all sorts crying, so be careful. Really, is better you use two bag, one inside each other.

Hit bread or flake with hammer until all fine, almost dust. Can also use rolling pin, but not so much fun.

Roll fish piece in crumb. Make sure is completely coat, like wearing little furry jacket. So cute.

Heat iron skillet very hot and put in lots butter. Fry fish on one side till brown, watching careful. Then fry other side. You wouldn't believe how many people I have to tell this part to. It just make me tired.

Serve with lemon juice or nice *Tartar* or *Dill Sauce,* *Chapter Twenty Two*. You can also do what I learn from sexy man from Alabama: use this hot hot sauce they have all over down there. This might be another story some time. Or maybe not.

Ingredient List:

- Lake trout, one three pounder
- Egg, one large
- Flour, one half cup
- Sea salt, one quarter cup
- Bread crumbs or crushed corn flakes, one cup
- Butter, one quarter cup
- *Tartar, Dill* or Louisiana hot sauce

Crazy Mixed Up Riba Balls

Here is way to make look like you catch more fish than you really catch. I learn this trick in one those cheap restaurant my cheap friend take me to. She think is "five star" because is five piece cutlery on table. She paying, so I not say nothing.

Can use any kind fish from lake. Remember take away bone from fish. **Put fillet in meat grinder.** One time my daughter use pencil sharpener. This not good idea.

Put fish in large bowl.

Fry onion in lots butter until clear and **mix like crazy** with fish.

Make hard bread crumb into very fine piece with heavy bag and hammer or rolling pin like I show you in *Fried Fish* recipe, above. Put somewhere in kitchen where you not forget about it. Maybe put note on fridge.

Now use soft bread crumb. Like I tell you before, no white bread. Blech. **Mix with milk,** unpasteurize from farm if you can find. Can also use buttermilk for tangy taste. Listen: I did not say use *Tang* for taste. **Soak crumb in: one stirred up egg, salt and crack pepper.** Don't cheat with bad pepper. Mix mix mix.

Add bread crumb mix to ground fish.

Here is tricky part. **You have to take these slimy thing and make into many small ball.** If I was you, I would put on rubber glove. If I was you, you would be so lucky. If I was you, who would you be? Never mind. Puzzle on philosophy after you eat delicious thing.

Latex glove good too, if this part of your usual wardrobe. **Put fish ball in second bowl.**

Now thing get slimier. Put on whole latex outfit, don't matter what colour. Check for pinhole. When you lift fish ball mix from bowl, is going to be liquid left behind. Get over this.

Fish and bread crumb ball now sitting in second bowl. Get it? Go find bowl of very fine bread crumb you hide somewhere in kitchen. If can't find, blame someone. If they say they not responsible for losing bread crumb, tell them, "I didn't say you was responsible. I say I'm blaming you."

Take each ball and dip in liquid, then in fine crumb. Each slimy ball is now look like little porcupine.

At this point, Baba hearing serious report that your fish ball may actual not be ball. My Irish friend name Kathleen, she say is like fish ball get mammogram. This is okay. Flat ball may not be fancy, but will still taste *smachnoho.*

Heat up fry pan very hot and melt butter. Fry fish ball till they brown but not black-brown. Make sure you roll them around, or they stay little bit raw and shape funny, like old man part that hang from short. Make you sick either way.

Put fish ball on platter garnish with tomato, cucumber and red pepper slice. Also parsley.

Put out bowl of *Tartar* or *Dill Sauce,* *Chapter Twenty Two.*

Ingredient List:

- Fish fillets, one pound
- Onion, one medium
- Butter, one half to three quarters cup
- Soft bread crumbs, one cup
- Whole or two percent milk OR buttermilk, one half cup

- Egg, one
- Salt and pepper
- Tartar sauce
- Garnish: as in recipe

Pan Fried Sole

This incredible tender fish recipe. Taste just like love between two people. Now Baba getting sentimental. Can't cook with tear in eye.

Get real. Love is nothing like fish! Shouldn't be, or something wrong with you. However, is nothing wrong with shouting order for recipe from massage table while man cook. This simple enough.

How you know if simple enough for him? If he find G-spot after only several lesson AND remember where is, he can make this recipe.

Here your order:

Wash massage oil off hand. Especially if have this fancy-shmancy yin-lang perfumey oil.

Take four fillet of sole, no bone left. Sprinkle little bit salt on fish, then turn this way and that on plate of flour.

This delicate taste, so yell at man, **"Shake fish real good!"** This take off extra flour.

Put fillet in pan with lots butter on medium heat. Make smacking lip sound while cooking.

Squeeze lemon and pour over sole. DO NOT use frozen juice or fake thing from bottle. Must be fresh lemon.

Cook fish until flesh is all white and flaky like that boyfriend you got rid of for this one.

Add more butter to pan and melt. Watch man careful with your good eye. If he try to use motor oil instead of butter, yell real loud. You think man won't try this? Then you not live long enough with man. First time you yell, he going to say, “But is clean motor oil.”

Put piece of sole on each person plate. Pour butter over top. Now everybody making moaning sound.

Very tasty with steam baby potato, skin on. Maybe first time your man cook, you should not challenge him to do this same time. Multi-task is not big male strength, and is possible is not something you want him to learn. You want man with focus.

Speaking on which, this where woman make very big mistake. She crying crying, oi yoi yoi why can't man be more like woman? Listen, you want man to be more like woman, is plenty these transgender people in all sort stage. Pick one who is still man but more like woman. These New Age people always meditating about "integrate inner male and female working part." Go make romance with person have several kind working part.

Why you boring your girlfriend with all reason husband is not like her, and pestering man with same thing? Look, woman is soft, not too hairy, and have, like we say in Art class, negative space. Man is hairy, focus, and hopefully hung like elephant. Only not so periscopic.

Your option:

***Put spoonful caper, rinsed, on each piece fish.** I learn this from boyfriend who visit me from Greece. His hand always full of scrape from thorny plant. He not understand I be happy with caper from market. That is okay. Harder man work for you, more he love you. Is call "woman secret."

***Fry very thin round slice lemon in pan with fish until light brown.** Serve on top of fish fillet.

*Put fish over this *Ukrainski Nouveau Fusionski* thing call **jasmine rice.** So sweet and delicate.

***Put fish on brown rice.** Big contrast in texture.

Ingredient List:

- Fillet of sole, one half pound per person
- Lemon, one large per pound of fish
- Butter, one half pound
- Rice or potatoes

Chapter Seventeen

Ocean Fish

Scurvy Dog Baba

Is one time Baba visit Odesa and become pirate for short while. Odesa is port city on Black Sea. What most people not know and Baba not going to tell you is this: Odesa have secret nude beach where few hundred people go every summer.

One day Baba pack picnic lunch. What she take, you want to know. You always have mind on food. Cold vegetarian *Holubtsi, Chapter Fourteen*, small flask horilka and plastic jar *Uzvar (Stewed Fruit), Chapter Twenty Three.*

I spread out red flower babushka on sand and am eating. I turn this way and that so I roast even, like good chicken in oven.

All of more sudden, pirate pop up from behind driftwood. He say, "Arrrrrrr, big sexy Baba, I want to give you massage."

He have fierce brown eye and thing we consider very beautiful in Ukraina: *chorny bravi*. Mean "black eyebrow." We very visual people. Baba not get fooled easy, but pirate with these kind eyebrow and massage oil is one my big weakness. She never miss Shemar Moore on *Criminal Mind.*

What Baba not notice while pirate working his hand and hook, is he mix something into massage oil. Is charcoal from beach fire. Pirate poke her accidental with hook. Baba open eye and scream because her skin all pitching black. She run into Black Sea to rinse off black oil, but no use. She is painted woman. You can see dilemma.

Pirate laughing so his gold tooth show. "Har har Baba!" he say. I don't know why he talk this way, but every pirate Baba meet do. Anyway, pirate tell Baba she have to come on ship and he wash her with organic soap.

We get in small rowboat and go to ship. You would do same thing, I know. Don't be judger.

Oy, pirate wash me good. He so careful with hook. But even that feel okay, as long as he keep using lots soap and circular motion.

Then I feel ship rocking and pirate say "Har har!" again. Now he start to annoy me, even though I am empathetic to stressful profession. We move out to sea and is too far for Baba to swim back through possible group of shark. Beside, he let me wear eye patch and practice lots with sword.

Baba stay out in sea for two week. I try to make best of. Gang of pirate teach me how to deep sea fish and make simple recipe. They name me *Scurvy Dog Baba* because I am always asking for fruit. Woman cannot live on fish, horilka and massage alone.

Ukrainian Pirate Baked Ocean Fish

This tasty way to make fish if you stuck with pirate. Otherwise known as your husband. Count your blessing, woman. My pirate was real good time, but not marriage material.

Catch ocean fish like perch, whiting, sole or haddock. **Take out head and bone. Throw fish fillet in air and slice on your pirate sabre.**

Steam two huge potato, but not till entirely soft. Should make bit of squeaking when you stick in fork, like last time you scare yourself with dog toy. **Slice potato.**

Grease casserole dish with salo or butter. Make kind of wall around inside of dish with potato slice.

Put fish slice in middle of potato slice. Say, "Arrrrrr, now you will be my dinner, matie!" Make sure kitchen window close so no one can hear your private life.

Sprinkle this with salt.

Make oven 400 degree F.

Sour cream sauce:

Mix smetana with soniashnyk (sunflower oil) or extra virgin olive oil. Is no such thing as extra virgin sunflower oil yet. This because being virgin is waste of life. There is organic kind, and is very tasty.

Now mix in flour with sour cream and oil. Should be no lump.

Pour this sauce over fish and potato. Do not stir, or you disturb their marriage.

Sprinkle whole thing with crack black pepper and tasty cheese.

Try: firm goat cheese, Swiss, mild to sharp cheddar, Bleu cheese from bleu goat or Stilton, etc.. Any kind have real flavour to make contrast with mild fish. Mozzarella not too good and cottage cheese out of question. What kind pirate eat cottage cheese with fish? Sheesh. Next you be serving on lettuce leaf along with little calorie count book. This not way to make most of adventure with pirate on Black Sea, poopchik. **Bake forty minutes.**

Ingredient List:

- Ocean fish, two pounds
- Potatoes, two huge
- Salo (fat) or butter, one quarter cup to grease casserole dish
- Sour cream, one cup
- Melted butter, one tablespoon
- Salt and cracked black pepper
- Flour, one tablespoon
- Cheese, one half cup. See recipe for suggested types

Pickled Whitefish

This going to be easiest pickle thing you ever make. And friend will think you work for hours. Is traditional dish for Sviata Vechera.

When Baba finally leave pirate ship with whole bag of coin and jewel from treasure chest, I also make sure to take package of fresh whitefish from Black Sea. Pirate think this mean we engaged. Trauma counselor say we have "different value system." Pirate have to pay very big bill to get over me. Is good thing he is thief.

Heat oven to 375 degrees F.

Put four piece fillet whitefish in small baking dish. About one pound fish.

Cut up onion into ring and spread over fish.

You going to make your own fish pickle soup:

In small pot, mix together dry mustard, whole coriander and one clove mince garlic. Pirate tell me to add rum. I disagree and put in dry white wine, which work much better for high class lady like me. Baba don't know why they call "dry" wine. Just don't use for dry cleaning, or you be sorry.

Add vinegar, cold water and you guessed it---chop fresh dill. No stem. **Add salt and pepper** and bring to rolling kind of boil.

Pour fish pickle juice over whitefish.

Cover baking dish and bake only five minute. That's what I say: five minute. Listen good to Baba or you not making *Pickle Whitefish.* I know every cell in your Canadian body scream, "She mean fifty minute!" No way. Then that be *Baked Fish, Chapter Sixteen.* You have my permission to make that recipe right after this.

Let cool to temperature of your room, which should be about seventy degree F.

Put in fridge few hour. Even better overnight. If people ask what is, say "Ukrainian sushi."

Is traditional to serve as appetizer. **Put out nice rye and pumpernickel bread.** This not traditional, but awful tasty: serve over cold sushi rice mix with mayonnaise.

End note: best tasting whitefish is one you catch while fishing in ice. This is something you send man to do, because is so boring you won't believe. Woman have to be careful. Baba is biggest feminist of all, but she avoid doing equal thing that is stupid.

Ingredient List:

- Whitefish, one pound
- Onion, one small
- Dry mustard, one tablespoon
- Whole coriander, one teaspoon
- Garlic, one clove minced
- Dry white wine, one cup
- Vinegar, one quarter cup
- Cold water, one quarter cup
- Fresh dill, one half bunch
- Salt and cracked black pepper

Oseledets (Pickled Herring)

Baba teach you how to make one quart jar pickle herring. Better if you put on black bread, and drink vodka. They eat lots of this in Odesa, where is fish. I learn from sailor boyfriend.

First, practice scary face in mirror at home. You need this to fight for best fish. Go to fish market first thing in morning, with good straw basket on arm. Put piece cloth in basket. Say to fish man or fish woman, “I need best herring you got. Don't you be showing me any kind not fresh.” Get two large one along with they milt.

What is milt? Baba not sure you ready for this. Is fish sperm. And let Baba tell you, is extra flavor package. Nothing like human.

There will be other women there, try fight you for best herring. Make scary face. When fish worker hand you herring, yell, “Mine!” in loudest voice and swing basket around you. Now put herring on counter and poke in eye. Should bounce back. If eye mushy, yell, "Cheat!" and throw at fish man. Even better, throw hand full milt. I promise you, he now give you best herring. Put basket and cover with cloth. Go straight home before fish start to smell.

Now you home. Pour glass good vodka and drink.

Put herring on cutting board, chop off head, tail and fin. Pull out all bone. Soak in cold water overnight. Change water two or three time. Baba know this three time more often than you change fish tank water in year, but try to keep up.

Next day, soak herring in cold black tea or milk for at least two hour to make mild flavor.

Mix up:

Water. Line up early at pump. Can't make recipe without.
Vinegar. Strong kind, smell make eye water.
Brown sugar. Eat tablespoon yourself, have another drink vodka.
Bay leaf.
Whole pepper. Put in strong plastic bag, get boyfriend to hit with hammer. Men love this kind thing. It make them hot. Or if you lazy, buy pepper already crack. Don't go to store manager and say, "I want to buy pepper crack." Baba make this mistake when she Canada newbie. Square kind manager only hear one word, and he make big fuss like when I grow poppy. See *Poppy Seed, Chapter Twenty Four.*
Mix pickling spice. Kind with little round coloured thing, look like birdseed. But not taste like it. Is good thing.

Put all this in medium pot. Make boil, watch whole time. Then put on tile to cool. Baba call this "pickle soup."

Put milt through sieve. Of all thing to make your day, fish sperm is lumpy. And you thought your life was disgusting. Baba try to get this fact add to *Trivial Pursuit.*

Mix big splash soniashnyk oil into milt. Pour into pickle soup.

Take out onion. Spanish best kind. There no Ukrainianski onion in Canada, anyway. **Slice onion into ring.** This only way you fit onto bread later. If you cut into fussy little piece, you be sorry. You can cut biggest ring in half.

Sterilize pickling jar. I know, I know, you hoping this mean just wash. No, it mean you put jar up to top in very hot water, and then make boiling for ten minute. Boiling water must go inside and outside jar. Take out with tong. Put on super clean dishrack to drain.

Slice herring into size piece will fit your mouth. Baba don't mean put in now! Make sure is no bone left.

Put all piece in jar, making layer: onion, herring, onion, herring. Pour cool pickle soup in jar. Make lid very, very tight, or your apron going smell like fish and pickle soup always. Shake a little

Put in fridge. If you can control self, leave two weeks. If you impatient, can eat as soon as forty-eight hour. Baba know you rushing to get ready for Sviata Vechera, and oseledets is compulsory religious food. Religion of excellent food on holiday, Baba mean.

In meantime, open jar now and then, push onion and herring around. Say to them, "Onion and herring, I am boss here." Pull herring at bottom up to top, so all fish get equal pickling. This not to be confuse with Communism.

To eat: Take big loaf heavy black or rye bread. Put herring and onion on slice bread.

Oseledets (Herring) Spread

This recipe not for people hard of herring. Ha!

Baba already show you how to shop for herring. You going to make delicious thing for party like no one taste before. I call "cheap man caviar."

Take one big salty herring. Right away chop off head, throw to chicken. Is good thing to keep house chicken for. I prefer Bantam kind. They small, red and cute. Not make much mess. Mine girl and boy, name Peep and Beep. When I need them to not be pooping all over, I put in play pen or outside. Also now is bird diaper! So much better than mean people who keep bird in cage whole time.

Soak fish in cold water one hour to take away extra salt. Throw away skin and bone.

Rinse fish under cold water and roll in cotton towel until dry.

Put fish through meat grinder or chop very, very fine like ground beef. Skin under armpit going to wobble. Start chopping. If armpit skin make figure eight you know you on right track. When I get too annoy at all this flapping, I wrap upper arm in duct tape. Only make sure pit is shave, or you going to yell when taking off later. Is "helpful hint" too for when you like to cut down wind resistance in arm wrestle.

Boil two egg so they hard, three minute. It help if you have TV in kitchen. Three minute equal six insulting commercial telling me I too fat, too ugly, too poor. Second thought, use egg timer. This better for your intelligence.

See *Eggs, Chapter Seven*, for instruction on boil and peel. Mash both white and yolk to paste. Make sure egg is cool.

Mix chop herring with mash egg plus chive or very mild chop onion, soft butter, crack pepper, dry mustard and good kind vinegar: balsamic, wine or apple cider.

If you think you going to like, **grate very small, sweet apple into this.** Not necessary if you use apple cider vinegar.

Again, you going to be mashing so armpit skin wobble. If you not take me serious first time about solution, do it now.

Put herring spread in fridge one hour to firm up little bit. Too bad can't do same thing with armpit.

Just before company come, **put out plate with many slice good heavy kind rye and pumpernickel bread on platter.** If you like fancy, make toast or put out fancy cracker.

Baba warning: not so good with goldfish cracker. This too much irony for good taste.

Put bowl of herring spread in middle. Garnish spread with parsley or chive.

Just before this, take good hot shower and peel away duct tape. You don't want to do this in middle of party, everyone hear you screaming.

Ingredient List:

- Salt herring, one large. Approximately one half pound
- Eggs, two large
- Chives OR very mild onion, one quarter cup
- Butter, two tablespoons
- Salt and pepper
- Dry mustard, one half teaspoon
- Balsamic, apple cider or wine vinegar, one tablespoon
- Apple, one small
- Dark rye or pumpernickel bread
- Parsley or chives for garnish

Sardine Spread

This sardine spread like from Old Country. Make nice change from this tuna in can everybody eating in Canada like is some kind national food. Sardine very healthy for your bone and skin, too. Between you, me and everyone else reading this book, it make Ukrainian saying for poor people true, *Ni zhyty, ni vmeraty!* Not enough to live, or to die!

Going to be lots mashing here. Like you do with herring spread, put duct tape on armpit for precaution.

Boil two egg hard, chill and peel. Mash. Put aside where you can remember to find. See *Eggs, Chapter Seven.*

Take lemon from fridge overnight so easy to juice.

Mash sardine so they smooth. Leave bone and skin.

Special Baba Instruction: you going to add one ingredient at time, mashing into sardine. If you too stubborn for duct tape, make sure to wear eye google. You don't want black eye from rebound.

Here we go. **One at time: mash in extra virgin olive oil, soft butter, soft cream cheese, two hard cook egg, green onion or chive, fresh lemon juice, crack black pepper and salt.**

Do not use margarine instead of butter. This terrible thing they invent to make turkey fat. It kill turkey, so they add little bit orange color and make you eat. Be little bit more smart than turkey, okay?

Spread on good bread open face, or make sandwich. Don't tell nobody is sardine. Is too much prejudice in this country. Tell them you pick up fish in specialty store. Don't worry, they not figure out as long as you wrap sardine can good in paper towel and plastic bag, take out to trash before people see.

Ingredient List:

- Eggs, two hard boiled
- Lemon, one
- Sardines, one can
- Extra virgin olive oil or sunflower oil, two tablespoons
- Butter, three tablespoons soft
- Cream cheese, one half pound
- Scallions, two OR half cup chives
- Salt and pepper
- Quality bread: black, pumpernickel or rye

Oseledets (Herring) Salad

Here is thing they call "acquire taste." Once you do, nothing be the same.

Take two big fillet like I show you in recipe for *Pickled Herring*. **Cut**

up in piece about size of small rubber eraser, the kind you use when cooking checkbook.

Steam dice potato. Leave skin on for vitamin. Let cool.

Steam and peel beet. It going to make everything pretty pink color. Let cool, then peel. See peel direction in *Beet and Horse Radish Relish,* under *Ukrainian Spring Traditions, Chapter Six*. If you impatient, use fan on kitchen counter to cool. Do not ever be so impatient you put hot vegetable in salad. It make funny part-cook place on fish and you be sorry.

Take core from and chop up one medium tart taste apple OR two crab apple. Can leave peel on if no worm hole.

Chop up dill pickle. Taste better if garlicky kind. Throw away both end of pickle.

Chop up scallion type onion OR chive from garden. Not from spot where dog pee. Onion from herring fillet jar not so good for this recipe, so leave alone and don't get fancy idea.

In big salad bowl, toss herring, potato, beet, apple, pickle very gentle like you rocking sick chihuahua. Otherwise vegetable get cranky, start fall into crumb.

Add pepper. Don't add salt. Herring salty enough.

Boil egg till hard, three minute.

Peel and slice into ring.

Dressing:

Mix smetana with vinegar. Taste better if you use apple cider, wine or balsamic kind.

Mix dressing slow into salad.

Make garnish with egg slice and more chive. Try spell out word with chive, express how you feel. Red or orange pepper ring also make nice decoration. If you bored, you can chop extra pepper, stand back from counter and make ring toss onto salad. This give it carefree windblown look.

Ingredient list:

- Herring fillets, two large
- Potatoes, one cup diced
- Beets, one cup diced
- Apple, one medium or two crab
- Garlic dill, one medium
- Green onion, one

- Egg, one large
- Pepper
- Sour cream, one half cup
- Vinegar, two tablespoons
- Garnish as in recipe

Chapter Eighteen

Pechenya (Stew)

Kalampetsya (Mushroom Stew)

This one those special recipe have every kind of nutrition in it: mushroom, different kind delicious green and white vegetable, meat, nut and cheese protein. It kind of like all-dress Ukrainian pizza. Diversity is Baba middle name.

If you on some kind restriction diet, close your eye and turn page. Also this recipe not for you if you are lazy bone. Many ingredient are cook separate from each other.

We now get party started:

Make mushroom into thin slice. Very important: See *Mushrooms, Chapter Twelve*. Quality mushroom like gold flake, so take time to select and chop.

Slice onion super thin.

Put soniashnyk oil (sunflower) into hot iron skillet. Add onion. Make fry until goldy colour.

Say to onion, "Shove over," then put mushroom slice in big space in middle of pan. Make heat medium.

Slow pour heavy cream into pan. Important you wearing apron. If you have gifted chest like Baba, be careful. Stir gentle because mushroom slice can break. **Cook until cream start to evaporate** and look sticky. **Sprinkle with salt and crack black pepper.** Not black powder. This stuff will not bring out taste of mushroom. Or of anything.

Baba show you shortcut if you have good timing like polka accordian musician. If you do, can steam all vegetable in one pot. If you not trust yourself yet, cook vegetable in separate pot.

How to cook shortcut vegetable:

Slice two large potato. "Large" mean at least size of rock you using for paperweight for that mess on your desk. Do not peel, but make sure to cut out eye or any green part. **Put in boiling steamer basket. Let cook maybe ten, fifteen minute.** Poke with fork. Potato should be half tender before you add brussel sprout. Should have stem cut off and outer leaf peeled.

After five minute more steaming, **add one large stalking broccoli.** Don't be wasting. Slice stem very thin along with flower part and it will be delicious. **Steam five minute and all vegetable should be finish cooking.**

Heat oven to 350 degree F

Grease large casserole dish with butter. Put layer of potato. This your foundation. All these ingredient going to have special relationship.

Cover potato with smoke or Canadian bacon like you putting quilt on sleepy Pomeranian. About as much as you put in two sandwich. Or one, if no one looking. Veggie pepperoni will taste good, too.

This very cute: put layer of brussel sprout on top of bacon. Step back from counter and admire green ball on meat.

Layer of delicious mushroom and onion go right in middle. When people bite, their eye go all big and they think you are hero.

Next put layer of broccoli. Do not substitute zucchini. That slimy relationship just not going to work out. Will feel like time you take cousin to dance as date. Maybe you take him every time as date. Baba don't know. Do not write to her about this.

Sprinkle broccoli layer with half pound pounded hazel nut. I been waiting to say that. This add dry crunch to relationship. Baba know you used to pounding nut in plastic bag with hammer, but you can run over with car tire for big thrill, instead. This make such good noise, you will laugh. For extra value as anger managing exercise, paint chalk picture of boss on tire first.

Cover all this with few cheese slice. Use cheese with mild taste. Is good thing if it get stretchy, too. Mozzarella, Gouda or jack excellent for this. Absolutely not this "process cheese." You will ruin all your good work with this crapola.

How you save money on expensive cheese is not to buy in block. Ask deli counter person to slice exactly amount you want. If they put thumb on scale, give good glare and make him feel guilty. This is good time to ask for little sample of this and that. Some day Baba go to several deli and have whole lunch this way. You should be wearing bra one size too large for this job. Ask for slice Gouda at first deli. Then slice corn beef. Keep up glare. Ask for little package mustard and mayo. Put sample inside bra. Go to next deli and do same thing. Make sure you wearing good support hose and bloomer so your thigh not rub together, because this is lots of walking. If you not already carry in purse: buy small loaf slice bread. This is hard thing to get for free. Go to park, take meat and cheese from bra and make sandwich. There you go, free lunch!

Baba warning: on hot day, get to park very fast. Otherwise will attract wrong kind of boyfriend.

Put stew in oven without using lid. You better remember your ingredient already cook. Just bake until cheese on top is melty and gold colour.

Your option:

***Use half cauliflower, half broccoli. Or broccoflower,** if you can find this interesting thing. Baba would like to say she invent, but would probably get stupid frivolous law sewage from person who really do.
***Use good Montreal smoke meat,** Black Forest ham, prosciutto or Jewish corn beef instead of smoke bacon. Veggie kind sausage also good.
***Add layer goat cheese in middle with mushroom.** Not feta, this too strong pickle taste. Is probably from old goat. "So is my husband," you say. Not same thing. Use good mild farm goat cheese like from my goat Sonya. See *Kutya* under *Grain, Chapter Twenty.*
***Fry very thin slice from small red or orange pepper** with mushroom and onion. Not green, this is icky. NOT your option: white generic mushroom you usual see in produce section. They going to ruin recipe.

Ingredient List:

- Onion, one large
- Mushrooms, one pound
- Sunflower oil, one quarter cup
- Heavy or whipping cream, one half cup
- Salt and pepper
- Potatoes, two large
- Brussels sprouts, one cup small
- Broccoli, one quarter pound
- Butter, one quarter cup
- Smoked or Canadian bacon, one half pound
- Hazel nuts, one half pound
- Quality cheese slices, one third pound

Ukrainian-Canadian Caribou Stew

After Baba husband die, she decide she going to learn speak English and become True North Strong and Free Canadian.

I find myself real Canadian boyfriend, Inuit guy name Tom. We move into house together in downtown Montreal to have cultural night life. Next thing I know, Tom calling me from airport, saying, "Baba, bring your Cadillac. My parent send us caribou rear end from north."

I open trunk and say, "Tom, don't let that blood drip on my cherry red finish."

Take both of us, try to stuff caribou in trunk. He put both his hand on my bumper. We push and push. Finally, we get tired. I put my *dupa* against big hairy caribou butt and Tom lean on me. We kiss for little bit, I kind of like way tongue feel where his teeth missing. Then we remember to close trunk. Security guard come out, say we not allowed back in airport.

We get home, and caribou rear end too big for fridge freezer. So Tom sit on kitchen floor, legs straight out in front him. He cut piece off with hacksaw, say, "Catch!" I catch piece at time, stuff in freezer. I say, "Tom, we are now real true multicultural couple."

Now Baba show you how to make real Ukrainian-Canadian caribou stew:

This not going to be fancy. Caribou taste very good plain. Just meat, onion, garlic and potato.

Take big hunk caribou. Fresh as you can find. Check meat over. If some hair still left on it, pull out with tweezer or singe with candle. Make sure you clean off wax if you use candle. Do not use these same tweezer to pluck hair from chin. They get blunt shape from caribou hair, not work so good. One time I try Tom electric shaver, but it get jam with sticky meat. Tom not happy, and I have no one to rub against for few days. This terrible thing.

Soak in half and half water and lemon juice or water and wine or balsam type vinegar overnight. Kind with monk on label, he praying vinegar going to turn to wine. Ha!

Add half cup olive or sunflower oil. This take away too strong game taste and make tender.

Chop up enough potato relative size to one-third caribou roast. Some people take off peel. I leave on for good vitamin C. Scurvy is bad thing. One day I tell you how I almost became pirate on ship from Odesa, people call me *Scurvy Dog Baba*. But not today. See *Chapter Seventeen*.

Put potato in big bowl cold water so he not turn brown.

Peel and chop up onion real fine.

Put pile corn starch in big bowl. Enough so you will be able to coat each piece meat. Can also use flour, but corn starch make not so sticky.

Pour in salt and crack black pepper.

Make second bowl with lots cold water.

Heat olive or sunflower oil in very big frying pan. You know how much! **Put in onion and fry** till about halfway soft. **Peel and chop two clove garlic very fine, put in pan.** Garlic burn easy, so I never put in same time as onion.

Baba law: if you burn onion or garlic, start over. These thing very cheap. Burn taste can make best recipe bad.

Pour marinade juice away from meat. DO NOT DRINK THIS, EVEN WITH MIX. DO NOT GIVE TO DOG. DO NOT GIVE TO HUSBAND.

Take very sharp butcher knife and cut caribou meat into stew size piece. I know other recipe book tell you so many inch. Pah. Why you need this? You going to take stupid tape measure and find out how big is piece meat? You be measuring and cutting all night. Just cut meat into piece big enough so feel nice to chew, but not so big people call you slob.

This also some kind method for choosing lover. Never believe man he say, "So many inch."

I once date man, he claim he, "One hundred fifty pound dynamite with eight inch fuse." Baba is big sucker for good dancer. This guy, he can really bend leg and swing hip. Plus, he smell great, make Baba tingle all over.

Baba say, "Show me naked."

"Ha," Baba thinking. "Nice chest. But eight inch? Where you measuring from? Could be from elbow, for all I know."

Use your good eye, sister friend. I teach this guy how to use what he have, anyway. You know I'm good cook, hate wasting thing. And five and one half inch is almost adequate if you short like Baba. But I learn something. Sometime man with not so huge stew meat, he have good energy around this thing. Kind of like radiant heater. Beside, this guy learn to hold off till Baba yelling, "*Matka Bozha*! Mother of God!" and have eye rolling back in her head two, three time.

Back to caribou stew.

Put piece stew meat in cold water, then in bowl with corn starch. Roll meat around till it have nice coat. If piece fall on floor, dog can have. See feetnote.

If fry pan really huge with tall sides, you will **cook meat with potato in here.** If not, put big pot on stove and boil enough water so one inch higher than potato.

Plug in kettle full of water.

Add more oil to frying pan. Put in stew meat and roll around. When meat is halfway brown, pour in enough water so piece halfway cover. Mix up. This making gravy. **Stir and cook** until meat brown and gravy little bit thick.

If pan huge, add chop potato. If you made pot with boil water and potato, put meat in there.

You know, I hear reason some Anglo men is so small, is because their culture value virgin before marriage. Is like some kind fetish. Woman not get to see or feel his thing, so she have no choice. Some time they not even take good look at face! This happen for sure with your Queen, and that Prince of hers. I don't understand. Wasn't she terrible scared what her children going to look like? And now it turn out Princess Anne is some kind mutant horse eater, because she get millions tax money from Canadian government who slaughter horse. Sheesh. Look first, people.

First time Baba see Anne's son, she jump back from computer and scream. People, before you marry and breed, take good look at partner face, too.

And listen. I hope you not thinking Baba telling you to take lover with small private part. This was not my point. Usually stew meat is better in larger chunk. So don't all you small dick men start chasing Baba around. I am cook, not magician.

In Ukraina we have saying, *Give Baba inch and she laugh at you.*

Cook until potato soft, at least one hour. If gravy too thin at half hour point, shake up tablespoon corn starch in jar with half cup water until lumpy stuff stop happening. Pour in stew.

Stew always taste better second day. But you going to wait to eat? I don't think so.

Your option:

*__Chop up little bit celery, little bit carrot__ and put in stew.

*This going in whole different fancy-shmancy gourmet universe, but you can soak **fancy Chinese mushroom,** chop up and put in stew. Or try boletus, porcini, chanterelle, oyster, any kind but those taste like soap. Kind stupormarket push in your face.

*__Put teaspoon cayenne pepper in flour with salt and pepper.__ If you have cold, after stew cooked put more pepper in your bowl. **Or hottie**

sauce from Louisiana. Cayenne pepper very good for cold, make your blood boil and kill germ.
*You can make deer, moose and elk same way as caribou. See *Road Kill Stew*, below.

Ingredient List:

For every five pounds of caribou roast:

Marinade

- Extra virgin olive oil or sunflower oil, one cup
- Vinegar, apple cider or balsamic. One cup

Stew

- Potatoes, two pounds
- Onion, one large
- Corn starch, one half cup
- Cooking oil, one half cup
- Cold water, large bowl
- Keep kettle full and boiling

Road Kill Stew

So, you thinking Baba is so big hillbilly she eat road kill? Joke is on you. Baba see you drooling.

Carpathian-Canadian Lamb Stew

Baba not eat this too often in Ukraina. Our farm have cattle and horse, not sheep. Woman from Carpathian mountain bring this to my wedding, and I never stop thinking about. After honeymoon, I mean.

Then Canadian doctor tell me I have "bad cholesterol", and tell me best meat is lamb. Virgin olive oil also make "good cholesterol." Doctor tell me to drink lots more wine and brandy. I keep this doctor forever, I think. *Nazdorovya!* To your health!

This recipe also little bit different, because I add some Canadian thing. Best lamb stew you ever taste.

Buy chunk called lamb stew. Or you can buy leg lamb or chops, and cut into cube. Keep in fridge till I tell you.

Use biggest frying pan. Fry big chopped onion in virgin olive oil until soft and clear. Medium heat. Oil must be virgin, make difference to taste. Not the same as in rest of life, Baba telling you this. Who care if you virgin or not? This Canadian thing. In Ukraina, we have spring festival, these young people they playing around and nobody say nothing. We hot blood people. How you think you know who best to marry, you not fool around little bit?

Some people shock when I tell them young people play sexy game after funeral. When is best time to celebrate life, I asking you? I meet my husband at his Dad funeral. He crying crying, I let him drip tear in Baba cleavage. "Poor thing, poor thing," I say. Next thing I know, I saying "Matka Bozha!" very loud. People think I am praying for dead man soul.

Back to recipe:

Add lots chopped garlic. This very necessary, I don't care how you think breath smell. Make sure you not burn garlic. If you do, throw out onion and garlic, or lamb have terrible taste. Don't be worry, dorahenka! Onion and garlic cheap, lamb not.

Add chop red pepper. Also can cut into small ring, doesn't matter. Don't use orange pepper, because later we add yam. Then everybody complain, "Too much orange food, Baba!" Not green pepper either. Have too strong taste, and get slimy. That why I pick off my pizza.

Add in dry basil leaf. Not powder. Or enough basil from one big plant, chop very fine. This only time I tell you better to use dry leaf from shaker. Basil so strong and holy plant, nothing you do can ruin. Even priest catch on to this in Ukraina, use to purify holy water. Like water is not holy just because is water. Crazy people.

In Ukraina, we know water is living thing. Sometime river is so full of energy, she turn into spirit creature you can see. We call these creature *Rusalky*. Rusalka will lure man to his death, she so beautiful.

Put water in big soup pot, one half full. Add teaspoon salt and make boil.

Peel two big yam. Can use sweet potato if have to, but yam have beautiful orange colour and more Vitamin A against cancer. Also help you see good at night, if Russian coming. **Chop yam into small cube, add to boiling water.**

While vegetables frying, put cornstarch in big bowl. About one cup. Bowl must be big so you not have big mess. Get it? Big bowl, no big mess. **Mix into cornstarch one teaspoon crack black pepper.**

When yam boiling about five minute, add rest vegetable to water. Turn heat to low-medium.

Put full kettle of water on to boil.

Put out large bowl ice water.

Pour lots virgin olive oil into same fry pan as was vegetable, medium heat.

Ah, now is time: take lamb cube from fridge. **Dip lamb piece in ice water, shake, then in cornstarch.** Plop! In frying pan. Be very quick, so meat cook almost all at once.

People ask why I use cornstarch instead flour. Is because cornstarch make silky kind gravy in stew, and also easier clean up than flour. Flour get hard like cement in damp bowl. One thing you need know, Baba love to cook, hate clean up. Make other people do it. Promise them anything. When they taste your stew, they forgive your lie. This big secret of life.

Keep stirring lamb in oil. Add more oil, if you need. Once it look like lamb only have little pink left, add little bit boiling water from kettle and stir more. Water must be boiling. **Make sure pan is full of meat, so water not splash on oil. Add water until lamb swimming in thick gravy. Can also use boiling beef broth.**

Lamb taste very good, this point. Your job make sure family not steal meat from pan while your back turned. Is terrible thing to make stew, then find is only vegetable. You only are allowed eat one, two piece, make sure is cooked.

If stew not thick in half hour, mix little bit more cornstarch in half cup cold water and add to stew. If too thick, add more boiling water to stew. Is something like giving bath to baby. You put in enough water to tub so can wash smelly kid, but not so much they drown while you holding your nose.

In meantime, **cook pot brown rice. Or whole wheat or egg noodle.** You will pour lamb stew over this. Brown rice full Vitamin B, do so many good things, especially for woman hormone.

Stew even tastier, leave in fridge overnight. Listen for sound of creeping feet in kitchen, trying to steal only meat from pot. One time neighbour come in from window, even after I tell him Baba not that kind of girl anymore.

Other good thing to do with lamb stew:

*To bowl full stew, **add half cup coconut milk, teaspoon *Patak's Vindaloo Curry Paste* and teaspoon brown sugar.** This not Ukrainian thing, but I am full equal opportunity, multicultural sophisticate person with great neighbor.

***Splash Louisiana hottie sauce** into bowlful stew. Not into whole pot stew. Some people might not like.

*One good thing I learn in Canada (there not be too much), is **rice called jasmine,** come from India. So good with stew! Uh oh, Baba can hear Ukrainian storm cloud gathering, because she is not traditional purist. Baba is wild creator!
***Add one quarter to half cup plain yogurt** to bowlful stew.
***Half hour before stew ready, peel and chop one huge potato into little cube, add to stew.** Never put potato in at beginning, make starchy taste, like tongue drying up.
*Some people like carrot better than yam. So **chop up carrot** instead, cook just like yam.
***You can add bay leaf,** if you like this taste. Can also try stew with no basil, and bay leaf instead.

Baba warning: because we visit BC. I get excited and try make lamb & salmon stew. Blech. Taste like stupid thing made by hippie-shmippie, after they smoke too much funny weed. Don't do this.

Ingredient List:

- Lamb, three pounds
- Onion, one large
- Olive oil, one half cup
- Garlic, three cloves
- Red pepper, two large
- Fresh basil, one quarter cup
- Salt and pepper
- Yam, two large
- Keep kettle full and boiling
- Cornstarch, one cup
- Bowl of ice water

Kapusta i Horokh (Sauerkraut with Peas) With meat, and vegetarian variation

Why is Ukrainian so big on dish from cabbage? We say, *If there are potato and cabbage, then house is not empty.* Baba herself never seen house with only these thing. Usually is at least chair and television. But you never know. She wouldn't doubt is some isolate American somewhere, carving couch from freakazoid big potato.

In Baba next book, she going to teach you make your own sauerkraut. Since you is beginner, she going to let you buy from stupormarket in big jar.

Soak dry pea in water overnight. This is NOT split pea. Baba mean whole pea and nothing but whole pea. Is going to look attractive in landscape of sauerkraut. Split pea would be mush.

First look pea over better than you did that guy you dating. Pick out gravel, twig and loose tooth. After you marry, let him do this him own damn self. Throw away ugly pea with bad complexion. **Wash them in big bowl water** so loose piece will float to top. Throw this water out and soak in fresh water.

Next day, drain this soaking water and start fresh for cooking.

Pour in cold water and make boiling. Turn down and simmer till soft, about one hour. Stop reading your magazine and check on them while they cooking so they not boil dry. If pea is showing above water, add boiling water from kettle. Make sure you stop cooking before they turn into mushola. This not *horokhivka* (pea soup). If this what you looking for, you in wrong chapter!

This is traditional method of cooking pea.

Baba find that fresh pea is out of world---if you can convince your *Domovyk* house elf* to shell enough to equal amount as cook dry pea once they swell. About one and one half time as much. Or sometime you can buy bag of shell pea at farmer market. Baba not believe she saying this, but frozen can be good if you really, really lazy and run out of time. Thaw completely before adding to sauerkraut. In fridge overnight usually work, or pour boiling water.

Drain and rinse sauerkraut in cold water. Kind from can taste like can. Jar or fresh only. **Add cup cold water and make boiling, then simmer for fifteen minute.** Sauerkraut was sleeping, this make sauerkraut taste come to life. Do not drain.

Turn oven to 350 degree F.

Next instruction is only if you NOT making for Sviata Vechera (Holy Eve). This holiday is meatless. If you making meatless, put your hand over ear while Baba talk about such thing as salt pork and bacon fat (salo) dripping all over sauerkraut. And butter melting on mushroom along with smetana. On second thought, you better go, “Lalalalala I can't hear you!”

Slice up good mushroom and fry in butter.

Crush two clove peel garlic, but don't fry.

Put aside mushroom and garlic, but don't forget about.

Dice up salt pork or bacon. Take out biggest frying pan and fry until meat almost yummy crisp.

Take meat from pan with holey spoon, and put in fine chop onion. Cook until it get that nice yellowy color, make you think of eating almost anything with it.

Throw in flour and stir around so flour get brown. If it get lumpy, pour in little bit oil.

Once flour have nice tan, drain sauerkraut. Pour this sauerkraut stock in and stir around to make, if you can believe this taste extravaganza, sauerkraut-salo-onion gravy.

Baba can see your eye rolling back in your head. This was complete unexpected from recipe title, she know. This what happen when you trust little bit and let her lead you into Ukrainian cultural secret. Baba also find this recipe make man extra hot. She remember her mama serving to field hand, and they chasing beautiful *Rusalka* water fairy down by river later. Too bad rusalka tickle them to death, but that is life in Ukraina.

Now if you going to believe it, this get better. **Stir gravy into sauerkraut, then add thing you almost forgot about while you passed out: pea, mushroom and garlic. For big finish, stir in smetana, salt and crack black pepper.**

You saying, "Enough, Baba. I can't take no more!"

Suck it up, *sestra.*

Quick put this whole mess into casserole dish and bake for forty five minute.

It serve as many people who can fight to get to it first.

For meatless:

This going to feel kind of like smoking cigarette after first good meal. Is pleasure, but different kind of pleasure.

Make recipe up till where Baba told you to cover ear.

Cook fine chop onion in soniashnyk, sunflower oil.

Sprinkle over onion and stir around till flour get goldie-brown.

Pour in sauerkraut stock and stir for gravy.

Pour whole thing over sauerkraut and mix around.

Crush two peel clove garlic, and add in.

Add salt and pepper. Baba sorry to tell you, no smetana in this meatless dish either. Also suck this up. If you so sorry for yourself, make alternate recipe Christmas day and eat till New Year.

Put in casserole dish and bake half hour only.

*For more about Domovai/Domovyk, see *Sichenyky i Zrazy, Chapter Ten.*

Ingredient List:

With meat

- Sauerkraut, four cups fresh or 32 ounce jar (not can!)
- Dried peas, one cup
- Cold water, four cups
- Salt pork or bacon, one cup uncooked
- Onion, one medium
- Flour, three tablespoons
- Mushrooms, one cup fresh or equivalent dried reconstituted
- Butter, two tablespoons for cooking mushrooms
- Garlic, two cloves
- Sour cream, three tablespoons
- Salt and cracked black pepper
- Sauerkraut, four cups fresh or 32 ounce jar
- Dried peas, one cup
- Sunflower or extra virgin olive oil, two tablespoons
- Onion, one medium
- Flour, three tablespoons
- Garlic, two cloves
- Salt and cracked black pepper

Vegetarian

- Omit salt pork, butter and sour cream. Have extra sunflower oil on hand

Chapter Nineteen

Kartoplyanky (Potatoes)

These potato recipe going to make you turn up your nose at fast food french fry. We have saying, *Potato is the second bread.* Is most common staple in Ukraina.

And is easy, too. You going to cry when you realize you could have thought of these yourself. But you didn't. Baba ancestor did. This why I laughing. Early bird get warm place to live.

Creamed Potatoes

Cut two large potato in half and boil or steam until almost done. How you know? Is about one finger joint size across part in middle of potato still crunchy. Use fork to test, not your mouth. Peel or don't peel, your choice. Baba prefer extra vitamin in peel. If you using baby potato, definite don't peel. Make one pound.

Take out medium size pot. Cut potato into chunk and put into pot.

Pour heavy cream over potato. Don't be substituting your diet-shmiet skim milk or some awful thing. Cooking is ancient magic. You not stick to Baba old time recipe, you kill magic and your life go prickly, like wire in hay.

Sprinkle chop fresh dill weed and chive into pot.

Add salt and black pepper.

Cook on low heat for ten minute. Watch pot like cat stalking early bird, or cream burn.

Hello Dolly! Is time to serve this easy, special potato thing.

Your option:

Okay, okay, Baba make acquittal here. She fall in love with this thing call **rice milk.** Can make substitute for cream with mixing one cup rice milk and big tablespoon cornstarch. Mix these ingredient together and kill all lump before you pour on potato. Do not use soy milk!

Ingredient List:

- Potatoes, two large or one pound baby
- Cereal or whipping cream, one cup
- Fresh dill, one quarter cup
- Fresh chives, one quarter cup
- Salt and pepper

Potatoes with Salo (Ukrainian Cocaine)

First we need to talk little bit about *salo*. Is Ukrainian tradition to use big piece pork or beef fat for tasty cooking. Before you get horrify, understand that for many thousand of year, we raise our own cattle and pig. We treat nice, make hot oil massage, invite into house as guest. For sure they never inject with hormone or eat some kind artificial feed. So fat is clean and healthy, instead of you run to healthy food store and paying big buck for *Omega* this and *Unsaturate* that.

Only rule Baba have is never eat animal you have name for. "Pig With Big Nose" good enough. Actual, Baba now stop eating pig altogether. Is just too hard to find not been abuse. Vegetarian meat slice like pepperoni is honest, very good.

So take fist away from mouth and read what I teach you in *Roast Beef, Chapter Nine.* You know you want this, carnivore.

How to make:

Steam potato like I show you above. Don't be worry. Law of physic not change since then, okay?

Put potato chunk into medium size pot.

Fry salo----pork or beef fat in iron pan. Can also use vegetable oil. For each large potato, about as much as one half teacup that queen Betty use. I call this *Royal Proportion.* If salo still chunky, take from pan and chop into crumb size.

Put salo in with potato.

Fry chop onion in same grease from salo.

Listen careful to Baba: do not fry garlic in this recipe. We want fresh fresh taste, not over-fry mess like bad hair day in Muscovy trailer park. **Make mince from clove fresh garlic and add to potato.**

Add salt.

I know you not expect this, but **add chop fresh dill weed** and toss very light with potato.

Baba promise you children not going to nag so much to go to this fast food place. And so much cheaper to make this.

Ingredient List:

- Potatoes, two large or one pound baby
- Salo, one quarter cup
- Onion, one medium
- Garlic, one clove
- Salt
- Fresh dill, one half cup

Oven-Fried Potatoes

Turn oven to very hot---450 degree F

Use only one medium to large potato for each person you feeding. This kind food not going to make good leftover, so don't all of sudden get ambitious.

Wash potato. Cut into long narrow strip or round piece about one half inch thick.

Spread potato on baking sheet. Make sure sheet is traditional kind with edge, not modern thing look like toboggan.

Melt salo, Royal Proportion as above. **Pour over potato and mix around** so potato all shiny like Christmas tree ornament. Do not put on tree. Is thing call simile.

Bake until they soft and brown. Make sure you watching oven instead of TV. Turn potato over few time when they baking.

Drain off leftover salo. Add salt and pepper.

Your option:

*Sprinkle with **crumble fried bacon or veggie substitute**
***Dip in *Ukrainian Mayonnaise*,** under *Salad Dressing, Chapter Three.*

Ingredient List:

- Potato, two large. About one pound
- Salo, one quarter cup
- Salt and pepper

Potato and Cheese Bake

This fast and easy recipe for when rude person drop in at suppertime, and you don't want them to tell everyone in neighborhood you don't cook supper. These people have some kind radar. You can work like donkey in Siberian salt mine all week, but they catch you one time you put swollen feet up.

Here is Baba strategy: show all your teeth and make this casserole real quick.

Steam one medium to large potato for each person, like above. Include rude person in this count, even though I know you don't want. Is not good time to practice passing-aggressive.

Mix dry cottage cheese with beat up egg.

Add salt and pepper.

Grease casserole dish with butter or oil. You don't have time to melt salo. Also, I wouldn't waste such precious ingredient on this person.

Have smetana stand by. You don't have to use farm smetana this time. If you like being sarcastic, use that white jello they call sour cream at corner store.

Make layer potato, layer cheese/egg. Do again until all ingredient get used. Pour smetana on each layer. This is elegant white on white colour scheme like only sophisticate Mafia people use.

Throw on enough butter bread crumb to cover casserole.

Bake for half hour while making more smiling. I see I am having some kind flashback. I get anxiety in this recipe because I make once when Communist official drop in. "Drop in" in Ukraina mean he kick in door with boot and say, "What is for dinner Baba?" We have saying for these kind people, *Dark soul wear white shirt*. You have to watch for them in all country.

Serve with nice green salad and hope Communist choke on it. Baba is not having good day.

Ingredient List:

- Potatoes, two large or about one pound
- Dry cottage cheese, two cups
- Egg, one large
- Salt and pepper
- Butter, one quarter cup
- Sour cream, one cup

Grated Potato Bake

Baba call this *Great Potato Bake*. It taste like several million buck, but you can feed as many as eight regular people for couple of buck. Maybe Euro dollar, I don't know.

Dice up chunk of bacon. Fry in medium frying pan. Not till crispy. You going to let it cook but still be floppy.

Put bacon on paper towel to drain. Mechanic hand towel is splendidski absorbent tool. Use clean one, made from paper. See *Spinach Sichenyky, Chapter Ten*, for full explanation.

Pour out most of bacon fat except for about two or three tablespoon. This make brilliant way to fry fine chop onion. Fry them until they get tan but not sunburn.

Take frying pan off heat. Don't just turn off. Baba say take off heat because will continue to cook. This is call *Physic Law of Train Conductor*.

Baba now going to tell you something else you not want to hear. **You have to grate potato.** Yes, peel first this time. Little piece of peel in grate potato look too much like dirt. But don't be thinking is so much work. Baba letting you make this grate be coarse, not fine. Maybe if you make smiley smiley at neighbor, she let you borrow food procession.

Wash grate potato several time, then squeeze in clean towel. Not one you used for bacon. "Oh! Squeeze out water!" you saying, "Maybe this why my other grate potato recipe have water sitting in bottom all my life."

"Oh you *yolop*!" Baba say back. Silly thing.

Heat oven to 375 degree F.

Put potato in hugest bowl you got. Also clean. These two thing should not be mutual exclusive. Baba hope you don't have to go whole way to barn to get it. Send dog. Use stiff brush to scrub saliva. Tooth mark don't matter so much.

Mix up potato good with coffee cream, hold coffee. **Separate three large egg and mix around yolk with fork. Pour this in. Add salt and pepper.**

Baba hope you saved egg white this time. **Beat till it get stiff and cranky. Put egg white gentle into potato mix,** using rubber speculum.

Butter up medium size round casserole dish. Will help matter if dish is attractive.

Still being very gentle, scoop whole thing into casserole dish. Put small dot of butter all over top.

Bake about one hour. You can tell is done when potato look brown and crunchy. If you not sure, poke in fork and taste. Try not to eat half of dish before you take from oven.

Ingredient List:

- Bacon, one quarter pound
- Onions, two large
- Potatoes, three pounds
- Cream or half and half, one cup
- Eggs, three large
- Butter, one quarter cup
- Salt and pepper

Deruny (Potato Pancakes)

Baba going to show you how to make delicious kind pancake from potato. In Ukraina, we eat this thing for breakfast. I eat shred wheat too, but not at same time. Blech. This very easy to make.

Peel off skin from six potato. Grate potato small. When you grating, do not rub knuckle on small weasel teeth. This hurt like sonumabitch. Even better, you tell other people, "You not grate, you not eat." Sit back and watch. Have medicine plant ready for bleeding knuckle. See *Ukrainian Medicine: Babka Plant, Chapter Twenty Five.*

Wash potato in cold water several time, then squeeze out water with towel.

Peel and grate onion. Wear google on eye, just like Baba tell you.

Beat up two egg. Soon you finish with beater, rinse with cold water so not make sticky mess.

Put potato, onion and egg in big bowl with flour. Pour in and crack black pepper. Mix mix mix until arm muscle sore. Make that Arnold Schwarznegger jealous, you be so pump.

Make sure you wearing apron. This going to be splashy thing. Kind that cover your chest, especially you stacked like Baba. Ha! Here is warning: every ten year, replace apron. You know and I know, chest keep folding down. If it reach knee, time to stop cooking and let other people feed you.

Heat sunflower oil or olive oil in big fry pan. Do not use stupid canola. Now they making from some kind corporate genetic material. You don't want eat thing made by crazy man in polyester suit, only thing made by real farmer.

Wipe blood from grated knuckle off from potato. Drop big

spoonful potato mix into hot oil. It going to make zzzzzzzzz sound and maybe jump around in pan. Watch careful, don't be playing video game with thumb. This not why human evolve, okay? **When brown like nice cookie one side, flip over** with speculum and let zzzzzzzzzz on other. When other side brown, use speculum to take out of pan and on to plate.

Best to eat hot, with lots smetana. Can also eat with sauce, preserves or jam. Druny is chameleon food. It change character with every kind sauce you use. **Try *Rozha Z Tzukhrom*** *(Wild Rose Preserves)* under *Desserts, Chapter Twenty Three* .

If you not make exactly like I say, there going to be leftover. Some people brag they can keep in fridge two, three day. But if people not like first time, why bother? Try again till you have enough practice to be perfect, like Baba.

Ingredient List:

- Potatoes, six large
- Onion, one large
- Eggs, two large
- Flour, two tablespoons
- Salt and pepper
- Sunflower or olive oil, one half cup
- Sour cream, one cup

Chapter Twenty

Grains and Beans

Banya (The Bath House)

Banya or bath house is sacred place in Ukraina. It serve similar spiritual purpose as sweat lodge to Aboriginal North American, except ours is big wood house or dig from side of hill. We relax and we meditate. We make steam on rock and beat friend with birch rod for circulation. Ukrainian bath house have extra occupant, cranky spirit name *Banyk*. Sometime he have cranky wife name *Baniya*, which make this extra dangerous and spiritual place to visit.

If you disrespect ritual of bath house, Bannyk and Banniya can be awful mean. You not suppose to make loud burping or have sexy romance on bench. This can cause spirit to suffocate you in steam. However, they don't mind looking out from under bench if you cute when you naked. Probably better you don't go there alone. Black Plague that decimate Europe, is much less problem in Ukraina, due to Banya. Also, we did not burn healers as "witches" or kill cats that eat rats.

Other thing that offend these old spirit is false Christian icon. This is since Viking woman name Olga call herself “queen”. Viking make deal with new Church to forcefully evangelize Slavs, who is just fine loving Nature and Goddess. Olga husband, Viking “king” Igor go round to village extorting all sorts tax. This is opposite of what Jesus do. See, they just pretending to be Christian. When one tribe get tired of Igor personal revenue service, they kill him. Slavs is also not too happy about some being drowned during force baptism.

Olga do what evangelist do so good. She show forgiveness. She lock Slavic Drevlyan tribe into huge new bath house and light bath house on fire. Lots people get so scare, they convert to this religion with all their pocket. Criminal Viking seize Slavic land and turn over to church they build. This is sad story of Indigenous people all over world, poopchik. Predator get baptize in order to have sanction for genocide. Eventual, knuckle dragger Viking make love match with Genghis Khan horde. After they murder and steal from even more Slav, they make baby together call *Muscovy*. Muscovy/Moscow is Mongolian tribute so unimportant, Mongols burn it down twice! It become country only in 1547, under monster named Ivan Terrible. Is only “Russia” since 18th century. This is so you fooled into thinking Muskoli Viking/Mongol is Slavic. "Rus'yan" mean Slavic, and is fraud.

Some Ukrainian women have baby in bath house. Is dark, comfortable and easy to clean with few bucket of water or spraying hosa. In Canada, Baba once take woman in labor to local recreation centre steam room. This not work out so good, even with her annual pass. Sometime Ukrainian, especially kozak, put hashish or hemp seed on hot rock. Old Greek historian Herodotus record this going back many century in our history. He say we like to howl in this ceremony. Bannyk not mind this howling. Ukrainian not into pothead outside of bath house. Is sacred substance, not for every day abuse. Poppy opium is for medicinal only. See *Poppy Seed, Chapter Twenty Four.*

We have special ritual for poor person who work very dirty job like chimney sweep or painter. Instead of community bath house, he crawl into huge village bread bake *pich* (oven). He splash water inside clay wall to make steam. Because is not room to bring friend, he drink beer and beat his own self with birch rod. Is sad thing, but sometime his friend who waiting for turn fire up oven too hot. Uh oh, too much steam bath. This one reason why we always leaving brown nose gift for Banyk so he protect us. He like perfume soap and fir branch best.

Banya is excellent place to find lover. Is advantage in seeing person naked first. No unhappy surprise like in single bar.

Baba address man here: If you going to be natural male, make sure you take soft blanket along for leading new girlfriend out to field. Stash behind banya. How else you going to snag natural woman. If she come by and want you, I mean. You understand, this kind woman not always shave armpit. What you care? She usually bring fresh condom and snack.

During *Koruksun* (Winter Solstice), women tell fortune in banya. Baba get this down to art, because is no-fail method to know what kind of New Year you going to have. She lift back of skirt and walk into banya this way. Not even thong to intervene in experience. If banyk spirit touch her soft and warm, is good luck. If she feel cold, prickly hand, this is bad news all the way. Time to run. She recommend this as rule of life whether you in banya or not.

Baba have high recommendation of this method. She love her tarot card, but here there is no wiggling room for misinterpretation.

Once you learn your fortune, have steam and throw cold water on self, you going to be hungry like steppe wolf. Best thing to eat at these moment is super warm and nutritional

Kasha (Buckwheat)

Baba thought she was going to actual put *kasha* in Ukrainian medicine chapter. This grain is relate to sunflower, not wheat or rice. It can help with so many condition. Vet are using it for cardiovascular disease in dog, even. Think what it can do for you.

Kasha is eighteen percent protein! This is about same as average hamburger. Baba trying to get them kind restaurant to carry kasha, but so far is no *McUke*™ burger. And they say *Big Baba*™ with fry is out from questioning.

It have lots rutin, which make blood capillary wall get strong and help circulation. For same reason, eat buckwheat if your ankle swell. You going to watch them drain like credit from your Mastercard. Can help with sugar diet beet and bad cholesterol, too. Also high in magnesium.

Baba publisher tell her she have to say, "Check with doctor."

Baba guarantee doctor not going to make argument if you eating more grain. Or if you substitute tiny bit strong, delicious buckwheat honey for all that sugar you stuffing in *McFace*™.

Baked Kasha

This is one those recipe is absolute mandatory for Sviata Vechera. Kasha is principle crop in Ukraina along with wheat. Best thing, it is very disease-resistant, just like hemp. No pesticide to make your body part go in mutant form.

Ukrainian eat kasha for breakfast like cereal, in place of potato for starchiness and as mainline dish. If you going to get ambitious for once and bake bread or muffin, you have to mix kasha flour with wheat. Kasha is free from bondage of gluten.

Wash medium kasha and check for rock. "Medium" mean hull been crack by some mystery process you lucky you don't have to do yourself.

Put kettle of water on to boil. Or heat up some kind meat, vegetable or dry mushroom stock. This will make uncontrollable lip smack.

Baba law: Never put straight tap water in recipe. Always boil.

Drain kasha real good and put in frying pan with egg. Scramble them together so egg can coat each grain. This make kasha grain separate and get goldie-brown. Some people say they now get "nutlike" flavor. Baba say, what nut you talking about? Still taste like kasha to her. This is like suppose to be. Scrambling around should take two minute or so on. **If you turn kasha dark brown, throw away.**

Dump kasha into medium size pot. Throw in some kind fat or oil. Salo (meat fat) and chicken fat is like soulmate to kasha. No one say you can only have one. It depend how big your own soul. But if you making for Sviata Vechera, remember no animal fat. Soniashynyk, sunflower oil, and hemp or flax oil is another kind soulmate to kasha.

Throw in salt and boiling water. Boil kasha, then turn down heat to medium low until it suck up most of water. Should take about fifteen minute. But honest, Baba know you going to buy kasha from stupormarket in bag. There is bylaw against threshing on downtown boulevard. Bag going to have instruction for how long to cook, because it depend on how coarse is kasha.

If all you can find is “whole” kasha, you don't have to fry with egg. Baba find *Safeway* brand is good stuff. They be phoning her any day to offer endorsement fee. Just throw whole kasha into pot and cook like above. This not have as intense flavor as crack kasha, though.

Kasha approximately triple in volume when cook.

Turn oven to 400 degree F.

Put kasha into medium casserole dish with lid. Use the one have no crack. Baba believe in crack-free existence.

Bake for half hour, then lower heat to 325 degree F for whole hour. This not instant cereal, people.

Kasha should be fluffy but not mushy. If is kind of disgusting this way, **turn heat to 350 degree F and bake it for fifteen to thirty minute more.**

Serve with more butter on top. Can be main dish or side dish.

Your option:

*Make as **filling for *Holubtsi*** *(Cabbage Rolls), Chapter Fourteen.*
*For tasty cereal with good protein, **heat up milk or cream with little bit honey** and pour on kasha.
*For quick lunch, **mix one cup cook kasha with one third cup cream cottage cheese.** Kasha does not have to go through bake process for this. Is handy thing to put in lunch thermos, too. Will give you lots energy to deal with job you hate, maybe even enough to quit.

Ingredient list:

- Medium buckwheat groats, two cups
- Egg, one large

- Fat, one quarter cup
- Salt, two teaspoons
- Boiling water or stock, four cups

Ukrainian Pilaf

Make Ukrainian pilaf by add big hand full shred cheddar or firm goat cheese to every two cup bake kasha.

Baba repeat: add cheese after kasha is bake, or you going to have to use your blow torch to clean casserole dish. Baba is not going to give blow torch instruction until next volume of recipe book, under *Handy Hint For Oven Clean.*

Kasha Casserole

Baba know your head spinning both from trip to bannia and whole new world of kasha. Here is more psychohallucinogenic dogma: you can use kasha as substitute for rice or other grain in any dish. Might even be something you want to try with kasha you never dare before.

Ukrainian *yizha dusha*, soul food, is powerful thing. Dusha, soul, is fierce vitality force. It is roaring flame you cannot put out, inside cage of thick flesh and hard bone. Not some kind airing fairy floating around like chiffon scarf. That is Nu Age barfola. Food is to create more life force, make nourishing for your soul as well as your physical body.

Here is some idea for casserole. Make alternate layer with bake kasha and:

*__Montreal smoke meat or corn beef and fry slice mushroom__
*__Fry onion and ground lamb,__ lean beef, venison or bison. You can also mix these thing right in with kasha so it all one dish. Baba think layer is more interesting. She give you this second option so you can think you fooling family into believe this is new recipe. If they love you, they not say nothing about treachery.
*Any of above, and **make one layer slice tomato.** Best to use tomato with heavy meat, not watery kind. Sun dry type make very nice layer.
*__Mix one cup dry cottage cheese with large egg and splash heavy cream.__

Baba warning: Don't make these all at once. Stop trying so desperate and you can graduate Al-Anon. Baba have lots more success in life since she watch her pushing-over friend suffer. Is big difference between generous and coding pendant. You need to get decoded. Ha!

Bake for half hour in 350 degree F oven.

Sauce can be plain smetana pour over top before baking, or just before serving. *Try Horse Radish, Smetana and Green Onion* or *Honey Onion Sauce, Chapter Twenty Two.*

Kasha Sichenyky (Patties)

Here is one recipe Baba try to sell to McUke. One day she will have chain of restaurant, you will see. Ukrainsky food is going to be whole new craze in North America. You going to be able to buy borshch in drive-through Grande go-cup. Baba going to count her many million dollar and laugh.

Boil water in small pot.

Throw in kasha and fine chop onion.

Make simmer on medium-low heat until kasha say, “Enough already!” It will take about fifteen minute for all water to disappear inside kasha. This mixture should be fluffy puffy.

This will make about three cup kasha.

Mix up kasha with four medium size egg and dry bread crumb. Crumb should be coarse like your landlord chest hair, and from good rye or pumpernickel bread. Tightie whitie defeat purpose of kasha nutrition. Now forget these two image and go back to cooking.

Have extra cup bread crumb fly standby in case this not make burger firm enough. Can be tricky, depending on size of egg.

Add salt and pepper.

Put on those latex glove Baba know you keep in every drawer of house. **Make kasha patty and throw in frying pan with soniashynyk, salo or butter.** Should be maybe five patty if you planning to put inside bun. Or ten if you making small one to eat with good sauce.

Serve which way you like. Is incredible as burger with **Ukrainian mayonnaise, or with firm goat cheese melt on top.**

If you serving as small finger patty, **put on bed of nice color lettuce.** Do not serve with finger.

Ingredient list:

- Boiling water, two cups

- Medium kasha groats, one cup
- Onion, one medium
- Eggs, four medium
- Coarse stale bread crumbs, one to two cups
- Salt and pepper
- Fat for frying, quarter cup

Kasha Loaf

Here is unique recipe Baba bet no one else going to make for Sviat Vechir. She work this out when son Sasha go through vegetarian phasing. If Baba can be frank for once, he was big pain in *shyya.** He turning up nose at everything and commandeering Baba best cook pot to make big disgusting gallon of raw soy bean at one time. It always go sour before he finish, but he give even bigger self-righteous lecture on our wasteful way.

Baba finally cook him something that not trying to look like meat. But is good protein and very tasty. Not too bad looking, either. What else you need?

Now his vegetarian friend all hanging out in my house, asking for me to show them recipe. Like Baba don't have enough to do.

Cook one cup kasha like for sichenyky, above, including onion.

Fry up quality mushroom in soniashnyk oil and one clove crush garlic. NOT CAN MUSHROOM.

Mix in ground soniashnyk, almond or pumpkin seed. You should have mortar and pestle like Baba Yaga for grinding. If not, put in heavy plastic bag and roll over it. You will have blender idea and think you are brilliant. Until you have to pick ground seed from around blade and scrape side of glass. Seed have more oil than you think, and it stick like crazy to everything.

Mix in one raw egg real good. This is what bind loaf, along with seed or nut. You could use Krazy Glue, but everyone at table will die.

Add kind of spice you like: thyme work for this, so does basil or savory. This not exactly Ukrainian spice, but cumin is oh so heavenly. Try half teaspoon of first two kind. **Cumin,** you can use heap teaspoon. If you enjoy little bit spicy, **add half teaspoon cayenne pepper or splash hot sauce.**

Turn oven to 350 degree F.

Cram loaf into greasy loaf pan. Pour half cup sauce on top so will soak in while baking. *Horse Radish Sauce, Honey Onion, Smetana and*

Green Onion, Chapter Twenty Two is delicious with kasha loaf.

On top of this sauce, make guilty lily with several slice butter.

Bake for one hour and serve in slice on beautiful plate. Baba say this because no matter what you do, kasha is delicious but still brown. You can also serve smetana or more of your choice sauce in side dish.

*Shyya: Neck

Ingredient list:

- Medium kasha groats, one cup
- Onion, one medium
- Quality mushrooms, one half cup when sliced
- Sunflower or pumpkin seeds, or almonds, one cup
- Egg, one large
- Spices as suggested
- Butter, one quarter cup for topping
- Sauce as desired

Kutya

This sweet grain recipe is favorite of my goat, Sonya, in Ukraina. Her name short for *soniashnyk*, sunflower. I call her that because she follow patch of sun around all day, lie in it. Oh, she love that. You know how sunflower follow sun with their face? Sonya have very good suntan. Every day I put little bit suntan oil on her so she get brown faster. She start summer all white, and by end summer, she be dark like raisin. She dorahenka, very dear goat.

Sonya like her tan very much. She come in house, first thing she do is look in mirror. She turn like this, like that. She look over her shoulder and smile at reflection.

One time mean neighbor complain to village council. She say I dress goat in bikini. This not true! Goat prefer naked when we home alone. But when company come, she put on very smart one piece. Bright red, with big yellow poke dot. Sonya fashionable kind of goat. Only thing too bad, she not smell so good as she look.

In Ukraina we have saying: *Smell is bane of goat existence. Otherwise, they all be fashion model.*

When Baba see Sonya serious about suntan, I make deal on black market for google kind sunglass. I wrap around her head with elastic. She especially wear when she float on back in pool.

How you have pool in poor Ukrainski village, you want to know? I walk far into wood and dam stream with log. I even make jacuzzi. All it take is eggbeater. Also very good exercise for upper arm. I best looking girl in village, wearing sleeveless. You women paying for aerobic. Ha! All you need is goat.

Just be careful if you have goat with floppy-shmoppy ear. It should not get too close to eggbeater. Very difficult to pull out.

Sonya love to eat kutya, which is homemade cereal so delicious. In Ukraina all family eat this dish first on Sviata Vechera, Christmas Eve, then serve to animal to honor them for not biting baby rabbi Jesus.

We say about somebody who is too slick salesman, *He put too much honey in kutya.*

All Ukrainian hear animal talk on Sviata Vechera. But I listen to Sonya and feed kutya to her all year. She healthy like horse and make many gallon milk. And hoo boychik, those village people better honor Baba midwife by bringing her kutya at this time. Else she going to bite somebody herself.

Same neighbor follow me to Canada. She make complaint I bring goat on bus. Crazy health department. Pah! Kid wipe nose on bus seat, but I can't bring clean animal. In Ukraina I bring goat on bus all the time. She sleep in house, too.

Here is how to make delicious kutya for goat or human:

Soak wheat berry (kernel) in warm water for twenty four hour. Strain. That right. No such thing as fast food kutya. Is sacred dish. In Ukraina, each grain wheat represent one soul. Take time to make this whole recipe.

Same time, soak poppy seed in milk so covered by liquid. Put in fridge overnight. This make seed soft. *See Poppy Seed, Chapter Twenty Four.*

Put wheat kernel with milk in pot. Drain poppy seed and use this milk. If you strict vegetarian, can use water or rice milk. Soy milk going to taste weird. Goat milk excellent, if you like taste. Sonya be honored.

Make boil. Simmer for three hour. This mean turn down heat so you still see bubble every once in while. **Check on wheat every hour.** Add more liquid if top of wheat kernel poking through liquid like underwire through old bra.

Heat oven to 325 degree F.

Once wheat done, drain but keep one half cup liquid in separate bowl.

Mix this liquid with one half cup honey. Best if you keep your own bee. If not, try to find honey in tree. Watch out for bear. If you really desperate, buy from stupormarket. Real Ukrainian taste is buckwheat honey, very strong. Where I live in BC is many nice kind from flower like fireweed, blueberry blossom and so on.

For more good Baba information about bee and honey, See *Ukrainian Medicine, Honey, last chapter.*

Baba digress. **Mix wheat and honey with poppy seed, slice almond (roast or raw) and dry apricot. If you like, add raisin.** Some people not like raisin when they swell up in liquid.

Add salt and cinnamon. Some people add splash sherry.

Put kutya in large casserole dish. Do not cover.

Bake for twenty minute.

You can serve warm or chill, depending on how your goat like it. Do not serve to her too hot.

Sprinkle with little bit cinnamon. Can also garnish with those candy cherry. Slice in half.

At *Velyk Den'*/Easter, Baba follow Ukrainian native religion out in church yard. She take kutya, mead and *pysanky* (blessed eggs) to ancestor grave. Sometime Sonya come along to trim grass.

Kutya taste best when prepare couple day ahead of time before eating. Baba always laugh when she read this in recipe. Who going to wait that long?

Ingredients:

- Wheat berries, one and half cups. Soak in warm water 24 hours
- Poppy seed, one cup. Soak in one cup milk overnight
- Milk, five and one half cups---including milk for poppyseed
- Honey, one half cup
- Sliced almonds or walnuts, two thirds cup
- Dried apricots, two thirds cup
- Raisin, one half cup if desired
- Salt, pinch
- Cinnamon, pinch

Fasolia (White Bean Pate)

If you like how fasolia taste when I introduce you them marry to borshch, you going to go wild when they single. This recipe much easier and cheaper process than Internet date. Enough for four Ukrainian-size main dish serving is about one dollar in 2016. If you reading this from time capsule in outer space, tall Starbuck coffee is one dollar and ninety five cent before tax. Eat your astronaut heart out.

This recipe is absolute necessary as one of twelve meatless dish on Sviata Vechera.

Soak little white bean in water overnight. Soaking make cook time shorter and cut out most of greenhouse gas effect.

Boil them in pot. Add pinch salt when they almost done. Should take about one and one half hour till they tender. Fasolia have extreme tenderness. Is no bit of shell that will linger on teeth and tongue.

Baba know you very busy during Winter Solstice. If you trying to juggle all twelve meatless dish PLUS sick dog and too many freeloader, you have dispensation. Buy two big can white or navy bean at stupormarket. These you don't have to soak and cook. Don't sound so relieve. Is comforting thing for people to walk into house where bean cooking. Could change life better than those self-helping books you always biting nail over. **White bean almost double in size when they cook. Kind in can is already swell.** Baba going to leave you to do math.

Chop onion so fine, is like lace. Fry in good glop extra virgin olive or sunflower oil till lace is soft and see-through.

Drain bean but keep liquid. Mash up bean. Potato masher work, so do vigorous forking.

Pour in bean liquid tiny splash at time until is consistency you can live with.

Mix onion with bean. When you wondering why you doing all this for, remember white bean is delicious protein that don't make hardly any gas once is soak. Is especially important with full house on holiday. DO NOT SUBSTITUTE KIDNEY BEAN. You be so sorry, and Baba will not care.

Here is three ways to add garlic:

***Crush two clove raw garlic and mix with bean.** This create bad breath, but if you plan right, everyone will smell. This is ideal situation.
***At last minute when onion is almost cook, crush raw garlic and throw in pan.** Do not let garlic cook long enough to get brown. Give up while you still have head.
***Roast one head garlic.** This mean you have to start recipe early. If you kind of person who like to cook your own bean, this should be good timing.

How to roast garlic:

Peel off outer layer from head. Chop off woody part on top. **Throw little bit oil on top and wrap in tinfoil.** Easiest way to handle in oven is to balance garlic head in muffin tin. Do not bake honey muffin at same time. This false economy.

Should take forty-five to sixty minute in 375 degree F oven.

Squeeze garlic from two to four clove and mash in with bean. Add salt and pepper. Save rest of roast garlic to spread on bread, add to soup or meat dish.

Fasolia can be eaten hot like is, or made into cold dip/spread for vegetable and good strong bread.

Baba warning: Do not try to pass off one dish cold and one dish hot fasolia as TWO your Sviat Vechir dish. With your luck, experienced Ukrainian will be at table. Bus-ted.

Your option:

*Baba know you going to love fasolia so much, you will eat more than once in year. In that case, you can **cook bean in soup stock.** Vegetable, beef, chicken, all will make different taste.

Ingredient List:

- White beans, two cups dry OR two 14 ounce cans
- Onion, one large
- Extra virgin olive or sunflower oil, one quarter cup
- Garlic, your choice of amount
- Salt and pepper

Kulesha (Cornmeal Pudding)

This kulesha is miracle food. It give you plenty energy and glossy teeth. Can substitute when you bored of potato or rice for side dish. Is also wonderful nutrition if you rescue starving dog.

It swell up at least three time its size, so be warn.

First, get DVD of half hour favorite rerun TV show from library.

Mix up stone ground cornmeal with cold water in medium, nonsticking pot. Dusty kind cornmeal have not so Ukrainski taste. Is more like what left over in your popcorn bag.

Make boiling.

Quick throw in salt and sugar.

Turn heat to minimize and stir around for minute or two. Put on lid and let it entertain itself for half hour. Go watch one TV episode.

Stir around some more, put lid back on and leave alone on lowly heat. Watch next episode.

Stir around one last time. Now you not going to have time for third Frasier rerun. You have to heat up salo (bacon or beef grease) and mix into kulesha.

Serve hot. It will keep for week in fridge or snow, and taste even cornier when reheat.

Reheat instruction: put butter or more salo in cast ironing pan. Cover with lid and let steam about ten minute. Microwave? Forget about this.

Ingredient list:

- Stone ground cornmeal, one cup
- Cold water, four cups (one quart)
- Sugar, one teaspoon
- Salt, one tablespoon
- Salo, butter or sunflower oil, one third cup

Fried Kulesha

Baba got big thrill when she was ranch hand in Texas. Not only because she get to sleep in bunkhouse with eight cowboy. Also some guy call "Cookie" make kulesha, too. He show Baba how take it one step more into extreme. This turn into type of super-nutrition pancake. Good for when you have to ride range all day.

If you make night before and tell your favorite cowboy you going to serve along with kobasa, is guarantee he will still be there in morning.

Make kulesha like above.

Grease loafing pan. Pour kulesha into pan.

Let kulesha not-meat loaf chill out on counter. Wrap in foiling and put in fridge for overnight. Be hopeful you won't have time to poke at it.

Next morning, ignore that your cowboy look and smell like he wrestle steer. Steer was *you*, remember? You just quicker into shower, dorahenka.

Dump kulesha careful onto plate and cut thin.

Heat up cast ironing pan and melt any kind fat you like. Fry kulesha slice so it get appetizing brownie color on both side. Don't try any fancy flipping. This is waste of time and don't impress cowboy. He know rope trick.

Put maple syrup or soft butter on table. Eat.

Chapter Twenty One

Lokshyna
(Egg Noodles)

These next recipe is for thing I call "comforting food." Nothing so good for this like lokshyna, homemake egg noodle. Especially with butter and cheese. *Smachnenko*! Delicious!

Baba need this kind of thing one day after I am out riding round on my horse, Taras. I call him this because all good horse is combination of poet and warrior, like Shevchenko and Bulba. I see you scratching your head, poopchik. Is time to study Ukrainsky history waaaaay past perogy and borshch*

Taras is big Thoroughbred. When I first come to Canada, my children give me some old kind slow floppy horse with big hair on toe. I say, "Pah! Without fast horse, Ukrainian is nothing. We domesticate horse six thousand year ago."

I make them drive me to race track. They selling this horse who run like Nazi after gold tooth, but he always coming in second. If Baba not buy him, they ship him to terrible slaughter house. In North America is Horse Holocaust, just like Stalin do in Ukraina. They butchering 200,000 horse alive in Canada every year. It even happen to Kentucky Derby winner, and most Mama mare and Daddy stud once they become infertile. Retirement in nice green pasture is fantasy, poopchik.

Taras is over sixteen hand high and black like that pot you never clean. He put his slobber lip in Baba ear and tell her he more interest in beautiful filly behind him than some testosterone contest. If Baba promise him girlfriend, he run like champion for her. See? Good horse is perfect combination: poet and warrior.

One day Taras and me waltzing around neighbourhood and see this huge field of green green grass. Horse is dancing underneath and Baba can't help herself, even though sign say *Property Private*.

We trot to edge and see grass is very short. No gopher hole to break leg in. Next thing I know, Taras rearing up and we galloping faster than he ever go on race track. Only he sinking little bit with every stride. And there is two men yelling and waving some kind shiny stick over head. Baba and Taras keep galloping over this grass like in Heaven. Then there is several more men with stick, and Baba turn horse to sidewalk. Crazy men chase Baba and Taras all the way into K-Mart parking lot. They lose her because beer belly make it hard to jump speed bump.

Next thing Baba know, she get visit from Neighborhood Watch. This fancy Canadian name for "lousy snitch." They tell me to go meet at golf course club house. There ugly Anglo men sitting at table. They tell Baba, "We have half of mind to not just make you pay for damage. We want to make criminal charge for you."

Baba say, "I believe you have half of mind. This what it take to make green gallop field into place you chase stupid pimple ball with club. Why you not play real sport? Or turn all this land into place to grow food for real people?" She also tell them Ukrainian proverb, because they so boring. *Nai bude zle, aby nove!* Let something bad happen, so long as is something new!

They don't charge Baba because she recent immigrant. And because golf course already in news; they playing stupid fake game on real Canadian grave. This handsome Canadian wearing shirt made from deerskin say to media, "That Baba, at least she European Aboriginal using our land for traditional purpose. We welcome her gallop Taras on Native land."

This all over TV. Baba ride in parade with First Nation people and her RCMP boyfriend all around golf course. They give Baba three beautiful mare to thank her. Taras is happy. This all so romantic, I know you jealous.

Maybe once you make Baba's *Lokshyna*, you be more brave and have big adventure too. **Baba want you to know how easy is to make noodle at home:**

Basic Lokshyna

You going to beat up four egg. Because Lokshyna is egg noodle, genius. **Save one eggshell** for magic trick. This recipe make about one pound noodle.

Put clean sheet on kitchen table and forget about till Baba remind you later.

Sprinkle flour on cutting or pastry board. Mix together egg, all-porpoise flour, salt and two or three splash water from one half eggshell like you know what you doing.

This turn into dough. Why I have to tell you? **Knead** with those knuckle you drag on ground until dough is smooth. Baba is not going to say, "Like baby bum," because this is not appetizing. Kneading happen from inside of dough, out.

Cover up dough with clean dish towel for half hour. If you not have dish towel, is okay to use your clean bloomer if you single and no one going to be disgusted. Don't use thong, or Baba going to be disgusted. You don't want this, believe me. Underwear have purpose in life.

Tear off one third of dough and put on floured board. Keep rest of dough covered while you working. Use rolling pin to make dough thin, in circle shape. How thin? Like that neighbor who look like X-ray. And remember, noodle going to bloat up in water later, like when same neighbor get stuck in bathtub drain and CSI come.

Now very careful, turn over thin dough so it will get dry. But not too dry so you get remind of your bad hair. Really, you need to hire Baba to come over and make supervision. Call

1-900-ASK-BABA. Very expensive, but so worth it.

Be gentle and put first round piece dough on sheet you have on kitchen table. Baba know what happen next. You thought she was making joke about sheet before. Now you running round house like *banyak,* trying to hold dough on one hand while you ripping sheet off from bed.

Okay, once you get life together, **roll out second third of dough. Do same thing with this.**

Let three round, thin dough piece dry out little bit on sheet maybe ten minute. Make sure end is not get brittle. Baba corporate daughter once try fix this with fancy-shmancy hair conditioner. Then she on phone making all sorts crying because it not work. Baba hang up.

Cut each piece dough in three piece each. Take out calculator. Three time three is what? You know answer---good for you, poopchik!

Sprinkle dough with flour, then stack piece on top each other. Get out sharp knife. Now is time you have to make decision. Uh oh. Do you want skinny shred noodle like chow mein, or broad egg noodle? You can also cut in little checker square. Very cute in soup.

If you know how to tie noodle in little bow, go for it. Baba don't have time for this. Man you cook for not going to notice, anyway. Might be good test to make if you in love and suspecting he is gay. If he going “Oooh!” and “Aaah!” over small bow, give up hope you find well-groom heterosexual exception. If he already have fluffy dog who wear clothes, you should know better in first place.

Once you make executive decision and cut up noodle in shape you like, **separate noodle with your clean finger and leave on sheet to dry.**

Pretty soon your family who been avoiding doing any work will come in. Make them **put big pot salt water on to boil. Drop in noodle very careful.** They will cook in five or eight minute, depending what shape you cut. How you know they done? Noodle will float to top of pot, holding its nose. Noodle will have swell up during this process. **Take out from pot with holy spoon and drain in colander. Rinse with cold water so they not stick together.**

Or you can let noodle dry all rest of day and put in storage container for later. Put cat outside so she not walking on kitchen table. Baba love *kitsya*, but kitty litter in lokshyna is not desirable flavor mix.

If you don't want no one feeding noodle to dog when you not looking, you can also store in freezer bag. You don't have to thaw noodle before dropping in hot water.

Toss lokshyna with melt butter and eat with main dish. Uh oh. Maybe Baba should have told you.

In meantime you supposed to be making:

**Roast Beef, Huliashi* or *Bytky Beef, Chapter Nine*, or maybe
**Chicken Soup, Chapter One*, or
**Chicken in Dill Cream,Chapter Eight* or
**Zrazy (Meatballs), Chapter Ten.*

I forget to tell you, so what? You got to take your Ritalin around Baba. Read entire recipe first, or else blame it on bossa nova. Blame it on anyone but Baba.

Ingredient List:

- Eggs, four medium
- All purpose unbleached flour, three cups
- Salt, one teaspoon
- Warm water, one half cup. Use your judgment how much makes dough the right dryish texture.

Lokshyna and Spinach Casserole

This is favorite Lokshyna recipe of my horse Taras. He love spinach kind, not so much kind with bacon (below). Taras make good friend with pig next door name Bob. He think bacon is bad politic. It hurt his finer feeling.

Cook egg noodle till they float to top. Drain them and mix with

chunk melt butter, grate cheese and salt.

Here we going to multi-task. If you have arm like octopus, is no problem. While you fixing up noodle, also **steam two big bunch chop spinach.** Make sure you already cut off stem. Kitchen window should be open so horse can poke in face. Feed spinach stem to him and also to pig friend. Pig is short like usual, so you going to have to lean out window, Baba telling you this. If you not wash spinach first, horse probably going to spit dirt on you. Good. You deserve this.

While you fixing up noodle, steaming spinach and feeding horse, also **fry chop onion in butter and grease baking dish.**

With your next hand, heat oven to 350 F.

Mix up steam spinach with onion. Add salt and crack black pepper.

Kitchen smell so delicious, horse going to bang on door with big fat foot. Throw him some grate cheese. This confuse him until you can make rest of recipe. Most horse is sensitive to dairy.

You scoffing with your nose at this information. Baba only telling you what Ayurvedic veterinarian say, okay?

Ooop. Baba forget to tell you: **also you should be rolling fine bread crumb around in hot butter,** if you have any hand or stove element left.

Make arrangement of layer in baking dish: noodle, spinach, noodle, spinach. How many layer, you want to know. One more than ingredient you have, so you can beat self up and read stupid overprice magazine telling why you have low self-steam so you buy more stupid overprice magazine.

Put butter bread crumb on top of casserole.

Bake for about half hour. Is no big crime if you mess up little bit with cooking time. All ingredient is already cook. Really, you just need cheese to melt and flavor to blend. **Take out of oven just before bread crumb catch on fire.**

Is Ukrainian tradition to make garnish with slice hard boil egg. See *Eggs, Chapter Seven*, so you not screw this up, too.

Your option:

*Throw **big pinch fine chop parsley** in with butter bread crumb.
*Throw **hand full grate parmesan on top of casserole** along with bread crumb. Good kind only, not cheese dust from bulky bin.
***Try different variety melty cheese** so recipe taste different every time. Sometime Baba serve same thing every day for week and no one complain. Of course, you have to have real personality like Baba to make this thing work. Try: mild to old age pension Cheddar, Swiss, Edam,

Gouda, Jack, Marble, Colby, firm goat.

Feed casserole to horse only when cool and ignore when he spitting out cheese. Mad horse with pig friend not someone to make mess with.

Ingredient List:

- Lokshyna, two cups
- Cheese, one quarter cup
- Salt and pepper
- Spinach, two cups total when cooked and drained
- Butter, one quarter cup
- Onion, one half small
- Bread crumbs, one quarter cup
- Eggs, two hard boiled

Lokshyna v Syr (Cottage Cheese)

This recipe so easy, Baba almost ashame to reveal Ukrainian secret: this is what we make when we too lazy to even make *Lazy Varenyky (perogies), Chapter Thirteen.*

For four people:

Cook lokshyna. Do NOT rinse with cold water, because you need them hot like Brangelina. Yes, Baba know you like them both. Is okay. Everybody do.

Mix in melt butter or *salo* (fat). Baba give you some leeway because she know you already biting fingernail with guilty conscience. Look, as long as you not eat this every day, you probably not going to drop dead too soon.

Just when you think you is unforgivable sinner, **mix in cottage cheese.** Two percent or whole.

Add salt or garlic salt.

Now Baba really sending you for emotional heart attack: **make topping with crispy bacon or salt pork.** Pork rind from convenience store is going too far. Ha!

Ingredient List:

- Lokshyna, four cups cooked
- Butter, one half to three quarters cup OR

- Salo
- Creamed cottage cheese, two cups
- Salt or garlic salt
- Fried bacon or salt pork, one half cup

Lokshyna with Eggs

This turn out like interesting kind scramble egg.

Make like *Cottage Cheese* recipe, but use four beat up egg instead of cheese.

Melt lots butter or salo in big fry pan and add lokshyna and egg. Noodle should already be cook, or you be one sorry camper.

Add salt.

Mix around like you mean it. Serve on plate. Toast is not necessary.

Garnish with crispy bacon or salt pork. Or not, if you had heart attack recipe yesterday.

Baba warning: Give to guest immediately. This one those recipe delicious fresh from stove, but believe me, like lump of glue when cold.

Your option:

***Mix in big hand full grate parmesan or Asiago cheese** while cooking.

Ingredient List:

- Lokshyna with Cottage Cheese recipe, minus cottage cheese.
- Eggs, four medium

Baked Lokshyna v Syr

This is not horse-friendly recipe. Probably not dolphin-friendly either. Baba don't know. Ukrainian not so stupid we feed lokshyna to sea life.

You going to fry eight slice bacon until crispy, then mix bacon and salo with cooked lokshyna. Add salt.

If horse is with pig friend and poking face in window, this where he already get disgusted and leave. Good. You won't want to share this.

Heat oven to 350 F.

Beat up two large egg. Make sure is large, because this what hold thing together inside oven. If you construction-minded person, egg is your plaster. Get what Baba tell you? **Mix this large egg with dry cottage cheese and four half eggshell full whip cream.** Using measure cup is easier, but eggshell for this recipe is so you have excuse to lick cream off wrist.

Grease baking dish.

Make layer of noodle, cheese, noodle, cheese. Same like in Lokshyna with *Spinach Lokshyna* recipe (above). Baba getting bored explaining.

Make pan full butter bread crumb and throw this thing on top of casserole. **Bake about forty minute.** This should serve four city people or two real one. Serve with salad to ease your artery conscience.

Your option:

***Stir hand full fine chop parsley or dill in** with butter bread crumb. Baba warning: don't be thinking that fennel growing in alley is good substitute for dill. You ever taste licorice with cheese and bacon? Yuck.
***Mix in big hand full chop fresh chive or fried leek** with cheese and egg. Regular fried onion is too strong taste for this recipe.
***Mix in quarter cup sun dry tomato** or half cup not juicy kind fine chop fresh tomato.

Ingredient List:

- Lokshyna recipe
- Bacon, eight slices
- Eggs, two large
- Whipping or cereal cream, one quarter cup
- Dry cottage cheese, two cups
- Salt
- Buttered bread crumbs, one half cup

Lokshyna and Meat Casserole (Can substitute veggie meat)

If you is master of all above recipe (as if), Baba give you permission to get little bit creative with this one.

Go to deli and get some delicious kind meat and hard cheese. Traditional Ukrainian meat for this recipe is regular kind cook ham. But Baba give you permission to try: *prosciutto*, corn beef, *capicolli* and other thing make you fog up glass on display case. Kobasa (garlic sausage) and summer sausage is also good thing. Ham and kobasa together is like ecstasy pill. Can also use Tofurkey or other kind vegetarian deli meat, for sure.

Get your choice cheese, too. Only use common sense. Don't be getting mixed up with that Brie and Camembert; they not welcome in Ukrainian food.

Ask butcher to grind meat for you. See *Kalempetsya*, under *Stew, Chapter Eight*, for instruction on how to get free lunch at same time.

For four people:

Mix cooked lokshyna with butter. Again, you not running cold water on noodle this time. Cold noodle and butter will not melt. Baba know you going to try this stupid thing at least once, then sit on kitchen floor and crying. This is why she treat you like idiot in first place. So you not actual become idiot, in last place.

Heat oven to 350 F.

Mix meat and grate cheese with lokshyna.

Mix this with two large beat up egg and cereal cream.

You probably don't need salt, as most deli meat very salty. But my family love salt in everything. One time Baba get tired adding salt. Always pinch in this, pinch in that. Booo-ring. I go to feed store, buy big red block like kind for cow pasture and pow! Put on table for everyone to lick. Social worker take one look at happy family, say she "speechless." Baba make big stinking about cultural diversity. Social worker agree she probably could use time better elsewhere.

Baba warning: if you having guest over, buy fresh salt lick for centre piece. Some people think they so special, they have allergy to thing is partial used. Can also find in decorator blue. Martha Stewart make her own. Baba laugh and tell her this defeat purpose.

Between you and me, Baba would not do this in Ukraina even if she at end of roping. She give up all sorts dignity when she immigrate to Canada. Is so much oppression here. People all concern with *Peace, Order and Good Government* instead of thing in US they call, "Getting Life." Why not this colony revolutionize for once? In Ukraina, where we so poor we can't hardly get dress, we still give Russia big end of finger.

In Ukraina, we don't have such thing as social worker, neither. We have thing call "help each other." Someone abusing child, no one call village council if this person all of a sudden accidental DIE. And Ukrainian woman, she descend from Amazon. No such thing needed as batter woman shelter.

Now for your one time lucky break. No layering to think about. **Just**

spoon all ingredient into grease baking dish while you writing your great novel in head. Sorry, this second time Baba going to say “as if.”

Make topping from butter bread crumb. Like in other lokshyna recipe, you can mix fine chop fresh dill or parsley in with bread crumb.

Your option:

***Add one cup chop fried mushroom.** Use best kind you can afford. In this case, add one extra egg so everything sticking together.

Ingredient List:

- Deli meat, one half pound
- Lokshyna, four cups cooked
- Hard cheese, one third pound
- Eggs, two large
- Butter, one quarter cup
- Cereal cream, one half cup
- Bread crumbs, one half cup

Lokshyna and Kapusta (Cabbage) Casserole

This recipe is for when you poor like church moose, can't even afford spinach. **Make recipe like for *Lokshyna and Spinach Casserole*, except use cabbage instead of spinach.** Make two cup shred cabbage wilt in pan with onion is only difference. Not wilt completely, you understand. Should still be little crispy before you put in oven. All Ukrainian thing have backbone.

If you even more poor thing than this, leave out grate cheese. Will still be delicious. But you going to have to figure out your protein. Baba not in mood today to talk about what we eat during Stalinist famine. I guarantee, horse and pig will come back to help eat this now. Baba know you was lonely.

Ingredient List:

- *Lokshyna and Spinach Casserole* recipe, omit spinach
- Cabbage, two cups shredded

Lokshyna Ring

This is one of absolute only time Baba going to tell you to make food in something call "ring mold." Good thing is, this recipe hold together with no extra gelatin. It don't jiggle when you set it on table. Baba have issue with jiggle kind food. She trying to tell you: THIS IS NOT JELLY SALAD. Would your Baba do that to you?

Mix up hot cooked lokshyna with grate hard cheese and lump butter.

Turn oven to 350 F.

Separate three big egg. Not from each other, dummy. Stop sentimental whining and take down small egg fence you building. Separate white from yolk by playing shell game, back and forth. **Beat up white part with salt until they fighting back.** You know this happen when they get stiff.

Beat up yolk until it surrender. It always do this, Baba don't know why. She don't know meaning of surrender. **Mix yolk with cereal cream.** For small, glorious moment, cream will be color of your boyfriend eyeball after he spend weekend with seventy-two and half beer. Just before you take him to hospital. Face it, dorahenka, you not so concerned he have yellow eyeball as you mad he only have energy to pinch you once in while. Baba was going to teach you recipe call *How to Fix Floppy Joe* next, but she decide she is milked with human kindness.

Add yolk and cream into lokshyna mix. Hoo boychik, she gonna love it. This tickle.

Fold egg white into all this. Baba not trying to trick you. For some reason, in English they always folding thing into recipe. What you care? You don't even fold laundry.

Butter up this ring mold. Is better if is actually in shape of ring, not stupid fish or peacock. Put that fancy mold back on your neighbor wall. Because when you finish baking, **you going to use centre of lokshyna ring for good helping of *Creamed Vegetables,*** *Chapter Two* **or *Chicken in Cream,*** *Chapter Eight.*

Taras and Bob also love this recipe, except for with cream chicken. I make lokshyna ring for Bob birthday with cream vegetable instead.

Baba warning: Lokshyna ring don't hold up birthday candle too good. Everything kind of fall over and get pink waxy. Bob eat anyway. Maybe you will too. Baba just saying.

Also, if you making this for birthday, you have to put on floor. Baba never seen no tall pig.

Bake lokshyna ring forty five minute. You going to have to use your judgment. Tilt mold partway. If any liquid running out, put back in oven five minute. **Before you unmold this recipe, put out nice platter. Tip mold upside down and let lokshyna slide out.** Be careful, like you delivering baby pig. Bob so thrill when he read this part.

Make garnish from: hard boil egg slice, parsley sprig, dill sprig or slice green or black olive.

Ingredient List:

- Lokshyna, two cups cooked
- Hard cheese, one quarter cup
- Butter, three tablespoons
- Eggs, three extra large
- Cereal cream, one half cup
- Salt
- *Creamed Chicken* or *Creamed Vegetables* for centre of ring, two or three cups, depending on height of ring mold.

Fried Cooked Lokshyna

This crazy good Ukrainian junk food. It will make your denture happy. Even better, is two kind of way to make it. Almost unbelievable, what Baba sharing with you. Is like some kind phony charity.

Pour good layer of fat into fryer. You know any kind recipe start this way is gonna be good. Baba see you excite already.

Cook so many lokshyna as you want to eat. Drain and rinse with cold water. This recipe work better if you made very skinny lokshyna, almost like hair on your toe.

Spread lokshyna out on big plate and chill for at least hour in fridge. Do not leave out on counter with fan, or same person in your house who eat kleenex going to get this.

Start deep fat fryer to 400 F.

Pull lokshyna strand apart like when you combing kids' hair for lice, only not so gross out. DO NOT USE KWELLADA IN RECIPE. Baba just making brilliant simile.

Fry hand full of lokshyna at time until they are medium brown. Put on paper towel and sprinkle with salt or garlic salt. Serve warm. If you have vibrator, put this under tablecloth so lokshyna is squirm. Tell people is Klingon *gagh* food. Probably better you not add real worm.

Alternative Way:

This if you just made fresh lokshyna and family is clawing at sheet on table.

Cut up dough like in first lokshyna recipe. Shred super thin and make separation. Fry just like above.

Baba guarantee, you going to save bunch of money from ripoff bag of chip if you make this. You going to put corporate chip thief out of business.

Can also put fried lokshyna beside meat on plate, on top of creamed kind food, meat loaf or thick soup like *Horokhivka (Pea Soup), Chapter One*.

Baba warning: Do not serve lokshyna as garnish on lokshyna. This put you under suspicion for something.

Baba law: If you serve something soft or creamy, also serve crunchy. This not to be mistaken for good nutrition, just good taste. Then people take you serious as cook. Even dog like biscuit with can food.

Ingredient List:

- Lokshyna in quantity desired, cooked or fresh
- Any kind of fat for frying

Egg Drop Noodles

My friend Oksana, she show me how to make this thing called egg dropping noodle. This when you too tired to roll out real egg noodle.

Between me, you and bedpost, Oksana not have have good English like me. Also, her family not like us intellectual, from close to Lviv. But that's okay. She help me run still to make lots good horilka. Is always good to be friend with those mountain Hutsul people, in any country. Stalin mostly leave Hutsul people alone, and they carry on deep, ancient Ukrainian tradition in ways that was stolen from us in other areas.

This recipe make smooth thing from beaten up thing (bytky). **Beat up egg, then beat in one tablespoon water, flour and salt.**

Boil pot of water or make pot of simmer milk. Stop milk before it get actual boil, or it will have weird taste.

This where you need steady nerve. **Take up big spoonful of mix. Hold as high above pot as you can handle. Pour in skinny stream**

into hot water or milk.

Egg dropping noodle will be ready in two, three minute. You can eat in hot milk or scoop out for soup. Baba guarantee your University kid will be making this in dorm room when everyone else sick from dry noodle in package. You going to have to fight with school over hot plate in room. Use cultural diversity argument #3.

Ingredient List:

- Egg, one large
- Water, one tablespoon
- Water or milk, one quart
- Flour, quarter cup
- Salt

Hrybok (Easy Omelet Noodles)

Woo-eee, Baba really letting you in on Ukrainian secret now. This is alternate way to make fresh egg noodle, for when rolling pin is soaking in sink to take out blood. Is beautiful in clear or vegetable soup, and it add protein. Everybody going to be thinking you genius. In alternate universe.

Separate two egg. Cream butter with egg yolk. Only put in one yolk at time for best creaming. Baba not yolking. Ha!

Make oven 350 F.

Beat in flour and big splash water. Beat some more. This is true original meaning of "smoothie."

Beat up egg white till they scream for mercy and go stiff. **Fold into mix.**

Butter up baking dish. Here is next secret of great hrybok: heat dish in oven before putting in egg mix. This is one those rare occasion Baba let you use microwave.

Baba warning: Do not put hot egg in cold pan! Same principle as, "Do not use hot water to wash off egg!"

"Oh," you saying.

"Oh OH," Baba saying. *Chy ty z byka vpau*? Have you fallen off an ox?

Pour in egg mix, bake in oven for about ten to fifteen minute. This is where Baba revoke microwave right. Under US Constitution to make bare arm when defending cook book. By way, I bet you not know

Thomas Jefferson study Ukrainian *kozak* constitution in order to write US one. He very interest in concept of "Free Man", which is what "kozak" mean. Also kozachka, "Free Woman." Ukraina have first democratic constitution in Europe: Bendery, 1710, by Pylyp Orlyk. Orlyk was Hetman, or leader, of Zaporizhian kozaky. Some people who don't know history because they read skewed Wiki version, think kozaky are "Russian."

Poopchik, being Slavic or Ukrainian is ethnicity. It is bloodline. When predator invade your country, this don't make you or your country theirs in any way. Any more than you sudden become ethnicity of whatever thief rob your house and steal your furniture. Just because they sit on your couch and eat your cracker, don't make them owner of your house.

Baba try to edit Wiki for real history, but they is clearly infiltrated by Kremlin. Most reference to Ukraina is soiled with lies about Russian ownership and genealogy. They even claim helicopter inventor Ihor Sikorsky, born in Kyiv, was Russian! All sorts these lies, and if you edit, editors will not only change back but make abusive emails to you.

Wiki history of Russia is such mess of twisted lies, will make your head split. Please refer to Baba's extensive bibliography, and stick to Encyclopedia of Ukraina and other reputable source.

President of Wiki, Jimmy Wales, send form letter to Ukrainians who in response to reports of this abuse.

Hrybok is done if it don't jiggle when you kick stove. When is cool, slice into noodle.

Ingredient List:

- Eggs, two large
- Butter, one tablespoon
- Water, two tablespoons
- Flour, two tablespoons
- Butter for baking dish
- Salt

Chapter Twenty Two

Pidlyvi (Sauces)

Ukrainian Sliva (Plum) Pidlyva

Cut six fat purple or red plum in half. Yellow plum make unattractive sauce

Put in sauce pan. Cover plum with water. How much how much how much, you want to know? I said, "Enough water to cover plum." Sheesh. Get life.

Put on medium heat. Put in sugar depending how sweet you like sauce. Can try honey, but much easier to burn if you amateur Ukrainian.

Cook fifteen minute, pour over plum varenyky.

Your option:

Pour on *Medivnyk *(Honey Cake),* or ***Yabluchnyk*** *(Apple Cake), Chapter Twenty Three.*

***Pour on vanilla or fruit flavour ice cream.** Not caramel or chocolate! Blech.

Use as dip for *Cottage Cheese Patties, *Chapter Fifteen.*

Ingredient List:

- Plums, six large. Red or purple
- Sugar, one quarter to one half cup OR honey, one quarter cup
- Water

Plum Butter

This is call plum butter because is butter made from plum.

Baba serve this over top plain *Mlyntsi* *(pancakes), Chapter Four*, and natural, on toast. Is recipe for late summer, when plum is juicy and sweet.

Will make you impressario in extreme when you casual take out jar and put on table with toast. This take couple of hour to make, but can take care of good chunk of your *Rizdvo* (Christmas) present list for nearly free. **This one recipe make seven pint jar.** Give away what is left after you scarfle down huge amount and are lying on couch with swollen belly.

Day before, put lemon on counter and two small plate in freezer.

Get someone to pick you nine pound fat sweet red or purple plum. While you waiting at bottom of ladder, yell, "Watch out for those wasp!" Insect know good thing when they see. Is excellent time to make them pick several more pound for your holiday plum varenyky, which you going to make and freeze.

Did you know some city have free harvest? People who have fruit tree in yard will let you pick yourself, with no cost. Some city people will actual let fruit drop to ground and rot. You should take advantage. Of course, you going to bring them back little present. Be good neighbor. Don't turn into Soviet, always taking, taking.

Prune plum is not so impressive as normal red or purple. It have pucker mouth and stingy attitude, even when not total wrinkle face. Yellow plum have sweet flavor, but to be frankly, stirring yellow mush for hour and half will make turn your stomach. See *Baby Food, Chapter Five.*

Pit those plum with your gourmet plum pitter. This would be your hand and sharp knife, poopchik. Do not peel! You want jewel color to shine through in butter.

Use your biggest frying pan and melt whack of butter. Slurp it around so whole inside of pan is coat. Once again, this is where Chinese wokking make beautiful instrument for Ukrainian food. You can tilt this pan every which way, and ingredient will not slop on stove. Believe you me Baba, you don't want to be cleaning inside of element when cook plum is done with it. Might as well throw stove out window and buy new one, like last time. Just don't use Teflon, as it will kill bird immediate, and is toxic to everyone.

Cook plum in this butter over low heat for twenty minute. Use wooden spoon you carve yourself in community centre class. As if. But Baba serious here. You got lots stirring ahead of you. Metal spoon will make metal taste in plum.

Strain these plum by hand or okay, in food processor. Drip in fresh lemon juice while you doing this.

Grate lemon and/or orange peel and have on standby.

If wokking got dried up plum in it, clean it out. Start fresh. Put on your best orthopedic shoe, because you going to stand over pan and make stirring for about one hour.

When plum mix looking like you want it, make test. Take plate out from freezer and drip little bit plum on it. Should be consistency like jam. If running away from you, keep cooking and stirring plum. Test again.

Stir in lemon or orange zest and sugar. Zest is optional. You could even try in half of recipe only, see how you like. You going to eat bowlful this stuff before canning, anyway. Might as well make zest sprinkle right now. Call in family to test this, too.

Some time during this long day, you should **sterilize seven pint jar.** See *Pickled Herring, Chapter Seventeen.*

There, now you have real genuine plum butter. **Spoon into jar, but leave about quarter inch at top to make breathing room.** Don't worry, plum don't need snorkel mask. They is cool with it.

You can eat this after only one day in jar, so you better make quick gift wrapping. Is gift especially welcome if you bring to special person with good rye or pumpernickel bread, and tell them to make toast. Maybe they will even unwrap in front of you and invite you to eat.

Other good suggestion is to **spoon some this butter onto vanilla ice cream.** Even in layer, so you make this Canadian thing call parfait. You not going to find this flavor at Daring Quean.

Is also lovely to serve with not-so-sweet traditional Ukrainian cake. Wait! Baba sure don't mean glop all over *Yabluchnyk* (Apple Cake) or *Perekladanetz* (Coffee Cake) like you trying to hide something from secret police. She suggesting that sometime your friend not used to less-sugary cake like we make, and they go better with little bit plum butter on individual slice.

And please, Baba beg you not to bring shame to yourself by making Plum Margarine.

Ingredient List:

- Red or purple plums, nine pounds
- Unsalted butter, one quarter cup
- White sugar, two cups
- Fresh lemon juice, one quarter cup

Optional: Orange and/or lemon zest, one quarter cup in total.
Cakes mentioned are in *Chapter Twenty Three.*

Khrin i Smetana (Horseradish and Sour Cream)

Don't read this story if you squeamish kind person. It have horse, soldier, spider and very strong horseradish.

My publisher make me write this disclaimer. I not care about you being big baby oversensitive-shmensitive to this and disturb by that. In Soviet Union I see thing every day make you have "environmental sensitivity." Like stealing, starvation and murder.

Toughen up and you hear damn good story:

My barn spider in Old Country name Hanya Oksanichka Sophia Slawka Alexandrichka. She name after ancestor. She big as man's hand and live fifty year. Every day she eat pile of bug as high my ankle.

I also have beautiful horse, white like snow with dark eye. When sun shine, she look like silver. She love to come in house and eat kasha from sink. Sometime she curl up by warm wood stove and snore little bit. She name Misha. She look just like unicorn, but without horn. Misha magic horse. One day Stalin soldier come to make this Communist collectivization. One try to steal my Misha. Spider drop, pow! on his head and bite him till he die.

I feed him to spider.

Don't be worry. I only feed one piece at time, so spider not be sick. I give rest to neighbor. He make good leftover. I'm hungry too, but have big trouble digesting Communist.

Then very terrible thing happen. Next soldier, he too much for spider. She bite his head, but his hair very thick. He take my beautiful Misha away. Soviet steal three million horse from people who first tame horse. Three million. They either put in pathetic Russian breeding program or they eat. Next thing I know, Soviet steal cattle and even our land. Is terrible sad thing. Then they make me work on collective farm for peanut.

I have to leave spider behind with neighbor when we finally run from Ukraina to Canada. Very sad. But my spider, Hanya Oksanichka Sophia Slawka Alexandrichka, she write me letter for many year. More faithful than one my son.

If you can stomach this thing that happen to me, you can stomach this hotsie-totsie sauce.

Mix fresh smetana with grate, clean *khrin* from garden. You have horseradish in garden, right?

Baba didn't think so. Good thing this recipe very easy, because I have doubt about you learning Ukrainian Gestalt. Okay. Off you go to stupormarket in car instead of nice healthy walk to garden. Or maybe you at least be on West Coast and ride bicycle. You look like dorking with fluorescent tape on pant and ugly sandal with sock, but at least you get some kind exercise for once.

Buy jar of prepare grate horseradish, any colour. Baba like red from beet juice, but white okay. Mix real good with smetana, white sugar and salt.

Put in fridge at least one hour to let ingredient talk to each other, come to agreement about flavour.

There. Long story, short recipe. Can eat this like spicy pudding, but probably you like on meat. **Horse radish sauce tasty on pork or beef. Incredible on *Sichenyky*** (meat patties) or ***Meatballs,*** both in *Chapter Ten*. Even on ***Holubtsi*** *(cabbage rolls), Chapter Fourteen*, or ***Beet Salad* or *Coleslaw,*** *Chapter Two.*

Not too shabbola on your corn chip, neither. You could serve this on football day and be life of party while men watching commercial, if this your sad ambition. Just don't dance in front of TV with tray, okay? Is more than one way to be dorking.

Baba warning: do not feed to horse or spider. It make them sneeze.

Ingredient List:

- Sour cream, two cups
- Horseradish, three heaping tablespoons grated
- White sugar, one teaspoon
- Salt

Tartar Sauce

Don't be thinking there be real Tatar in this sauce. They just one more people who make Slavic people life miserable as slave. At least they leave behind one good recipe. Baba going to practice little bit forgiveness, because Tatar leader make positive statement on behalf Ukraina during Russian aggression. We is now good neighbor.

Here is more kind of mashing I teach you in other fish spread recipe. See *Herring Spread* and *Sardine Spread,* in *Ocean Fish, Chapter Seventeen*. Get duct tape ready, cuz there nothing else to do in this recipe but mashing. Hoo boychik.

First, hard boil six egg. See instruction under *Deviled Eggs, Chapter*

Seven. You only going to use yolk. If you not have pig, feed egg white to your bodybuilding boyfriend on dry toast. Make smiling whole time. Don't tell him this is substitute for real thing.

Mash egg yolk with extra virgin olive oil. This tastiest kind and make good cholesterol.

Mash in French mustard, apple cider or balsamic vinegar and horseradish. If you want tartar sauce to be very cute pink, use red horseradish. If idea of green dill pickle floating in pink sauce is blow your mind, use white.

Add smetana, fine chop dill pickle and pinch salt.

Pour into glass jar. Good in fridge about one week. If you make right and use on good fish recipe like I show you, should be none left week from now.

Serve with:

***Fish**
*****Syrnichky*** *(Cottage Cheese Patties), Chapter Fifteen.*

Ingredient List:

- Eggs, six
- Extra virgin olive or sunflower oil, two tablespoons
- French mustard, one teaspoon
- Apple cider or balsamic vinegar, one tablespoon
- Horseradish, one tablespoon
- Sour cream, one quarter cup
- Dill pickle, one large
- Salt

Kropova Pidlyva (Dill Sauce)

This where Baba going to insist you be real discipline person. Absolutely must have fresh dill if you going to make dill sauce. Sauce is thing that can make good meal ecstasy, or rescue other terrible thing you cook. This dill sauce so good, Baba once serve over dog biscuit (home made) when secret police visiting, and they not notice.

How to make perfect:

Leave lemon on counter overnight. Then squeeze out juice.

Chop bunch dill. Throw out stem, duh. Baba going to repeat herself here. Poopchik, this is dill sauce. If you even having single suicidal thought about using dry crap from jar, call WASP crisis line right now. 1-800-GETLIFE. Is run by volunteer.

Then call Baba at 1-900-ASKBABA. $4.99 per minute. Talk to her for hour or two. You decide which is better value.

Melt butter. Mix in flour or corn starch. Only cook for minute or two. You don't want flour to turn brown. This delicate, delicate taste.

Pour in clear soup from chicken or vegetable. Mix mix mix. This supposed to get thick like when you make yogurt in saddlebag. Take away from stove.

Mix in that lemon juice, cereal kind cream, salt and very fine dill.

Baba warning: Like I say, first take away hot thing from stove before mixing in last few ingredient. Else you going to have one more thing to cry about, even after you tell crisis line about your boring day.

Ingredient List:

- Lemon, one large
- Fresh dill, one heaping tablespoon chopped
- Butter, two tablespoons
- Flour, two tablespoons
- Soup stock, one cup
- Cereal cream, one half cup
- Pinch salt

Smetana and Green Onion Pidlyva

If you can dig up those new baby potato to eat with this sauce, you will be grateful forever. Baba in da house.

Chop up green onion so they look almost like grass clipping.

Glop thick smetana into medium pot and make boiling. Double boiler give you best odd of not burning. This is where one pot fit inside other. Water boiling is in bottom pot, and smetana is in top. Also best for melting chocolate (but not in this recipe).

Throw in onion and laugh how they making green design on white. **Turn heat down to low simmer,** which is about four on your burner. **Shake in salt and crack black pepper.** Leave alone to develop like photograph for half hour. Sauce will get thickness, but not enough to glue potato together.

Ingredient List:

- Sour cream, two cups
- Green onions, one half cup
- Salt and pepper to taste

Honey Onion Pidlyva

This sauce is about as easy as can get, and so traditional. Ukrainian was making this back in day when we fighting cave bear for honey from tree. We was digging wild onion and garlic, too. This because it was best thing to put on fry mammoth.

First house was in Ukraina over twenty thousand year ago, made from mammoth bone. Several interlock jaw form foundation, and rib make archway to hang skin. We make drum from mammoth skull too, with groovy red design better than rocking roll drum kit.

We draw huge mural with mammoth, and write about it 24,000 years ago. Here is first evidence of most oldest Great Goddess Inanna, who was previous thought to be Sumerian. We was Mesolithic. We have Ukrainski Stonehenge, only lots older than UK one. Ours is call *Kamyana Mohyla*, in Southern Ukraina, just outside town of Melitopol.

This Stone Mound is natural result of Samartian Sea retreat 14 million years ago. Around it is several oldest statue, maybe 9000 year. Guess what they call? *Stone Baba*. This blow what is left of your mind, does it not? Baba think is stone groove.

When Muscovy ("Russian") invade Eastern Ukraina, they invade our ancient place of worship, our very soul, our human origins.

What Baba is saying is, we ate lots mammoth like you eating *Burger King*. Every day, same damn thing. Is a bit dry too, so sauce was essential thing.

Heat soniashnyk oil in big frying pan, medium heat. If you can find organic or cold press, this it more Ukrainian taste.

You going to need that, because here is Baba secret: she discover wok. She like its curvy side very much, because she can be wild creator. Baba like to pour and throw ingredient from distance, and wok don't make splashing onto stove.

Peel and make quarter from three big onion. Not quarter like money. That would be *koshmar*, nightmare. Slice very thin like onion paper. Ha!

Mince up clove garlic. Put onion and garlic in oil together. They say, "Howdy doody." Baba learn that when she cowgirl in Texas. Also, "Yuppie kayak," and, "Butter my bum and call me biscuit." That last one in Canada just make people stare at you. Y'all not so friendly like Texan.

Cook these ingredient for twenty minute. Keep your good eye on it and stir lots. Should be very tender but not burn.

Add beef stock. Home made is best kind. Turn heat to medium-high and cook until liquid is half its original size. This should take five or seven minute, and is what fancy-schmancy cook call "reduction."

Throw in liquid honey. Buckwheat has most Ukrainian taste.

Stir in glop Dijon mustard and big splash apple cider vinegar. If you substituting plainer ingredient, Baba not going to guarantee her work. **Turn heat down to medium low and simmer all this tasty mess for fifteen minute.**

Remove from stove element and let sit for fifteen minute before serving. Sauce have best taste when serve warm, not hot hot heat. Kitchen going to smell like honey sauce heaven, so be ready to slap family hand when they try to taste too soon.

This sauce is excellent not only on **mammoth meat, but on vegetable and *Kasha*** *(Buckwheat), Chapter Twenty.*

You going to come out with about two cup sauce, enough for two meat loaf or casserole dish roasted vegetable. If you like to make double recipe, you can freeze without losing taste. But fresh is always better, no matter how much your husband like mammoth jerky.

Ingredient List:

- Sunflower oil, one quarter cup
- Onions, three large
- Garlic, one clove
- Beef stock, three quarter cup
- Dijon mustard, two teaspoons
- Apple cider vinegar, two tablespoons
- Honey, two tablespoons

Chapter Twenty Three

Desserts

Kupala (Summer Solstice)

Baba really know how to get party started. She especial like to make *Cherry Charlotte, Almond Crescent Horn, Poppy Seed Cake* and *Kozak Honey Mousse* for excellent holiday call *Kupala*, which mean "she bathing."

Kupala/Kupalo is also proper noun, god and goddess of Love and Harvest. She/he represent Sun Queen and King. In case you not already guess, this is pair of sexy twin. They represent science of astrology as Gemini. Christian get it all mix up with story about John Baptist. They mix up holiday and make boring. Baba love Jesus, but he was not boring. He big bicep man running around overturning Wall Street table. He was first in *Occupy Movement.*

Ukrainian celebrate Kupala for several thousand year. On summer solstice, whole village bathe together. This is because sun reflect in water for longest time on this day. We bathe together to get super charge for rest of year. Is first official kind of solar power.

On Eve of Kupala, men and women make many bonfire near stream or pond. We light these fire with flint or rubbing our body together, because fire have to be new. Sometime Kupala/Kupalo jump right in there and light fire with twin drill. They grin lots. We jump over these fire and make wish, while flame burn away what we don't need no more. This include guilty conscience, expired herb medication and stained crap Canadian would dump on charity store.

We build straw figure who represent waning Sun Twin, dress them up and make good fun of them all night. This represent sun going slowly to sleep like *baba* or *didukh* (grandma or grandpa). Some people burn him, some people drown him or tear him apart and scatter in field for next year fertility. You think this barbaric? Other culture make human sacrifice at this time. In North America, is no dignity involved in deposing worn out Queen or King. You just throw egg at losing candidate. Dignity is important thing in life.

Ukrainian have lots fun at Kupala Love Harvest funeral. We dance and sing song about best part of life. Man song have lyric like, *Oh pretty girl, put your hand on my big sweaty horse,* and *I want you to polish my sword, chickie babe.* Woman answer with, *Your horse can have a drink in my well/Uh oh, horse better not slobber* and *Is that sharp sword in your scabbard, or you just happy horny kozak?*

Then there is old chestnut about man giving woman re-re-re-respect. You think Aretha Franklin first one to sing this? Uh uh. This was word for good time in Ukraina for many century. We have old song about woman who respect husband but love all the other.

We play *Blindfold Kissing Game* and *Pass Apple Around With Anything But Your Hand Game.* Ukrainian have real good balance.

Women wear all kind flower and herb on body and garland in hair. This attract man who is dying to pick flower. Is nothing subtle about Ukrainian romance. Maybe you already guess. Is very beautiful, though. Later, women throw garland on water to read their fortune for next year. If no flower left, she pretty well guess how it gonna be.

Village wise woman hang out nearby. Woman who don't want to wear eyeglass ask her for wreath made from mugwort. They wear this and stare into bonfire to strengthen their good eye. When this *vorozhka* is not healing burn from fire or rug, she tell your fortune by tarot card, candle wax and if you sleep with village idiot.

After all this, we walk through dark wood. Is not easy, because on this night, all tree move and talk. We hunt for *tsvit paporoti*, fire fern flower. This one night it glow in dark and make all your deepest wish come true. When you find, you have to make magic circle around flower and fight *nychyste syla*, dirty demon who try to chew off your face. Mind you, by this time we is pretty well buzz on mushroom and magic herb we put in our varenyky and horilka. After one person find fire fern flower, we all go in couple to celebrate life. If we go in threesome, this call *Having three well on your property*. Ukrainian civil servant exam not like any other, Baba guarantee.

Most traditional thing to eat on Kupala is egg and varenyky. Egg is for fertility and varenyky is one kind symbol of crescent moon. Young people also feed each other *Poppyseed Cake, Chapter Twenty Four*. Poppy seed is thing that scatter everywhere, so is good example if you want to do this yourself.

Here is Baba favorite Kupala recipe. Easy to make and very sexy. Baba can hear some people whining, "But Baba, is not strictly of Ukrainian origin!" Baba say politely, "Maybe you need more time with kozak and his horse, dorahenka."

Vyshnia (Cherry) Charlotte

Make someone else **pit fresh sweet *vyshnia*. Put these in bowl with vanilla sugar and big splash cherry liqueur or kirsch**. One time Baba want to tell that Chicken Colonel, "Who you telling to have finger licking day?" but she kind of feel kindred spirit. She know you already licking finger and moaning.

You need three dozen lady finger pastry, total. Put enough just to cover bottom of springform pan. No, put them on top and hope they hover like hummingbird. Baba give you permission to actual buy these for Kupala. Probably from story you understand you need to weave flower garland and get bikini wax. When you having bath with all your neighbor is not time to be making fussy pastry, okay? Sheesh.

Springform pan is kind with buckle on side, like that chastity belt you pretending you going to wear on holiday. Ha!

Throw about one third of cherry in blender with huger splash cherry liqueur.

Wait. Baba know this not all going into recipe. Throw in extra cherry and liqueur to tide yourself over.

After blend and drink, **use cherry/liqueur liquid to make ladyfinger moist.** Matka Bozha, Baba feel like she reliving Kupala right now.

Make bowl full real whip cream with more vanilla sugar. Do not use kind from spray can, or for sure you will not be one to find fire fern or get her flower pluck.

Put layer of cherry on ladyfinger. Cover with whip cream. Keep doing this until ingredient all gone or you pass out. Finish with layer of ladyfinger.

Put *Cherry Charlotte* in fridge for couple of hour. Unbuckle from pan. Before you take to party, put on more sweet whip cream.

This meant to be serve to special person with your bare hand.

If friend not serve you back same way, send him into wood to fight crazy demon by himself. Grab fire flower when he not looking. Run.

Vanilla sugar:

You can buy or you can make. **Get one vanilla bean for every two cup sugar.** This more subtle taste than liquid vanilla. Recipe already have plenty alcohol. Like you ever get enough. But still, Baba trying to make you sophisticate in every way.

Slice side of bean. Scrape seed into airtight jar with sugar and mix up. Then bury bean pod in sugar and leave alone for at least whole week. Occasional you will hear noise from container. They just having their own Kupala. Ignore.

Ingredient List:

- Pitted cherries, one and one half pounds
- Cherry liqueur or kirsch, one half cup. One quarter cup goes
- with cherries, one quarter cup in blender.
- Vanilla sugar, one half cup. One quarter cup goes with cherries, one quarter cup in whipped cream.
- Ladyfingers, three dozen
- Whipped cream, two cups
- Springform pan

Next Kupala recipe, non-alcoholic:

Rohalyky (Almond Crescents)

This dessert is full of heavy symbolism. Golden moon crescent is on head of Kupala/Kupalo for their royalty. Because they sexy royalty, is also symbolize animal horn and is full of creamy filling. You not going to find anything like this around palace of your Queen E, Baba telling you this.

This also just as easy to make as that doughboy stuff. With Baba pastry, you can be much more proud.

Leave butter on counter overnight. Put some kind heavy cover over top so cat won't have to put on big innocent act in morning.

Mix together unbleach flour with full yeast. Use bowl. Cut in soft butter with whisking thing until it all look like that crumbly cloud you ignore on your wedding day. Uh oh. Is running make up.

Beat up two egg yolk and add to cloudy thing. Put egg white in fridge. Throw in big splash *smetana* (sour cream).

Go wash your hand. Baba not going to say “again,” because then we both be liar. **Mix dough into ball with hand,** but don't be kneady, or dough will get tough. Just give little massage. Baba get annoy when you get kneady. Ha! **Wrap this up in wax paper and chill for two hour.** If you done this last Kupala, you wouldn't have stretch mark now.

Filling:

Make oven 375 degree F.

Grind up toasted almond, but don't make into dust. This filling going to be surprise kind, creamy but crunchy. Just like when you stay up all night to make your own peanut butter. As if.

Mix up almond with brown sugar.

Beat up two egg white with pinch salt till they begging to be with almond and sugar. This is good practice.

Take dough from fridge, and divide into three smaller ball. They going to have to be smaller, or something wrong. You got yourself inside shrinking universe by mistake. Baba have no idea what you should do. Maybe call Stephen Hawking or something.

Take rolling pin out from bedroom and sprinkle flour both on it and on table. Roll these doughball out into three circle so thin like your stinking boss pretend is his wallet. About one eighth inch.

Cut each circle into eight wedgie. Here is little bit tricky. You going to look back and forth, dough to filling, dough to filling. Make executive decision and **spread one twenty-fourth of filling onto each piece dough.**

Baba warning: Do not mix this up with one quarter of filling, or you going to be calling yourself *durna diuchina*, stupid girl, all night. This is not conducive to making best fern-plucking.Whoever tell you stupid is sexy, just want all good man for herself. Remember object of recipe in this section!

Start rolling from wide end. Keep rolling to skinny end, then pull up dough into nice smile shape. Keep point on bottom, or else crescent will open in oven.

Put almond crescent on baking sheet you coat very light with soniashnyk, sunflower oil.

Bake half hour or maybe forty minute, until they all beautiful goldie color and have puffy face, like time you made disaster with collagen.

Name *rohalyky* is derive from rohy, two horn. Some idiot going to make joke about your horny pastry. This is not person to choose on Kupala. Baba advice about stupid and sex apply to all kind sex.

Your option:

See *Poppyseed Rohalyky, Twenty Four*, for alternate filling.

Ingredient List:

Pastry

- Unbleached flour, two cups
- Dry yeast, one tablespoon
- Butter, one cup
- Egg yolks, two
- Sour cream, one quarter cup
- Waxed paper

Filling

- Ground, toasted almonds, two cups
- Brown sugar, three quarter cup
- Egg whites, two
- Salt, pinch

Kozak Honey Mousse

This recipe remind Baba of Led Zeppelin song, *Black Dog*. Is how she feel inside most of time.

Is again something to feed each other with hand. Is real good thing you taking bath together right after.

Make separation of eight big fertilize egg if you want to get pregnant. Otherwise, use only from virgin chicken. How you tell? Is no way. You have to put chicken in house at night, keep eye on her every minute and have rifle handy. This work out with your family history real good, Baba know.

Beat eight egg yolk while dripping in liquid honey. If you already Ukrainian, use buckwheat honey. Very strong taste. Go slow with honey, just like with love. Baba like to invite young man to watch her make this. Or get him to beat yolk while you dripping honey. Sometime this recipe take whole day.

Cook egg honey mix on low heat. Keep stirring with wood spoon. Do not lick, spoon will be extremely hot. Burning tongue before Kupala is tragedy you won't forget. This is good time to remind you not to lick side of metal trough when you visit barn at Winter Solstice, too.

Take egg honey mix off stove and let cool till is room temperature.

Whip those eight egg white into frenzy. They should be stiff and begging for honey.

Fold them into egg honey mix. Put mousse in one big bowl or keep in several small bowl. Depends: how many well you want on your property?

Put in fridge for two three hour. They going to have goose bump. What you care? Is in interest of good romance.

Garnish with several slice of fresh fruit.

Ingredient list:

- Eggs, eight large
- Liquid honey, two and one half cups
- Fruit for garnish

Baba interrupt story on Kupala Eve because she can't wait for dessert. Now she back.

Day of Kupala: Alternate name is *Day of Hangover and Sore Thigh.* This pretty wicked, too. Dew of Kupala very, very important. Guess what dew symbolize in Ukraina? Let's just say dying Sun twin leave behind fertility present. Sick people roll around in morning dew, farmer drive cattle through wet field, and woman run through field barefoot. If she really, really determine to get marry, she leave pretty bowl outside overnight and wash her face in this super-juice. Like Baba say, really really determine.

In Ukraina, we tease pregnant not marry woman by singing to her, "Shouldn't have run around in dew barefoot, dorahenka." Honest, this stuff is everywhere. Sometime Baba just shock by Nature.

Kozak Crab Apple Pie

Recipe for Adult Only: Has Liquor

Make double pie crust. Most important thing, you do some practice. Big secret: what make pie crust tough is when you handle dough too much. You need develop confidence, this area.

Pie is not tradition in Ukraina. But when Baba learn to bake pie here, she take to it like duck to bathwater. Beside, in Canada no one believe is cookbook by "grandma" unless have plenty pie.

Okay. Get children and grandchildren to take stepladder to crab apple tree. You think Baba going to pick apple with arthritis and in skirt? You out of your rocker. Is good way to hurt self and snag good support hose. Make family pick as many they can. Best crab apple is kind have rosy skin. You stand bottom of tree and yell, "Hey, not that one, it have worm!" Make them carry big basket of apple into kitchen and wash very well.

For one big pie, you going to need:

Lots crab apple. Use brain for how much. Okay, because you Canadian, I hold your hand: should be **about six cup apple slice.** Best part this kind pie, do not peel apple. Peel is very thin and tasty. Slice and take out core.

Lemon. Leave lemon on counter so be warm. Use one with thin skin. Squeeze and pour over apple. Give unusual little taste, no one guess what. Also keep from going brown.

Brown sugar. If apple very very sour, little bit more. Check on sugar night before. If all in one hard lump, put in big piece potato for make moist. You do this same time you check on your supply of

Horilka. This Ukrainian word for strong liquor. When I have pirate boyfriend from Odesa, he get me best spice rum for crab apple pie. He also very cute, with black eyebrow. We drink horilka & dance *hopak*. If he stop saying, "Arrrrr, Baba," maybe I stay with him.

Four Rose Whiskey very good, but not so much for pie.

Also can try vodka or liqueur horilka flavor: raspberry (*malynivka*), strawberry, (*tertukha*), gooseberry (*agrusivka*), plum (*slivovitz* or *slivanka*), rose hip (*shypshynyk*), apricot (*morelivka*), cherry (*vyshnivka*), lemon (*tsytrynivka*), orange and clove (*mokrukha*) , orange or lemon rind (*mokhena*), black currant (*kontabas*). Is all very, very good. In future cookbook, Baba going to teach you how to make some these yourself. Then you won't be lying to liquor store how you buying "for friend."

You going to soak crab apple in horilka and spice overnight. Enough so bowl of apples just covered. They will drink. If they don't drink all horilka, pour off extra next day and drink with friend while wait for pie to bake. This very medicinal. I f you get sick anyway, it help you forget. **If you using fruit liqueur,** pour only little bit on apple and stir around to coat all pieces. Very strong and so expensive!

Add cinnamon, ground clove and nutmeg. About less than quarter teaspoon each. If you use spice rum, leave out cinnamon. Stir around spice in apples.

Throw in tiny pinch salt. Put filling in fridge to soak until next day.

When you ready to bake, make:

Perfect Pie Crust

You think you know how to make pie crust? By time Baba finish, you going to be one holy roller.

First thing you need to do is make fat and liquid chill. This keep them isolate and then they pow! Make their magic in oven. This is step so many people miss, and it make whole thing more easier. Where Baba learn this trick? Her friend from Siberia make flakiest pie crust in world. Difficult thing there is to find place to bake pie.

Mix up flour with salt in huge bowl. If you was planning ahead, bowl would be in fridge.

Take out pastry blender thing from fridge. Mix in cold butter and cold shortening. You heard Baba. Both. Butter make eye-crossing taste, shortening is flake-maker.

Cut up this mixture until it look good and crumby. The colder the fat, the crumbier it look. This is positive direction. Believe Baba when she say not to make these crumb smaller than size of *horokh*, green pea. She know this don't look like your crazy blender protein shake. Live with it.

Here is next trickola: **beat up two cold egg yolk with juice from lemon.** Acid test will give small zing! Flavor in crust, and also more tender. No one will know why your crust is double extra special.

Have icy water ready. Stir in enough to egg and lemon juice so you have about two third cup liquid.

Here is trickster part. **Stir in little bit of egg mix to flour/fat mix at time. Use fork. STOP when dough just start to stick together. Pick up dough couple of times, flip over and drop, just like when you mad at underwear in sink.**

If there is bunch of dry thing in bottom of bowl, add tiny splash cold liquid. If you put in too much liquid, you will use more flour to correct. Then you will have too much flour. You will add more liquid, more flour. Soon you will have crust that is just little bit tougher than your shoe. Better to be careful from getting-go.

Sprinkle flour on counter. Press dough down into round shape, then divide in half. Put in fridge for at least half an hour. If in fridge for more than three or four hour, let it sit on counter for fifteen minute before you start to roll. There is chill dough, and then there is hypothermia. If dough is too cold, it will be too busy shivering to roll out.

Roll out in two pieces on barely any flour. Flour make crust tough. Baba find this silicone pie rolling mat in Canada she really like. She can use less flour, because it hardly stick.

Always make rolling from centre out, from centre out. Else you end up with grubby stretched thing, look like your possession after divorce.

Press half of dough down into pie pan, save other half for top crust.

If you getting drift of Baba instruction, go for gold. **Put pie pan with dough back in fridge for half hour. Do not put in filling yet, or it will be soggy.** Is okay. Apple don't mind soaking up horilka for few minute more. Also put top crust in fridge, on top of plastic or pan. If you going to make crissy-crossy top crust, cut up strip just before laying on top of filling. Do not lay on top of filling yourself, even if no one looking.

Here is Siberian chemistry: when cold fat melt in oven along with cold water, it make million tiny steam pocket. Pastry will puff up while tasty fat is running along bottom of this steam pocket. Is why people from cold climate look very self-contain, but are hot like bannia in private. See *Lokshyna/Bannia, Chapter Twenty One*.

Make oven 375 degree. If you have wood stove, you know how to tell.

Melt and stir two with brown sugar. Then mix into apple.

Put all apple into crust. What you think, you do something else?

Make fancy crissy-crossy with dough strip on top. If you like just one piece crust, lay carefully on top apple, and press edge into rim of bottom crust with fork. Dip fork in water every three time you press. Poke little hole in top crust, so pie not explode in oven. Oi, what mess that be! If you also making pie for children, mark crust so people know difference between one with horilka.

Bake pie about 45 minute. Check to see top crust goldy brown. You understand, you have to watch these things, Baba can't be there whole time, make sure you being smart.

Ingredient List:

- Crab apples, four cups cored and unpeeled
- Brown sugar, one half cup
- Butter, two tablespoons melted
- Liquor of your choice, three cups or just enough to cover apples
- Lemon, one half

- Salt
- Cinnamon, ground cloves and nutmeg. One quarter teaspoon each
- Pie crust, top and bottom

Pie Crust, top and bottom for 9" pie

- All purpose flour, four cups
- Salt, one and one half teaspoons
- Butter, two thirds cup
- Crisco or similar shortening, two thirds cup
- Egg yolks, two medium
- Fresh lemon juice, three teaspoons

Tell children "No!" they try to eat this pie. If parent try to feed children this pie, slap hand with wooden spoon, and **serve children:**

Crab Apple Pie

Recipe for Everybody: No Liquor

Pick apple and make crust just like before. Only this time, you bake for children and people who not like horilka. If you make both kind pie, you make sure you mark crust some way so people know difference. Children drunk make Baba mad.

Night before, instead of soak apple in horilka, you make very thick mixture from:

Orange juice or one these kind syrup: raspberry, black currant, strawberry, cherry, or any kind you like. Even some people like hazelnut. If you very cheap, wait until barista person at Starbuck not looking. Finish you coffee in paper cup. Squeeze squeeze squeeze some their fancy syrup into empty cup. Take home and pour over slice apple. Next day, pour away what apple not drink.

If police come from Starbuck, say you thought because coffee so expensive, syrup was "refill," like in real coffee shop. I don't know, maybe you too young to remember when people was human.

Because syrup sweet, you **add only small handful brown sugar to fruit,** or even none. Is your taste, your decision. They say we in free country.

Bake like other pie, 45 minute at 375 degree.

Ingredient List:

- Same as for *Crab Apple Pie* above, except substitute three cups orange juice for liquor. Or dilute flavored syrup 50/50 with BOILED water.
- Reduce sugar by half to all.
- Pie crust, top and bottom

Other Kind Pie

These kind you make almost like Crab Apple, except different fruit.

Cherry, Apple and Raspberry

Only thing different, **mix two tablespoon cornstarch into little bit soaking liquid, pour over fruit.**

Peach or Nectarine

Leave skin on peach. Taste fruit first. If very sweet, use less sugar. **Mix two tablespoon cornstarch into little bit soaking liquid, pour over fruit.** Use only pinch clove, not cinnamon or nutmeg. Taste incredible with raspberry or strawberry vodka or liqueur.

Saskatoon

Do not add spices. **Mix two tablespoon cornstarch into little bit soaking liquid, pour over berry.**

Gooseberry

Same same as Saskatoon.

Blueberry

Also same same.

Rhubarb Pie

Pick rhubarb stem yourself, because leaves are poison. Even good idea to make little fence to keep children away. Wash hands with soap after picking. Pink kind most tasty.

Make oven 450 degree.

Make dice from raw rhubarb and mix with sweet kind apple (not crab). Baba strong recommend you try different kind this heritage apple. Go to farmer market and ask to see different kind.

Put fruit in pie shell, then sprinkle with brown sugar or honey, flour or cornstarch, cinnamon, salt and grate orange rind.

Put two thick slice butter.

Put top crust on pie. Cook at 450 degree ten minute, then turn down to 350 degree for thirty-five, until crust goldy brown.

Ingredient List:

- Rhubarb, four cups. Pink part only.
- Sweet apple, two cups. Mac and Delicious are good. Sunrise, Pink Lady, Ambrosia and Pippin, incredible.
- Brown sugar or honey, one half cup
- Flour or corn starch, one quarter cup
- Cinnamon, one tablespoon
- Salt, pinch
- Orange zest, one tablespoon
- Butter, two tablespoons
- Pie crust, bottom and top

Rhubarb Strawberry, Raspberry or Blueberry Pie

Just **put in two cup berry instead of apple** with rhubarb. Don't use plum or gooseberry.

Pumpkin Pie

In Ukraina, pumpkin is bad luck for young man. If he make proposal to young woman and she accept, she tie beautiful embroider scarf on his arm. If she not like him, she throw pumpkin at him. This is why Baba mother and father have to grow huge garden of pumpkin. She throw one at least twice a week.

Therefore, is no such thing as pumpkin pie or cake in Baba recipe book. Is unlucky.

Tasty Sugarless Pie

Best thing I find in Canada is fruit juice, made powerful concentrate. Anytime you not want sugar in pie, use half cup apple concentrate. Grape juice tasty with gooseberry and blueberry only.

"And bring us a lot of horilka, but not of that fancy kind with raisins, or with any other such things — bring us horilka of the purest kind, give us that demon drink that makes us merry, playful and wild!"---*Taras Bulba*, by Nikolai Gogol. No, is **not** "Russian" literature.

Uzvar (Stewed Fruit)

We make fruit stew for good dessert, very healthy. You want more fancy-shmancy, you call fruit "compote." Not me. This make me think that funny little man who write something about Cold Blood and also that gangster, Al Compote. They scare me while I eat. So I be plain person, show you how to make fruit stew.

Pick all kind your favorite fruit from orchard. I know you not have glorious kind like in Mother Country, but do your best. Fruit orchard in Ukraina make you cry, so beautiful. If no orchard, buy fruit from stupormarket. You poor thing.

In medium sauce pan, put each these kind fruit: dry apricot, wrinkle like your face gonna be when you ninety-three year old. Prune, especially if you like to be regular person. Otherwise, two fat plum. Take out stone in middle, what you think? Slice peach or nectarine OR dry pear slice. If you do both of last thing, too mushy.

Cut up nice big juicy yabluchka, apple. Take out core but leave peel for vitamin.

If your family like raisin, put in handful.

Can also add if feeling frisky: strawberry, raspberry, blueberry, saskatoon or blackberry. Remember some berry will make whole fruit stew colour blue. You like blue food? Then like grandchildren say, "Go for it."

Stupid idea: grape, kiwi, orange, grapefruit, gooseberry and especially, tomato.

Cover fruit so is one inch water on top. Squeeze in lemon juice to make zing zing taste. This fruit stew sweet by itself, but **some people like sugar or honey.** For very strong Ukrainian taste, put in buckwheat honey.

Other thing you can do: instead water, use apple cider or juice. Cider is stronger taste.

Make boil, then turn down right away. Make simmer for twenty minute, stirring with spoon. Turn off heat and let fruit sit for fifteen minute. This make fruit all soft and flavor like one magic thing. I promise, it taste like nothing else in world.

How to eat:

***As traditional dish at Sviata Vechera.** You should multiply this recipe several time for guest. You can also pour out some of resulting liquid and **serve as separate drink, *Pyva Bozha.* Drink of God**. Not taste too bad with horilka, either. Baba kind of like to use this as mix for her Wild Turkey.
*Just like this, in nice bowl with cross-stitch design.
***Pour on vanilla or fruit flavor ice cream.** Not chocolate, or you be sorry.
***Pour on fruit varenyky.**
***Sprinkle with seed from organic soniashnyk, sunflower. Or chop almond.** With lemon juice (above), you now have nice crunch crunch with zing zing.
***Put piece real honeycomb in mouth and chew** while eat stew. Make sure is no bee part still in comb. This hard to pick from false teeth.
With *Yabluchnyk (Apple Cake), next recipe
With *Medivnyk (Honey Cake)

If you feeling generous, give some to neighbor who have tight little mouth. See if I care. Maybe she tell you, "None you business if I constipate."

Don't call me if she slam door in you face.

Ingredient List:

- Prunes, dried apricots and pears. One half cup each. Can substitute two whole plums for one half cup prunes. If using fresh fruit, decide between fresh pears and peaches/nectarines One large fresh apple, unpeeled. Or dried apple slices, one half cup

- Berries, one half cup
- Fresh lemon juice, one tablespoon.
- Sugar or honey, one teaspoon
- Unsalted sunflower seeds or chopped almonds, one half cup

Yabluchnyk (Apple Cake)

This recipe is apple in my eye.

You going to love this kind cake, Baba guarantee. Apple in Ukraina is called *yabluchka*, and we have so many kind in orchard. Acre of field cover in beautiful tree hanging with red, yellow, pink and green apple. Look like Christmas tree all summer. In Ukraina, we have holiday call *Yablochnyi Spas* to celebrate fruit harvest.

I strong suggest you find heritage kind apple with unusual taste. There even some people in Canada work to preserve this. You can make cake taste little bit different every time. Just like when you make boyfriend wear wig in bedroom. My daughter say, "This too much information." Baba say is not quite enough.

One thing you need know. Ukrainian cake not necessarily going to be sweet and homogenous like some sawdust thing from mix in box. We take food serious, especially bread. Yabluchnyk less sweet in bread part. Then everyone be surprise when apple very sweet. This call **Baba Law of Contrast.**

How to make:

Put butter on counter early in day so soft. Do not use stinking margarine or recipe going to not turn out with Ukrainian *dusha*, soul. Like my homeboy say, you feeling Baba?

Sift pastry flour with brown sugar, salt and baking powder.

Take pastry tool and cut in butter. Dough should look crumbly.

In small bowl, use eggbeater on one egg and thick farm cream. Never mind trying save calorie here. Stir egg and cream into dough, but don't take too long. So that dough stay tender, should be handle as little as possible. I have trouble with this minimal handling part, as do Madonna. She my girl.

Butter baking pan measure eight by ten inch. You have trouble with these measurement, this good time to call 1-900-ASK-BABA, $4.99 for minute. I know, is cheap joke, but is going to cost you. You lucky. Think what it cost to ask Madonna.

Pat dough very gentle into pan.

Heat oven to 375 degree F.

Mix brown sugar with cinnamon.

Cut apple into thin slice. If peel is beautiful pink or red, leave on. If green, not so attractive and people get gross out. Peel away green.

Spread apple slice on dough. Sprinkle real good with sugar and cinnamon mix. If you using crab apple with tart taste, use more sugar. Also can substitute honey.

Take several small piece butter and put on apple. Don't be stingy.

OR make layer cake. This not traditional, but is my preference. Is also better, because is Baba invention:

Pat half of dough into grease pan. Put apple, sugar-cinnamon and butter on top. Put rest of dough on apple. Cut up one extra apple to decorate top of cake.

Bake for half hour. Use your common sense: if you stick knife in cake to see if done, apple in middle always going to be moist. Watch you don't over bake cake till dry.

What send yabluchnyk right over topping is if you serve with *Rozha z Tsukrom* (Rose Petal Preserves), recipe coming up next. These thing serve together are powerful love spell. Watch careful who you serve to. Baba make this cake at music studio where she teach power metal singing. Next thing she know, have five "underemployed" guitarist sleep on her couch, making love eye at her in morning. Actual, they nauseous till noon. Adjust your thinking to time change.

Yabluchnyk option:

You can use imagination and **replace apple with slice fresh peach, cherry or plum. Raspberry and strawberry** out from this world. Try combination of fruit. This much better than fruit salad from tin can. If you try tell people this still Apple Cake, you just look like goofy.

***Serve with Uzvar** (Fruit Stew). Warm or cool.

Serve with *Plum Sauce, *Chapter Twenty Two*. Do not use stuff from bottle!

Ingredient List:

- Butter, one half cup plus another quarter to grease cake pan
- Pastry flour, one and one half cups
- Brown sugar, one quarter cup. If this cake is not sweet enough the first time you try it, add more sugar next time. It is meant to be eaten with a sweet topping and not be overly sugary.

- Baking powder, two teaspoons
- Salt
- Egg, one large
- Cereal or whipping cream, one third cup

Topping

- Brown sugar, one half cup
- Cinnamon, two teaspoons
- Apples, sweet. Four large
- Butter, one quarter cup

Rozha z Tsukrom (Wild Rose Preserves)

We going to make preserve from wild pink rose. This so romantic thing, you will not believe how tasty. It make men act like fly.

First, you find big bush full those kind pink wild rose. Kind in Canadian domestic yard have too thick petal, hard to eat. In Ukraina we grow special kind, but in Canada you have to go hunt with flashlight when neighbor asleep.

If they can reach, send grandchildren with hose to give rose bush shower with spray hose. In Ukrainian we call this *spraying hosa.* If stupid social worker come to ask why children spraying bushes at night, pull your hair. Say, "Oi yoi yoi, they always walking in sleep. Help me get funding for good counseling." Baba guarantee she not come back.

Pick only rose petal, leave yellow part alone. You can pick rose hip for tea. See *Ukrainian Medicine, Chapter Twenty Five.*

At home, **sprinkle petal right away with lemon juice so not turn brown. Or pour scald hot water over petal when they in sieve.** This last thing also make leftover bug rise to top. Or at least kill them. Sometime I leave few little bug if I going to serve to men, so they not be thinking I make them eat complete lady food. Men funny that way.

You going to need **two cup white sugar for every tight cup rose petal. Also need one lemon for every two cup petal. Make boil one cup water for every cup rose petal.** This recipe always remind me Ukrainian proverb, *You not appreciate sugar until you have to eat lemon.*

When this all boiling, turn down heat and let simmer fifteen minute. Keep stirring. Best if with wooden spoon. Rose petal she very delicate, and metal spoon hurt her feeling.

Cook until syrup is thick enough to coat back of spoon without

sliding off. Ukrainian cook don't bother with candy thermometer nonsense. How you like if you be pretty pink petal and some hamfist *koshmar*, she just come from barn, stick big fat thermometer in your eye? Not so much, I'm telling you. You not good cook until you can see good and use your instinct. Either practice or buy your rose petal preserve from Baba. Call 1-900-BUY-BABA.

Squeeze lemon. Is better if you left lemon on counter overnight. Warm easier to squeeze.

Mix in juice from fresh lemon for each one cup petal. But again I telling you, be proactive cook. Taste while you making something. But not too much, or nothing left for later. Just enough so friend not pointing at you on street, saying, "Your cooking stink!"

Spoon preserve into sterilize jar. Use small jar, because you not going to eat lots of this at once. Give jar little tap tap with finger while you filling to release air bubble and make last insect float to top.

Your option:

*__Serve with *Yabluchnyk,*__ *(Apple Cake)* **or *Medivnyk*** *(Honey Cake)*
***Ice cream**
As filling for *Pampushky *(Doughnut)*
With** ***Nalysnyky *(Crepes), Chapter Four*

Ingredient List:

For every two cups of packed rose petals

- White sugar, two cups
- Lemon, one large to make two tablespoons juice
- Boiled water, one cup
- 8 ounce sterilized jar

Honey Cake (Medivnyk)

Ukrainian invent honey cake because we have most and biggest honey bee in world. Buzz buzz buzz, they so cute. Look like chubby little stripe kozak kissing flower as if pretty girl.

Best kind this cake, you get honey from buckwheat. This strong Ukrainian taste. Clover honey is weak kind, meant for tea only. The darker is honey, the more good mineral it have inside. Baba know you not always obey her. Your loss, for sure. Just make sure honey is liquid for *medivnyk* recipe.

Baba law: also get honeycomb and chew this like gum while you cook. It give you right rhythm for good cake. When you visit bee keeper, get me bottle honey wine, or I want to know why not.

Make sure you going to be home while cake bake. Is not okay to run to boyfriend down hallway in meantime. This not some ugly powder thing from box with woman in bad haircut smiling because she make so much money from you. This serious project from sacred ingredient.

Make honey boil, then let cool. Watch honey whole time. It not take long to boil, and you don't want burn.

Heat oven to 350 F.

Make cream brown sugar and soft butter. Not this slimy "margarine" thing.

This next thing sad, but have happy ending. Tell four free range organic egg, "I have to separate you, but only for little while." Do it, even if they cry. If egg have blood spot, this good. Mean is fertile and came from smiling chicken. **Put four egg yolk, one at time, into sugar and butter. Beat up.**

Pour cool honey into batter and beat more. You chewing that honeycomb like Baba tell you? Rhythm, rhythm!

Sift cake flour with baking soda, baking powder, salt from Black Sea, cinnamon.

Baba tell you secret of why her cake better than neighbour cake: **add nutmeg and ground clove.** Sifting dry thing also important. Make batter fluffy and well-mix.

Add to batter one cup dry thing, then half cup smetana. Another cup dry thing, half cup smetana. Pay attention to TOTAL: one cup smetana, three cup dry thing. Because last time I check, you can't do math. Last cup dry thing. See chapter on smetana. Nowhere but varenyky (perogy) recipe is it more important that smetana come from farm in jar. Sure, you can use this white jello from stupormarket and cake will turn out. But smetana make big difference.

If you like walnut, date, dry currant or raisin, you can stir in one cup of one kind or mixed kind. One cup total. But not necessary to real good honey cake. Peanut no good.

This where you keep promise to egg for reunite. **Use egg beater in white part until your bicep swell. Egg will look like snow drift. Mix into batter.**

Grease pan with butter. Best kind pan is with tube thing in middle, so honey cook even. Pour in batter.

Next Baba trick for honey cake: **Oven start at 350 F for first fifteen minute only.**

Cake will bake total of fifty or fifty five minute. Turn oven down to 325 F and bake here for next fifteen minute. Then turn oven down to 300 F for final twenty or twenty five minute.

Honey burn real easy, so make sure you listen to Baba about this. Playing with temperature will also make nice crunchy crust on cake.

Check with knife. If middle still sticky, put back in oven five more minute.

Honey cake get better as it age, just like woman. You will not resist taste when you first bake, but try mostly control yourself. Or you can do like Baba, and make two in first place. Don't lie to self about appetite, poopchik. This is big part of life pleasure.

Wrap first cake in foil or plastic, and put up on high shelf where no one else can touch. At Christmas, I make one month ahead so honey have "cure" taste, just like good horilka. Remember honey is living thing, come from living creature who work hard. Medivnyk is evolving thing, not ready-mix.

If you made two, go back and start eating first one before children get home.

Serve with *Uzvar* fruit stew, on side. **Or with my special *Plum sauce***, *Chapter Twenty Two*. **Also good with real whip cream.**

Drink with glass cold goat milk. If unpasteurize, even better. I prefer from brown goat, but you can't have everything. In Canada. Big surprise: also very good with plain taste rice or almond milk.

Your option:

For many present to friend, **make bigger recipe and spoon batter into clean, greased coffee can. Or even little soup can.** I know, I know, Baba wrong to even suggest you not making all soup from scratching. Take out cake from can before giving to friend.

Ingredient List:

- Buckwheat honey, one cup
- Butter, one half cup plus enough to grease pan
- Brown sugar, one cup
- Eggs, four large
- Cake flour, three cups
- Baking soda, two teaspoons
- Baking powder, one half teaspoon
- Salt
- Cinnamon, one teaspoon
- Nutmeg, one half teaspoon
- Ground cloves, one half teaspoon
- Bundt pan. Absolutely necessary so cake bakes evenly.

Medivnyk (Honey) Muffins

Baba warning: Muffin is not traditional Ukrainian thing. Muffin is so cheap person can count how many you eat. You can't sneak bigger piece, like cake and bread.

I learn muffin from woman name Muffy. She tell me this Canadian word while we watch her husband play polo. Polo is game for baby. You not even allowed knock anyone off horse. Pah! Personal, I like good fast game *bazkashi.* This Afghani thing I introduce to Ukraina, where I become champion on my white horse, Misha.

Bazkashi is on field whole country long and have no rule except WIN. On centre line is head of dictator. You want real winning strategy, you pretend is Stalin or Putin. These day, things sad in Europe. You have to settle for head of minor politician. Whole group gallop gallop gallop their horse to this head, and hit with mallet until it fly into enemy goalpost. On way, you make lots good screaming and collision with your horse into people. Is something like NASCAR for Klingon.

In Canada, they say, "Oh, we so democratic, we so anti-Soviet, we so anti-Nazi." But you have to improvise, make pretend head by paint face on cabbage. Bo-ring.

Anyway, make muffin for Muffy friends after good game bazkashi or sissy polo.

Here what you do:

Make recipe for *Medivnyk*, above.

Spoon batter into greased muffin pan. Recipe will make maybe two dozen muffin. Try to share. If any muffin pan space still hollow, fill with water. This will keep pan from wrinkling in oven, and will make muffin even moister. Bake just like honey cake. **Will take less time, so turn down heat more often. About forty minute, total.** Take toothpick from your mouth and check, you lazy bone.

Baba law: The smaller thing is, the faster it cook. Is because more surface area is expose. This is call *First Law of Thermal Underwear.* You should have learn in physic class if you paying attention. Is why you should never bring baby in hot tub.

Ingredient List:

- As for Medivnyk
- Greased muffin pans, 24 count

Chocolate Medivnyk (Honey Cake)

Baba have big confession to make to you. She not always as sincere and honest as you know her. During terrible time in Soviet regime and Holocaust---because Ukraina always get best of both world---Baba have hard time letting go of some habit. Like living.

Then she come to Canada. When little granddaughter Rosie old enough to walk to drugstore, her favorite thing is chocolate Easter Bunny. She so cute, always point to biggest one on shelf, kind who make wide candy eye. Unfortunate, Baba is poor. It break her heart she cannot buy Rosie this major chocolate rabbit.

Here come bright side to starvation in Europe: Baba can carry entire live turkey in her bloomer. Chocolate is literal piece of cake. She just point and say, "Look over there, Rosie!" and pow! rabbit is swoop under long skirt.

Baba limp little bit going home, but she tell Rosie straight up that arthritis in knee is pretty bad today. Someone have to teach child honesty.

Baba teaching you to make chocolate medivnyk. She give you lucky break. This recipe only require one big fist full unsweeten chocolate. Should be plenty room in your bra, from what Baba see is diet situation in Canada.

You ready for this honey and chocolate extravaganza? Here we go:

Leave hunk of butter on counter overnight so you don't have to argue with next day. Baba is sure you going to forget, then try to make soft in goofy microwave. Here is what will happen. Butter will get melt in puddle partway, and stay cold and hard partway. This is terrible disappointment. Avoid, I am telling you this.

Melt chocolate in double boiler, not fry pan where you make bacon. What is double boiler, you want to know. Is one pot go inside other, like that crazy dead German import Russian Katerina. She think she so great. She absorb part of Ukraina, then part of horse. She think they go together like *rama lama lama ka ding a da ding de dong.* Mix of guilty conscience and heavy horse kill her in end. Double boiler is lots more functional. Katerina is who Peter I use to steal Crimea, first time, right after Muskoli rename themselves "Rus'yan" to make fraudulent claim of Slavic heritage. Rus' mean Slavic. Which they are not!

You boil water in bottom of boiler to melt delicate thing on top part. Good chocolate burn easy, so is good idea to invest in chocolate protection. Mix in liquid honey, but don't taste. If you sincere about becoming Ukrainian, get buckwheat honey. Is very strong taste, so if you don't want to overwhelm taste bud, go slow. Baba know honey and chocolate together is irresistible, but control yourself or you going to burn off your good lip. Then how you going to lie to fascista? **Put boiler aside so honey chocolate can cool.**

Turn oven to 350 F.

Make sifting with flour, baking soda, salt and bake powder. Do this twice, and don't get amount of each powder thing mix up. You been back to that honey chocolate with finger, and your head already spinning. **Put dry thing aside.**

Make creaming with butter in huge mix bowl. Everything heading in this direction now, okay? **Mix in white or brown sugar little bit at time,** so butter have time to adjust to new relationship. Butter and sugar is one of best love match in world. **Add good splash vanilla.** Can substitute whiskey, Baba find out the hard way. **Beat in two egg, one at time.**

Pour in that wild honey chocolate. Can you believe we in world where all these thing can make life together?

Have cake flour and buttermilk waiting. Add hand full flour, then splash buttermilk. Hand full flour, splash buttermilk. Keep going and mixing till each ingredient is used up. You can lick spoon now. As if you waited.

Butter eight inch by eight inch baking pan. Pour in batter.

You can also double recipe and bake in bundt pan.

Bake forty minute. Oven start at 350 F for first ten minute only.Turn oven down to 325 F and bake here for next fifteen minute. Then turn oven down to 300 F for final fifteen or twenty minute.

Honey burn real easy, so make sure you listen to Baba about this. Playing with temperature will also make nice crunchy crust on cake.

Check with knife. If middle still sticky, put back in oven five more minute.

Is second good ending to this Easter Bunny story. Baba not know this till recent, but family who own drugstore actual see her take chocolate. They send bill to her children every time. Nobody want to embarrass woman who survive everything Baba has, especial in front of little Rosie. This was in Winnipeg, where is excellent refugee and immigrant community. In BC, they would probably hold Baba hostage to be drug mule.

Ingredient list:

- Buckwheat honey, two thirds cup
- Bitter chocolate, three ounces
- Baking soda, one teaspoon
- Baking powder, one half teaspoon
- Salt, one half teaspoon
- Butter, one half cup
- Brown sugar, two thirds cup
- Vanilla, one teaspoon
- Eggs, two medium
- Cake flour, one and three quarters cups
- Buttermilk, three quarter cup

Syrnyk (Ukrainian Cheesecake)

Last year Baba go out to New Year party stagola. Boyfriend don't renew Viagra prescription, say he want Baba to accept him as "natural" man. Baba say, "Fine. Then I go natural, too. I am forgetting my denture, hair color and deodorizing. And I don't wear foundation garment in front your friend, neither." Not to mention I don't cook no varenyky or holubtsi on holiday. Boyfriend can just eat "natural" food. Raw out from freezer. Is some good birdseed in backyard, too.

Once he go stomp out from house to suck beer with his loser friend, Baba quick take off her old person shoe, shave her leg and put on all New Yearing gear. She hop into her Cadillac with Rocket 88 engine and find swingingest party in whole town. Soon she is dancing *hopak* with forty year old man she can tell is not going to need no Viagra. He is tall and dark and he like to give her floppy eye. It turn out he is Denzel Washington long lost brother, who was out for many year exploring kozak life in Ukraina. He look like he can really ride those steppe. Angelina Jolie adopt him and bring him to North America. For which he also need date who interpret Ukrainian into excellent English. This is probably perfect for Baba. She always up for two in one experience.

Hoo boy, here come that midnight mass. We is counting down, and he is holding Baba hand so tight, she is glad she didn't waste energy cooking for her natural boyfriend. Suddenly is "Happy New Year!" and this guy put his warm lip on Baba. He is some kind romantic paramedic; he give her the kissing of life.

We is all fire up and ready to go.

At home, Baba serve him *syrnyk* by hand. This is most romantic recipe ever. Is *actual* Velyk Den' (Easter) traditional recipe, but you going to be making it all time, Baba guarantee.

Leave butter out overnight so is soft. If butter is scared, leave it by night light.

Make separation from six egg. Baba know, is hard to hear this when you just getting used to conglomeration. Don't be worry, yolk and white get together later. They meant for each other.

Beat egg yolk very thorough with sugar until mix in bowl is perfect pale yellow like you wish your kitchen could be.

Beat in butter, then baking powder. If you say fast enough, this is also Baba vocal lip warm up exercise.

Now come what we all been waiting for: cheese. This should be farmer kind or dry cottage.

Strain through sieve so it make that zizz zizz sound. Plunk this in rest of mixture and beat up whole thing until is smooth like your New Year wax leg.

Stir in lemon zest and lemon juice. Remember lemon will give up more juice if it happy and warm from sitting on counter.

If you like raisin in cheesecake, this is where they make their wrinkle entrance.

Now your egg white going to stop its pining, just like Baba promise. **Beat them until they turn into small white mountain. Insert them gradual into rest of batter.**

You going to bake in slooooow oven. This mean you have to say everything twice. Not really. It mean you using low heat for best baking of syrnyk. **300 degree F if you can stand, 325 at maximum if you little bit impatient.**

Butter one those chastity belt springform pan.

Now come magic substitute for crust: sprinkle pan all over with soft bread crumb. This one of few time Baba going to let you use white crumb. Syrnyk crust is for looking good, not nutrition. Same way you wear those six inch heel and have air traffic control bikini wax that make you scream. Is for vanity, not sanity.

Pour syrnyk batter into pan and bake about one hour. Watch it for when it shrink away from side of pan. Is kind of hard to tell when anything with syr, cheese, is bake using Baba prefer and brilliant method of chopstick. You just going to have to stick your eye on it.

Take syrnyk out from oven and let sit. Baba even chill it for couple hour in springform pan. Then she sure cake will not crumble when she release it from its prison. You going to serve it cold, anyway. **Unbuckle pan and slide gentle gentle onto good looking plate.**

Baba know, you feeling like something is missing. You have one reflex hand on economy size can cherry pie filling. Made mostly of corn syrup and food color. Listen, traditional syrnyk is so damn fine, it don't need no topping. Topping is if you make big flopping. Baba once had surprise at Jewish deli. They was adventurous enough to give baking work to Anglo-Saxophone. They serve her some kind Episcopalian New York cheesecake with whip cream. Oy yoi yoi, she almost swallow her tongue.

If you want to decorate syrnyk, use fruit slice. This is not same thing as topping, Baba telling you this. Decoration is to enhance what is already perfect. Fresh peach is beautiful, as is fresh cherry, raspberry or strawberry.

How to serve: Feed boyfriend one piece fruit. Then hand full cheesecake. Kiss him while mouth is still full. Feed nother piece fruit. More cheesecake. Kiss him and kiss him and kiss him. This is all you need to know, Baba promise. He going to kiss you back till his good fluffy lip is chap. Them Anglo-Saxophone with their whip cream don't know nothing about nothing.

Ingredient List:

- Eggs, six large
- Sugar, one cup
- Unsalted butter, one cup
- Baking powder, one teaspoon

- Dry cottage or Farmer cheese, four cups
- Lemon zest, one tablespoon
- Lemon juice, one half cup
- Soft white bread crumbs, one half cup
- Optional: one half cup raisins

Perekladanets (Coffee Cake)

The other day Baba is standing in line at coffee shop. Some *koshmar*, nightmare person, start arguing with nice clerk that their coffee cake don't have coffee in it.

Baba tap him on shoulder. “Excuse me,” she say, because Baba always polite. “Do you not understand this mean you eat with coffee?” I show him all my denture.

“No,” he snarling, “Carrot cake have carrot, and coffee cake suppose to have coffee.”

Baba have good answer ready. “But date loaf not mean you ever going to get one. Ha!”

Ukrainian coffee cake is extreme baking. It have all sorts layer and filling, like torte. Because you amateur, Baba going to start you on bunny slope version. It don't have coffee inside it. Complicate kind going to be in next book.

This is traditional dessert at both Velyk Den' and Sviat Vechir. You have to treat it right.

First ordering of business, **test your yeast like in *Kolach,*** *(Circle of Life Bread), Chapter Eleven.* **For Perekladanets, you going to use quarter cup water and one big pinch sugar.** If yeasty beast get bubbly like good hairdo, is usable for recipe.

Scald milk. See *Hrechenyky* (Buckwheat Pancakes), *Chapter Four.* **Then let cool to luke. Beat together with flour. Add yeast mix to this mess. This going to be call your “sponge.”** Don't eat any other kind. Baba use this term with neighbor, and she have to go to veterinarian for surgery.

Put clean towel over this mix and shove aside on counter until it bubble again. Should take about ten minute. If it don't bubble this time, your milk was too hot. You going to hate Baba, but start over. You wish you had done this time you knew you weren't exactly cutting along skirt pattern. Hate Baba now, love her later. She is Home Economic Dominatrix.

Okay, you got yourself together? **Take out biggest mixing bowl.**

Beat up two whole egg with three extra egg yolk and salt. Add sugar while you beating. Give egg white to neighbor who eat sponge. Is part of strategy against law suit.

Melt butter in small pan. Mix this into egg along with vanilla. If you don't have horilka handy, take sip of vanilla. Will keep you from tasting slimy batter in progress. And use real vanilla. Will make all difference to your cake.

Pour in spongy thing. Sift flour. Mix in flour with big strong spoon. Baba prefer wooden one she carve herself. Pull yours out from where is keeping window open. Mixing go better if all in one direction. Otherwise, dough get confused. Some people knead this dough, but this kind pretty soft. Baba have concern you going to get gross out and give up. If you not naturally hands on person, use spoon.

Cover up and let dough rise up to double its size. Maybe half hour.

Give it knockout punch in *zhyvit*, cover and let it try to get up off canvas. Warning: This is not last time for this kind of action. If you starting to whine, just remember is always good idea to read recipe through first so you can plan your life.

Take out biggest tubing pan you got and smear with soft butter. Sprinkle with very fine soft bread crumb. This is one of few time Baba going to give you dispensation to use white bread.

Chop up kind of nut you like. Cashew, walnut, almond. But not peanut. Everyone will think you cheap. **Mix together with brown sugar and hallelujah, even more vanilla.**

There is going to be two layer to this cake, so conduct yourself accordianly.

When dough is twice its size, use big spoon to put half in pan.

Sprinkle dough with half of nut mix. Put on rest of dough, rest of nut mix. This way no one can say cake is half nut. Ha!

Put aside dough in warm place to make double again, while you finish rest of vanilla.

Heat oven to 375 degree F. Make sure rack is in centre of oven. Do not put cake in oven until that little red light go out unless you want floppola on your hand. **Bake for ten minute. Then you going to turn down heat to 325 F and bake for forty good minute. If you cover with foil, is less chance of top burning.**

This Perekladanets is delicate, ladylike cake, not corporate thing that get ship all over country. Once you take gentle from stove, **let sit for at least ten minute** before you try to flip over onto plate. Get help, which is what Baba been telling you all along.

Ingredient List:

Dough

- Sugar, one teaspoon
- Lukewarm water, one quarter cup boiled
- Yeast, one package
- Scalded milk, three quarter cup
- Cake flour, one half cup
- Eggs, two whole and three yolks
- Salt, large pinch
- White sugar, one half cup
- Melted butter, one quarter cup
- Real vanilla, one teaspoon
- Sifted flour, two cups

Filling and Topping

- Chopped nuts, one half cup
- Brown or demerara sugar, one half cup
- Vanilla, one teaspoon

Pampushky (Filled Doughnuts)

Pampushky is Ukrainian doughnut with big surprise in middle. Traditional is to fill with rose petal preserve, *Rozha Z Tsukrom*. This literal mean "rose with sugar." If you learn good from Baba how to roll your rrrrrrrrrrrrr, you now have exciting new name to call your sweetheart. Or new horse. Think of yourself prancing into show ring and they say, "Here come *Rozha z Tsukrom*," just before you fall off.

Baba just kidding. She know you clinging too hard to that saddle horn to ever lose balance.

See *Kolach, Chapter Eleven*, for yeast testing instruction. See *Rozha Z Tsukrom, Chapter Twenty Three*, and have this Ready Freddie.

If your yeast test positive, Baba give you green light. **Mix one half cup warm water with two tablespoon white sugar, then sprinkle two envelope yeast on top.** Let it hang out till it look kind of spongy.

Make milk lukewarm. Mix this into yeasty mix. Mix in three quarter cup flour. Beat this whole thing up real good.

Make cream from butter and sugar. Little extra is always good, because this where taste testing portion of our show begin.

Beat up all egg material. Yes, ingredient list is correct. You going to have more yolk than white. Baba know you been waiting for this; she is not yolking.

Throw in that zesty lemon, real vanilla and yeasty mix to egg and butter. Use nother clean spoon to taste, then throw in sink.

Mix in rest of flour and knead with hand for ten minute.

Baba warning: This is end of taste test time. If you lick dough now, will be sticky mess for later. Will also retain embarrassing tongue mark.

Cover up dough with towel that is little bit damp. Please, damp with clean water, not from wiping forehead. This is baking with Baba, not aerobic class. **Let dough get double, about half hour.**

Give dough good punch and knead little bit. Cover and let rise again.

Get out compass. Divide dough into four piece, one for each compass direction. First piece of dough must face north, or Ukrainian sky God *Dazbogh* will be mad.

Gotcha! Dazbogh got nothing to do with making pampushky. He don't mind it, though.

Roll one piece dough into thin rectangle. Turn over couple of time while you rolling, and use tiny bit flour.

Put glob of rozha z tsukrom along dough, every two inch or so.

Roll out next piece dough to same size, and make covering of first piece. Pink filling will show through dough. Baba know, this is some kind sexy doughnut recipe.

Take round drinking glass, kind you drink water from when you not swilling horilka. **Cut out dough so filling is exactly in middle.**

Sprinkle little bit flour on cookie sheet, and put pampushky here.

Do exact same thing with next two piece dough.

Let those pampushky rise on cookie sheet one more time. Yes, believe it or nut, they will get double again! This is miracle of nature never stop amazing Baba.

In meantime, **heat up lard or soniashnyk oil to 375 sizzling degree in deep fryer.** Very deep skillet will work if you have to do it this way. Watch that temperature. If fat start smoking, this mean it is burning. Avoid this.

You can test if lard is hot enough by dropping in dough scrap and crossing your finger it turn goldie color real quick. Of course you have dough left over. You could not possibly eat that much raw dough in last half hour.

Uh oh.

Fry only six pampushky at time so they cook quick and don't get too greasy. If they is in a skillet, flip over with your expert wrist so they get goldie on both side. They will be like puffball, and even have sort of white ring in centre.

Sprinkle them with icing sugar after they have drained themself on paper towel.

There you have it. Is pink seduction doughnut personified. Your husband going to stop spending his evening in *Tim Horton*, flirting with policewoman.

Ingredient List:

- Sugar, two tablespoons
- Warm water, one half cup
- Yeast, two envelopes
- Two percent or whole milk, three quarters cup
- Flour, five cups
- Unsalted butter, one quarter pound
- White sugar, one half cup
- Eggs, two
- Egg yolks, three
- Salt, one teaspoon
- Vanilla, one teaspoon
- Lemon zest, two teaspoons
- Icing sugar, one quarter cup
- Lard or sunflower oil, one quart
- Rozha z Tzukhrom, one cup

Chapter Twenty Four

Mak (Poppy Seed)

First you have to grow poppy. Many row, right up to front door and down to front gate. I bring mak, poppy seed, in lining of skirt to Canada. In Ukraina, we even have *Makovyi Spas*, summer holiday to celebrate poppy harvest. Here, they not want you brew nice cough syrup, make you sleep. I go talk to pharmacist about this. She try to sell me cough syrup, tell me I can't make from poppy seed.

I say, "What in this super duper cough syrup, so expensive?"

She say, "Come from poppy seed."

I get mad, say, "What I trying tell you? You some kind thief, tell me I can't grow my own poppy seed to make cough syrup." Next day, RCMP come talk to all Baba in neighbourhood.

But I too smart for them. I show them patch poppy from stupid weak Canadian seed, not kind make cough syrup. They smile and say, "Please," and "Thank you," like I crazy old woman, not know what they want. Soviet Union terrible, but at least when soldiers come, they not act polite, and I know they coming steal my thing.

Then this real handsome RCMP officer come back after work. He take me out and show me his big black horse. We laugh and drink horilka, then go for musical ride. He tell me he going to fix it so I never be bothered about poppy again. Ha! Baba always get her man.

Anyway, once poppy come out of ground with pointy leaf, every day you have to talk to them. I know you read book tell you tell big story to plant, play them music, and so on like New Age thing. I show you Old Age thing. Baba stand over baby poppy, point finger and say, "You! Bloom!"and she bloom. Make big red flower, so beautiful.

Once poppy bloom, pick whole bunch and hang from rope on ceiling until they dry. Then shake little seed into brown paper bag until you have whole cup. This not take so long as you think.

If you need syrup for bad cough and sleep, you come see Baba. Also if you want have baby with no big pain.

Mak (Poppy Seed) Cookies

This national cookie of Ukraina. Baba make plateful, and soon all children in neighbourhood running round with little black spot on teeth.

Very cute, like albino ladybug.

You promise me, you never tell no one how easy to make. Just serve and let them say is "exotic." Which is stupid thing people say. It mean, "Don't belong in North America, like white bread do."

Day before you baking, put *mak* in milk. This make it soft. Put in fridge. And remember, you not going to find mak at Mac store. Ha!

Same day you baking, leave butter on counter for few hour. Best kind butter is from Jersey or Brown Swiss cow, kind look like little deer with long eyelash. Is bad luck to eat this cow, by way. Must keep as pet. This first secret why your cookie going to be better than neighbor cookie.

In meantime, **leave sour cream out so is room temperature.**

Mix mix mix sugar with butter in big bowl until make fluffy and white goldie like you wish your hair look, instead of that fried egg you wearing on head. Can use white or yellow sugar. White sugar make more like Marilyn Monroe hair.

Beat up two egg with beater thing. Be very firm with egg, tell them they have to be all one thing, white and yellow.

Put together egg and sour cream into butter/sugar mix. This point where you look over shoulder to see no one looking. Take clean spoon and taste. Lick lip, taste again to make sure you mix completely.

Take mak from fridge, pour off milk. If you real Ukrainian, you warm up this milk and drink with coffee and chicory for Slavic latte. Can't find that at Starbuck. Ha! Even better if you have kind poppy little bit like medicine syrup. Good luck finding in Canada, chickie babe. **Mix mak into butter/egg/sugar/cream.** Mix real good, so no one mad their cookie not have funny little black spot.

Get grandchildren help sifting pastry or all purpose flour. This fun thing, tell them. **Sift in baking soda and little pinch salt.**

Baba warning: Make sure grandchildren sifting this over big bowl. Even cleaner if bowl sitting on kind of big foil thing you bake turkey on at Thanksgiving. Afterward, let children use foil thing to pretend they making thunder, drive parent crazy. Even better if one of them is playing thunder bass on piano, same time. Show him how to make rain with right hand, too. This how you pay your children back for driving you crazy.

Pour dry thing into wet thing. Do I have to tell you how important is good mixing?

Here is next secret of best kind cookie: **put dough in fridge for at least two hour, let get real chill.** I know you try to save time, but don't put in freezer where so cold like Siberia. Why I have to tell you?

Heat oven to 375 degree.

Put dough on floured board and roll thin. Using pastry flour best. Sorry, you hippie-shmippie, whole wheat flour make too thick and sticky.

Traditional mak cookie is round. You can show grandchildren to press down with open side of drinking glass and twist. Just don't give them shot glass. Cookie too small and they get funny idea. Or use cookie cutter, make any shape you want. My sister she sell special cookie cutter at some kind erotic party, but I think this not classy to give out body part in neighborhood. But, everybody work out trauma their own way.

Grease baking sheet. Put cookie in oven. No, put on your big toe. Like that going to work. Not really. **Watch cookie get little bit brown on edge, maybe ten minute,** depending on if you ever clean your oven. If oven catch on fire from grease, cookie bake a little faster. Eat with Jersey milk.

Ingredient List:

- Poppy seed, one half cup
- Whole or two percent milk, one half cup
- Butter, one cup
- Brown or white sugar, one cup
- Sour cream, two tablespoons
- Eggs, two large
- Pastry or all-purpose flour, two and three quarter cups
- Baking soda, quarter teaspoon
- Salt, pinch

Mak (Poppy Seed) Cake

This kind cake you take to grandchild PTA meeting. No one else going to make anything else like, because they showing up with some kind crappy cookie they make from box. They be thinking they all want to be like you. Good idea you practice being humble in front of mirror before meeting.

Pour milk over mak. Cover bowl and put in fridge overnight. This sacred Ukrainian ritual. Most opium come from poppy, keep kid quiet in school. See feetnote.

If you can find, goat milk always make better cake.

Next day **find tube kind pan** somewhere in that desert you call kitchen. If not there, go to second hand store to find where other loser give up on baking. Buy their stuff for peanut.

Wash second hand pan real good. Baba going to smarten up your hygiene too. You bet.

Way to make best mix batter: over bowl of wet thing, put flour, pinch salt and baking powder into large sieve. Mix around dry thing with spoon until all sifted through.

Now is moment you all been waiting for. **Pour mak and milk into batter.** Don't worry it going to turn temporary gray color. This all come out in wash. Only you not going to wash nothing except your hand. Never mind why.

Put electric mixer on medium Put butter on counter to make soft. This not going to take too long, so heat up oven now. 350 degree F.

Butter tube pan and dust with flour.

Take out large bowl. Do not use dog water bowl or she be growling at you whole time.

Cream together cup butter, lemon zest and one and sugar.

What is zest? Oh, you kidding me. Take peel from lemon and grate. Stop just before knuckle bleed. Give zing! taste to cake.

Make four large egg white. Be careful here, is technique to this. Have two bowl ready. **Crack each egg gentle and scoop white from shell to shell like circus trick.** Save yolk for something else, like decorating salata. Cook first and crumble on salad.

Pour egg white into butter, lemon zest and sugar. You can use wooden spoon and do aerobic for fifteen minute, or set electric mixer on high. **Beat up till fluffy, either way.**

This also how I like my hair, but you try mixer on me I going to stop feeding you. You going to keep scraping side of bowl so all mixed even. Will look beautiful, like me or Christina Aguilera on good day. See? I told you gray color going to disappear, just like good dye job.

Pour batter into pan and bake forty-five to sixty minutes. At forty-five minute you going to check with wooden skewer. This safer than toothpick and don't make as big gash as knife.

Take cake from oven and let sit five minute to settle itself. Then turn very careful upside down onto wire rack and let cool. If your hand reach out to taste, slap yourself. We have one more thing to do so this cake perfect.

We going to make glaze:

In large bowl, stir icing sugar, soft butter and three teaspoons fresh lemon or two teaspoon fresh orange juice and one teaspoon lemon.

Baba warning: Using lazy bone canned juice is first way you going to ruin this cake. Baba know you going to think of so many other way, but she is not psychiatrist.

Once and only once cake is cool, dribble glaze over top. If you impatient and put on warm cake, glaze going to sink into cake and be like weird pudding. Believe me, you cannot hold head up at PTA meeting like this. Everyone think you make from some terrible mix and you be apologizing like idiot all night long. I hate when women apologizing.

Your option:

*You understand this is not classic Ukrainian, but Baba is constant inventor. **Make substitute for lemon or orange juice in glaze with these kind juice:** pomegranate, mango, papaya, raspberry, strawberry, blueberry, saskatoon, apricot, cherry, black currant. **Mix two teaspoon one these kind with one teaspoon fresh lemon.**

Grape and grapefruit not too tasty. If you thinking tomato juice, is time for you to buy other recipe book with all kind jelly tuna salad. Put this one back on shelf, because Baba give up on you.

Feetnote: Just kidding about kid.

Ingredient List:

Cake

- Whole or two percent milk, three quarters cup
- Poppy seed, three quarters cup
- Butter, one cup
- Lemon zest, one teaspoon
- Sugar, one and one half cups
- Egg whites, four large
- Pastry or all purpose flour, two cups
- Salt
- Baking powder, two teaspoons

Glaze

- Icing sugar, one cup
- Butter, two tablespoons
- Lemon or small sour orange, one half. Three teaspoons juice

Makivnyk (Poppy Seed Roll)

Poppy seed is yet nother kind of symbol for fertility. By now you having idea: almost everything in Ukraina is some kind symbol for fertility. When we not doing it, we baking, singing or making poetry about it. Now we going to roll in it, which is what you been waiting for.

Even if you that poor, is always possible to make romance. And somehow, we always find enough food for our *diutyny,* children.

This *makivnyk* is little bit more complicate than poppy seed cookie or cake. Very impressive on holiday table. Baba make for boyfriend as birthday cake, and he was relieve to not have some frou-frouing frosty icing thing. Roll have more attractive look to man. It look kind of like shock absorber.

Test your dry yeast with sugar in warm water. If it don't bubble, throw out. Yes, this happen, even to Baba. Is fault of yeast for being past expiring date or being store in too warm place. Your fault, really, but Ukrainski psychologist say is healthier to blame somebody. Baba always do.

Lukewarm scald milk. This mean you boil but never till it burn. If it burn, you know what to do.

Sift flour. Put aside one half cup.

Mix milk, yeast mix and half cup flour into pasty mess. Baba know this don't look like promising start. **But next come mixing butter, sugar, egg and salt, and add to yeast mix.** Now we cooking with gas. Whatever that mean. Sound almost like you should take little walk outside.

You back already? Situation has even improved around here. **Mix in lemon zest, real vanilla and rest of flour.**

Here is, for you anyway, bad news. You going to knead this mix ten whole minute. Is not going to get tough elastic feel like bread dough, so don't keep nagging at it.

Lift ball of soft dough into biggest bowl you grease with maslo, butter.

Cover with cleanest cloth you got and go away till dough is double up or nothing. About forty minute.

Give it good punch till it say, "Oooof!" then leave it alone to rise again.

Make rolling so dough is one big rectangle sheet, about one quarter inch thick. Keep picture in your mind you going to need to roll this sucker around filling. Too thick, and it will be like when you trying to roll sleeping bag on camping trip. Too thin, and you will look like *I*

Love Lucy episode.

Once you is sure you know what is going on, **beat up one egg white and brush this onto surface of dough.** Save yolk for your hangover. You have one now? Quick make Bleeding Mary and throw in yolk. Swallow quick.

Makivnyk Filling:

Don't turn on oven yet. Makivnyk got one more rising to go.

Mix together ground mak with lemon or orange zest and liquid honey. Like always, Baba promoting that unique Ukrainian taste, buckwheat honey. And she have nother trick: **mix together fresh orange and lemon juice**, not one or the other. Between these two flavor, not even most sneak head gourmet person will be able to guess how your filling made. Unless you cooking for Ukrainian cultural centre. Then all baba will surround you and fight how much of each you actual use, and in which province mak was harvest.

For makivnyk, mak is not soak in milk first. You would never get blender clean again.

Spread filling nice and even on dough. Roll roll roll like jelly roll.

Grease up baking sheet. Put makivnyk on this, and let rise again about half hour.

Turn oven to 350 degree F.

Make several slash with knife on top of roll in diagonal way. This is anger management exercise. Not really. It help steaming escape so makivnyk don't end up looking like blowfish. Or blown shock absorber, if you cooking for man.

Bake ten minute, then turn oven down to slooooow, or 300 degree for fifty minute.

If you didn't swallow that egg yolk, you going to beat it up and brush it on makivnyk ten minute before she finish baking. Take out of oven first. And this way Baba expect you to read whole recipe through first. Otherwise you ending up with egg on face.

One extra super special bonus: Baba promise you back in *Rohalyky* (Almond Crescent) recipe, *Chapter Twenty Three*, you can make *mak rohalyky*. Is true! Just stuff them with mak filling, like she just show you.

Ingredient List:

- Yeast, one package or one tablespoon
- White sugar, one teaspoon
- Warm water, one quarter cup

- Milk, one half cup
- Cake flour, three and one half cups
- Butter, one quarter cup plus extra to grease bowl
- White or brown sugar, one third cup
- Eggs, two medium
- Salt, one quarter teaspoon
- Vanilla, one half teaspoon
- Lemon zest, one teaspoon
- Flour, three cups

Filling

- Poppy seed, two and one half cups ground
- Lemon or orange zest, one tablespoon
- Fresh lemon juice, one tablespoon
- Fresh orange juice, one tablespoon
- Liquid honey, one half cup
- Egg white, one to brush on dough before filling
- Egg yolk, one to brush on makivnyk while baking

Chapter Twenty Five

Ukrainian Medicine

In Canada is against crazy law for me to tell you to make Ukrainian medicine at home. Just like was illegal under Soviet Union. This medicine shtick belong to doctor, and big pharmacy company who make big profit.

So Baba have to tell you this: if you sick, see doctor. Even if you have to wait six hour in stinking waiting room where forty people groaning and your sraka hanging from blue gown. This going to cure you, for sure.

On other hand, you can try these thing, hypothetical situation.

Rose Hip Tea

One my boyfriend like to call me "Rose Hip." He say I know how to make even funny looking thing taste good, which is another big secret of life. See *Yeast Infection*, below.

Never you minding about what he mean. If Baba have to tell you, you never get it. But at least I show you how to make zooming Vitamin C in your life with rose hip tea.

After your grandchildren pick all petal from rose for preserve and they wasting time on XBoxing, send them back to pick rose hip. They going to whine and cry. Tell them Ukrainian proverb, *Fly can't sit on boiling pot.* Believe me, they not going to care. But at least you educating them.

I know, you hoping Baba going to say, "Just pour hot water over rose hip and drink tea like is some kind boring pre-manufacture tea bag." Wrong. You know Baba better by now. **You have to boil rose hip for good ten minute.** Or else it taste like one them over price "flavor water" everyone pretend to like. Which have no medicine value.

Boil two tablespoon fresh rose hip in two pint water. This lots of fun if you have those kind pot made of glass. You can see little hip split and seed come out. Tea will turn pretty pink colour. If you not have glass pot, at least use ceramic so tea not get metal taste.

Strain and put in some honey. Some people like to add pinch dry mint, too. I call this "Ukrainski Julep." I drink after good fast game bazkashi. See *Medivnyk (Honey Cake),* under *Desserts, Chapter Twenty Three*. Make me feel like Kentucky countess. I give some to good horse, too. Make sure is cool, because horse have big fat lip and buck teeth. This give him trouble spilling little bit into saucer to sip. Don't make fun of your horse lip and teeth, though, Baba telling you. If you physical perfect like horse and your lip and teeth only funny looking part of body, you should be so lucky.

Rose hip tea have very high source Vitamin C so your teeth not fall out. Don't be thinking Baba have denture because of not drinking her rose hip tea. Some time after Soviet and Nazi steal her land, rose hip all she have to eat. Her teeth fall out from starving, because soldier too disgusting to eat. Mostly. Unless you marinate.

Anyway, you can drink as much this tea you like. No such thing as too much Vitamin C. Is what you call water soluble. How you know if body have too much, is you pee every few minute. Is terrible drag at party.

Med (Honey)

Did you know to make one pound honey, bee must fly twenty five thousand mile? This farther than flying around whole earth. This call *Art for Art sake*. You should kiss bee little stripe butt. Bee do Ukrainian special favor. He fly to sun to get beeswax for making sacred pysanky egg.

When God was creating earth, Devil try to imitate by making ugly kind of reverse earth. Bee spy on Devil. Pow! Devil catch bee in claw. He say, "I let you go as long as you give message to God. Say, 'Devil tell you to eat bee poop.'"

Bee buzz, "Oooookay." He fly back to God and tell him what Devil say. God say, "That is fine. From now on, bee will have sweetest poop in world. Ha!"

This is why honey so good medicine for all people. Bee is first real anarchist healer.

Baba tell you how *Plantain* or *Babka* is good wound healer, below. Honey have even extra power because it kill germ. If you can convince bee farmer to give you unpasteurize, is better medicine. In Ukraina, we have holiday call *Medovyi Spas*, to celebrate honey harvest. We have holiday for everything. We always thanking Nature and God.

Let's say you cutting wood for stove and you miss. Uh oh. Is hole in leg. While you screaming at top of lung, yell for honey. First clean out wound with soap and water. Then pour lots honey in wound. Thin layer will not work so good. Baba know this burn. You big wimpola. Is good thing you not Ukrainian kozak. On battlefield, they pour gunpowder in wound and light on fire. Baba warning: If you going to try this, do not substitute crazy sparkler or stupid firecracker. *Ty durniy*? You some kind dum dum? If kozak not have honey after this procedure, he pack wound with chewed bread and cobweb. Is better if chewer not also have tobacco in mouth. This is toxic.

Do not use solid kind honey and try to melt. Too much heat kill germ killer. Use unpasteurize honey, and Melaleuca is best kind.

Here is recipe for comfort kind tea when you have cold, or just long day weaving basket:

Honey Lemon Tea

This recipe will soothe sore throat and give real Vitamin C boost. Baba make recipe for lots, so you only have to boil one big pot, then reheat. She not recommend put in microwave, as death ray will kill good microbe in honey.

Put one small hand full Orange Pekoe or any other black tea you like in cheesecloth bag. Grate fresh lemon peel from one large lemon. Also put this in bag and tie up. Not with twist tie; it will rust. Use cotton thread.

Popeye quiz: You already know from reading recipe in this book WHAT ABOUT LEMON?

Is right. Leave on counter overnight to make easy squeezie. Squeeze one lemon till it screaming, "Uncle Tom!"

Boil up one and quarter quart water. Why one quarter? To make up for what evaporate. Is basic science.

Throw in lemon juice and cheesecloth bag. Boil for five minute, then let steep for ten.

Stir in one half cup liquid honey. We do this last to make preservation of germ killer.

This tea recipe give sleeping comfort like no other.

Some people say adding cup horilka help kill germ. Maybe, maybe not. But it make you sleep better, anyway. **Warm whiskey separately and add to this tea.**

OR, just mix together honey, whiskey and lemon juice.

Baba warning: Do not give this version to children. Yes, you can create alcoholic, for all you banyak who still giving to children. Their little system get use to alcohol and they start to crave. Duh. Is why woman who drink and drug in pregnancy give birth to damage and addict baby. Aren't you glad Baba here to connect those mole on your back?

Ingredient List:

- Loose tea leaves, one quarter cup
- Lemon peel, one tablespoon
- Lemon, one large
- Honey, one half cup

Arthritis Remedies

Oi, how Baba arthritis hurt her. But pain go away pretty fast when she get young man to rub honey medicine into her joint.

Mix one teaspoon cinnamon into quarter cup honey. Mix in enough warm water to make pasty thing. Is also good time to whip up *Kozak Honey Mousse, Chapter Twenty Three*, so young man don't have time to think of you as old lady with creaky joint. With all men, distraction is key. If you ever worry about if you can keep attracting man, think of how many will get excite over rubber doll.

When you is live woman, man is piece of cake. You take off your clothes, and in general he pretending you is Playboy bunny. Is sad truth. Use to your advantage.

Next arthritis medicine is oral. **In morning and night, get same or different young man bring you cup of hot water with two tablespoon honey and teaspoon cinnamon. For breakfast variety, both you can eat lots honey and cinnamon on bread.** This formula also take care your bad breath all day. Make lots good kissing, Baba say.

Ask him to rub in honey paste again, even if you feeling great. With Baba Ukrainian remedy, you never have to smell like old person again.

Facial Mask

There is reason she call Queen Bee. This queen look young till day she give up hive. Why? She bathing in honey fume all time. You going to learn secret.

Spread honey on face and leave on as many hour as you can stand. Can also mix in small hand full oatmeal. If you want astringent toning, add teaspoon cinnamon.

Baba warning: Do not use premix kind oatmeal, because fruit and nut will fall off your face all over house.

This formula will make skin smooth and cure pimple. Pimple on nose, pimple on thigh, it don't matter.

If pimple is on *dupa,* you going to have to be extra mindful how you sit. My property manager friend Aleksander put newspaper down to protect chair. Next thing he know, he have classified car ad permanent on his rear. Not this don't suit him. Everyone say it do. And much cheaper than tattoo.

Baldness

My friend husband get freak out because he start to lose hair. First it just get thin, then real bald patch grow on top. He start pulling hair over bald patch this way and that way till it look like checkerboard. Was tragic.

Finally, he borrow her vibrator to stimulate hair growth. He end up pulling out rest of hair. He is left with small fringe around ear.

Don't let this happen to you.

Here is remedy you can try: make paste from tablespoon honey, two tablespoon extra virgin olive oil and one teaspoon cinnamon. Rub good into scalp and forget about for fifteen minute.

Cat will try to lick your head. Baba know this feel good, but remember her caution story.

Baba law: If professional vibrator not make hair, cat tongue don't have chance.

WASH HAIR. Do not walk around street like this.

This may or may not regrow some your hair, but at least it make what is left extra shiny. Smell good, too. Maybe people will want rub your smooth honey taste scalp, with or without hair. See also *Yeast Infection* for Baba opinion on baldness.

Is kind of honey call *Manuka*, have best healing property. It come from Tea Tree. Is available on Internet and hippie health store.

What Else Honey Good For?

*If you get dry or sore place inside your kvitichka (vagina), **pour liquid honey in and insert regular tampon.** Replace honey and tampon at least four time in day. If you not have helper, use big syringe or turkey baster. Take these thing from bedroom and wash before company come. If was used to inseminate horse or girlfriend, you make DAMN sure you wash good before. "Why Baba telling me this?" you asking. Poopchik, you wouldn't believe.

***Pour liquid honey on kvitichka just for hell of it.** Remember what Baba tell you about young man. He is there to be your helper and admirer. Make sure to put old sheet on bed.

*See *Babka Plant* (plantain), for herpe remedy. **After you use Babka, you can dot on honey** to help keep infection from spread. This is not cure, so don't be fool.

***Honey really help digestion**. If you have sore stomach and farting like old cow, eat more honey before and after meal. If is your husband with gas problem, make him *Kozak Honey Mousse* all time, or just drip honey in his mouth when he not looking. Honey help relieve ulcer pain. Between honey and Babka plant, you almost going to be able to laugh.

***Honey help heal burn** and reduce scar tissue.

*If you use honey on wound and top with gauze, **honey will pull dirt from wound when you remove gauze.** Is wonderful when children skin knee.

***Honey work well on animal wound** too, if you can keep them from licking. For this reason, most effective on cow and horse. Make best poultice for abscess, especially inside hoof. Veterinarian now using this, just ask.

***If you have crack nipple from nursing, put honey on gauze pad and press.** Baba find this help her frostbite. Listen, if you gallop horse on Ukrainian steppe with jacket open, you get chap nipple too. Sheesh.

Babka (Plantain)

Plantain is kind plant some dummy call "weed." This W word is political way to dismiss plant that heal you without dangerous and expensive drug. Is justify by saying this plant grow everywhere, so is not valuable. Actual, this plant grow everywhere because Nature want you to be healthy for free. Plantain is especial precious to me, because Ukrainian word for it is Babka, which is kind of Baba who is cuddly. That is me if you nice to me. Sometime.

I learn how important is Babka-plantain when my pet chicken Beep stub his big toe. Beep is red bantam. He weigh only about two pound and is completely harmless. I have several Beep and his girlfriend Peep since. I call them Peep and Beep II, Peep and Beep III, Peep and Beep IV.

Anyway, my daughter Odarka she teaching Beep I and his girlfriend Peep I to go down her slide. She put grain of oat on step and the two chicken follow grain, then wheeeee! Slide down slide. Soon they not need oat to go on slide. They just two chicken in sunlight, having fun.

Tragedy strike. Beep get little bit egotist like rooster do. He not bother to flap wing when he close to bottom of slide, and boom! He land on big toe. He flopping around in sand, beeping and my daughter making all kinds crying. I run there and see his toe broken and also bleeding. I quick make splint from popsicle stick. I pick plenty Babka, shove in my mouth and chew until green juice run out my face. Then I press plant on wound.

Bleeding stop so fast you would think you imagining more thing than usual. I bruise more fresh Babka and wrap up his sore splint toe with surgery tape. Beep limp around for few day, but his broke toe heal faster than Russian running after political advantage.

Baba warning: If you not experience with animal medicine like Baba, you should take chicken to veterinarian. This the only kind Western doctor Baba sometime trust. She take her son Ivan quick! To vet when he swallow ball.

Is simple as that. **Pick many leaf and press on wound or bruise.** It stop bleeding and speed up healing.

Other use:

*This plant is purify blood and help when you bloating like sick cow. You can make tea with leaf. **Put one teaspoon dry leaf in cup hot water. Do not boil. Let sit for ten minute, strain and drink.** Have one, maybe two or three cup a day. Especially if you have period.

*If you get bee sting, small burn or cut, **quick pick Babka and chew in your mouth.** Make lots saliva. Then **press spit leaf on hurt part.**

*If you ambitious kind person who walk around lots, **put leaf in shoe.** It help so you not get terrible blister.

***If things not looking so good in your kvitichka (see *Yeast Infection*, Baba keep telling you!), press mashed up Babka leaf there.** Will make herpe sore feel better. See *Siberian Kartoplia, Chapter Two*, for advice on how to work with **impacted thong.** Get enough Babka leaf to make tea solution in whole bathtub for this emergency.

*Baba really getting down to it now. **If you have hemorrhoid or just**

itchy in your sraka, of course this leaf help you, too. Since we are in general geographic area, Baba going to tell you **three cup Babka tea in day sometime cure diarrhea.**

***Babka tea make ulcer in stomach feel softer.** If doctor give you ulcer medicine, take plantain tea few hour in between medicine time.

***Tea help with sore throat and cough.**

***Take away itch from poison ivy**. Often time when you see poison ivy bush, is babka growing nearby. Baba want to know: if you see bush, why you walk into it?

If you leave Babka alone, it will grow tall stem with seed. You pick this and give to your chicken or budgie. They be so happy.

Baba warning: Make sure you search for photograph of this plant before you pick. Do not confuse with skunkweed, or you be stinky beside sore. Who going to look after you then?

Do not pick plant from roadside or where people walking. Will have toxin from car and dirt from bottom of shoe. Go to nice open field and make sure is no insecticide.

Malyna (Raspberry)

This medicine almost fail Baba one summer. Every day I look in garden, and baby *malyna* growing on vine. They beautiful, red and juicy and smell very fragrant in sun. All of sudden, my malyna start disappear act. This make no sense, because Baba make her son build six foot chain link fence around acreage to keep out deer and keep in her two red Doberman.

But day after day, less and less raspberry. Then one morning at nauseate time like six am, Baba follow her two dog out when they go pee. She see them walking up and down between garden row and plucking baby malyna off bush. Then they lick leftover off each other nose. Just like Soviet covering each other crime.

"You traitor!" Baba yell.

But they use lip on plant so delicate and look so much like small deer, she can't stay mad. Just start laughing at Doberman humor. Doberman is not dog for stupid person to have. Those people have pit bull. Wait, I take back. Stupid people should not have any kind animal. This another one of Baba box of soap. We talk more later.

You going to be so happy to hear this: **Next time you have bad cold, bad period, dire rear or arthritis attack, send husband to garden for**

big pail malyna. Eat as much you want while you lie there look pathetic. He try to eat some, slap his hand,. Tell him, "This is woman remedy. Now rub my back, Mister Buster." **Malyna make you sweat, is anti-inflammatory and have good iron.** Also, it smell way sexier than Vicks.

Husband get cut on finger from rose he pick on way back? Tell him to put on fresh malyna leaf to stop bleeding.

If you have sore eye from smoke or just from usual cause---poking finger in eye when drunk---**boil water and drop in hand full malyna leaf. Let water get cool for good hour, then wash your eye.**

Malyna leaf is excellent tea for period cramp and gentle douche. It love your uterus like no one going to in your life, dorahenka. **Three glass every day during last two, three month of pregnancy make uterus get good tone.** Also work on **morning sickness.** Sometime baby pop out and smell like malyna. Baba not joking here. What you got to lose, anyway? Worse thing can happen, you get too much Vitamin C. Which you will pee out. And it will smell like malyna, too. Ha!

If you that kind of person into making funky kind **home skin cream or healing salve, try malyna leaf.** If you need buy malyna leaf, call Malyna Factory, Inc. 1-900-ASKBABA, just like always.

Baba's Patented PMS Cure

Baba know all about this PMS, and she not mean Pig Man Stalin. PMS is happen all over world, ever since woman not in charge. We store up hormone, and boy, they angry. In Ukraina for many century, woman train horse and ride side by side into battle with man. Then things get little funny with Western idea of somehow man better with horse and bow. Suddenly, women start to get this PMS.

You hear how in some culture women have menstrual hut? Ha! Baba second husband have to build himself little hut in back yard, go live there for few day each month. He take small TV, power drill and good*bye*. Sometime Baba hear little bit drumming, too. He learn this on "man weekend." Baba call this PLSS, *Pan in Leisure Suit Syndrome*. Man direct from Ukraina have no need of this. He already know how to dance, sing, ride horse and play instrument. These essential man skill. Canadian man...well, you know.

Okay, never mind crazy husband. Here is what make Baba feel better. **It get her in touch with Nature and build her iron blood:**

Find nice thick juicy piece steak. Should have big bone in. Have nother small, very tough piece steak for each dog you have. Call dog inside, but leave husband out.

This very important so you can let all hanging out: close curtain everywhere you going to be in house.

Next, take off all clothes. You already know Baba is some kind nudist, now she going to teach you how this to your advantage. Throw towel on floor to sit on.

Throw your piece steak in hot fry pan with butter. Leave only few seconds, then flip over. Put on plate. Do not take out cutlery. Throw piece tough steak to dog. Sit on floor with your almost raw piece and start chewing. Is very important you make growling noise. Think how much you hate PMS and how is strange that husband is insensitive jerk once every month. Dog will start to growl. He will be scared at first. He should be. Growl louder. Say to dog, "Get over it, *pasyk.*" Soon dog will start to growl with you, not at you.

Let steak juice run down your boobala. Do not wipe, except hand in your hair.

Baba warning: do not wipe hand in dog fur. This will make PMS worse when you to clean up.

When you finish meat, chew on bone and keep growling. If you is vegetarian: Take big chunk tofu and cut in half long way. Take small paintbrush and make steak drawing with extra thick soy sauce. Eat this and growl because taste weird. Sorry, this is best Baba can do.

If you like, can finish therapy session with big slice cheesecake. DO NOT SAVE ANY FOR HUSBAND. This is not good time to go sudden coding pendant and ruin all good work Baba show you.

Take long hot bath with good expensive candle and smelly oil. Dog will try to lick off steak juice before you get there. Baba don't want to know what happen, so don't write letter about it, okay? Deal with own conscience. Baba have enough crazy picture in her head to last several lifetime.

Kalyna

People! Do not burn the trees! The red kalyna heals the heart, the forest and grove heal the soul. ~Stepan Kryzhanivs'kyi

Kalyna is cranberry, and is woven through Ukraina folklore, medicine and art, and has come to symbolize Ukraina itself. Kalyna have intimate connection to female body, especially *kvitichka* (see *Yeast Infection*, below) and uterus. Ukrainian make tincture from kalyna bark to make **less bleeding from birth haemorrhage and menstruation.** If you want to make sarcasm to man, give him kalyna for his **hemorrhoid**. Say nothing. Let him look it up.

Kalyna is also **good for lung and throat**. We cook up infusion for **coughing, asthma and sore throat**. Make sure you add honey, or someone going to spit red crap all over your little nurse outfit.

Even Western doctor like a little natural magic, because he prescribe kalyna juice to **stop bladder infection**. Is incredible **anti-inflammatory and antibiotic** that work on both surface wound and deep in gut.

Here is only thing that modern industry improve on. Kalyna usual grow on bush, all across Ukraina. Some company grow in boggy place, so is easier to pick. Increase sunshine on berry mean increase medicinal potency.

To break the kalyna also mean first time romance. *Oh, I did not break the kalyna alone, my lover broke it, too, while I bent it down.*~Lemko folk song.

Kalyna stain look just like virgin blood, in case you can squint real hard and remember. In Ukrainian song, losing your *kalyna vinok* (wreath) was same thing. Lose how you like, Baba say. Just don't lose vinok on bus. Is against law in some place.

Baba working on catchy chorus for this song, like Temptations, *Break kalyna down, oh yeah, bend it down, break kalyna down down down.*

Yes! Baba say, do not do this kind of thing alone. Breaking kalyna is not actual possible by horseback. You need accomplice.

For wound, you can press crushed kalyna directly on top. Is great antibacterial. For same reason, gargle with unsweetened juice **kill your dragon breath.** Don't use every day, as juice is very acidic and will wear on enamel.

You want soft, fresh, youthful skin like Baba? Good luck! Just kidding. Here is her secret, worth price of whole book: Mix up kalyna juice with honey and smear on face.

Leave this mess on for at least twenty minute and think how much better you will look when you rinse off. Attitude is half of beauty. Kalyna, inside and out, even work like horse to **fight against your pimple, blackhead, eczema, thin hair, even cancer.** It is full of flavonoid and anti-oxidant. Reading her own chapter, Baba wonder why she just not eat kalyna for every meal.

Yeast Infection

Let's say you have itchy *kvitichka*. Yes, this is right. In Ukraina, one thing we call women pretty private thing is “little flower.”

I tell my daughter and granddaughter, “This your flower. If you like man to sniff and pluck, is your business. If man pluck flower when you not like, is his shame. Is never your shame.”

I tell you story. My granddaughter, when she four, five years old, she like very much word for frog, *zhaba* (pronounce “z” like “s” in treasure). She make rhyme with “Baba.” She jump up and down, and all day she say, “Baba zhaba, Baba zhaba, Baba ZHABA!”

She so cute, jump from foot to foot, wearing little stripe shirt. I cut her hair with soup bowl, and it bounce up and down. Sometime I laugh so hard, I wipe eye with apron. I tell my friend, and they laugh too. I walk into Ukrainian Hall to play bingo, they all raise glass horilka and yell, “Baba Zhaba!”

Not long time ago, my granddaughter turn twenty year old. She come in house with face white like sheep. “Baba,” she say, “Why you not tell me zhaba frog is other slang word for women private part?”

“Ha ha!” I say, “Because you so cute and funny calling me Old Cunt.”

Okay. Your little flower also called zhaba because smooth and slippery and make many egg. Itchy? You know I have to tell you, “See doctor.”

You know, in Canada you think you have democracy. Freedom of speech, freedom of press, freedom of choice. Democracy, democracy. Pah! I spit on your democracy. Soviet Union terrible, terrible place. Is like hell. But at least you know not to print pamphlet or not say nothing against government. Or else soldier come at night and bang bang bang knock on door and take you to Siberia.

But Canada is worse hell. Here you all talk “democracy.” But you say wrong thing against government, men come in nice suit, wearing white glove and carry briefcase. They say, 'Please ma'am, please sir, sign this paper.' If you not sign, boom! They take you to Siberia.

In Ukraina we say, *Black soul wear white shirt*. Democracy, democracy. Here you cannot even choose your own health care. When Stalin take away all Baba medicine herb from village, we all know is evil thing. Here many people think is for your “protection.” I spit on your democracy.

Back to yeast infection. In Ukraina, if we scratching in not so polite way, we not see doctor.

Are no doctor, anyway. My sister, she die from gangrene because Soviet would not treat broken leg, and they take away my medicine herb.

If you scratching like this, you will not get husband. Most important: do not marry man who scratch there!

Here is what you do: take one clove garlic and make peel so bald and shiny. You know, like when you hang on to man have head like bowling ball.

Second Last and Most Important Baba warning: Grab his both ear, or you be sorry! Is not bad idea to ask him to take out denture. Baba once date man she don't like only for this reason. Not saying this is fair, but life is not fair. Really, who take loss at end? You think bald toothless man going to call police, say, "Oy yoi yoi, that big sexy Baba, she make me get naked so she can grab me by ear and make me smell pretty flower"? Not happening, poopchik.

Cut off both end of garlic so not scratchy. You going to put this inside your kvitichka/zhaba at night. Take out in morning. Put in fresh one next night. Should take only three night, and itch completely gone. You not smell like sucklehoney, but who want man near you when you itch like crazy?

I'm going to say one thing about this uber-Ukrainian Ayla in "Clan of Cave Bear." She probably put garlic up kvitichka too. But I think maybe she look too much like big Barbie with long nail to do this safe. You have to shove garlic inside so up firm against cervix. Otherwise you be chairing business meeting or taming wild horse, and smelly thing come shooting out your zhaba like SCUD missile. Positive thing: this could be end of twerking in your lifetime.

Last Baba warning: use fresh garlic every time for medicine and cooking! You probably think Baba talking down to you. But you ever read warning on tampon box? Apparent, some poor Canadian women so not used to touching kvitichka/zhaba, they do all sort crazy thing.

Some women with long nail/long zhaba tell me they make applicator type thing from tampon cardboard. Long nail dangerous, you can scratch inside flower skin. You try. I keep nail short and use finger for everything. This not techno-Baba here.

I would tell you "have fun," but probably you won't.

The End

Get Famous.

Review **Baba's Kitchen** on *Amazon, Goodreads, Library Thing* or your own blog.

Visit Baba's website. Hear her read from the book, and get her free newsletter with additional recipes:

www.ukrainiansoulfood.ca

Now available: *Rosie's Rescue.* Meet Baba's family! Find out more on her website.

Baba's Kitchen: Ukrainian Soul Food is on *Facebook.*

Visit your Baba daily!

Heart to Heart

The Essential Guide to Animal Communication

Excerpts from an upcoming book
by Raisa Stone

You've read about the close connection Baba has with animals. Animal telepathy is an ancient Ukrainian tradition, without which we could not have domesticated the horse and wolf. In the Christmas chapter, Baba discusses how all Ukrainians speak with animals on Sviata Vechera (Christmas Eve).

This detailed guide will teach you how to communicate with your own pets by developing your natural intuitive skills.

Introduction

"You should try to hear the names the Holy Ones have for things. People name everything according to the number of legs they have. The Holy Ones name them according to what they have inside."
~ *Rumi*

Do you remember what it was like to be first introduced to the wonder of animals? You were probably overwhelmed with their sheer magical presence. Those knowing eyes! The soft fur and feathers! You were amazed by every movement, breath and sound.

If you're like me, you remember the thrill of the first time you saw a horse, or touched a dog or cat's fur. Or felt a bird hook her little feet around your fingers.

Then, you were taught to give orders. To make animals obey. And during this time, you were probably given all sorts of messages about human superiority over dumb animals. You were told they only understand one word commands, and otherwise operate entirely by instinct.

It's quite possible that as a child, you actually heard animals speak, or otherwise knew how they felt and thought through your various intuitive senses. But this was drummed out of you, with jokes and admonitions about "not letting your imagination run away." And maybe a caution about being "crazy."

It wasn't your imagination, and you aren't crazy. You really did know what animals thought and felt. You were *taught* to disregard their voices because of a vast societal hypnosis which tells us that to harm animals for certain purposes, is okay and even desirable. That animals don't feel and think, and that we can't hear them, is a relatively new concept. And it is utterly, completely wrong. In fact, it is societal insanity.

I've listened to animals since I was born. I've communicated with countless animals, starting with Prince the Irish Setter who slept by my crib. Before I could even form words, Prince and I exchanged mental images and feelings that were unmistakeable and clear communications.

I help people understand animals from the **animal's** point of view. I descend from thousands of years of animal communicators and trainers in my Native country of Ukraine. We wouldn't have been able to domesticate the horse or wolf without this gift. Though many of our ancient ways have been diluted by non-Indigenous beliefs, we still have an Animal Communication Day: Christmas Eve. On that night, every Ukrainian honours their animals by serving them a beautifully prepared vegetarian meal. And on that night, every one of us hears them speak---not just the people who've chosen this as a profession.

With the help of Animal Communication, I've won awards at shows and successfully trained aggressive and traumatized animals.

In this book I'll help you awaken your gift of animal communication.

I call it ***Awaken** the Gift*, because animal communication is something your ancestors knew. And so did you. It's only been asleep inside of you, due to societal conditioning. I have countless stories about the things animals have told me, the problems I've helped solve. And oh boy, do I love telling those stories!

You may have read other books on the topic, and been told vagaries such as, "Meditate to let animal messages enter."

Most people tell me they give up right there, seeing themselves forced to assume some impossible posture and trying to keep their minds still for an hour or more daily.

I despise the Lotus position too, and trying to keep my mind still is like jamming too many pantyhose into a tiny drawer. I've sat in countless meditation workshops that gave me plenty of time to detail my grocery list, worry about my pets at home and think about the new song I want to learn.

Instead of telling you to "quiet your mind", **I *guide* you in specific, extremely visual and sensory meditations that place you, boom! directly inside animal consciousness.**

I'll share my ages-old ancestral secrets with you. I didn't learn my skills in a weekend New Age workshop; **my people have been doing this for thousands of years.** We couldn't have survived the Ice Age without Animal Communication. In order for my people to have been the first to domesticate the flighty, hyper-alert horse, they had to create a solid intuitive bridge.

It's so simple, it's difficult. In *Heart to Heart*, **I've simplified what *should* be simple: harmonious communication with our loved ones.**

Besides our busy minds, the main reason traditional meditation is so difficult for learning Animal Communication, is this means listening with the wrong organ: the brain.

Genuine connection and intuition with animals comes from the heart.

Animal Communication is very much about developing and trusting your intuition and your heart centre. If you've ever known who was calling at the moment the phone rang---without caller i.d, or you had to take a different route---then discovered you narrowly averted disaster---you're already in touch with your intuition. **I'm going to teach you to be more confident in listening to yourself, and to those we're told are voiceless. Animals are far from voiceless.**

Do you need hundreds of pages of exercises to awaken this gift? No! Becoming an Animal Communicator is just like that old joke:

A man asks a stranger on a New York street, “How do I get to Carnegie Hall?”

The stranger replies, “Practice!”

Once you learn the basics, everything else is about returning to these again and again. Like a musician, you practice scale notes, harmonies and structures, then put these elements to work on as many songs as possible. But those songs mean nothing without the element of heart.

An Animal Communicator learns the essentials, then listens to as many animals as possible. Simple, but difficult. Easy, but requiring effort. Just like a musician, how skilled you become will depend on how well and how often you practice. A scale becomes a song. One song learned, gives desire and confidence to try the next. One intuitive “Aha!” leads to several more.

Intuition coupled with heart energy informs, heals and connects.

Heart to Heart is about teaching you essentials, quickly and easily. Once your heart gets involved, learning accelerates. So do results.

I've included plenty of stories about my personal experiences speaking with animals. Where pet guardians have given their permission, I've used real names and details. Otherwise, the stories are "mash ups" of several experiences (with disguised names) to illustrate a point. I carefully guard the confidentiality of my clients, so recognizing a specific pet or client here has been made impossible.

You're reading this book because you love animals and Nature. You trust that it's possible to reawaken the wonderful gift of Animal Communication. I'll teach you the way back to that miraculous state you knew in childhood...

Talking with animals is like entering an alternate Universe. To me, it's far more real than the one of noisy vehicles, cell phone addiction, computers and TV. If you're fond of books like *The Lion, the Witch and the Wardrobe,* animal-related stories by Ursula K. LeGuin, or those fabulous pieces of art depicting people with unicorns---well, it's like that. Every time I enter an animal's consciousness, I find myself deep within an enchanted forest, where the understanding of each other runs as clear as a mountain-fed stream. Here's an encounter I had with two wild rabbits.

Two Rabbits

After leading a ceremony to send Light and Love to Easter bunnies, I went for a solitary walk through a wilderness area.

A wild rabbit hopped onto the path in front of me. Just ten feet away, she said, "Hello," and relaxed. She watched me intently with her huge, soft eye. I stood in wonder.

Maintaining centred energy, I stepped forward. I wanted to know if she was truly interested in interaction, or frozen in fear. I was truly amazed by her boldness. Instead of scampering into the bush, Ms. Bunny circled me. This was fun. I stepped forward again. She circled me and began grazing off to the side. This is how bunnies play "tag" with each other! We circled once more, then she slowly grazed her way back into the woods. She'd satisfied her curiosity about a human.

Two minutes later, another bunny hopped out in front of me. He stopped only four feet away. He nonchalantly nipped at the path side grass, and sent me lovely, gentle vibes.

He then did something I've sure only a hand full of people on this planet have witnessed from a wild rabbit: he sat on his haunches and trustingly groomed himself. His right paw went to his mouth. Out came the small pink tongue to wet the paw. He firmly passed the paw over his crown, his long ear, down his shoulder and side. He did it again. I was entranced.

One bright brown eye remained fixed on my face.

"You're dif-fer-ent," he said, leaning heavily on each syllable. His speech pattern was distinct; it was clearly an effort to speak with a human.

He sent me a mental picture of people who enter his turf with energy that doesn't honour animals as equal, sentient beings. He was greatly puzzled by their behaviour. "Why do they come in here like *that*?" he asked. Images filled my head of children who chased after him and his family, people talking loudly and tramping on delicate vegetation without care.

He showed me that he felt my energy as "safe." The vibe I emit is purely harmless and loving towards all animals. What an honour, to be viewed this way by a vulnerable prey animal!

The rabbit then took me on another shared mental movie. He invited me into his consciousness, where I was reduced to his size. I felt what it is to run at lightning speed under fallen trees, enjoy the damp moss brushing against my belly, be exquisitely sensitive to every sound and nuance of movement. I have never smelled air so clean, felt sunlight so clear. Its warmth felt as if it went into my bones.

We communed for about 20 minutes, until dusk compelled me to leave the woods.

Here's a review of a vital animal communication fact. I hear from many people who get frustrated when they attempt animal telepathy. As humans are so focused on oral communication, we tend to think that only *hearing* a pet's words in a distinctive voice is legitimate.

In fact, clairaudience (hearing) is only one of the six intuitive gifts. The others are: seeing, smelling, tasting, sensing, and knowing. Hearing is the rarest gift. I have all six gifts, and they vary in strength. I've identified my strongest ones, and build upon them. Think of it this way: if you love to dance or play a sport, do you work endlessly at a discipline that doesn't "click," or do you focus on improving in the areas that do? What's really cool is that focusing on your strengths will build skills in your weaker areas.

In this *Heart to Heart* meditation, you may find one, a few, or all of your intuitive senses come into play. **Have your journal and pen ready** to note the details. Impressions may come rapidly, and be fleeting, even though they feel unforgettable in the moment. Write down everything, no matter how unlikely it seems.

Here's how animals speak with us: They sometimes show us brief images and symbols. They have a unique point of view...At times, the message you receive may be uplifting. At other times, it may give you a jolt. **Pets are Master Teachers, not "yes men."** They come into our lives to teach deep truths, and to help us grow our souls. When your pet seems agreeable to most things you say and do, he is communicating, "I love you unconditionally," not, "Yes, you're always right."I learned a striking lesson about unconditional love one Valentine’s Day. Striking, because it came from an animal whom I’d not previously met.

My Funny Valentine

How special is animals' love.

One Valentine's Day, I was walking in the park with a fellow. A large brindle dog came galloping toward us, mouth gaping.

It was strange; I'd normally raise an arm and say, "Stop," or "Slow down." Next would be rolling into a ball on the ground. Instead, my body instinctively kept a loose and open posture.

As my friend looked on in slack jawed horror, the dog leaped for my face---and planted a kiss on my lips.

When he landed, I asked him to sit. I crouched down and said, “That was a lovely kiss. But you have very sharp teeth, and could hurt someone. You can’t do that again.”

The dog responded, "But I loved you from the moment I saw you."

I told the dog that in order to get kisses from me, he would have to sit at my feet. No more jumping.

His guardian strode up with a, “What has he been up to *now?”* expression. I explained what had happened. She took on a skeptical air.

As we chatted with his guardian, Tony (the dog) returned from his Nature exploration to stand at my feet. He gazed at me adoringly and said, "I love you. Kiss?" He tilted his head charmingly.

“Tony,” I replied, “What is it you need to do to get a kiss?”

His behind hit the dirt. I crouched, and we kissed. After his kiss, he ran off to sniff some more bushes. He returned three more times. The third and fourth, I didn’t need to remind him.

His Mom said she'd never seen him behave this way. We parted reluctantly.

Thank you, Tony *My Funny Valentine*, for reminding me of the pure and innocent nature of love.

Naturally, the fellow who stood by in slack jawed helplessness will not have the privilege of being my Valentine companion again.

I'm going to mention the primary guided journey, *Awaken the Gift*, one more time. Doing one meditation right after the next will create an incredibly powerful experience. You'll find your connection to animals expanding in ways you'd never imagined after putting these two meditations together. The next chapter will take you into *Heart to Heart.*

The Awaken the Gift and **Heart to Heart guided journeys** are also available as digital recordings on my website:

http://www.reisastone.com/

Click on *Learn Animal Communication.*

To be updated on this and other books by Raisa, subscribe to her mailing list on the website above, or at

www.ukrainiansoulfood.ca

Do you have an animal loving child in your life? Give them ***Rosie's Rescue,*** Raisa's book about Ukrainian perspectives on animal rescue. Meet Baba's granddaughter Rosie! Detailed descriptions of pony care and riding lessons, with a touch of magic. Available through

www.ukrainiansoulfood.ca

Parting Notes:

Thank you for buying *Baba's Kitchen: Ukrainian Soul Food With Stories from the Village*. I hope the stories and recipes serve you well.

Though I completed the manuscript in roughly four years, it has taken my lifetime to collect and write. I laughed a lot, and sometimes cried at recalling or discovering devastating bits of history. In middle age, it was a shock for this rebel to find her nationalist father's words about needing my Motherland, to be true. As a child, I was embarrassed by the blue and gold flag flying in our Winnipeg yard. These days, I'm looking to purchase one.

I'm grateful to my ancestors for my love for and talent with horses and other animals, a love of good food and a belly laugh. Also inherited from my family and Ukrainians in general, a gift for design and drawing, writing and dance. We say, *Without Art, there is no life.*

Please respect that writing this book has been a lifelong, unpaid labor of love. If your friends and relatives would like to read it, ask them to purchase it. Copying or forwarding the material in any manner is a violation of copyright, whether it be the entire book, or sections you reprint in your blog/Facebook. I much appreciate your help publicizing Baba's Kitchen. If that is your intent, please contact me through:

www.reisastone.com
www.ukrainiansoulfood.ca

I am interested in developing a line of frozen gourmet foods, clothing and natural cosmetics based upon the book. Serious offers, backed by a sound business plan and track record, will be seriously considered. I am also available for readings, storytelling/singing performances and voice/storytelling workshops. And of course, animal communication.

Dai Bozha i Smachnoho!

Raisa Stone

The USSR, Soviets and Russia

In the Bibliography, you'll see the struggle I had discriminating as to purely Ukrainian sources. Countless times, I have been met with the discouraging remark, "Oh, you're working on a book about Russia." Certainly not! Researching this book was a maze-like reclaiming of my heritage, as Russians have illegitimately claimed so much of our culture.

Ukrainians are the Indigenous people of Eastern Europe. In a sweeping statement: Russians are largely descendants of Viking and Mongol invaders whose predatory time line distressingly echoes the oppression of Indigenous peoples in the Americas.

Ukraine has been the site of continuous habitation by complex, civilized people for 44,000 years. There is DNA evidence that some Slavs traveled directly to Eastern Europe from humankind's birthplace, Africa's Rift Valley, without settling in the Middle East.

The Viking invasion of our home occurred in the 900's AD, relatively late in history. Kyivan Rus' ("Rus" means Slav) had already existed for 500 years, and was the most powerful nation state in Europe. Until the barbarian invaders cunningly had themselves baptized in order to sanction the looting, rape, murder and land seizures they called "Christianity." In the 1200's, they allied with Genghis Khan's Mongolian hordes to ultimately devastate Kyivan Rus'. Though historians argue about the forces that eventually created Russia, it is impossible to believe that Indigenous Slavs welcomed Vikings. Documented history demonstrates that Slavs killed self appointed Viking "king" Igor who demanded we support him financially. Igor and "queen" Olga's grandson, Vladimir, showed his disdain for matriarchal Slavic traditions as well as Christianity by tearing down his grandparent's church and using its materials to build an elaborate altar to the formerly minor Slavic war god Perun.

Viking loot lined the pockets of Kyivan bureaucrats, particularly patriarchs of the newly planted Church. Over time, some Slavs began to feel that being extorted was spiritual duty or, that perhaps it was simply safer to go along with their government's alliance with the barbarians. This mimics the politics of the European Inquisition, which overlaps the same historical era. Separation of Church and State was not a reality for many chapters of human history. Defying either/both carried severe penalties and was psychologically binding.

I do not wish to dismiss the sincere Christian faith of many Ukrainians, but it is not to our benefit to ignore the truth of history. We are in a life or death struggle with the people who have repeatedly subjugated, murdered and stolen from us for 1100 years. I myself am of dual faith. Along with most Ukrainians, I combine the symbols of Christianity with those of our pagan (Nature worshipping) ancestry. Russians are not our brothers, and "brothers in Christ" is a mockery. They murdered our brothers and sisters.

It is also impossible to believe that a cultured, strongly matriarchal people welcomed Vikings as romantic partners. Viking women were subjugated to the roles of servants and broodstock. While the Slavs had for millennia venerated the Divine Feminine and the earth, the invaders forced the concept of a Sky God. Weavers of intricate clothing, Slavs kept themselves rigorously clean, as evidenced by both oral history and said steam baths; Vikings and Mongols were notoriously lacking in any semblance of personal hygiene. Not marriage material.

Once they had depleted Kyivan Rus'and its surrounding Slavic tribes, the Viking/Mongol people moved to the East, and grandiosely called this newly claimed land *The Grand Duchy of Muscovy.* Even then, it was not formally a state until 1540. As of 1187, Ukraina was documented as a sovereign nation in The Primary Chronicle. To divorce themselves from Ukraine's Aboriginal people, the Muscovites used no hint of a Slavic name. Until the 18th century, when Czar Peter I realized that assuming the name *Rus'sia* (Slavic) would help his tribe stake a claim to Slavic lands once again. Crimea, for example, was violently stolen from Ukraine in 1783, then ceded back in 1954. The recent referendum was a reclaiming of hot property.

Ukrainians have been a sovereign people for centuries, and our beautiful country has never been part of Russia. The aesthetically pleasing parts of Russian culture: its music, art, dance, cuisine, etc., are largely appropriated from Eastern Europe's Indigenous people. Ukrainians were first to domesticate horses, roughly 5000 years ago. Baba's claims of inventing the first oven, the bow and arrow, trousers, horse tack and the wheel are legitimate. Trousers, of course, are a lot more comfortable than robes when on horseback. Wear found on the teeth of horse skulls proves our invention of the bit. Stirrups allowed us to stand up and shoot arrows more effectively.

Imagine what it was like for a highly cultured, creative, politically evolved, scientifically advanced (we built pyramids before the Egyptians, without slaves!), skilled, egalitarian people to suddenly be set upon by a violent gang. This systematic terrorism has not ceased. We have been murdered and exiled in order to impose the Russian language, and to steal what was valuable from our culture. I lost about twenty million of my tribe during the Stalinist purges, Holodomor (engineered famine) and World War II. Then more to the 1986 Russian-created Chornobyl disaster. Which they sent Ukrainian men to clean, without so much as protective clothing. When my father's mother (my Baba) broke her leg slaving for the Soviets, she was denied medical care. And of course, they had already destroyed our native plants and medicines. She died a prolonged, excruciating death from gangrene.

It's obvious to any discerning eye and confirmed by world leaders that most of the current "pro-Russian separatists" are financed by Putin's government. What is not so well known: Stalin's famine-genocide of up to 12 million Ukrainians in 1932-33 was for the purpose of moving Russian citizens into the empty death camps. Here they raised their families, amid corpses. Yes, there are genuine separatists in Eastern Ukraine. They are illegal squatters without conscience.

Current events are a continuation of the barbarians' long term efforts to exterminate Ukrainian's Indigenous people, and claim our tribal lands. We now know that even the word "Ukraina" means *Homeland*, not "Borderland" as previously asserted.

A quote from a Communist leader speaking in the Kharkiv region in 1934: "Famine in Ukraine was brought on to decrease the number of Ukrainians, replace the dead with people from other parts of the USSR, and thereby to kill the slightest thought of any Ukrainian independence."~V. Danilov et al., Sovetskaia derevnia glazami OGPU_NKVD. T. 3, kn. 2. Moscow 2004. P. 572

Today, thousands of Ukrainian girls and women are enslaved and sexually abused by the Russian human trafficking network, the largest in the world. Thousands more live in such dire poverty, they're marketing themselves as "mail order brides" to callous men. I recommend the documentary *Love Me*. The Russian Mafia conducts a brisk trade in black market human organ sales. All this suffering, which became systemic and epidemic through 1100 years of subjugating the feminine.

Ukraine has a tradition of preserving history through *kobzars*, wandering troubadours. Thousands of years of knowledge, from battles to songs to current political news, is passed along by these accomplished storyteller musicians. This is also how we have provided dignified employment for the disabled----most kobzars are blind. In 1929, Stalin invited the kobzari to an Arts conference in Karkhiv. Most attended. He executed them. Hundreds of lives and much of Ukraine's history was lost. History, they say, is written by the winners. *Baba's Kitchen* is, for me, an act of resistance and restoration. I collect fragments of our legends and present them as a storyteller, wistfully knowing I can never be a full-fledged kobzara.

Indigenous people have been murdered, brutalized in residential schools, and herded onto reservations. In Ukraine, reservations were called collectives---most of my relatives remained in Soviet collective slavery until 1991---and every school became a tool of oppression and genocide. Sharing an alphabet is not the same as sharing a language.

At the time of publishing this book, Ukrainians are once again suffering Russian aggression. What Baba describes under Soviet rule, exists in a new form. What is different: the revolution is being televised.

It is exhilarating to see the warmth, humor and creativity of my people: the blue and gold piano in front of police lines, my people enthusiastically singing; citizens blocking a military compound outside Kyiv but bringing the police and soldiers hot tea; huge vats of hot soup being cooked and served to protesters; the iconic toppling of Lenin's statue, with *Slava Ukraina* (Long live Ukraine/Glory to Ukraine, the words with which I dedicate this book) written on his rear end---then traditional musicians playing music and reciting the poetry of freedom fighter Taras Shevchenko at its base. If Baba were there, she'd dance in her fine red boots and hope the world was watching.

Despite Russia's obvious role in the atrocities and their homophobic policies, the Sochi Olympics went ahead. Piles of slaughtered dogs lay in silent testimony to the brutality of these people. In their innocent, painful deaths I see the millions slaughtered of my people, including my grandmother. The Russian narcissistic response to the world's condemnation of their behavior is a resounding echo of Viking and Mongolian warlord values. Violence, lies and gain through crime are cultural norms. I have no doubt that some of the allegedly pro-Russian people in Eastern Ukraine are neither paid Putin-ites nor squatters, but simply terrified of their psychopathic neighbor. As just one example of how Russian was "taught" in Ukraine: in 1951, the graduating class of a Kharkiv college requested to write their final exams in Ukrainian. The Russians executed 33 and sent 800 to a Siberian gulag, from where they never returned.

My Baba and all Babas, their families and friends, look forward to a new experience for Ukraine. One where our status as an Indigenous people and independent nation is solidly based on our human right to live freely and prosperously, with no brutal masters and a prosperity that flows back to us, rather than enriching the exploitive.

Dai Bozha i Slava Ukraina!

Two Love Poems

Love Ukraine
by Volodimir Sosiura
Who was forced by the Russians to recant

Love Ukraine, as the sun loves,
As do the wind, the grass and the water...
Love her in fortunate times and in joyous moments,
Love her even in time of stormy weather.

Love Ukraine in dreams and in waking,
A Ukraine covered in cherry blossoms.
Her beauty is eternal,
Her speech is tender as the nightingale's.

In brotherhood like an abundant garden,
She shines through the ages...
Love Ukraine with all your heart,
And in everything you do.
For she is the only one in the world
With all of space in her sweet cup...

She is in the stars, in the willows,
And in each beat of her people's heart.
In flowers and birds, and shining lights,
In every epic and in every song,
In children's laughter, in maidens' eyes,
And in the purple banners above the roaring throng...

As the bush that burns, yet doesn't burn
She lives in the paths, in the oaks
In the dark howling, in the waves of the Dnieper
And in small purple clouds.

In the cannonade of thunder that scattered ashes,
When strangers in green uniforms
Bayoneted the darkness, opening the way for us
To a bright and candid spring.

Young man! Give her your approving laughter,
Your tears, and all you are until you die...
For you cannot truly love others Unless you love your Ukraine.

Young woman! As the sky is blue, Love her every moment.
Your beloved will not want you,
Unless you also love your Ukraine.

Love her in love, in labor, and in battle,
As if she were a song that pours from the stars...
Love your Ukraine with all your heart and all your might,
And we will be Hers through eternity.

-1944

The Horsewoman of Chornobyl

by Raisa Stone

My blood aches.
My blood family is sickened
Crouched humble to a supper
Of bread
They have wrestled
From Her arms

(She is Holy, Holy)

A new kind of seasoning
Spills across the table
By the gate, our horses
Shudder in their flaming skins.

In our Mother country
Bread and salt are offered as "welcome"
To the stranger or
The weary expatriate returning home
There shattered, here poisoned.
Grains of wheat are human souls
Grain ground into bread, community.

(We are Holy, Holy)

Salt is antidote to nuclear sickness.
We are sprinkled liberally
With one
And dying from lack of
The other.

Always from my kozak grandfather
And now
Through bright atomic haze
I dream the horses
Red gold black.

(They are Holy, Holy)

They gallop the steppes
Tails flagged glorious
Higher than the melting towers
Older, swifter than melting time.
With my grandfather's saber
With my words
I wage war
With our hard rain.

Published in *Nasha Doroha*, national Ukrainian magazine, to commemorate the 20th anniversary of the Chornobyl disaster.

Bibliography

Aaland, Mikkel. "The Russian Bannia: History of the Great Russian Bath." Abstract: CyberBohemia: 1998. www.cyberbohemia.com

Anthony, David W. *The Horse, The Wheel and Language: How Bronze Age Riders From the Eurasian Steppes Shaped the Modern World.* Princeton University Press, 2008

Andrusyshen & Kirkconnell. *The Poetical Works of Taras Shevchenko.* University of Toronto Press, Reprinted 1977

Artyukh, L. "The Green Murmer of Polissya." Abstract: www. Ukrfolk.com.ua

Auel, Jean. *Clan of the Cave Bear.* First book in the Earth's Children series. New York: Crown, 1980 A fictionalized but plausible anthropological study of neolithic Eastern Europe, focusing on Ukraine. Followed by: *The Valley of Horses, The Mammoth Hunters, The Plains of Passage* and *Shelters of Stone*

Baby Names: Ukrainian. www.mybirthcare.com

BBC News. "Russia Medics Face Organ Retrial. The re-trial of four Russian doctors accused of illegally removing patients' organs has begun in a Moscow court." Http://news.bbc.co.uk/2/hi/europe/4133110.stm

Boryak, Olena. "The Midwife in Traditional Ukrainian Culture." Midwifery Today: 2003. Excerpted from the Slavic and East European Folklore Association (SEEFA) Journal, vol. VII

Campbell, Joseph. *Flight of the Wild Gander: Explorations in the Mythological Dimension.* New York: Viking, 1960

Chirovsky, Nicholas. *An Introduction to Ukrainian History, v 1-3.* New York: Philosophical Library, 1984-86

Conquest, Robert. *The Great Terror: A Reassessment.* New York: Oxford University Press US, 2008. A definitive account of the Stalinist purges.

Conquest, Robert. *The Harvest of Sorrow: Soviet Collectivization and the Terror-Famine.* New York: Oxford University Press US, 1987. The Terror-Famine is known as the Holodomor, and was a deliberate act of genocide by the Russians against Ukrainians. A must read if you want to understand the bitter side of Baba.

Davis-Kimball, Jeannine. "Warrior Women of Eurasia." Abstract:

Archaeological Institute of America. 50.1. January/February 1997

Eisler, Rianne. *The Chalice and the Blade.* Cambridge: Harper & Row, 1987

Dictionary of Greek and Roman Geography. London: Walton & Maberly. Ed. William Smith LLD. 1854. One source for information about the Neuri "wolf shaman" tribe and the origin of the werewolf myth.

Ellingson, Irmgard Hein. "Easter Water." The Bukovina Society of the Americas Newsletter (Ellis). 14.1. March 2004: 1

Farley, Marta Pisetska. *Festive Ukrainian Cooking.* University of Toronto Press, 1998

Firouz, Louise L. "Turkoman Horse Origin." Abstract: The Turanian Horse Website: 1998. www.turanianhorse.org/origins.html

Gibson, Arthur C. "The Pernicious Opium Poppy." Essay: Economic Botany course, UCLA. www.botgard.ucla.edu

Gimbutas, Marija. *The Civilization of the Goddess: The World of Old Europe.* San Francisco: Harper, 1991

Gimbutas, Marija. *The Gods and Goddesses of Old Europe, 6500-3500 BC.* Los Angeles: University of California Press, 1982

Gimbutas, Marija. *The Language of the Goddess.* San Francisco: Harper, 1989

The Goddess Remembered. Dir. Donna Read. Video. National Film Board of Canada, 1989

Gogol, N.V. *Taras Bulba.* Trans. Isabel F. Hapgood. New York: Crowell, 1886

The Great Famine-Genocide in Soviet Ukraine, 1932-33. www.artukraine.com/famineart/index.htm

Gregorovich, Andrew. "Ancient Inventors of Ukraine." FORUM Ukrainian Review. Scranton, 91. Fall-Winter 1994

Groushko, M.A. *Cossack: Warrior Riders of the Steppe*s. New York: Sterling, 1992

Herodotus. *The History of Herodotus, bk. IV.* Trans. George Rawlinson. 440 B.C.E. www.classics.mit.edu Direct observation of the Scythian culture, precursor to contemporary Ukrainian culture

Herodotus. Herodotus' Tenth Logos: Country and Customs of the Scythians. 4.1-82. http://www.livius.org/he-

hg/herodotus/logos4_10.html
Hippocrates. *On Airs, Waters and Places. Parts 17, 18 &19.* Trans. Francis Adams. 400 B.C.E. Www.classics.mit.edu Direct observation and mythology of the Scythians. Verification that the legends of the Amazons arose from Scythian culture.
Hodges, Linda. *Language and Travel Guide to Ukraine*. New York: Hippocrene, 2004
Hodges, Linda. *Ukrainian Language, Culture and Travel.* www.pages.prodigy.net/l.hodges/ukraine.htm
Hrytsa, Sophia. *Ukrainian Christmas Carols.* www.houseofukraine.com
"Jarilo." Wikipedia. www.wikipedia.org
Johnson, Kenneth. *Slavic Sorcery.* St. Paul: Llewellyn, 1998. Take this book with a grain of salt. While it has some marvelous information about Slavic spirituality, the author makes no distinction between Ukrainian and Russian beliefs and practices. As well, some of the spiritual exercises may not be of Slavic origin at all, but rather an amalgamation of Far Eastern with "New Age." As you know, Baba prefers Old Age.
Kidd, Sue Monk. *The Secret Life of Bees.* New York: Penguin, 2003
Kish, Walter. "Ni Zhyty, Ni Vmeraty." Abstract: InfoUkes website. No date.
Kliuchevskii, V. O. and Marshall Shatz. *The Time of Catherine the Great.* Trans. M. Shatz.
London: ME Sharpe, 1997
Kononenko, Natalie Dr. "The Domovyk: The House Spirit, also Called Khoziain, or Master of the House."
Kononenko, Natalie Dr. *Ukrainian Minstrels: And the Blind Shall Sing.* New York: ME Sharpe, 1998
"Koroksun." Wikipedia. Www.wikipedia.org
Kotsiubynsky, Mykhailo. *Shadows of Forgotten Ancestors.* Trans. Marco Carynnyk. Littleton: Ukrainian Academic Press.
Kyiv Traditions. Www.whatson-kiev.com
Le Vasseur, Guillaume. *A Description of Ukraine.* Trans. A. Pernal & D. Essar. Cambridge University Press, 1993
Lemkin, Raphael. *Soviet Genocide in the Ukraine.* Essay: Ukrainian Civil Liberties Association, 1953.

http://www.uccla.ca/SOVIET_GENOCIDE_IN_THE_UKRAINE.pdf

Littleton, C. Scott and Linda A. Malcor. *From Scythia to Camelot: A Radical Reassessment of the Legends of King Arthur.* London: Taylor & Francis, 2000

Loeb, Louisa. *Down Singing Centuries: Folk Literature of the Ukraine.* Trans. F.R. Livesay. Winnipeg: Hyperion, 1981

"May, Month of Saints and Heroes." The Ukrainian Weekly (Parsippinay). April 24, 1977. No author attribution

"Merheleva Ridge." Wikipedia. www.wikipedia.org.

Mills, Yaroslava Sumach. "The Pysanka: Ancient Talisman." The Ukrainian Weekly (Parsippinay). April 3, 1983

Nestor. *The Primary Chronicle.* Kyivan Rus': 1113. A history of Ukraine compiled by a monk, covering approximately 850 to 1110 AD. The name *Ukraina* was documented in this widely respected manuscript. Not to be confused with the title "Russian" Primary Chronicle, which the Russians have hijacked. There was no Russia until the 18th century.

Owens, D. W. "A Small Dictionary of Pagan Gods and Goddesses." Abstract: www.waningmoon.com

Petrusha, Luba. www.web.mac.com/lubap/PYSANKY/Pysanka_Home.html. Comprehensive site on the ancient origins and creation of pysanka, Ukrainian sacred eggs.

Picknicki, Jeff. "A Glance At Ukrainian Traditions of the New Year Period." The Ukrainian Weekly (Parsippinay). January 1, 1989

Plokhy, Serhii. *The Cossack and Religion in Early Modern Ukraine*. Oxford University Press: 2001

"Pylyp Orlyk Institute for Democracy." Abstract: www.usukraine.org. The 1710 Bendery Constitution, largely drafted by kozak Pylyp Orlyk, was the world's first such democratic document. It predated the US Constitution by over 65 years, and was studied by Thomas Jefferson. "Kozak" means free man, "kozachka," free woman.

Ralston, W.R.S. *The Songs of the Russian People: As Illustrative of Slavonic Mythology and Russian Social Life.* New York: Haskell, 1872. Reprinted 1970. Again, barely any distinction

between Ukrainian and Russian beliefs and practices. About three quarters of the songs are Ukrainian.
"Red Fife Wheat, Canada." Slow Food Presidia. www.slowfoodfoundation.com. Information about wheat brought from Ukraine in the 1800's. The foundation wheat of the Canadian grain industry.
Reid, Anna. *Borderland: A Journey Through the History of Ukraine.* Boulder: Westview Press, 2000. A must read."Resolving Canada's Conflicted Relationship With Margarine." In Depth: Food. www.cbcnews.ca. July 9, 2008
Roberts, A. "The Kozaky Reenactors Handbook." Unpublished, 2008
Ruzhynskyy, Dmytro. "Ukraine's Pagan Rituals." Abstract: The Ukrainian Observer, issue 200.
www. Ukraine-observer.com
Ryan, W.F. *The Bath House at Midnight: An Historical Survey of Magic and Divination in Russia.* University Park: Penn State Press, 1999. Yet another book chock full of Ukrainian or general Slavic information, but attributed mainly to Russian culture.
Stechishin, Savella. *Traditional Ukrainian Cookery.* Winnipeg: Trident, 1957. This was the "bible" at the centre of my family's kitchen. Whatever my grandmothers and mother (and then I) couldn't remember by heart was referenced in this classic. My mother still has the first edition family copy, stained with butter, beets and a little horilka.
Shadows of Forgotten Ancestors. Dir. Sergei Paraganov. Film. Dovzhenko Studios, 1964
Shukhevych, Volodymr. "Christmas Among the Hutsuly of Ukraine: A Look At Our Past." Trans.
Snyder, Timothy. *Bloodlands: Europe Between Hitler and Stalin.* Philadelphia: Basic Books, 2010
Stone, Merlin. *When God Was a Woman.* New York: Barnes & Noble, 1976
Orysia Paszczak Tracz. From Hutsulshchyna, v 4. Lviv: Materyialy do Ukrainsko-Ruskoyi Etnologiyi.Reprinted in The Ukrainian Weekly (Parsippinay). January 3, 1988
Tracz, Orysia Paszczak. "About Our Ukrainian Easter: More Than Just Easter Baskets." The Ukrainian Weekly (Parsippinay). April

3, 1988: 6
Tracz, Orysia Paszczak. “A Good Way To Go.” The Ukrainian Weekly (Parsippinay). November 22, 1998: 7
Tracz, Orysia Paszczak. “Christmas Fabric.” The Ukrainian Weekly (Parsippinay). January 5, 1997: 8
Tracz, Orysia Paszczak. “Our Christmas Traditions: Wheat, Poppy Seeds and Honey.” The Ukrainian Weekly (Parsippinay). December 24, 1995
Tracz, Orysia Paszczak. “Our Christmas: Nothing's Really Changed.” The Ukrainian Weekly (Parsippinay). January 4, 1998
Tracz, Orysia Paszczak. “Songs Your Mother Should Never Have Taught You: Erotic Symbolism in Ukrainian Folk Songs.” Lecture. Vancouver: Ukrainian Cultural Centre, May 30, 2008
Tracz, Orysia Paszczak. “Ukrainian Easter Traditions: Velykden---Great Day.” The Ukrainian Weekly (Parsippinay). April 23, 1995: 11
Tracz, Orysia Paszczak. “Ukrainian Rizdvo: A Lunar Christmas.” The Ukrainian Weekly (Parsippinay). December 28, 2003
Stechishin, Savella. *Traditional Ukrainian Cookery.* Winnipeg: Trident, 1957. This was the “bible” at the centre of my family's kitchen. Whatever my grandmothers and mother (and then I) couldn't remember by heart was referenced in this classic. My mother still has the first edition family copy, stained with butter, beets and a little horilka.
Trckova-Flamee, Dr Alena. *Lycaon.* Encyclopedia Mythica online: 2006
http://www.pantheon.org/articles/l/lycaon.html
Ukrainian Catholic Women's League of Canada, Eparchy of New Westminster. *Ukrainian Traditional and Modern Cuisine, 3rd ed.* New Westminster, 1992. If you find any of these wonderful little cookbooks self-published by Ukrainian churches and women's groups, be forewarned that quite a few of the recipes are simply each woman's “best dish.” They are not all necessarily Ukrainian. The narrative will not inform you. They assume you are Ukrainian and will know the difference between syrnyk and Lazy Daisy cake.
Ukrainian Women's Association of Canada. *Ukrainian Canadiana.* Edmonton, 1976
Ukrainian Women's Association, Olena Pchilka Branch. *Cooking*

Ukrainian Style. Yorkton: Yorkton Branch, 1977

Walker, Barbara. *The Women's Encyclopedia of Myths and Secrets*. San Francisco: Harper, 1983

Wilson, Josh. "Maslenitsa, Blini!: The Food and Celebrations of the Russians." Abstract: School of Russian and Asian Studies (Woodside). September 3, 2005. www.sras.org. While this author is correct about the Russian term "blini," he incorrectly attributes the winter holiday of Maslenyitsa to Russia. It is firmly of Ukrainian origin.

Winter, Sarah K. I. "Moist Mother Earth." www.winterscapes.com. A directory of Slavic gods and goddesses. I checked this information against many other sources. Some was dead on, some dubious or neopagan fanciful. However, it was a good springboard for organizing research into the Slavic pantheon.

Zakydalsky, Oksana. "Orysia Tracz Tells Toronto Audience: Baba Was Right All Along!" The Ukrainian Weekly (Parsippinay). 49.1. December 4, 2005. But you knew that.

Websites

brama.com Ukrainian Arts and culture resource.

en.wikipedia.org/wiki/Cucuteni-Trypillian_culture I would appreciate knowing who wrote this excellent article about the largest settlements in Neolithic Europe, shared by Ukraine, Romania and Moldova. The Cucetini or Trypillian culture existed from 5100 to 2750 BC. Please ignore the superfluous references to Russian names, they are irrelevant.

encyclopediaofukraine.com

hermitagemuseum.org Russian museum housing artifacts from the Paleothic, Neolithic and Bronze ages. Scythian gold. Bird and goddess statues. Sarmatian and Hun pieces.

infoukes.com A comprehensive resource directory.

travelwestukraine.com Ukrainian customs

ualberta.ca University of Alberta website. Countless pages of information about Ukrainian history, language and customs. Compiled by Professor Natalie Konenenko, author of *Ukrainian Minstrels: And the Blind Shall Sing*. Also the home of "Canadian

Association of Slavists".
arts.ualberta.ca Home of the "Peter and Doris Kule Centre for Ukrainian and Canadian Folklore".
wumag.kiev.ua Home of "Discover Ukraine Magazine"

NB: Please be careful when using Wikipedia. It has been pervasively infiltrated by Kremlin propagandists, and assigns Russian credit to many Ukrainian heroes and other facets of our culture. Three examples of many: Ukrainian Ihor Sikorsky, inventor of the helicopter, renowned Ukrainian painter Mykola Pymonenko and the entire history of Russia.

End Book

About Raisa

Raisa Stone is a professional singer, storyteller and animal communicator who loves to cook, dance, and make people laugh. She spent nearly 50 years compiling this book, starting with pureed borsch as baby food and cutting dough circles for perogies as soon as she could reach the table top.

Her narrator, Baba, is a composite of the personalities who fed her and told outrageous and heart wrenching stories of the Soviet, Nazi and immigrant experience. She is available to perform at your special event in person, or by webcam.

Raisa's poetry was chosen to commemorate the 20th anniversary of the Chornobyl disaster by national Ukrainian Magazine *Nasha Doroha.*

Raisa's animal communication practice is an extension of the reverence in which Ukrainians hold both animals and the spirit world.

www.reisastone.com

Sign up for Baba's free newsletter:

www.ukrainiansoulfood.ca

Just released: ***Rosie's Rescue.*** This lovely book explores the Ukrainian creation myth, and is where the character of Baba first emerged. For animal lovers of all ages. Meet Baba's family!

Visit Baba on Facebook & Youtube, under:
Baba's Kitchen: Ukrainian Soul Food

Support Ukrainian authorship:
Review Baba's Kitchen on Amazon or Goodreads

Made in the USA
Charleston, SC
10 April 2016